ADMIRAL OF THE FLEET
EARL BEATTY

Admiral of the Fleet

EARL BEATTY

The Last Naval Hero

———◆———

AN INTIMATE BIOGRAPHY

STEPHEN ROSKILL

COLLINS
St. James's Place, London
1980

William Collins Sons & Co Ltd
London · Glasgow · Sydney ·Auckland
Toronto · Johannesburg

First Published 1980
© S. W. Roskill 1980

ISBN 0 00 216278-4

Set in Bembo
Maps by Brian Elkins

Manufactured in the United States of America

*Dedicated to the memory of
the late George Godfrey-Faussett,
and to Iris, Lady Leslie
and the 3rd Earl Beatty
but for whom this book
would never have been written.*

ERRATA

Shortly before publication I was informed that the copyright of material, from which I had successfully applied to the Third Earl Beatty for permission to quote, was legally vested in the Executors and Trustees of the Second Earl, Sir Arthur Collins, KCVO, and Mr David Dixon.

In these circumstances I would like to acknowledge that the Trustees are the copyright owners of some of the material used in this book and I apologise to them for my mistake.

I am grateful to them for drawing my attention to errors in the attribution of two illustrations, the portrait of Lady Beatty by Laszlo and the Death mask, both of which are vested in the Trustees.

And I take this opportunity to correct some errors of my own and misprints, namely:

page 31, line 12. For '1890' read '1899'.
page 167, line 19. For 'south' read 'north'.
page 324, line 6 from foot. For '93' read '94'.
page 361, line 8. For '101 and 93' read '100 and 94'.

STEPHEN ROSKILL

Contents

Illustrations

Maps and Diagrams

Foreword and Acknowledgements

My interest in the career of Admiral of the Fleet Earl Beatty dates to
the early 1960s, when my publisher suggested that I might write a
new study of the Battle of Jutland (31st May 1916) for publication on
the fiftieth anniversary of that clash. I therefore began to collect
material about the battle and to interview survivors of it; but when
Professor Arthur Marder visited me at my Hampshire home to
discuss his own work on the naval side of the 1914–18 war, he told
me that his intention was to devote a whole volume to Jutland, and
exhibited understandable anxiety about the possibility that I might
produce a rival account. I therefore changed my mind, handed over
to him all the material I had collected (of which he has made good
use in his third volume of *From the Dreadnought to Scapa Flow*), and
decided to devote my energy to a study of Naval Policy from 1919
to 1939 in order to fill the gap between the Official Naval History of
World War I by Sir Julian Corbett and Sir Henry Newbolt and my
own work on World War II. That decision resulted in the publication
of my two volumes titled *Naval Policy between the Wars* here and in
the USA in 1968 and 1976. I would record that Professor Marder has
recently reciprocated my action over the Jutland papers by obtaining
for me on loan from the University of California the microfilm of
the papers of Admiral of the Fleet Lord Wester Wemyss which he
had made and which I badly needed for use in this book.

Though I abandoned my prospective book on Jutland I was aware
that Professor Marder did not intend to deal with the protracted
controversy over the production of the various officially sponsored
accounts of that battle in the 1920s; so I continued to collect material
on that complicated and somewhat unsavoury *fracas*. But I soon ran
into a serious difficulty over publication of the results of my
research. The 2nd Earl Beatty generously invited me to spend several
quite long periods at his lovely home Chicheley Hall, Buckinghamshire, in order to study his father's papers in tranquillity and to take
copies of those which I needed; but I quickly realised that he was
totally opposed to publication of an intimate biography of his father,
and particularly opposed to a critical study of his part in the Jutland
controversy.

I therefore accepted that it would be hopeless to try and obtain the
2nd Earl's permission to publish material of which he owned the

copyright; so I held my hand. This *impasse* continued until the 2nd Earl Beatty died in 1972. I then approached his son, the 3rd Earl, to ascertain his views on the use of material the copyright of which had of course descended to him. I was delighted to receive a very cordial reply giving me the complete freedom which is essential to any biographer who intends to make a serious study of an important public figure. My first acknowledgement is therefore to the 3rd Earl Beatty, for permission to publish such of his grandfather's letters and papers as I desired.

My second great debt is to the late George Godfrey-Faussett who not only raised no objection to publication of Admiral Beatty's letters to his mother, but provided me with a great deal of information about the admiral's relationship with his family. He also bought at Christie's 57 of Beatty's letters to his mother which had come on to the market, added to them 99 more from his own family archive, and presented the whole collection to Churchill College, Cambridge for my sole use initially. Not content with those acts of generosity he bequeathed to the same college the whole of the papers and diary of his father Captain Sir Bryan Godfrey-Faussett, who was Naval Equerry to King George V from 1901 to 1936. It was a source of great sorrow to me that George Godfrey-Faussett died in March 1979, though he had, most fortunately, already scanned the parts of this book which deal with Beatty and his mother.

My third stroke of good fortune derives from my friendship with the late Sir Shane Leslie, Bart., which goes back to my early days in the navy. Leslie was a close personal friend, confidant and admirer of Admiral Beatty, and was in fact the author of parts of the biography planned soon after his death. The original intention was that Leslie should handle all the family and personal side of Beatty's life and that Rear-Admiral W. S. Chalmers, who had served on his staff during the war, should write the accounts of his battles. But the 2nd Earl Beatty took exception to Leslie's draft because, so he told me, they dealt too fully with the admiral's turbulent marriage and his extra-marital liaisons. He therefore suppressed it. Leslie then handed his drafts and much other Beatty material over to Admiral Chalmers, who completed the authorised biography in 1951 but only dealt very discreetly with those aspects of Beatty's private life about which Leslie was of course fully informed. Unfortunately quite a lot of the letters and papers which Leslie had collected about the admiral were lost either in transit between him and Admiral Chalmers or stolen from Castle Leslie in Eire by visitors or temporary inhabitants in about 1965 – to the very great distress of their owner.[1] Though I greatly regret being deprived of this irreplaceable source material enough remains for me to present what I believe to be an accurate account of that side of the admiral's life. Moreover the losses were to some extent counter-balanced after Leslie's death in 1971 by his widow Lady (Iris) Leslie going to great trouble to assemble and transfer to me in accordance with her husband's oft-expressed wish all his surviving naval papers. These documents have now been placed in the Churchill College Archive Centre, and as they overlap closely with the Godfrey-Faussett collection they have been catalogued together under the symbol SLGF. I have now transferred to the same Archive Centre the greater part of my own papers, which include much Beatty material and which have been catalogued under the symbol ROSK. The rest will follow when I have finished with it or after my death.

I would say that although my own papers and Sir Shane Leslie's contain notes on or copies of a great many of Beatty papers, including selections from the enormous number of letters which passed between him and his wife, I have been unable to check them with the originals because the Beatty collection is now in the possession of the family's lawyers pending, so I have been informed, a decision by the Treasury regarding acceptance of it in part payment of the duties to be levied on the 2nd Earl's estate. As it always takes a very long time for the authorities in Whitehall to reach a decision on such a matter I have not thought it wise to await the day when the papers again become available. I have therefore here accepted that the copies of Beatty letters and other documents in my possession are accurate, and where no specific source reference is given in my notes the reader should assume that the original document is in the Beatty papers – which have not yet been catalogued.

It will be appropriate here to say a little more about Beatty's many holograph letters. If, as Shane Leslie wrote, letters are 'the pith and marrow of biography' Beatty certainly fulfilled a biographer's need in abundance. Unfortunately his handwriting, for which he generally used old-fashioned quill pens, though large is often very difficult to read. In consequence I have placed question marks in the quotations here reproduced where I am unsure of any word. Moreover Beatty's style of writing included the very frequent use of capital letters – which will appear both ugly and unnecessary in print. However, I have after some thought decided to leave in the capital letters – because I consider it basically wrong for a historian to tamper with the text of original material he is using. Beatty's punctuation was often erratic or even non-existent – a defect in which he resembled Nelson. I have therefore sometimes inserted punctuation marks, but only in those cases where it has seemed to me that his meaning would otherwise not be clear to the reader. In all other respects the original letters are here quoted exactly as written.

Admiral Beatty was an intimate friend of King George V, who always showed great admiration for and confidence in him. The Royal Archives at Windsor Castle thus contain a large number of letters written by the admiral, as well as many references to him in other documents. All the material culled from the Royal Archives is here published by gracious permission of H.M. The Queen, and I am deeply indebted to Miss Jane Langton, the Registrar of the Windsor Castle Library, for finding every possible document dealing with my subject and having copies made for me.

Though the research I carried out for some of my earlier books, especially for my biography of Lord Hankey, (*Hankey : Man of Secrets*, 3 Vols., 1970-74) and my history of *Naval Policy between the Wars* referred to above provided me with a great deal of material about Beatty, the preparation of this book naturally necessitated going over some of the ground again, and also exploiting a number of completely new sources. Being now in my 77th year I find constant travel and the labour of patient and thorough research tends to overtax my strength. I have however been exceptionally fortunate in gaining the help of a number of young, able and energetic scholars who were interested in my work or engaged on studies which in one way or another overlapped with my own. I am particularly grateful to the following:

Mr. John Campbell for allowing me to exploit his very thorough and detailed analysis, based on German as well as British records, of the hits received and obtained by both sides in the naval battles of World War I, much of which has been published as *Warship Special No. 1. Battle Cruisers* (Conway Maritime Press, 1978), and for reading and criticising my chapters on the Dogger Bank and Jutland battles.

Mr. Peter Sanderson, now Deputy Warden of London House, for offering to undertake research on my behalf, for combing the papers of Earl Lloyd-George, Lord Beaverbrook, Andrew Bonar Law and Lord Davidson, now in the House of Lords Library, for Beatty material, and also for obtaining what I needed from the Naval Library, Fulham.

Dr. R. J. Knight of the National Maritime Museum for searching for Beatty material in the papers of Admiral Lord Chatfield, Admiral K. G. B. Dewar, Admiral Sir Henry Oliver, Admiral Sir Herbert Richmond, Admiral Sir Walter Cowan and other collections held at Greenwich.

Mr. Jon Sumida of the University of Chicago for allowing me to exploit his very thorough and highly revisionist work on the Fisher Era in general and the problem of naval fire control in particular, which will be the subject of his Doctoral Thesis due for completion in 1980.

Mr. Anthony Pollen for the gift to Churchill College of some of the papers and correspondence of his father Arthur Hungerford Pollen and for the promise of the remainder after he has completed his biography of his father; also for much correspondence and many interviews about Arthur Pollen's naval inventions, lasting over a period of more than ten years.

Dr. Nicholas Rodger of the Public Record Office for looking up references I needed in the Cabinet and Admiralty papers and for providing me with copies of many of them.

Miss Marion Stewart, Chief Archivist of Churchill College Cambridge, and her assistant Miss Clare Stephens for finding Beatty material in the many collections held in that college's Archives Centre, notably the papers of Admiral of the Fleet Lord Keyes, now transferred to the British Library, Admiral Sir Reginald P-E-E-Drax, Admiral Sir John de Robeck, Admiral Sir Reginald Hall, Admiral Sir Frederic Dreyer, Admiral Sir Horace Hood, the 1st Lord Hankey, the 1st Viscount Weir, Mr. A. H. Pollen and various memoirs written by officers who were near contemporaries of Admiral Beatty or knew him well.

Though responsibility for the selection of the letters and documents here published and for the accuracy of my text rests of course entirely with myself it is right to record that I could never have completed this work without the cordial help and co-operation of the men and women I have mentioned above. All quotations from documents held by the Public Record Office are published by kind permission of The Controller, H.M. Stationery Office.

In addition to the foregoing I must express my gratitude to the following for the gift of papers and for permission to quote copyright material:

The late Admiral Sir Geoffrey Barnard for copies of the papers of his uncle Admiral Sir Hugh Evan-Thomas and for permission to make unrestricted use of them.

Mr. John Barnes of the London School of Economics for correspondence and discussions about Beatty at Chicheley Hall and in London – though we are not in agreement on one controversial issue.

Mr. Charles Beatty for recollections of his father and of his uncle the admiral.

General The Viscount Bridgeman for a copy of his unpublished memoir of his father the 1st Viscount and for permission to print quotations from it.

The Baron Chatfield for permission to print unpublished letters by his father Admiral of the Fleet Lord Chatfield.

Dr. The Hon Alice Cunnack for permission to make unrestricted use of the papers of her father Admiral of the Fleet Lord Wester Wemyss.

Admirals Sir William Davis and Sir Angus Cunninghame Graham for their memoirs and for permission to use them without restriction, and for many valuable letters about the 1914–18 war.

The late Admiral The Hon Sir Reginald Plunkett-Ernle-Erle-Drax for depositing his papers in my college and granting me unrestricted use of them.

Admiral Sir Desmond Dreyer for the papers of his father Admiral Sir Frederic Dreyer and for permission to make unrestricted use of them.

Captain G. A. French for valuable letters about the naval side of the 1914–18 war.

Professor Paul Halpern of the University of Florida, Tallahasse, for copies of letters he had found in the Keyes papers and for much valuable correspondence about the naval side of the 1914–18 war.

The Viscount Hood, elder son of Admiral Sir Horace Hood who was killed in the battle of Jutland, for valuable recollections of the Beatty family and of the society in which they moved.

Captain Basil Jones for permission to reproduce an extract from his privately printed autobiography, *And So To Battle*.

Admiral Sir Charles Madden, Bart for permission to reproduce unpublished letters by his father the Admiral of the Fleet of the same name.

Admiral Sir Ian McGeoch for memorable anecdotes about Lords Beatty and Chatfield.

Mr. Robert Rhodes James for permission to reproduce extracts from his biography of Lord Davidson *Memoirs of a Conservative*.

Mr. Anthony Ryan of Liverpool University for drawing my attention to Beatty material and for valuable correspondence about him.

I have made every effort to trace the ownership of copyright in unpublished material I have used, and if I have failed in any instance I trust that my lapse may be excused.

As to published works which have been particularly valuable to me Professor Marder's five volumes on the naval side of the 1914–18 war (*From the Dreadnought to Scapa Flow*, Oxford 1961-70), Professor A. Temple Patterson's two volumes of *Jellicoe Papers* (Navy Records Society, 1966–68) and Mr. Martin Gilbert's authorised biography of Sir Winston Churchill (vols. II to V, Heinemann 1969-76) all come within that category.

I feel that I should here say a few words to explain why I devote considerable space to the subject of the fire control equipment fitted in the major British warships of the 1914–18 war. It has long been known that those ships suffered from serious defects in material, which vitiated both the offensive performance of their functions and their capacity to withstand heavy blows. The former has heretofore been attributed mainly to the provision of inefficient armour-piercing shells, while the latter has been explained chiefly by the faulty design of their cordite propellant charges and by dangerous practices in the handling of them between the magazines and the gun houses. Though there is a great deal to be said for both the above explanations I have long been convinced that they are far from being the whole story. During the last decade that conviction has been strengthened by my association with Mr. Anthony Pollen, whose work on the voluminous papers of his father has recently borne fruit in his biography of him (*The Great Gunnery Scandal*, Collins 1980). While Mr Pollen and I were in constant correspondence and discussion on the subject Mr. Jon Sumida arrived from Chicago University and soon devoted his great ability to thorough research in the Admiralty's records and in other primary sources which cover the subject of the equipment supplied to the Royal Navy before the 1914–18 war. Though I do not wish to anticipate the publication by Mr. Sumida of his full analysis and conclusions I am sure that he and Mr. Pollen have, at the very least, made out a strong case in favour of the argument that the Admiralty made a disastrous and quite unnecessary mistake over the choice of fire control equipment provided to the fleet; and as Beatty's battle cruisers were the spearhead of that fleet's offensive power it was they who were the principal sufferers from it.

The reader will naturally ask why he should accept such a thesis as is outlined above more than fifty years after the battles in question were fought, and in face of the conclusions drawn by other historians who have ploughed this particular field. The answer lies in the Admiralty's treatment of its records, which all who have worked in them have long agreed to be nothing short of scandalous. Only recently has it been discovered that there originally were no less than thirty-six volumes of 'Pollen Papers' in the Admiralty's records, and that all of them were destroyed during the process known as 'weeding'. Had those papers been available to earlier historians I am sure that they would have probed that aspect of the navy's material deficiencies. As it is we have had to await the exhaustive studies made of the Pollen papers in his son's possession and other untapped sources – supplemented by what remains in the Admiralty's records and in private collections.

As regards the strength of Beatty's ships in defence, though I fully accept that the ammunition troubles referred to above were important contributory factors, I hope to show that inadequate armour protection (of which Beatty became aware after his first clash with the enemy) has been unduly neglected; and that the entire policy of the Admiralty during the long period when Admiral Fisher's influence was paramount, and in particular his oft reiterated view that armour should be sacrificed to speed, requires re-assessment.

Miss Edith Eales has once again typed and often retyped my manuscript with exemplary care and accuracy, while my wife has not only provided me with a stable and happy home to work in but has greatly helped by checking my typescript and in other ways too many to mention.

Mr Richard Ollard of Collins & Co. has once more proved an ideal editor and a greatly valued friend. It is not on his advice but because of the economic problems facing the printing industry that I have placed my source references at the end of the book instead of on the page to which they refer, as I did in most of my earlier works. Finally I must thank Mr. Douglas Mathews for the care with which he has compiled the Index, Mr. Brian Elkins for the skill with which he has drawn the maps from my rough sketches, and my colleagues at Churchill College for their stimulating company and for electing me into a Pensioner Fellowship after I had passed the University retiring age.

Frostlake Cottage,   Churchill College,
Malting Lane,   Cambridge.
Cambridge.

NON VI SED ARTE

ADMIRAL OF THE FLEET
EARL BEATTY

CHAPTER ONE

Early Years

DAVID, EARL BEATTY, VISCOUNT
BORODALE OF WEXFORD, BARON BEATTY
OF THE NORTH SEA AND OF BROOKSBY,
KNIGHT GRAND CROSS OF THE MOST
HONOURABLE ORDER OF THE BATH,
ORDER OF MERIT, KNIGHT GRAND CROSS
OF THE ROYAL VICTORIAN ORDER,
COMPANION OF THE DISTINGUISHED
SERVICE ORDER
DOCTOR OF CIVIL LAW, DOCTOR OF LAWS

Such were his final style and titles. He was also a Privy Counsellor, but the pundits declare it to be incorrect to include the letters PC (though it is often done) on the grounds that it is 'an office and not an honour'.[1]

Beatty was beyond doubt the best known fighting Admiral of the Royal Navy – and perhaps of all navies – of the first World War. Extremely handsome and possessed of outstanding courage and a very high degree of charisma, he was the youngest British Admiral since Nelson;* and he won the devotion and unbreakable loyalty of all who served with or under him – both high and low. Yet there are aspects of his life and character which were rigidly suppressed when it came to writing his authorised biography, and only recently has new material come to light which enables, and indeed calls

---

*It is interesting that the Greek word 'Charisma', translated in Liddell and Scott's famous Lexicon as 'grace, favour' and as 'a gift of God's grace' does not appear in the 1961 larger OED though 'Charism' and 'Charismatic' appear in it. Apparently following American dictionaries (e.g. Webster, 1971) 'Charisma' does, however, appear in the 1972 OED Supplement where it is defined as 'a gift or power of leadership or authority; aura' and as 'applicable to a certain quality of an individual personality by which he is set apart from ordinary men and treated as endowed with supernatural, super-human, or at least specifically exceptional powers or qualities'. It is of course in this sense that it is used here.

for, a reassessment of his career and his place in history.

The future Admiral was born on 17th January 1871 at Howbeck Lodge, Stapeley, the small country house in Cheshire then occupied by his parents. We know that one of his great-grandfathers fought under Wellington (then Sir Arthur Wellesley) at Talavera in 1809, and as he bequeathed a Waterloo medal to his heirs he was also presumably present on 18th June 1815. On one occasion the Admiral described himself as being 'of the Irish persuasion with a dash of the French in me';[2] but I have been unable to find how or when any French blood came into his ancestry. When he was already famous he answered an autograph-hunting Irish schoolgirl's question by saying that he was 'entirely Irish and proud of it too'.[3] That self-description of his lineage was apt, since he came of old Irish stock from the 'famous County of Wexford', which his first would-be biographer Sir Shane Leslie, himself an Irishman, called 'the least Gaelic of the Irish counties' but 'in revenge one of the most rebellious'. Beatty's ancestors were, according to the same authority, 'bold riders and country gentlemen' as well as 'Warriors at Bellona's call'.[4] Though statistics and records concerning the people of that wild country are sparse it is known that his grandfather, also David Beatty of Borodale – their home in the Enniscorthy district, and commemorated in the Admiral's titles – was Master of the Wexford hounds for 40 years. His father, David Longfield Beatty of Borodale, served in the Fourth Hussars, mostly in India, and married Katherine (or Katrine) Edith, daughter of Nicholas Sadleir of Dunboyne Castle, County Meath.

The family was sufficiently well off to move from Ireland to Cheshire early in their married life, and four sons and one daughter were born of the marriage. They all seem to have run true to the family tradition of gallantry on the field of battle and recklessness in the hunting field. The eldest son Charles, born in 1870, served in the South African war and won a D.S.O. He then became a well-known gentleman jockey and steeple chase rider, gaining second place in the Grand National of 1897 and fourth place on the same horse (Filbert) in the following year.[5] He rejoined the Army to take part in World War I and died of wounds in 1917. The David of this biography was the second son; William Vandeleur (born 1872) was the third; and he too served with distinction in South Africa and in World War I, and became a

well-known owner and trainer at Newmarket. The fourth son
George (born 1882) served in the Indian Army and also made
his name as a gentleman jockey. He died in India in 1915. The
last child was Kathleen, the only daughter, who was always
known as 'Trot'. She married Colonel Miles F. Courage, a
member of the brewing family, who was Master of the
Hampshire Hunt during and after World War II. David always
remained devoted to Charles and 'Trot', the only members of
his family he had the chance to know well.

It is a fair assumption that the future Admiral's good looks
came from his mother, and his love of field sports, especially
of fox hunting, from his father. He grew up in the normal
carefree way of a comparatively well-to-do county family in
the 19th century, but unlike his brothers he soon developed a
strong interest in ships and the sea and a determination to join
the Navy. That he accomplished, after a year at a well-known
'crammer's' establishment at Gosport, in January 1884 at the
ripe age of thirteen. As he passed into the *Britannia* training
establishment 10th out of 99 candidates he obviously possessed
reasonable though in no way brilliant academic ability. The
records of his time in the *Britannia* show that he was a
high-spirited youngster, and not too amenable to the very
strict discipline then enforced; for he was punished 25 times as
a cadet for 'minor offences' such as 'skylarking'. Three more
serious offences, for one of which he was severely beaten, are
also recorded against him.[6] He was not selected as a Cadet
Captain, and passed out at the end of 1885 18th in his term of
33 – which was well below his place on entry. Thus it
certainly cannot be said that he showed outstanding promise at
an early age.

The system of training naval cadets which was in force
when Beatty joined the *Britannia*, and which continued little
changed for more than another half century, now seems
extraordinarily ill-conceived. Though it is true that some
boys came through it with little apparent harm, and ultimately
became fine officers who rose high in the service, others were
undoubtedly ruined by it and either left the navy totally
disgruntled at the first opportunity or served on with
increasing dislike of the life which they had chosen, or which
had been chosen for them by parents, to become thoroughly
bad officers. The system was based on forcing cadets into a
pre-conceived and rigid mould by the application of harsh,

even inhuman discipline. Obedience to orders was the
hallowed principle of the system, and woe betide any boy who
was deemed to have transgressed that tenet. Any signs of
originality or independence were severely frowned on – if not
actively suppressed; while intellectual accomplishments always
came a bad second to athletics. Though other officers who
came through the mill of cadet training have written very
critically about it my own experience is perhaps worth
recording.[7] I was born on 1st August, which was the starting
day for one of the three annual cadet entries. If I had been born
a day earlier I would have been automatically placed one
'term' earlier and so four months senior; but the rigidity of the
system was such that cadets could only choose their friends
from among those belonging to the same four month age span
as themselves, and in particular from those who slept (in
alphabetical order of surnames) in the same dormitories. Every
order in the dormitories ('Clean your teeth', 'Say your
prayers' etc) was signalled by a Cadet Captain ringing a bell;
and junior cadets could be, and frequently were, severely
beaten by boys who might well be only a few months older
than their victims. It was not surprising that, despite ameliora-
tive efforts made by some of the more humane and understanding civilian masters, this system should have stifled any
tendency to show originality. Perhaps the most revealing
comment on the system was made by an officer of my own
generation who had the misfortune to fall into Japanese hands
after his ship was sunk in the Java Sea Battle of 27th February
1942 but later achieved Flag rank. When asked about his
experiences as a prisoner-of-war he replied, doubtless partly in
jest, 'After four years at Dartmouth a Japanese prison camp
was quite a picnic!'[8]

As Beatty was, in his own later words 'entirely Irish' we
may attribute the tribulations he suffered in the *Britannia*, at
any rate in part, to the natural rebelliousness of his race. But in
his case no lasting damage was done – perhaps because some
of the staff evidently tolerated his high spirits. Moreover it
was even then obvious that he possessed an attractive
personality; and from the earliest times he possessed what
Nelson called 'interest'.

On leaving the *Britannia* Beatty was appointed, thanks to the
influence of his very determined mother, to the *Alexandra*, the
flagship of the Mediterranean fleet, whose Commander-in-

Chief at the time was Queen Victoria's second son Alfred Ernest Albert, Duke of Edinburgh (1844-1900). Though certainly not one of the most admirable members of the Royal family of the period he had gained a reputation for being a good handler of ships and squadrons. He and his wife, who was the Grand Duchess Marie Alexandrovna, only daughter of Tsar Alexander II of Russia, took a great interest in Beatty, and allowed him the freedom of the lovely gardens of the San Antonio Palace outside Valletta where they lived. There Beatty had what was probably his first flirtation – with Marie, the eldest of the Duke's four vivacious daughters (1875-1938), who had the unusual distinction of being a grand-daughter both of Queen Victoria and of Tsar Alexander. Marie, then aged about 12, obviously fell for Beatty and after they had parted she wrote him a number of affectionate letters. Rather oddly she always addressed him as 'Dear Beatty'; but that was probably merely a reflection of the fact that in those days, and long afterwards, naval officers in general and midshipmen in particular always addressed each other by their surnames, and Marie was merely following the practice of her playmates. In those letters, which Beatty carefully preserved, she later recalled the happy, care-free days which they had enjoyed in Malta. In 1892 Marie, then aged 17, married Ferdinand, nephew of Carol I of Roumania, who succeeded his uncle to the throne in 1914. Marie was then influential in counteracting the pro-German sympathies of Carol and his entourage, and so contributed to her country joining the Allies instead of the Central Powers – to whom it had in fact been tied by a secret treaty of 1883. Though this change of sides led to disaster at first, Roumania did in the end gain greatly through having fought on the winning side in World War I. But from our point of view those events lay far in the future, and what probably mattered in 1886 was that it was through his friendship with the Edinburgh family that Beatty first came into touch with Royalty and the aristocracy.

The *Alexandra*'s gunroom included an extraordinary number of midshipmen who later became Admirals and who served under Beatty in the 1914-18 war – including Walter Cowan (who became a life-long devotee), Richard Phillimore, Reginald Tyrwhitt and Richard Webb; and among the commissioned officers were several who were to be intimately connected with the Court – notably Colin Keppel, The Hon.

Stanley Colville and Charles Cust. It is surely fair to conclude that the young Beatty's three years as a Midshipman gave him the taste for aristocratic society, which later became a marked feature of his character.

After leaving the *Alexandra* and all the gaieties enjoyed by the flagship's officers in 1889 Beatty was appointed as a Sub-Lieutenant to the corvette *Ruby* (still rigged for sail) for training in the more serious business of seamanship. Eighteen months ashore for technical courses followed, and during his time at Greenwich College Beatty appears to have taken full advantage of the proximity of London – despite a chronic shortage of ready cash. The ladies of the stage evidently proved an irresistible attraction, and a contemporary recorded that 'his cabin at Greenwich was full of photographs of actresses, some of which were signed in the most endearing terms'.[9] Not surprisingly he did not do well in his Sub-Lieutenant's examinations, ending up with a first-class certificate in Torpedo, seconds in Seamanship, Gunnery and Pilotage and a third in Navigation – which deprived him of maximum seniority on promotion to Lieutenant.

Two not very exciting appointments understandably followed; but in July 1892 he was selected to serve in the Royal Yacht *Victoria and Albert* for the summer cruise, and Queen Victoria then allegedly described him as 'the nicest mannered boy' on board.[10] It was of course this period which again brought Beatty into touch with Royalty and the aristocracy; and in those days 'influence' still counted for much in the lives and careers of service men. But one may reasonably find in such appointments the origins of a less attractive side of Beatty's character – namely the virulent anti-Semitism which we will encounter later and which undoubtedly reflected the attitude of many titled people at that time. If anyone still believes that anti-Semitism existed only in Tsarist Russia and National Socialist Germany he should study the attitude and sayings of the wealthy and aristocratic British.

In August 1892 Beatty was promoted Lieutenant and appointed once more to the corvette *Ruby*, then commanded by an officer described by one of his contemporaries as 'a hard bitten old sea dog'.[11] During the following year, spent in the West Indies and South Atlantic, the young watch keeping officer doubtless learnt about the handling of sails in all weather conditions, which probably hardened him physically but cannot have helped to develop his intellectual capacity – at a time moreover when the navy should have been facing up to the implications of the vast changes brought about by the introduction of steam propulsion and the invention of new weapons of every type. The effect of such changes must have been brought home to Beatty in his next appointments, which were to the comparatively modern battleships *Camperdown* and *Trafalgar* built in 1885 and 1887 respectively. They both belonged to the Mediterranean Fleet and neither was equipped with sails, so giving Beatty his first experience of the technological revolution then in progress, and of the new manoeuvres known as 'steam tactics'. Unhappily those developments led to the disastrous collision between the *Victoria*, flagship of the C-in-C Admiral Sir George Tryon, and the *Camperdown*, flagship of the second-in-command Rear-Admiral A. H. Markham, on 22nd June 1893 when the former was sunk off Tripoli on the Syrian coast with the loss of 358 lives including that of the C-in-C.[12] In the light of subsequent events it was a curious coincidence that among those saved from the *Victoria* was her Commander John Rushworth Jellicoe, who was actually in bed with a high temperature at the time of the collision, and that Lieutenant David Beatty joined the *Camperdown* a few months later. As regards Beatty this period of service in battleships at a time when 'spit and polish' was regarded as the royal road to promotion was little to his liking, since he longed for action or, if that could not be provided, for sport in the hunting field at home. In consequence his enthusiasm for the navy waned, though only temporarily.

The opening of the Suez Canal in 1869 greatly enhanced the strategic importance of Egypt and the Sudan to Britain; since by far the greater share of her military and mercantile traffic to India and the Far East thenceforth flowed by the new route rather than the long haul by the Cape of Good Hope. British interests were greatly increased by Disraeli's purchase of the bankrupt Khedive's Suez Canal shares for £4 millions in 1875; but France also had strong cultural, financial and strategic interests in the country, dating back to Napoleon's invasion of 1798. With Ottoman Turkey's hold on her empire steadily weakening throughout the 19th century the possibility of a major clash between the two powers most concerned in the stability and control of the country was always present.

To understand the circumstances which first brought Beatty the opportunity to prove himself as a fighting leader it is here necessary to make a brief digression to review events in the Sudan in the 1880s. The chief characters on the indigenous side were Mohammed Ahmed, a deeply religious man of humble birth who declared himself a 'descendant of the prophet Mohammed' and so 'Mahdi', or 'the guided one', and Abdullah, Khalifa of the Sudan, who provided the political and military leadership on joining forces with Ahmed. Their purpose was to eject the Egyptians from the Sudan, and when their revolt began in 1881 they achieved quick successes. While the Sudan was in turmoil and Egyptian control collapsing the revolt of Arabi Pasha against British and French control broke out in Lower Egypt. When the French declined to take joint action Gladstone's government author-ised the bombardment of Alexandria (11th July 1882) and the landing of strong forces which defeated Arabi at Tel el Kebir. The occupation of Cairo and the exile of Arabi followed; but the cost and difficulties of countering the Mahdist movement in the Sudan were so great that in 1884 the fascinating if exotic character General Charles Gordon, who had previously served a long term (1874–79) in the Sudan, finally as Governor-General, was recalled and sent to Khartoum with orders to evacuate the Anglo-Egyptian garrisons. By May 1884 he was cut off in the city, which fell to the Mahdist (or 'Dervish') forces on 25th January 1885 after a siege of 317 days when the tardily sent relief expedition was almost in sight of its objective. In the following year General Sir Herbert Kitchener, 'Sirdar' or C-in-C of the Egyptian army, was authorised to reconquer the Sudan and avenge Gordon's death. Substantial Anglo-Egyptian forces, equipped with modern weapons, were assembled, and it was Kitchener's request for gunboats to operate on the Nile in support of the southward advance that produced Beatty's opportunity.

The officer chosen to command the gunboats was Stanley Colville, who had been Beatty's commander in the *Trafalgar*, and it was at his request that Beatty joined the expedition – actually on loan to the Egyptian government.

Here it must be emphasised that the support which river gunboats could give to the army depended very largely on the level of the Nile waters, which varied greatly at different seasons, and on the ability to navigate the series of dangerous rapids and cataracts, of which there were four between Wady

Halfa and Khartoum. As Colville had served with the relief expedition sent to Khartoum in 1885 he was well informed regarding the navigational hazards on the great river, and took active steps both to discover the best channels and to make his polyglot flotilla as efficient as possible for the work to be undertaken. At the time of his appointment there were already four gunboats and some small river steamers on the Nile, and three more gunboats were being shipped out from England in sections for assembly on the spot.

By the end of July 1896 the original boats had concentrated a short distance above Wady Halfa and were hauled through the first series of obstacles by 2,000 men – though not without serious difficulty. However, by late August seven vessels had reached the open waters of the next reach in safety. Meanwhile the railhead from Cairo was being pushed south and the new gunboats had arrived in sections. Kitchener, however, decided not to wait for the latter to be ready, but decided to continue his southward advance, supported by the available craft. One gunboat struck a rock during the passage of the next cataract, but those commanded by Colville and Beatty as well as a third gunboat and three small steamers got through safely – despite fierce resistance from the Dervishes lining the river banks. It was during this passage that Beatty's gunboat (called the *Abu Klea*) was struck by a shell which lodged unexploded in her magazine. Beatty promptly picked it up and threw it overboard. Though he narrowly escaped injury from the hot fire poured into the little craft he came through unscathed. Colville was less lucky and was seriously wounded, so command devolved on Beatty who decided to press ahead and try to outflank the Dervish position. Despite the strong current and heavy fire he covered safely the 35 miles to Dongola, whereupon the enemy evacuated their main positions further downstream. After a pause to allow the army to come up with him Kitchener resumed the attack, and on 22nd September Dongola was captured. With his communications dangerously stretched he then decided to call a halt, and thus ended the first phase of the campaign.

After a spell of home leave, mostly spent hunting in the Shires, Beatty returned to Egypt for the 1897 campaign at Kitchener's special request. By the time he arrived the new gunboats were ready, and the Sirdar immediately ordered an advance. The river flotilla was now commanded by Colin

Keppel, and two of the gunboat captains were Horace Hood and Walter Cowan, who were to be numbered among Beatty's most devoted friends and admirers, and whose outlook, courage and interests were very similar to his own. As Beatty's 'Rough Record of Proceedings' for the second phase of the Nile Expedition has survived we have a fairly full account of the adventures which beset his ship the *El Teb*;[13] and Churchill has provided a vivid account of how she was capsized in the next cataract and her Captain and most of his crew of 15 were swept down river and picked up by another gunboat.[14] His own vessel having been lost, with all his personal equipment, Beatty took command of the *Fateh*, and in her the next cataract was successfully negotiated, though not without hair-raising difficulties. Between October 1897 and August 1898 Beatty was constantly in action, working ahead of the army and engaging every target he could find, and on 2nd September the climax came with the Battle of Omdurman. Though chiefly remembered today for Churchill's vivid account of the charge of the 21st Lancers it is fair to claim that the victory, which resulted in the immediate recapture of Khartoum, would not have been possible without the constant support of the river flotilla; and we may recall the description given by Beatty, who had watched the battle from the crow's nest of the *Fateh*, when Churchill asked for his impressions. 'It looked', said the sailor on their meeting many years later when Churchill was First Lord of the Admiralty, 'like plum duff: brown currants scattered about in a great deal of suet'.[15]

After the fall of Khartoum the reconquest of the whole Sudan soon followed; but the intended withdrawal of the British forces was delayed by the receipt of reports that a strange force, including some Europeans, had arrived at Fashoda, some 400 miles further south on the White Nile. This possible challenge to British-Egyptian control of the vast and long disputed area had to be investigated, and if necessary countered. So Kitchener pressed on south embarked with his troops in the invaluable gunboats – including Beatty's. In fact the foreign force was French and consisted of only eight Europeans and about 120 natives under Captain Jean Baptiste Marchand, who had accomplished the amazing feat of crossing the African continent from Senegal; but their presence could have provoked a major international incident, and great tact and diplomacy were required to persuade Marchand to recognise the Egyptian flag and to withdraw his men. After some anxious days the French flag was lowered on 11th December 1898, and in the following March the Anglo-Egyptian 'condominium' over the Sudan was officially recognised.

If in the light of recent history the whole British involvement in the Sudan appears to be a waste of lives and of money it is fair to emphasise that not only did a period of comparatively stable and efficient government follow but the Arab slave trade from the African hinterland to ports on the Red Sea was effectively checked – though it was not finally eliminated until well into the next century. The chief credit for that humane accomplishment of the 1890s must be accorded to the famous explorer and administrator Sir Samuel Baker (1821–93), General Gordon and their tiny band of devoted collaborators – most of whom were British, and all of whom worked devotedly in a hostile environment and an unhealthy climate. Thus the intervention, if mainly inspired by strategic and financial interests, had a strong humanitarian purpose as well.

In his first despatch on the Sudan campaign (dated 21st October 1896) Kitchener commended the work of the gunboats and their crews very warmly with the result that Beatty was gazetted a Companion of the Distinguished Service Order – a very unusual award for so junior an officer to receive. In his final despatch (dated 30th September 1898) Kitchener enlarged on the contribution they had made to his success. The result was that, among other honours and promotions, Hood and Beatty were promoted Commander on 15th November. His age was at the time 27 and he had served 6 instead of the usual 11 to 12 years in Lieutenant's rank. Thus did he place his foot firmly on the lower rungs of the ladder leading to the top of the naval tree; and, perhaps more important, he had demonstrated to seniors and juniors his energy and drive, his organising ability and capacity for improvisation, his unflinching courage in face of danger and his ability to co-operate cordially with the sister service; while his brief encounter with Captain Marchand may have given him an introduction to the conduct of international diplomacy at a time when power-seeking European nations were engaged in dangerous rivalry.

CHAPTER TWO

China, 1899 and Marriage, 1901

On his return home from Egypt Beatty found himself something of a popular hero, and many social functions were organised in his honour. He spent most of his four months' leave hunting in the Shires, but he also visited his old home in Ireland. There is no doubt that he was attractive to women, and he must surely have been aware of it. Among the women he met at this time was Ethel Tree, the beautiful wife of Arthur M. Tree and only daughter of the enormously wealthy pioneer of the chain store system Marshall Field of Chicago.[1] We will return later to Beatty's courtship of her.

In April 1899 Beatty was appointed Executive Officer of the small battleship *Barfleur* (10,500 tons, 4-10 inch 29 ton guns, completed 1894). She was flagship of Rear-Admiral James Bruce, second-in-command of the China Station, and her Captain was Stanley Colville, under whom Beatty had served in the *Alexandra* and *Trafalgar* and in the first Nile campaign. It is reasonable to suppose that Colville had asked for him as his second-in-command.

The first twelve months of the *Barfleur*'s commission involved her in nothing more exciting than the normal routine work of a flagship on a foreign station; but after May 1899 events took a very different turn and Beatty again found himself on active service. The 'Boxers' were a fraternity or secret society of a type common in Chinese history. Its members were recruited mainly from the peasantry, and like other such societies they indulged in the cult of magic. Their reckless bravery was inspired by a belief in ritual practices which claimed to make members immune to injury from bullets. Their ritual included pugilistic exercises, and it was from them that the soubriquet by which they were known was derived. They first gained prominence in Shantung province in 1899 shortly after the Germans had seized the port of Kiaochow, and they quickly became symbols of resistance both to foreign penetration and to the ruling Manchu dynasty. Attacks on foreign communities soon increased to an alarming degree, and many European missionaries and Chinese converts to Christianity were massacred by them in Shantung and neighbouring provinces. The Dowager Empress Tzu-hsi, often referred to as the 'Western Empress' or, less reverently, as 'old Buddha', who had been the dominant influence in Chinese politics during the previous three decades, hoped to deflect the Boxers' activities from opposition to her dynasty by allowing them to develop unchecked; and she even gave them some degree of encouragement. In the early summer of 1890 the Boxer rebellion reached Peking, where the German Minister was murdered and foreign residents were forced to seek safety in the Legation Quarter. Chinese Government troops now joined hands with the Boxers, and railway communication with Tientsin, the important Treaty Port on the lower reaches of the Pei-ho River, which was the capital's chief link with the outside world, was soon cut. On 31st May Admiral Sir Edward Seymour, the British naval C-in-C, sent guards to Peking; but they proved quite inadequate for the protection of the foreigners. Seymour therefore sent ships of the China Squadron to Taku Bar at the mouth of the river, which was the nearest point to the capital which they could reach. There they were soon joined by Russian, French and German warships, all with Admirals in command, and by some Austrian, Italian and Japanese units as well; but Seymour was the senior officer present, and all the other nationalities agreed to serve under his command.

When an urgent warning was received telling Seymour that unless help arrived quickly the Legations would be overrun and their occupants probably massacred he acted without awaiting authority from home, and 2,000 men were landed from the warships with the object of forcing a way up the railway line from Tientsin to Peking. Seymour himself took command of the heterogeneous and ill-equipped expedition, and proceeded to act with more courage than judgment. By the time he had progressed about half way to his objective his force was completely held up by strong and well-armed bodies of Boxers, who had destroyed the railway line for some miles ahead. After five days of endeavouring to advance further Seymour learnt that the line was also being destroyed in his rear. He therefore accepted that the attempt had failed and that

he must at once retreat to Tientsin and await reinforcements.
The disengagement proved costly and hazardous, and only
after a mainly Russian force had sortied from Tientsin did the
survivors fight their way through to that city.

On 11th June (the day after Seymour had left on his forlorn
expedition) Beatty landed with 150 men from the *Barfleur* to
help in the defence of Tientsin, where a mixed brigade about
2,400 strong, whose equipment had been stripped to provide
the Peking relief force with weapons, was under attack by
about 15,000 well-armed regular Chinese troops supported by
a horde of Boxers. On the night of 16th the Taku forts at the
river mouth were bombarded and captured, so ensuring that
communications between the fleet and Tientsin were kept
open. Fierce fighting followed in and around the Tientsin
foreign concessions and the railway station, with Beatty
always in the forefront; but on 19th he was wounded in his left
arm and wrist. After a few days in the extemporised hospital
he got himself discharged, shortly before a relief column got
through to the beleaguered garrison from the fleet. On 24th
June he set out in command of the British contingent of the
mixed force hastily assembled to go to the relief of Seymour,
whom they joined the next day. The survivors, who included
over 200 wounded (among them John Jellicoe, Seymour's Flag
Captain) were successfully extricated to Tientsin on 26th.

More soldiers of many nationalities had by this time arrived,
and they gradually took over from the sailors and marines; but
Beatty and his men from the *Barfleur* stayed with the Tientsin
Defence Force. His journal gives a graphic description of the
fighting, but it ends on 13th July.[2] Shortly afterwards the
whole of Tientsin was in allied hands. Three weeks later a
force of about 20,000 men set off to relieve the Legations.
Beatty volunteered to go with them despite his wounds –
which were in fact a good deal more serious than he admitted;
but the Navy's part in the undertaking was over, and the
Legations were successfully relieved, after heavy fighting, on
14th August.

Beatty, who had again shown high qualities of leadership
and courage, as well as the ability to work amicably with
sometimes difficult allies, was now ordered to return home.
He gained a very warm commendation from Captain E. H.
Bayley under whose orders he had worked during the siege of
Tientsin, and from the C-in-C in his despatch on the

operation.[3] The outcome was that he was one of four Commanders who were specially promoted Captain to date 9th November 1900. His age was only 29, and he had served no more than two years in his previous rank.

We saw earlier how, before he left for China, Beatty had been strongly attracted by Ethel Tree. No doubt she was exquisitely turned out and beautifully mounted for the hunting field; and that, together with her thrustful, even reckless riding, must have presented an irresistible appeal to a man of Beatty's character, interests and temperament. Nor can he have been unaware of the advantages to be gained from her vast wealth. They soon exchanged letters, which on Beatty's side, reveal the strength of his determination to win such an attractive prize; but the correspondence languished because, so Admiral Chalmers suggests, he learnt that she was 'flirtatious', which was certainly no exaggeration of her attitude towards the other sex. The same biographer suggests that before Beatty went to China there may have been 'an arrangement' between them – by which he presumably meant a decision to marry as soon as she was free to do so. Beatty's early letters to his inamorata were always signed 'Jack', perhaps as a deprecatory description of himself as a simple Jack Tar; but Leslie considers it may have been intended to disguise his indentity during what he calls the 'slightly surreptitious days' of his courtship.[4] What those letters undoubtedly do make clear is that his aim went a great deal further than the desire to establish a friendship. But Ethel was a married woman, and in those days an officer who allowed it to become known that he was the lover of such a person, or who married a divorced woman, exposed himself to social ostracism and risked his whole career. No doubt this explains why Beatty decided, like Agag, to walk delicately. However, when he landed at Portsmouth and received a telegram and a letter from Ethel which were a plain invitation to resume their association of two years earlier, Beatty responded with avidity. In September 1900 he had to undergo a tricky operation in order that he might regain the use of his left arm, and until that was over he could neither progress his courtship nor return to his and Ethel's common interest of fox hunting.

Here we may note two aspects of Beatty's character which were to endure throughout his active life – namely his almost childlike superstition and his sentimentality. The former may

have been a product of his Celtic ancestry, but the Mrs.
Robinson whom he consulted about his future prospects on
9th November 1900 (the date of his promotion to Captain)
was by no means the last fortune teller whose allegedly occult
powers he sought in order to enhance his confidence about
what the future held for him. Incidentally among the many
prominent people to consult Mrs. Robinson, who was very
well known in the West End of London, was according to
Leslie, his first cousin, then 'a youthful subaltern living in
Great Cumberland Place' called Winston Churchill; and she
long preserved the letter of appreciation he wrote to her.[5]
After his marriage Beatty and his wife both consulted another
prophetess, Edyth du Bois about the number of times he
would take part in battles;[6] and in Edinburgh he found during
the war yet another called 'Josephine'. One day when Beatty
was at sea and hopeful of action he signalled to the captains of
the ships in company, no doubt partly in jest, 'Does Josephine
hold out any hopes for today?'[7] He was also known to surprise
his staff by bowing three times to a new moon when on the
bridge of his flagship – a relic of paganism which, curiously,
the great novelist Thomas Hardy seems also to have practised.[8]

As to Beatty's sentimentality, when he was able to resume
fox hunting only a few weeks after the operation on his arm
had been successfully carried out, he wrote to tell Ethel how
he had revisited the very spot where he had first sighted her,
and how he longed for the day when they could be 'together
always'. Thus Ethel cannot have been unaware of the fact that
if her marriage to Arthur Tree was dissolved she could be sure
of marrying Beatty as soon as the decree was made absolute.

During the following months both parties conducted
themselves with extreme discretion. While serving in China
Beatty had neither said nor written anything which revealed
his infatuation, and Ethel for her part allowed, and probably
encouraged, her husband to file a divorce petition against her
in the U.S.A. on the grounds of her desertion. It was granted
on 12th May 1901, and Arthur Tree was given sole custody of
their son Ronald (1897-1976) who later became a member of
the British House of Commons (Conservative), Joint Master
of the Pytchley Hunt and Parliamentary Private Secretary to a
number of Ministers in the Baldwin, Chamberlain and
Churchill governments. Churchill used his beautiful country

house Ditchley Park, near Oxford, and only a few miles from
his family's seat Blenheim Palace where he had been born,
when it was considered unsafe for him to stay at Chequers
during his World War II Premiership.*

Both parties experienced family opposition to their marrying. According to Beatty his old father 'fell flat on his back'
when told of his son's intention; and his sister Kathleen
('Trot'), to whom he was devoted was, very reasonably
apprehensive of the effect on her brother's career. Expectedly
Albert Baillie,[9] an old friend in Holy Orders and future Dean
of Windsor, who acted as a sort of unofficial chaplain to the
Beatty family, was totally opposed to the marriage. On
Ethel's side her father, whose Nonconformist principles were
as rigid as his dedication to making money, was also strongly
opposed to her divorcing her husband and re-marrying.
Ronald Tree has recorded the cataclysmic effects on both his
father and himself of the desertion of the former by his 'wilful
and beautiful mother', and how when he was 16 and Arthur
Tree died at the age of only 52 he flatly refused to go back to
Ethel. However, a reconciliation took place later, and Ronald
became 'absolutely devoted' to Beatty, for whom he
developed a profound admiration.[10]

Despite the parental opposition Ethel's divorce went
through without comment or scandal, and on 22nd May 1901
she and Beatty were married by special licence at Hanover
Square Register Office. He was 30 and she 27, and between
them they had steered a fairly safe course between the Scylla of
social ostracism and the Charybdis of ruining his naval career.

But if the immediate difficulties and dangers had been
successfully surmounted the future was, at any rate from
Ethel's point of view, far from cloudless, since in Leslie's
words 'Under Queen Victoria a divorced woman could go
nowhere. She was received in no stately home unless her lover
possessed one. Other women lifted their trailing and dusty
skirts as she passed. The woman was awarded a social
sentence, and very few dared to face the condemnation of their
sisters'.[11] Though the same prudishness continued during the
next Monarch's reign Ethel set herself to overcome such

*The house is now (1979) the property of the Ditchley Foundation for
Anglo-American Studies. For an account of its history and restoration see
Ronald Tree's autobiography *When the Moon was High* (London, 1975).

obstacles with all the passion and determination of which she
was capable; and in the end she succeeded – at any rate in some
degree.

It is difficult to say how much if at all Beatty knew about
the defects in Ethel's character – her mental imbalance, her
arrogant pride based on nothing but money, her rabid jealousy
and possessiveness – before they married; but the most
probable answer is 'very little'. Leslie on the other hand, who
got to know both Ethel and her husband very well indeed, and
became a great admirer of the latter, saw her defects clearly
and recorded them both in his private papers and in his draft
biography of the Admiral. In the latter work he recorded that
she had 'a will of iron', and that although her wealth helped
Beatty's career by enabling him to enter the highest social and
political circles,★ she also 'marred his happiness', and at times
reduced him 'almost to despair.' He recalled the poem 'Modern
Love' in which George Meredith agonised on the disaster of
his own first marriage, and applied to Beatty and Ethel the
metaphor used by the poet in his own case. 'These two were
rapid falcons in a snare'.[12] As he several times referred to her
resemblance to that beautiful if deadly bird of prey he was
evidently impressed by Meredith's metaphor. She was, he
wrote in retrospect 'beautiful, opulent, ambitious and
unhinged by her hereditary fortune and by an insane streak';
and again 'She brought him many gifts: great beauty, a
passionate and a jealous love, sons, wealth, houses and a
personality he could not conquer, for against him was arrayed
a distraught spirit which brought their home life to utter
misery'. He also recorded how, much later, Beatty had
described himself as 'the most unhappy man in the world', and
remarked 'I have paid terribly for my millions'.[13] Leslie also
commented astringently on the *'folie des grandes maisons'* from
which Ethel always suffered; for she bought or rented at
various times, and often simultaneously, Hanover Lodge in
Regent's Park and 17 Grosvenor Square in London, Dingley
Hall and Brooksby Hall in Leicestershire for hunting with the
Quorn and Cottesmore foxhound packs, Grantully Castle in
Scotland for the grouse shooting, and Reigate Priory in Surrey

★The extent to which the Beattys moved in the highest society is shown
by the fact that King George V's diary records them coming to lunch or
dinner at Abergeldie Castle or Balmoral five times between 1906 and 1914.
In addition Beatty twice took part in Royal shoots. Royal Archives.

– which Beatty particularly liked because it had been the home of Lord Howard of Effingham (1536–1624), who became Queen Elizabeth I's Lord Admiral and held the chief command against the Spanish Armada in 1588; and of course when Beatty became 1st Sea Lord the official residence Mall House was also available to them.[14] The truth surely is that Ethel was the prototype of 'the standard dissatisfied rich woman' personified by the wealthy and utterly spoilt Madame Odintsov created by Turgenev in his novel *Fathers and Sons* (Paris, 1888), recently analysed and dissected so brilliantly by Sir Victor Pritchett.[15]

But few if any of the foregoing ominous indications regarding Ethel's character can have been apparent to Beatty when he married her; for they wrote or telegraphed to each other almost daily when they were separated, and his letters bear every mark of an utterly sincere, indeed overwhelming, love and devotion. It is, as Leslie remarked, curious that both sides of 'this amazing correspondence' have survived: 'hers sealed with mauve wax and his in the envelopes addressed with the [diagonal] slant' which became as characteristic of him as the tilt at which he always wore his naval cap. His letters, wrote Leslie, 'tell the story of his [naval] life', while hers were 'iridescent, amusing, gossipy, intolerant, passionate and often quite incredible'.[16] Though Admiral Chalmers used a number of her letters in the authorised biography, he suppressed virtually all the stigmata noted by Leslie – which in fact gave warning of the troubles to come.

Here two persons who were to play an important part in Beatty's life must be introduced – Bryan Godfrey (later Captain Sir Bryan) Godfrey-Faussett (1863–1945) and his wife. The Godfreys were a Kentish family which can be traced back at least as far as the 15th century. In the early 18th century they were linked by marriage with another Kentish family called Faussett, and in the mid 19th century their names became permanently linked together. Bryan was the eldest son of Godfrey Trevelyan Godfrey-Faussett and an Irish girl from County Kilkenny named Jane Morris. He joined the Navy in 1877, seven years before Beatty, and soon became a close friend of the Duke and Duchess of York (later King George V and Queen Mary) whom he accompanied on their tour of the Dominions in 1901. On conclusion of that tour the Duke was made Prince of Wales, and appointed Bryan as his Equerry.

He accompanied the Prince and Princess to India in 1905-6, and after the Prince had succeeded to the throne, to the Delhi Coronation Durbar of 1911. Bryan served as Equerry-in-Ordinary to George V until his death in 1936, continued in that office during the brief reign of Edward VIII, and finally became an Extra Equerry to George VI from his accession until he died in 1945.[17]

Eugénie Dudley Ward was descended from an obscure Alsatian called Louis Mayer and a remarkable girl born Fanny Kreilssamner who, after Louis had conveniently disappeared, married Colonel John Gurwood. He had fought with distinction in the Peninsular War and at Waterloo and became the editor of Wellington's despatches.[18] Gurwood committed suicide in 1845, but it was through him that Fanny was accepted by London society – fortunately for the four daughters born of her first marriage, one of whom, named Eugénie, married William Baliol Brett, a future Master of the Rolls and 1st Viscount Esher, in 1850.[19] One son and one daughter were born of that union, and the daughter married William Humble Dudley Ward. It was their daughter Eugénie Fanny Eveline whom Bryan Godfrey-Faussett married in 1907. Portraits and photographs show her to have been a beautiful woman with long golden hair. To Bryan and their intimate friends she was always known as 'Babs' – which Beatty must have become aware of; but perhaps because he regarded that nickname as the prerogative of her husband, he never used it. Incidentally the use of babyish nicknames seems to have been fashionable among the upper class at that time, and Ethel Beatty was always referred to as 'Tata' by her husband and their circle of rich friends.

Bryan Godfrey-Faussett's early letters to his fiancée telling how he broke the news of his engagement to the Prince of Wales and his consort make it plain that she was at once accepted into the Court circle.[20] The very detailed diary kept by Bryan throughout his naval service and his long period as a Courtier will prove an invaluable source to social historians of the first half of the 20th century;* and it was almost certainly

*Now in Churchill College, Cambridge. It may be remarked that Eugénie Godfrey-Faussett was a sister-in-law of Freda Dudley Ward with whom Edward, Prince of Wales (later Edward VIII) had a long and passionate love affair, but whom he later callously discarded in favour of Mrs. 'Wally' Simpson – whom he married after his abdication in 1936. See Frances Donaldson, *Edward VIII* (Weidenfeld and Nicolson, 1974) pp. 57-8 and 159-60.

through Beatty's friendship with the future King George V that he became intimate with Bryan and his attractive wife. The manner in which the fate and fortunes of the two families became intertwined will form an important part of the tale to be told here.

CHAPTER THREE

Problems – Naval and Matrimonial, 1902-1913

Despite the successful surgery on Beatty's arm, and the fact that he was able quickly to resume fox hunting, almost two years elapsed between his being wounded at Tientsin and the Admiralty's medical board passing him fit for sea. His first appointment as a Captain was to the cruiser *Juno*, a comparatively modern ship (launched 1895, 5,600 tons, eleven 6-inch guns). She was allocated temporarily to the recently formed Home Fleet, then commanded by the redoubtable Admiral Sir Arthur K. ('Tug') Wilson. After exercises, in which Beatty showed he was a good ship handler and no stickler about the rigid naval etiquette which then prevailed, in August 1902 he took the *Juno* out to the Mediterranean, which was her proper station. The separation from Ethel, who never took the sacrifices demanded of her by the navy well, was evidently a lachrymose affair on her part.

After calling briefly at Gibraltar, the strategic importance of which evidently impressed Beatty, he sailed for Malta. His letters to Ethel of this period show that he had difficulty in bringing the *Juno*'s crew to the state of efficiency he considered essential. However, under his firm leadership it was not long before she was placed at the top in the gunnery practices and other competitions by which the efficiency of ships was then, and for many years afterwards, assessed.

The *Juno* had nearly reached the end of her commission when Beatty took her over, and after three months he transferred to the *Arrogant*, a slightly more modern ship (launched 1896, 5,750 tons). She belonged to a class known as 'Ram Cruisers' which had been designed to take advantage of the somewhat adventitious evidence regarding the effectiveness of ramming the enemy produced by the Austro-Italian battle of Lissa in 1866. Again Beatty's period of command was brief, and in October 1904 he transferred to the modern and larger County class cruiser *Suffolk* (launched 1903, 9,800 tons, fourteen 6-inch guns). During the last part of this period of Beatty's service on the Mediterranean station the C-in-C was Admiral Lord Charles Beresford, whose rigid system of training and discouragement of initiative did not appeal to him. However, they always remained on good terms – helped perhaps by the fact that they were both Irishmen and both horse lovers. This was the time when, under the dynamic influence of Sir John ('Jacky') Fisher, who became First Sea Lord on 20th October 1904,* the navy was adapting itself, albeit with widespread reluctance among many officers, to a multitude of new weapons and techniques – such as wireless telegraphy, torpedoes and the replacement of coal by oil firing. Though the wealth which Beatty now enjoyed, and the expensive pursuits such as polo which it made possible, aroused jealousy among some officers it could not be denied that in competitions and recreations the *Suffolk* came out at or very near the top. One incident which was widely repeated in the fleet showed Ethel at her most arrogant. Despite warnings from his Chief Engineer her husband over-drove his ship in order to get back quickly to Malta, doing serious damage to her main machinery. When there was talk of disciplinary action being taken against him Ethel is alleged to have remarked 'What – court martial my David? I'll buy them a new ship'. Whether true or not such a tale did the young Captain no good.

On 22nd February 1905 Ethel, who had come out to join her husband, gave birth to a son at Malta – to Beatty's great delight. He was christened David Field, but was long known as 'Dadie', which was how he pronounced his name as a baby. From the start Beatty became an adoring father.

Towards the end of 1905 the Beattys returned home in order that he should take up the appointment of Naval Adviser to the Army Council. Co-operation between the two services was not assisted by Fisher's tactlessness and ruthlessness, but Beatty got on well with the soldiers and had a hand in planning the transport of an Expeditionary Force to the continent. However, combined operations (in the modern sense) then had a low place in Admiralty plans and were not seriously investigated until much later – an omission for which

*Not on Trafalgar Day (21st Oct.) as Fisher was later fond of saying and many writers have repeated.

a heavy price was to be exacted.

Beatty left the War Office in December 1908 to take command of the battleship *Queen* (15,000 tons, four 12-inch and twelve 6-inch guns), in the Atlantic Fleet. She formed part of the concentration of warships in or near home waters which was the key to Fisher's strategic policy. As with Wilson and Beresford in the Mediterranean Beatty soon got on excellent terms with Prince Louis of Battenberg, the C-in-C, from whom he won golden opinions. But he was severely, and justly, critical of the lack of originality and imagination shown in the fleet's tactical exercises at this time. In July 1909 he wrote sarcastically to Ethel that the recent two days at sea 'have been most productive, principally in demonstrating how unpractised our Admirals are in the manner and methods of handling large fleets. It is not their fault. We don't do enough of it . . . We have a very fine Fleet and the best materials . . . But we have eight Admirals, and there is not one among them unless it be Prince Louis, who impresses me that he is capable of a great effort and 34 Captains among whom there is really fine material, which seems wasted for the want of a guide or leader. . . .'[1] Though one should probably discount such strictures in part as coming from a young and ambitious officer it is a fact that, except for the time when Admiral Sir William May was in command of the Home Fleet (1909-11), training suffered from what Admiral K. G. B. Dewar, one of the 'naval intellectuals' of the period, has aptly stigmatised as 'tactical arthritis' – by which he meant the rigid conformity enforced on Captains and junior Flag Officers who were merely required 'to follow the Admiral's motions'.[2] Any tendency to unorthodoxy or originality was severely frowned on – which plainly rankled with Beatty.

Although in his letters to his wife Beatty was often critical of senior officers he kept clear of the deadly feud which developed at this time between Beresford and Fisher, and which split the navy from top to bottom. Early in December 1909 he learnt that he would get his Flag when the next vacancy occurred; but as his time as a Captain was less than that prescribed for promotion to Rear-Admiral a special Order in Council was necessary. On 1st January 1910 Beatty, then just under 39 years old, became the youngest Flag Officer in the navy since the late 18th century.* His and Ethel's delight

*Rodney became a Flag Officer at 31 and Keppel at 37. Nelson became Rear-Admiral of the Blue at 39.

in this exceptional proof of the high regard in which he was held was enhanced by another son being born to them on 2nd April 1910. He was christened Peter Randolph Louis – the last in compliment to the young Admiral's C-in-C, who stood sponsor to the infant.

In the spring of 1911 Beatty attended the Senior Officers' War Course at Portsmouth, and took a house at Ryde, Isle of Wight, in order to have his family near him. Though he told Bryan Godfrey-Faussett that the course was 'in parts interesting and instructive and in other parts purely a great waste of time',[3] it was in truth a poor substitute for a proper staff training, such as Beresford and a few far-sighted officers had long wanted to introduce;[4] but another seven years were to elapse before that deficiency was fully remedied. The trouble lay in the fact that too many senior officers, including Fisher and Wilson, considered training for staff duties to be quite unnecessary.

Beatty's early promotion appears to have whetted Ethel's determination to overcome one of the handicaps under which divorced women then laboured – namely the strong opposition to allowing them to be presented at Court, or indeed to participate in any Royal functions. A letter written many years later by Eugénie Godfrey-Faussett, to Shane Leslie recalled most amusingly the scene which she made in order to achieve her purpose. It is worth quoting.

Hampton Court Palace
January 25th 1948

My dear Shane,
        . . . It was a long drawn out battle to get poor Ethel (A) to Court or (B) to the Coronation of K.G.V. You remember how sticky were the laws in those days of [? towards] those who wished to attend the Court as opposed to the Divorce Court? Poor old Godfrey had been entrusted with this ticklish business,* and had been requested to read the whole of the Divorce proceedings to prove Ethel's innocence etc. Godfrey was doing his best to help. The Lord Chamberlain was looking down his nose.[5] David was threatening to leave the Navy. Ethel was putting on one of her hysterical acts . . . I remember my astonishment on

---

*Though Eugénie here refers to her husband as 'Godfrey' their son George assures me that in the family he was always referred to as 'Bryan'.

entering the drawing room [of the Beattys' house at Ryde, where the Godfrey-Faussetts were staying] to find Ethel in floods of tears and Godfrey standing with his arms folded and a heavy scowl looking like the well known picture of Napoleon! Godfrey later explained to me that she was saying that she would force David to leave the Navy unless she was received at Court and he was answering that he would drop the whole business unless she swore she would do no such wicked thing! Godfrey won the day, David remained in the Navy, and some years later the embargo was lifted and Ethel duly made her bow. Do come down here whenever you can. . . .

Yours ever

Eugénie's memory is substantiated by the letters which passed between Beatty and her husband and between him and the Lord Chamberlain's Office, which have survived apparently complete; but she does not mention that shortly after the painful exhibition put on by Ethel at Ryde she did send Godfrey-Faussett an abject if somewhat ungrammatical apology 'for my very silly and weak behaviour when talking to you on Sunday. I fear the only excuse I have to offer is a very stupid one, that for the last few weeks since Jack first talked to me about giving up the sea, I have been most frightfully worried. I have always been so anxious for him to go on, and that I, in no way, should be a hindrance to him. The thought of his making perhaps a fatal mistake on my account came upon me as a great shock and so for a few days quite unnerved me. So do please forgive me'.[6] That letter probably decided Beatty's *amicus curiae* to persevere on his behalf.

Meanwhile the machinery of Court etiquette was moving exceedingly slowly. From that quarter the story begins early in March 1909 when an official in the Lord Chamberlain's office told Godfrey-Faussett that 'several anonymous letters have been received by [the] Lord Chamberlain about Mrs. Beatty', which makes it plain that poisoned pens had got to work. Although the writer declared that such letters 'do not influence the question' he thought it right that Godfrey-Faussett should know 'that her having been *divorced* and we understand having lived with Captain B. before the trial [which was almost certainly untrue] makes her case a little shady – *not "snow white love"* I fear'. He concluded none the

less that 'if the Judge who tried the case can supply the
required notes on the trial – which go to prove that ALL *the
blame* is on the side of the other husband (who divorced her) –
then the case can be considered on its own merits. But it is too
late for this year and the two Courts are full. . . .'[7]
It was probably the above quoted letter which caused
Beatty to go into action to obtain evidence of his own
innocence, and in October 1910 he sent Godfrey-Faussett 'a
certified copy of the Evidence' given in the divorce court in
America. He stressed that Ethel 'first left Tree BEFORE I knew
her', and left him finally 'in March '99 when I was in
China!!'.[8] Godfrey-Faussett's reaction was to advise him not to
'fuss about it any more', and not to 'apply for a "Court"' . . .
at present at any rate';[9] but as time passed and activities in
London became increasingly concentrated on the Coronation
of King George V without any sign that the existence of the
Beattys was to be recognised at that climax to the season, his
patience evidently began to wear thin and he repeated to
Godfrey-Faussett his threat to leave the navy. He wrote that
while doing the Senior Officers' Course he had 'ample time
for reflection' and in consequence was 'beginning to consider
the desirability of leaving the service altogether'. His reason
was that 'my little lady likes the good things of this world
including the gay side of it. She has a nice house in Town and
is sufficiently supplied with the necessary to be able to live in
London and enjoy the entertaining and being entertained that a
season produces. And it has undoubtedly struck her that my
being in the services for ever precludes her from anticipating
[? participating] in such and [in] what to her . . . provides
something of the joy of Life'. He also protested that his wife
was 'not permitted to have her patriotism and loyalty
stimulated by being present at Court', and concluded by
asking for 'a command to attend the Court Ball' in order 'to
tide over the feeling of depression and of being overlooked'
from which they were suffering.[10] This lengthy and rather
pathetic plea produced a suggestion from the Lord Chamberlain's office that as Ethel had 'been to a Court Ball in the last
reign' and 'she is such a personal friend of Their Majesties' the
latter might 'wish some alteration [to be] made in her status'.[11]
The Coronation, however, took place on 9th August without
any sign of further progress; but the King does seem to have
taken note of what his equerry told him, since Ethel was

commanded to attend a Court Ball a little later, and so, in Leslie' words, was able 'to make her bow'. In consequence her husband gave up all thought of abandoning his naval career.

It may be useful here to quote what Leslie wrote in his draft biography of Beatty about the relations between him and Ethel, and the correspondence that passed between them. That each was jealous towards the other, and that they watched each other closely for any sign of interest in another man or woman, appears again and again in their letters; and Leslie's picture is the more valuable because he knew them both well, and was certainly no uncritical admirer of Ethel.

'Until the war broke out' wrote Leslie 'he employed every means of correspondence to keep in touch with her, to keep her humoured or amused, to keep her roving affections within the unfailing orbit of his love. Telegrams were exchanged every day and he was miserable when she forgot to send hers or if the mails were late. He toiled at plans for meeting her and bringing her to ports he would touch or hotels he could reach. When she could join the Fleet the Admiral's barge was at her untiring disposal. . . .

He always hated leaving her or seeing her depart for the London season, for Ascot, Sandown, for Paris, for Monte Carlo but he drew satisfaction if he felt she was being admired and amused. Restless and relentless she cruised south in search of pleasure, occupation, frivolity, friends and admirers. At home she passed rapidly from the pursuit of one house to another. He indulged her in all her whims and wishes, though in his letters he tried to curb her with a silk snaffle . . . He was so faithful to his dream of her that he could not bear to think she could be otherwise to him. If she did not keep all these things in her heart she kept every letter and every scrap he wrote in her treasury. Although she wrote in reply she was careless in addressing or sending them. He was always writing almost like a schoolboy of his continual disappointments when the post arrived. Again and again he wrote out the simple form of his address, but she had a weakness for mixing the names of ports; and of course it is impossible to receive letters which actually have not been written. . . .

His letters came down to routine and formula: endless inquiries and hugs for the two "Sonnies", the utmost consideration for Ethel's plans and pleasures, cheery response to all her gossip and very careful but unfavourable accounts of any ladies he met. A number of fair ladies, considered highly in their day, would have been surprised at the poor estimate they met in the Admiral's letters to his wife . . . Other ladies crossing his path fared even worse and received the lowest possible marks in any beauty competition. He was jealous of her companionships but could not bear her to travel on the Continent or hunt in the Shires without male escort. Out hunting he implored her to pay attention to hounds and less to conversation at the covert's side. He begged her not to use beauty make-up while she was still young and beautiful.'[12]

Many years later, when Leslie was working on his biography of Beatty, he asked one of the Admiral's intimates Captain Augustus Agar VC, whether he thought Ethel's vast wealth had been a handicap to Beatty's career. Agar replied that before the war Beatty had been the subject of criticism on that score, not all of which came from within the navy, but that after the battle of Jutland it was never heard again.[13] Probably such criticism had no firmer base than jealousy for the good things of life which Beatty was able to enjoy after his marriage.

Soon after the Palace squall over Ethel's presentation had subsided she decided to follow the example of other very wealthy people of those days and add a floating and mobile home to the considerable number of static homes she already owned or rented. Beatty looked around for a suitable vessel and thought he had found one called *Glencairn*, a substantial ship of nearly 900 registered tons (1,570 tons gross) built at Leith in 1908. However, it turned out that she had already been bought by Lord Tredegar, the owner of vast estates in South Wales.* Beatty unwisely telegraphed to Tredegar offering to buy the yacht at a premium – and asking whether, if she was not for sale, her owner could recommend another vessel. The reply he received may be classed as the epitome of the snub aristocratic. 'The *Glencairn* is not for sale', telegraphed Tredegar, 'and I am not a ship broker'.[14] Search for an alternative was accordingly renewed, and Beatty entrusted the job to a certain Captain Grint – about whom tantalisingly little is to be found in the Leslie or Beatty papers – except the fact that he became the devoted and life-long friend of both

*Courtenay Charles Evan Morgan, 3rd Baron and 1st Viscount (2nd creation) Tredegar. (1867-1934).

the Beattys. Grint soon recommended a steam yacht of about 210 tons registered (680 gross) called the *Sheelah*, built by John Brown on the Clyde in 1902. She was bought almost on the nail and at an undisclosed price.[15] To Ethel she was a godsend because she never suffered from seasickness, and when she was afloat her tortured and unstable mind probably came nearer to finding peace than at any other time.

Before the trouble over Ethel's presentation at Court had been resolved another crisis which threatened Beatty's career blew up. In July 1911 he wrote to the private secretary to the First Lord, Captain E. C. Troubridge,* about his employment after the 15 months spent ashore doing the War Course. Beatty had evidently asked for command of either the 1st or 2nd Division of the Home Fleet or to be appointed as Director of Mobilisation in the Admiralty when that post fell vacant. Troubridge replied that the First Lord, Reginald McKenna, could not promise either of the sea-going posts mentioned – which was surely understandable since Beatty's name stood at the very bottom of the Flag List and the claims of more senior officers obviously had to be considered. But Troubridge gave warning that Beatty 'not wanting [the] 3rd Division or [the] Atlantic [Fleet] has rather narrowed the choice'; so he was 'somewhat at a loss' to give 'any definite reply'.[16] Beatty's reasoning was that whereas service in the North Sea or Channel was likely to bring opportunities of action in the event of war with Germany, the Atlantic Fleet, based chiefly on Gibraltar, held no such prospects; but he certainly took a serious risk in pressing his wishes to the point of refusing whatever appointment the Admiralty might offer him; for in those days, and indeed for many years after the 'Commissioners for Executing the Office of Lord High Admiral' were very conscious of their dignity and took a poor view of officers who argued the toss with them.

At first the prospect for Beatty looked favourable, since less than two weeks after Troubridge had written so dubiously, McKenna himself asked the young Admiral to come and see him. Though Beatty got the impression that the First Lord understood and accepted his unwillingness to go as second-in-command of the Atlantic Fleet, either he read more into the First Lord's words than was intended or McKenna changed his

*Later Admiral Sir Ernest Troubridge (1862–1926)

mind – perhaps under pressure from senior officers who viewed Beatty's meteoric promotion with envy. At any rate on 21st July McKenna wrote 'in pursuance of our conversation' and offered him the very post he had indicated he did not want.[17] Five days later Beatty replied at length explaining why he wanted to serve in the Home Fleet and disliked the Atlantic Fleet job. He claimed, apparently correctly, that he had asked Troubridge to note his name for the former, that the secretary was well aware that 'the one appointment I have always stated I'd not wish to be considered for . . . was that of 2nd in Command Atlantic Fleet'.[18] Troubridge replied the same day, with rather brutal if justified frankness, that 'The fact is that the Admiralty view is that officers should serve where they i.e. the Admiralty wish and *not* where they themselves wish';[19] and it can hardly be denied that acceptance of the latter as a matter of principle would have produced chaotic conditions. It is, however, certainly true that even in the early 20th century officers who possessed influence often did succeed in getting the appointments they wanted; and when, as in Beatty's case, they enjoyed such wealth as to make them prepared to stand out against Their Lordships' wishes a serious clash was obviously a possibility, and could only have ended with the enforced retirement of the recalcitrant officer.

Beatty's reply to Troubridge's somewhat minatory letter began with a sermon about the principles stated by the secretary with regard to Admiralty policy. 'If I had lived to a hundred' he wrote sarcastically, 'I would never have guessed them'. He continued on an angry note, writing that 'There is something peculiarly subtle in inviting the poor devil yearning for employment to state his desires and hopes and then offering him the one thing they know he doesn't want'; and he ended with an ill-mannered attack on the outlook and methods of the Admiralty.[20] He then went to Scotland for the grouse shooting on the Invercauld estate, which Ethel had rented from the Farquharsons; while in London rumours circulated that he had acted impetuously and in pique. These rumours evidently reached Beatty's ears, since in August he wrote at length to the faithful Godfrey-Faussett setting out his side of the story of his conversations and communications with Troubridge and McKenna. Godfrey-Faussett took this somewhat one-sided statement of the case to Bolton Abbey, where the King was enjoying the shooting on the Yorkshire estate of the Duke of Devonshire, and read it to the Monarch who, according to his equerry, said he was 'sorry about it and perfectly understands your feelings and is not surprised at your being disgusted at the way you have been dealt with'. But as he continued with a tally of the game killed ('yesterday 790 brace without the pick-up') and gave no indication regarding whether the King would take the matter up with the First Lord, Beatty may well have felt disappointed.[21] It thus came to pass that, except for the few months of the senior Officers' War Course, he remained on half pay for the two years following his promotion to Flag Rank. Admiral Chalmers considers that Beatty's refusal of the Atlantic Fleet appointment 'was a courageous decision' and stressed that he was 'always ready to dice with fate'.[22] But it can surely be argued that, without his wife's wealth and with a family to support, he could hardly have faced such a long period of reduced emoluments with equanimity; and his dealings with Troubridge and McKenna suggest that the distinction he had earned on active service in the Sudan and in China, and his very early promotions, had produced a very high degree of confidence in his own ability and more than a touch of arrogance.

The chief purpose behind Asquith's ministerial reshuffle of 1911 was to improve relations between the War Office and the Admiralty, which had been far from cordial during Fisher's time as First Sea Lord and had reached a nadir when Sir Arthur Wilson held that office. The issue came to a head when in the spring of that year the French sent a military force to Fez in Morocco and the Germans, seeing this move as a first step towards annexation of that country, sent the gunboat *Panther* to Agadir on the Atlantic coast – allegedly to protect German interests and subjects. In fact German actions, in which the Kaiser had a big hand, had a far deeper political and strategic purpose – namely that Germany should participate with France and Spain in carving up Morocco. To the British government the prospect of a potentially hostile naval base being set up on the flank of one of her most important trade routes was alarming. The crisis revealed that the navy was far from being ready for the war which at one time seemed likely, and that no war plans existed except in the mind of Admiral Wilson. Though the crisis blew over in October and was resolved by Germany recognising a French protectorate over

Morocco in exchange for a slice of French Congo the aftermath rumbled around Whitehall for a long time.

If war had come an attempt by Germany to invade Britain was considered to be a real possibility, and invasion had in fact been almost continuously in the foreground of the deliberations of the Committee of Imperial Defence ever since 1904. The problem produced a split between the 'Continental School', who considered that in the event of war an Expeditionary Force should be sent to support the left flank of the French Army and the 'Maritime School', which held that although a serious invasion was not a practical operation of war as long as our fleet commanded the North Sea, a raid in considerable strength on the East Coast – or 'Bolt from the Blue' – was a real possibility, especially in foggy weather. In their view strong land forces should therefore be held at home in order to contain such a force until the fleet could reach the scene and deal with the enemy transports and escorting warships. The crisis came at the famous C.I.D. meeting of 23rd August 1911, when General Sir Henry Wilson, the Francophile Director of Military Operations, completely outclassed his namesake Admiral Sir Arthur Wilson, the First Sea Lord, in the presentation of their cases.[23] One pregnant result of this victory of the Continental School was the abandonment of the concept of Amphibious Warfare until Fisher revived it in 1914. Beatty, very naturally, favoured the Maritime School (though with qualifications about Fisher's wilder schemes for assaults from the sea); but he did not yet carry heavy enough guns to make his views heard in high circles.

On 23rd October 1911 Churchill was moved by Asquith from the Home Office to the Admiralty, and McKenna took over the former appointment. Though the new First Lord accepted the despatch of the greater part of the Regular Army to France he also soon made his advocacy of amphibious assaults plain. But the flaw in his strategic concepts lay, firstly, in his insistence on the adoption of 'offensive' measures from the very beginning of a war – with scant regard for the resources available and the need for specialised equipment and intensive training for such notoriously hazardous undertakings; and, secondly, in the fact that although his ideas were imaginative they were often wildly impracticable. We will return to that subject later.

Churchill's arrival in the Admiralty marked a climacteric in

Beatty's career. Although Churchill had not previously met him he was familiar with his exploits in command of gunboats on the Nile during the campaigns of 1896–98, when he had been serving with the 21st Lancers.[24] He has also recorded his admiration for Beatty's fearlessness and prowess in the hunting field and on the polo ground. At their first meetings Beatty also impressed Churchill by his ability to view 'questions of naval strategy and tactics in a different light from the average naval officer', that he 'thought of war problems in their unity by land, sea and air', and that he expressed himself in speech and on paper with clarity and brevity and freedom from technical jargon.'[25]

It is certain that the Sea Lords took a dim view of Beatty's intransigence over the Atlantic Fleet appointment, and were reluctant if not downright unwilling to offer him further service; but Churchill took a different line, and he has told how his first meeting with the young Admiral 'induced me immediately to disregard this unfortunate advice'.[26] The outcome was that on 8th January 1912 he appointed Beatty as his Naval Secretary – the key post which Troubridge had recently vacated.*

Meanwhile Churchill's dissatisfaction with Admiral Wilson as his chief naval colleague had come to a head, and at the end of November 1911 he dismissed him. The choice of a successor did not, however, prove easy. Churchill undoubtedly considered Prince Louis of Battenberg,[27] but even at that time – before the wave of xenophobia had swept the country – his German ancestry was held in some quarters, notably by Lloyd George, to rule him out. In the end the colourless and uninspiring Sir Francis Bridgeman was appointed; but after a few months relations between the two of them had deteriorated badly, chiefly because of Churchill's interference in every aspect of the Admiralty's business. In November 1912 Churchill seized on Bridgeman's dubious health as grounds for another change. But when he told the House of Commons of his intention, and quoted from private letters written by Bridgeman to Battenberg and Beatty in which he admitted that his health was indifferent, he came under heavy fire from the Conservative benches.[28] Inevitably Beatty was involved in

*Soon after Beatty's appointment the title was changed from 'First Lord's Private Secretary' to 'Naval Secretary', presumably because Churchill brought in his own Private Secretary.

the fracas at the top of the naval tree; and he appears to have shown tact and diplomacy in handling it.* It is worth quoting what Churchill said on the subject of the physical and mental stamina demanded of a First Sea Lord.

'The duties of the First Sea Lord', he declared, 'are of vital importance to the country . . . it is essential that the First Sea Lord should be thoroughly fit and capable . . . He must be able to transact a mass of detailed business day by day without being unduly fatigued. He must have good health and strength, not only sufficient to bear the daily strain, but to bear any extra or sudden strain which circumstances may throw upon him. If the First Sea Lord is not thoroughly fit and capable for reasons of health, it is the duty of the First Lord to tell him so, to suggest his resignation of his office, and, if necessary, to supersede him. . . .'[29]

One cannot but feel that Churchill himself deviated widely from the principle he laid down in Parliament both when he recalled Fisher to the office of First Sea Lord in October 1914 at the age of 73 and when he retained Admiral Pound in that office during the Second World War long after there was strong evidence that his health by no means came up to Churchill's standard.[30]

Beatty's correspondence shows that although he held no very high opinion of Admiral Bridgeman's ability he liked him personally. In December 1912, about a year after Churchill had dismissed him from the office of First Sea Lord, Beatty as Naval Secretary became involved in a controversy with the Palace over whether Bridgeman or the maverick Lord Charles Beresford, who enjoyed the King's friendship, should be promoted to fill the one available vacancy as Admiral of the Fleet. He told Lord Stamfordham, the King's private secretary, that although such promotions rested with the Monarch, a search for precedents had proved that the Admiralty always submitted recommendations. As Bridgeman had held all the high commands possible, including the office of First Sea Lord, and the Admiralty had declined to recommend Beresford for promotion, he was confident that the King would not be placed 'in an awkward position' if the former was preferred to the latter. The King evidently accepted this advice, since

*On 26th Nov. Bridgeman wrote to Beatty that he had begun to draft a letter of resignation but had changed his mind when he felt better in health. Quite properly Beatty probably showed it to Churchill.

Bridgeman was promoted; and so ended what Beatty described to Stamfordham as 'this lamentable controversy'.[31]

Because there was no proper Naval Staff at the beginning of Beatty's time as Naval Secretary he evidently acted not only as personal Staff Officer to the First Lord but as a sort of one man Naval Staff – which certainly reveals an extraordinary state of affairs in Whitehall. At any rate there exist in his papers a number of cogent memoranda in his hand which were produced for Churchill at this time. They dealt with such matters as which bases should be developed for the Home Fleet (he favoured Scapa Flow in the Orkneys, and Cromarty Firth and Rosyth on the east coast of Scotland),* the threat to surface ships from mines and submarines (in appreciating which Beatty was far ahead of nearly all his contemporaries), the need for powerful light forces to be based on Harwich and Yarmouth, the probable strategic employment of the German Navy, the functions of our own battle cruisers, co-operation with the French Navy and a multitude of other subjects. Though these papers make it evident that Beatty had not yet mastered the art of clear and concise literary expression, they do show the wide range of his thinking, and how wrong were those who regarded him only as a gallant and rather swashbuckling character. It is also a fact that many of the ideas Beatty propounded at this time were adopted during the next two or three years.

Churchill always subjected his professional colleagues and advisers to intense pressure, and Beatty's letters to Ethel written in 1912-13 while she was on the Continent – usually gambling at Monte Carlo – are of particular interest in revealing how he reacted to and withstood that pressure. His two years on half pay, his comparative youth, and his sporting interests probably all contributed to his ability to cope with Churchill's restless and dynamic energy, and also to his ability to view far-ranging problems with a clear eye. What Beatty lacked, as did Churchill, was knowledge of the technical side of modern warfare; and decisions had been taken during the Fisher era which vitiated both the capacity of our big ships to stand up to heavy punishment and their ability to inflict such punishment on an enemy. But it would be unfair to blame

*See Map 1, pages 74-5

Churchill for the lack of magazine safety arrangements, the inefficiency of our armour-piercing shell, and the rejection by the Admiralty of an advanced fire control system capable of producing good results at long ranges, since the crucial decisions had been taken some years earlier. We will revert to that subject in the next chapter.

We have seen how Lord Charles Beresford, for all his defects of character and of conduct, had long favoured the creation of a Naval Staff and as a first step had initiated the Naval Intelligence Department as early as 1887;[32] but little was done to develop the idea for more than a decade. In 1908 Maurice Hankey, the remarkable Marine officer who had just become Assistant Secretary to the C.I.D., produced a paper stressing the need for such an organisation;[33] but he was not yet influential enough to get it adopted in face of the opposition of many top Admirals, including Fisher and A. K. Wilson. Churchill, however, needed no persuasion on such an issue, and on 1st January 1912 he announced publicly that a Naval War Staff was to be created.[34] Though his scheme was a long overdue step in the right direction it suffered from the serious defects that the Chief of the War Staff had no executive authority, that the First Sea Lord was not also made Chief of Naval Staff, and that no trained Staff Officers existed to put flesh on Churchill's skeleton proposals. It thus came to pass that the Navy entered the war handicapped by faulty organisation at the top. Beatty was well aware of the need for a Staff and supported Churchill's efforts to conjure one into existence; but, as with Hankey in 1908, he did not yet possess the rank and influence to overcome what the influential American naval historian Captain A. T. Mahan called 'the inertia of a conservative class'.*

A few months after Churchill promulgated his staff proposals it became known that the German Admiralty was pressing for an amendment to the Navy Law of 1900 – the legislative measure which had first aroused British apprehensions. The

---

*Mahan was actually referring to the long interval which frequently elapsed between weapon developments and the changes in tactics which should result therefrom; but the same argument can reasonably be applied to changes in administrative methods such as the need for a staff arising from the same cause. See Allan Westcott, Ed. *Mahan on Naval Warfare, Selections from the writings of Rear-Admiral A. T. Mahan*, (Little, Brown, Boston).

new 'Novelle' as it was called proposed that three new Dreadnoughts should be laid down in 1912, 1914 and 1916 and that a third fully commissioned squadron of battleships should be created. If carried out these measures would make the existing British naval building programme quite insufficient to maintain the 10% superiority in capital ships over the next two largest naval powers established in 1889 and redefined in 1908. Hectic negotiations between the two countries followed, in which Beatty was only concerned as a sort of personal staff officer to Churchill. First the enormously wealthy Anglo-German financier Sir Ernest Cassell took advantage of his friendship with Albert Ballin, the head of the Hamburg-Amerika Line, to pave the way to persuading the Kaiser to modify the Novelle.[35] Then followed the famous Haldane Mission to Germany of 1912;[36] but none of these comings and goings succeeded in getting the German proposals modified, and in May the Reichstag voted to adopt the Novelle as it stood. The consequence was that Anglo-German naval rivalry was intensified, and Britain and France drew closer together. The road to Armageddon was now clearly signposted, and because Germany could have 25 fully manned battleships in the North Sea by the end of 1913 the British fleet was reorganised to increase the Home Fleet to 33 battleships in full commission plus eight in reserve with nucleus crews at the expense of the Mediterranean forces. Beatty was naturally in full accord with Churchill over these measures.

Meanwhile other developments were exerting a profound influence on British naval strategy and dispositions. The 1912 naval manoeuvres had brought out the submarine threat to surface warships clearly – a threat which Fisher had foreseen as early as 1904 when he wrote to Admiral May, then Controller of the Navy, 'It's astounding to me . . . how the very best among us absolutely fail to realize the vast impending revolution in naval warfare and naval strategy that the submarine will accomplish!'[37] The lessons drawn from the 1912 manoeuvres impressed Churchill far more than his principal naval colleagues. Though Beatty certainly sided with the First Lord the view that the submarine threat had been exaggerated prevailed. These developments did, however, have the important result of bringing about the abandonment of the long-held strategy of adopting a close blockade of the German North Sea bases. Instead an 'Observational Blockade' was first adopted; but that was dropped in favour of 'Distant Blockade' from bases in the far north, shortly before the outbreak of war – despite the fact that Churchill, who always belonged to the 'seek out and destroy' school, deprecated any strategically defensive measures and did not like the change.

Churchill delighted to use the luxurious Admiralty yacht *Enchantress*, a converted passenger liner of some 4,000 tons, to visit naval bases, ships and squadrons, overseas as well as in the British Isles – so much so that he spent a total of six of his first eighteen months as First Lord on board the yacht. Beatty, however, was a good deal less fond of these expeditions than his master – probably because Churchill always brought along with him a crowd of political colleagues whom he wished to impress, and his Naval Secretary had perforce to join in entertaining them; but he was impressed by Churchill's determination to make himself informed about every aspect of naval strategy and administration, telling Ethel that 'Winston talks about nothing but the Sea and the Navy, and the wonderful things he is going to do'.[38] Professor Marder has written that Churchill was 'a great trial, personally, to most of his colleagues';[39] but that does not apply in general to Beatty as his Naval Secretary, since it was at this time that a strong bond of affection and admiration developed between them. On 9th December 1912 Prince Louis of Battenberg moved to the appointment for which he had been considered a year earlier, and during his term of office relations between the dynamic, if sometimes erratic, First Lord and his naval colleagues entered a more settled period. Beatty undoubtedly welcomed the arrival of Prince Louis, with whom he had long been on friendly terms.

In the summer of 1912 very important exercises were carried out in the North Sea to investigate the ability of the Germans to land an invasion force on the East Coast and the likelihood of the navy successfully intercepting such a force. It was probably to test Beatty's capacity as a sea-going admiral that Churchill gave him command of a squadron of six old armoured cruisers for the period of the exercises. Beatty chose as his Flag Captain Ernle Chatfield who, like himself was to rise to the highest rank and hold the highest office which their service could offer. Beatty hoisted his flag in the *Aboukir* on 2nd July, and Chatfield, who had not previously known him at all well, has recorded that his six weeks in that ship 'were

illuminating and exciting', and that he quickly realised that he
'was with a man of exacting character'.[40] They only had a
very short time to bring the squadron, all of whose ships had
for some years been in reserve with only skeleton crews, to
the state of efficiency Beatty required; but he and his
command came through this severe test satisfactorily, and so
confirmed Churchill in his high opinion of him.

When in the spring of 1913 command of the Battle Cruiser
Squadron fell vacant Churchill had no hesitation 'in appointing
him [Beatty] over the heads of all to this incomparable
command'.[41] When Beatty turned over his duties as Naval
Secretary to the First Lord to Rear-Admiral (later Admiral Sir
Dudley) de Chair he told his relief that 'You have to have a
bloody awful row with Winston once a month and then you
are all right';[42] which shows how clearly Beatty had come to
understand the need for subordinates to have the moral
courage to stand up to their superiors, no matter how difficult
they might be.

CHAPTER FOUR

The Battle Cruiser Squadron and
Preparations for War, 1913-14

Beatty hoisted his flag in the *Lion* at Devonport on 1st March 1913. He again chose as his Flag Captain Ernle Chatfield, whose abilities and character he had been able to assess in the *Aboukir* during the previous year's exercises. Chatfield thus became Beatty's *fidus Achates* and his most loyal disciple and admirer – at times excessively so, as we will see later. But he was without doubt one of the ablest officers of the 20th century, though he lacked his mentor's charisma. During the years they served together or in close proximity Chatfield had a better opportunity than anyone else, except perhaps Beatty's secretary, of observing and assessing his conduct on the bridge of his flagship in action, at the First Sea Lord's desk in Whitehall, and in conferences with politicians and celebrities of many nations. His opinion must therefore surely command respect. His description of Beatty is that he was 'a thoughtful strategist and tactician, planning how best to utilise his forces', and that he was not, as some writers had suggested 'a mere Prince Rupert, dashing and happy-go-lucky in the spirit of the hunting field'.[1] None the less it is certain that in his correspondence Beatty did often employ the language and metaphors of the hunting field in describing the movements of his ships in searching for and pursuing the enemy. This was especially so in his letters to Ethel and to his sister 'Trot' Courage, and in those to Roger Keyes and Walter Cowan, two of his most intimate naval friends; but all of them were of course deeply imbued with the spirit of the chase, and fully familiar with the fox hunter's peculiar etiquette and jargon.

If Beatty acted wisely in selecting his Flag Captain his choice of The Hon. Reginald Plunkett* as his Flag Commander was equally judicious; for Plunkett was an 'intellectual' at a time when officers with that bent were too often looked at askance

*Later Admiral The Hon. Sir Reginald Plunkett-Ernle-Erle-Drax
(1880–1967)

in the navy. He had an original mind and was one of the founders of the Naval Society in 1913, which still publishes its quarterly journal *The Naval Review*. Early in April 1913 Beatty told Ethel how he had 'trotted my round little Flag Lieutenant for a good long walk ashore. I like him very much, more so than I did my first one. In fact I like all my staff. They are all intelligent and charming. . . .'[2] The 'round little Flag Lieutenant' was Ralph Seymour, whom Beatty had brought in to replace Charles Dix – the officer he had inherited from his predecessor Admiral Sir Lewis Bayly. But Seymour, unlike Dix, was not a qualified signal specialist. He did, however, come of an aristocratic family, and one wonders whether Beatty placed excessive emphasis on the social duties of a Flag Lieutenant, and whether the snobbery to which both he and Ethel were subject influenced his choice. If so the outcome in war was, to put it mildly, unfortunate for Beatty – and ended in tragedy for Seymour.*

Much happier than Beatty's choice of Seymour as Flag Lieutenant was his selection of Fleet Paymaster Frank Spickernell† as his secretary. As with Chatfield he continued to serve close to or under Beatty throughout the active career of the latter; and he proved a tower of strength to the admiral in handling the many intricate and delicate issues which fell to his lot as Commander-in-Chief and First Sea Lord. Beatty was also fortunate in getting the service of able Engineer Captains to serve successively as Fleet Engineer Officer – F. R. Stettaford and C. G. Taylor, who played a vital part in keeping the battle cruisers' main machinery capable of very high speeds.

The *Lion* was refitting when Beatty joined her, and he was probably justified in thinking that the work in hand could best be left to the supervision of Chatfield and his specialist officers. So within 24 hours he left for Monte Carlo, where Ethel was gambling heavily – and unsuccessfully – at the Casino.

---

*Ralph Seymour (1886-1922) was a son of Sir Horace Seymour (1843-1902) Deputy Master and Controller of the Royal Mint, and of Elizabeth Mary daughter of Colonel Frederick Romilly. He was thus a descendant of the 1st Marquess of Hertford (1718-94), whose family name was Seymour. Ralph was also related to Admiral Lord Alcester (1821-95) and General Lord Gleichen (1863-1937).

†Later Captain (S) Sir Frank Spickernell (1885-1956).

Perhaps it was typical of the man that he rejoined his flagship with the narrowest possible margin of time – during the night before the squadron was to sail for exercises. However, his first sea experience with his new command, though with only four of his five ships – *Lion, Princess Royal, Indomitable* and *Indefatigable* – proved satisfactory.* In March the squadron took part in exercises under Admiral Sir George Callaghan, the C-in-C, Home Fleet in the presence of a distinguished company including Churchill on board the *Enchantress;* but Beatty's intention to deploy at high speed across the 'enemy's' van was frustrated by a tramp steamer and the 'set piece' was therefore a fiasco. Beatty was, however, quite unperturbed. An interesting point brought out in Beatty's report on the 1913 exercises is his remark that 'The transposition cypher used for wireless signals is one which can be discovered [i.e. broken] by any student of cryptograms in about an hour';[3] and it is indeed true that British cypher security was grievously faulty in the early stages of both World Wars – though the Germans only took full advantage of it in the second one.[4] Another serious weakness – namely lack of training in night fighting, is nicely illustrated by a memorandum circulated to the First Fleet as late as March 1914 in which it was stated that 'the number of rounds to be fired with main armament guns at night is laid down annually by the Admiralty', but the allowance was 'very small'. It was recommended that it should be fired at a fixed target, in which purpose it might prove 'a useful means for drawing attention to the effect of blast, flash etc. from heavy guns!'[5] Rarely can a more short-sighted memorandum have been given the seal of official approval.

At this time Beatty was giving much thought to the tactical employment of his squadron in the event of war with Germany. His long memorandum of Easter 1912, mentioned earlier, though mainly concerned with strategy, had shown his awareness of the threat from submarines and mines; but it was the question of fighting at unprecedented speeds which began to concern him once he had taken command of the battle cruisers. As the Germans had adopted a similar design to that of his ships, and some of their battle cruisers had already entered service, the possibility of an engagement of that nature

*The *Invincible* was refitting when Beatty hoisted his flag, the *Queen Mary* had not yet completed and the *Australia* and *New Zealand* were overseas.

was plain to him.* Despite opposition he won his point, and on Chatfield's recommendation he next turned his mind to carrying out main armament firings at far longer ranges and higher speeds than the 9,000 yards and 14 knots heretofore insisted on by the Inspector of Target Practice – chiefly because those limitations were convenient for competitive gunnery firings. Beatty got his way and in 1913 his ships engaged towed targets at 16,000 yards, which brought out problems such as the effect of vibration on rangefinding.† Nothing could, however, be done to remedy these defects before war broke out – even had the high Admiralty authorities not frowned on Beatty's unorthodox thoughts and actions.

In view of the serious weaknesses in long-range fire control which became evident during Beatty's battles, a technical digression may be useful to the reader's understanding of what follows. In 1904 Captain Percy Scott, one of the most original thinkers of his generation on gunnery problems, had con-

---

*The first German ship classed as a battle cruiser, though in reality she was a large armoured cruiser was the *Blücher* (1906 Programme, twelve 8.2-inch guns), but the first genuine battle cruiser was the *von der Tann* (laid down 1908, eight 11-inch guns). She was a substantially better fighting ship than any of the British battle cruisers armed with 12-inch guns – the three *Invincibles* laid down in 1906 and the three *Indefatigables* laid down 1909-11 (all with eight 12-inch guns). The next German ships were the two *Moltke* class laid down 1908-9 (ten 11-inch guns) which corresponded to the two British *Lion* class laid down 1909-10 (eight 13.5-inch guns). Then came *Seydlitz* (ten 11-inch guns) and the *Queen Mary* (eight 13.5-inch guns) both laid down 1911. In 1912 the Germans laid down the two *Derfflinger* class (eight 12-inch guns), while the British only started the *Tiger* (eight 13.5-inch guns).

†In the stereoscopic rangefinders used by the Germans the operator, who had to have excellent and identical vision in both eyes, placed a 'Wander-mark' over the target which could be as ill-defined as a smudge of smoke. The 'Coincidence' rangetakers of the Royal Navy had to bring together the two parts of a vertical or near vertical object such as a mast – which might well not be available to them. A stereo rangetaker might lose his special vision in the excitement of battle or through fatigue; but *given equal light conditions* the advantage probably lay with him in the vital early stages of an action. After the war the British carried out prolonged comparative trials with German instruments against their own; but the decision taken was to adhere to the coincidence type. The probability is that accuracy was influenced more by light conditions (which were never the same for both sides) and by the performance of the fire control system fitted than by the type of rangefinder used.

cluded that only by placing the controlling sight for the main armament guns high up on the mast could the severe handicap produced by cordite and funnel smoke and by spray at high speeds, which often blinded the gunlayers and obscured their targets, be eliminated. He called this new system 'Director Firing' and took out a patent to cover it in 1907. Unfortunately the usual opposition to all innovation proved extremely powerful; and Scott's cantankerous personality did not make it easier to get his inventions adopted.[6] The fitting of Director Firing accordingly proceeded extraordinarily slowly, and by the outbreak of war only eight ships had received it – and for their main armaments only. The first of Beatty's ships to be fitted was the *Tiger*, which did not join his squadron until October 1914 and then needed a long period to work up efficiency.

A corollary to the possible (though not proven) inferiority of the British rangefinders and the lack of Director Firing was the inefficiency of the Royal Navy's main armament fire control system at long ranges. At the beginning of the century Arthur Hungerford Pollen, a brilliant inventor who had studied the naval fire control problem closely, produced proposals for a highly advanced system capable of accuracy at long ranges and offered it to the Admiralty. Fisher, then First Sea Lord, at once appreciated its importance. He told the First Lord in September 1906 that *'Pollen's invention is simply priceless'*, and pressed for the Admiralty to obtain its sole use.[7] A start was made by ordering a set of the instruments known as the 'Argo Clock' for trial, and a large sum was promised for monopoly of manufacture. The key to the problem was that in its final and most advanced form the Pollen system produced constantly up-to-date ranges and bearings of the enemy, and corrected them automatically for the changes produced by the movements of both sides' ships during the projectiles' time of flight. Jellicoe as DNO 1905-7 as well as Fisher initially supported Pollen's design; but Jellicoe received a sea appointment in August 1907 and was replaced by Captain R. H. S. (later Admiral Sir Reginald) Bacon. He took a very different view to his predecessor and supported the simpler, and so cheaper, but less accurate system produced by Captain F. C. (late Admiral Sir Frederic) Dreyer; and Bacon had the support of that hardened sea dog of the old school Admiral Sir Arthur Wilson, who succeeded Fisher as First Sea

Lord in January 1910. Jellicoe later became strongly anti-Pollen, remarking that it had fallen to him several times to turn down his inventions;[8] but such remarks could of course have been inspired by reluctance to admit that, as Controller of the Navy 1908-10 he had been seriously wrong when the decision to adopt the Dreyer system and reject Pollen's was taken.

Professor Marder describes Dreyer as 'a gunnery genius'[9] and quotes without comment Fisher's description of him as having 'the brain of a Newton' – which was in fact an example of the admiral's capacity for wild exaggeration.[10*] Though Dreyer did have a flair of invention, which he used – though at first with scant success – from the beginning of his sea-going career,[11] the more prominent and enduring traits in his character were his burning ambition and his ruthlessness in furthering his own ends; nor of course was he a trained designer and technologist. He became a very close intimate of Jellicoe's and acted as self-appointed apologist for the admiral almost to the end of his life.[12]

In the early days of Pollen's work on producing the best possible solution to the long-range fire control problem he had the help and support of Lord Kelvin, who was a colleague on the Board of the Linotype Company, perhaps the most brilliant inventor and applied physicist of the period, and who enjoyed the confidence of the Admiralty; but Kelvin died in 1907 which probably weakened Pollen's position and prospects. Jellicoe as Director of Naval Ordnance 1905-7 also supported Pollen's ideas, but as Controller of the Navy 1908-10 he turned against him. It was almost certainly the influence of A. K. Wilson and Bacon which resulted in the summary rejection of the Pollen system by Fisher in favour of Dreyer's early in 1908, which was repeated two and four years later; and it seems improbable that the mathematical principles and design subtleties of Pollen's invention were understood by the later DNOs (Archibald Moore 1909-12 and F. C. T. Tudor 1912-14). As to the Controllers who followed on Jellicoe, the first was Charles J. Briggs (1910-12) a somewhat

*In fact Dreyer passed out of the *Britannia* 5th in his term of 58 cadets. When he qualified as a Gunnery Officer he was 5th out of 18 candidates in the theoretical course at the R.N.C. Greenwich and 2nd in the practical course in H.M.S. *Excellent*. On returning to Greenwich for the Advanced Course he was 1st of the three officers selected to take it.

shadowy figure who appears to have left no personal papers;[13] but Professor Marder has drastically revised his early opinion of him, in which he accepted 'Jacky' Fisher's contemptuous view, and that his 'BMG' (Briggs Must Go) campaign were justified. Marder's final assessment is that Briggs was 'a fine officer of unimpeachable character', but that he was 'not a conspicuous success as Controller'.[14]* Be that as it may Briggs certainly wanted a competitive and comparative trial between the later models of the Argo Clock and the Dreyer table to be carried out in 1912; but it was vetoed by his superiors.[15] The next officer to hold the office of Controller (1912–1914) was the Archibald Moore who had recently been DNO. Beatty developed a very poor opinion of his ability, and he was certainly not the man to force through a major change of policy in fire control equipment in face of what had become a powerful vested interest.[16]†

Beatty took no part in the controversy between Pollen and Dreyer and their respective supporters in the early stages; for technical issues were never his forte. But it will be told later how by 1916, with two years' war experience behind him, he had become convinced that faulty fire control was one of the defects in what he called the Royal Navy's 'system', and had become a strong supporter of Pollen. This is not the place to go into the details of the Pollen system, which another historian will be describing in full detail in the near future, but it is relevant to state that in its final form (Argo Clock Mark V) it could by 1914 have given the navy more accurate and 'helm free' gunnery (that is the automatic correction of range and bearing to compensate for the firing ship's movements) than the Dreyer system. As, however, the final Pollen system was turned down without a trial we shall never be able to quantify its superiority except in theory and by taking account of the unquestionable success of the early models. As regards British capacity to manufacture the more complicated Pollen system in the required quantity, the designer of it at any rate had no doubts; for in 1912 he wrote to Captain Moore, who

*Compare this view of Briggs with that printed in *Fear God*, II, pp. 417, 442 and 446, in which Fisher's condemnatory letters are printed without comment, and with *Dreadnought*, I, p. 418 where Briggs is described as 'pretty impossible' and the Fisher view of him reproduced.

†This summary of a complicated story owes a great deal to the very thorough research carried out by Mr. Jon Sumida of Chicago University.

succeeded Bacon as DNO in 1910 and was about to relieve Admiral Sir Charles Briggs as Controller, that 'There would not then be the slightest doubt about being able to get our clocks for the [*King*] *George V* class ships at the date you mentioned to me yesterday. Indeed, I see no reason why we should not be able to supply them at two a week within six months of commencing manufacture'.[17]

Though Pollen later became stridently anti–Jellicoe, and some of his journalistic activities were lacking in balance, Professor Marder's dismissal of him as 'the naval journalist' and his description of the early model of the Argo Clock as 'Pollen's gadget' show lack of appreciation of his importance as an inventor.[18]

To go back to 1910-12, for the reasons outlined above the eponymous 'Captain F. C. Dreyer's Fire Control Table' was fitted in practically all the Royal Navy's capital ships which took part in World War I. Furthermore it remained in all big ships (cruisers and above) completed before 1920 or left unmodernised right up to World War II – notably in the *Hood* when she was sunk by the *Bismarck* in May 1941. The reasons why Fisher and Jellicoe, who had supported Pollen in the first instance, switched their allegiance to Dreyer is not the least puzzling aspect of this story; but there is evidence that they considered the simpler system adequate for fighting at the medium ranges (about 9,000 yards) and comparatively low speeds then expected. It has already been told how in 1913 Beatty tried, though not with any marked success, to introduce high speed battle practices.

The final outcome of the Pollen versus Dreyer conflict came in 1923 when, in Professor Marder's words, the former 'received £30,000 from the Royal Commission on Awards and Inventions for the Argo Clock, *which the Admiralty cribbed in "Captain F. C. Dreyer's Fire Control Table" in 1912*' (italics supplied).[19] In 1916 Dreyer received £5,000 from the Admiralty for his 'invention'; and the Royal Commission declined to recommend him for any further award. On the other hand the Commission found that the Dreyer system worked 'substantially on the same principles' as the Argo Clock – or to put it more bluntly was a plagiarisation of Pollen's invention; and it was for that reason that the Royal Commission recommended that the large award mentioned should be made to him. However, it was not until the 1920s, when the 'Admiralty Fire Control Table Mark I' was fitted in the *Nelson* class battleships and (in various Marks) in all later capital ships and cruisers, that the navy obtained the degree of 'helm free gunnery' offered to it before the 1914-18 war.

It was Reginald Plunkett, whom we have already encountered, who produced the great majority of the tactical papers for the battle cruisers at this time. The outcome was that in April 1913 Beatty set down (once again in his own hand) the functions of the battle cruisers as he then envisaged them, and the principles on which his Captains should fight their ships.[20] The functions of his force he summarised as follows:

'(a) To support a reconnaissance of fast light cruisers on the enemy

(b) To support a blockading force [see above pp 56-7 regarding the abandonment of 'Close Blockade' and substitution of 'Distant Blockade' in July 1914].

(c) To form support between the cruiser force and the battle fleet when cruising.

(d) To support a cruiser force watching the enemy's Battle Fleet.

(e) Finally, to form, a fast division of the Battle Fleet in a general action.

Although, as Admiral Chalmers has remarked, (c) and (d) above were perfectly normal functions for cruisers, whether large or small, Beatty's principles did bring together in admirably concise form the duties which would probably fall to them in war. The tactical principles stated were only slightly modified by the C-in-C, Sir George Callaghan, and were ultimately embodied in the Grand Fleet Battle Orders.

Ever since the American naval historian Captain Alfred Thayer Mahan had published the first of his three studies of the 'Influence of Sea Power' in earlier wars in 1890 the dominance of what may be called the 'Decisive Battle School' over the 'Control of Sea Communications School' had become very marked in British naval circles.[21] Mahan's influence, especially in Britain and Germany, was both wide and deep; for he appeared to provide the explanation for the acquisition and retention of a vast Empire by the former, while to the latter, and especially to Kaiser Wilhelm II and his chief naval adviser Grand Admiral Alfred von Tirpitz, who became State Secretary of the Imperial Naval Office in 1897,[22] he appeared to provide the clue to achieving comparable power and wealth. But it is now plain that Mahan's arguments were based on far too narrow and selective a study of history, and that his explanation of British success was too facile; yet his works completely overshadowed those published a short time earlier by the brothers Captain Sir John Colomb RMA and Admiral Philip Colomb,[23] who had suggested that there were serious fallacies in the belief, common in the earlier 19th century, that naval warfare was a matter of heroic officers fighting decisive battles – often against odds. John Colomb particularly argued that, provided the homeland was secure, the protection of sea communications was both the cardinal duty of naval forces and the source of the nation's strength and power; while Philip produced important studies of blockade, the convoy strategy and defence against invasion. It is noteworthy that the Colombs' works were ignored by the Admiralty and despised by 'Jacky' Fisher, who exerted immense influence on British naval policy and strategy early in the 20th century. It was he who inaugurated the race in building ever larger big gun ships with the design of the *Dreadnought* of 1906.[24] In 1911 Julian Corbett, whose historical research went far deeper than Mahan's, published his important study *Some Principles of Maritime Strategy*, a deeply pondered synthesis of his earlier works. In it he argued that statecraft and naval efficiency must be combined to make a strategic offensive possible, attacked the view that the introduction of steam had made trade defence more difficult, analysed the true meaning of 'command of the sea', and accurately forsaw the essential elements for success in combined operations. Though Fisher admired Corbett's works, and frequently used him to further his own purposes,[25] virtually all senior naval officers of the pre-1914 era regarded his views as entirely heretical; for they were, almost to a man, devotees of the 'Decisive Battle School'.[26] Beatty was certainly better informed and more widely read on historical matters than his principal collaborator and superior Admiral Sir John Jellicoe, who was almost illiterate in such subjects; but his training in the *Britannia* and afterwards, had, perhaps inevitably, made him a disciple of Mahan rather than of Corbett. It will be told in due course how the 'Decisive Battle' was always in the forefront of his thought and purposes, and that the function of the navy to control the sea communications, on which not only overseas expeditions but his country's very survival depended, was only forced on him reluctantly and never superseded the hope of accomplishing another Trafalgar.

Although by 1913 Beatty had developed clear ideas on the tactical functions of the force he commanded, he had no clear grasp of the world-wide issues involved in the application of a maritime strategy; but he had of course not yet reached a position where such understanding was vital to the prosecution of the nation's purposes. He had, however, become conscious of the potentiality in sea warfare of what he called 'Aerial Force' – by which he meant the German Zeppelin rigid airships – for reconnaissance, and possibly for attack purposes; and he remarked how 'it behoves us to move rapidly and provide the means of defeating them'.[27] Though that brilliant but iconoclastic gunnery officer Percy Scott[28] was in the end to be proved right in his view that 'submarines and aeroplanes had entirely revolutionised warfare' he actually exaggerated the influence of the latter,[29] and the day when aircraft made the battleship totally obsolete was a good deal further off than he anticipated. The Admiralty, after prolonged hesitation, ordered eight airships early in 1914; but none was ready when war broke out, and we continued to lag far behind the Germans in design of such craft – until we were forced to copy the Zeppelin model in 1917.

We have already seen how the possibility of a German invasion of the British Isles was constantly debated between 1905 and 1914. The 1912 and 1913 manoeuvres were both designed to test the practicability of flinging a raiding force ashore. The earlier exercise was however conducted under such highly unrealistic conditions that for the next one some soldiers were actually embarked in real transports. 'War' was declared on 23rd July, and the 'enemy' under John Jellicoe succeeded theroetically in getting 48,000 men ashore at Blyth and Sunderland.[30] The opposing battle fleets failed to make contact, but the defenders under Callaghan were adjudged to have lost heavily to submarine attacks. Early on 28th Churchill hastily cancelled the exercise – lest the Germans should learn too much. On the last day of the month the exercises were resumed, and the 'enemy' failed in his chief object of establishing a base in the Shetlands. Beatty's force operated with Callaghan's defenders, but played no significant part until the two battle fleets 'engaged' each other on 1st

August.

The chief outcome of the above exercises was the re-examination of the whole problem by the C.I.D. Sub-Committee on Invasion.[31] It reported in April 1914, and the conclusions which most affected the Admiralty and the Navy were, firstly that the 'War Book', in which every department's action on the approach of hostilities was set out in great detail, should be brought up to date; and, secondly, that a Territorial Force should be organised and equipped to defend the homeland against 'small raids', thus compelling the enemy to send such large forces that interception by our fleet would be practically certain. We now know that the Germans never seriously contemplated invasion in World War I (as Hitler certainly did in 1940), and that the 'Blue Water School', to which Beatty belonged, was far more realistic in its appraisal of the difficulties and possibilities than its military and Foreign Office rivals of the 'Bolt from the Blue' school.

Though Beatty was fully aware of the probable effect of the submarine on naval strategy and tactics, when it came to trade defence he suffered from the same blind spot as virtually all naval men except Fisher[32] – namely the belief that the convoy strategy had been rendered obsolete and impossible of execution by the replacement of sail by steam driven merchant ships, and by the enormous increase in seaborne trade since the mid-19th century. The opponents of the historic convoy strategy also argued that the assembly of convoys could not be kept secret, that during their passages they would provide inviting and easy targets, that if they arrived safely they would cause unacceptable congestion in the ports, and that the 'turn-round' of shipping would be badly delayed. To the 'historical school' of thought these were hoary and discredited arguments; but they provided Churchill with ammunition to press the case for 'hunting forces', and for the 'seek out and destroy' strategy which he always favoured. The price paid for this error was to be enormous in both World Wars of the 20th century. It must however be remarked that Beatty later changed his mind about convoy.

To turn to economic pressure on Germany, which was in the end to prove decisive if slow acting, pre-war naval thinking did in general attach high importance to it – though Sir Arthur Wilson was exceptional in arguing that it 'would have little or no effect on the result'.[33] But as Beatty was not called to give an opinion on the matter we can defer consideration of his views until, as C-in-C, Grand Fleet, he was required to play a large part in applying such pressure.

One important tactical issue on which he did express strong views in 1913 concerned the use of the battle cruisers in a semi-independent role during a fleet action. Though he argued strongly for 'divisional attack and divided tactics', with a wide discretion given to himself, the view that the fleet should fight in single line ahead was favoured by Fisher, Wilson, Jellicoe, Bridgeman and many other admirals, and by the outbreak of war it was generally accepted. This was not the only case where excessive tactical rigidity, and conformity to the C-in-C's movements inhibited initiative by subordinate commanders; but it exemplifies the extent to which the navy had by 1914 reverted to the concept which had led to many indecisive engagements in the late 17th and early 18th centuries, and which the genius of Nelson had shattered in the French Revolutionary and Napoleonic Wars. It is no exaggeration to say that in the late 19th and early 20th centuries the whole of British naval training emphasised conformity and obedience to orders, and discouraged originality and initiative. Though Beatty unquestionably stood among the few officers who wished to encourage initiative in subordinates he did not at the stage we have reached possess the authority to institute the far-reaching changes needed – which would in fact have had to permeate the entire system of naval training before they had percolated through to the highest ranks.

To illustrate Beatty's attitude on this important matter we may quote from the Battle Cruiser Orders which he issued before the war. The conclusion he had derived from study of earlier conflicts was that 'Cruiser Captains and Battle Cruiser Captains, to be successful, must possess, in a marked degree, initiative . . . Orders should be complied with in spirit, but it is not desirable to be tied by the letter. . . .' Then, probably recalling Nelson's famous Trafalgar Memorandum,* he wrote that 'Much must be left to the initiative and judgement of Captains. They are relied on to act promptly in battle for dealing with cases such as the following . . .'; and he went on to enumerate cases in which initiative would be essential.[34] It

---

*'Something must be left to chance . . . no Captain can do very wrong if he places his ship alongside that of an enemy'. Memo. of 9th Oct. 1805. Sir H. Nicolas, *Dispatches and Letters of Lord Nelson* (Henry Colburn, 1846), pp. 89-92.

will be told later how Beatty's subordinates, who had of course been trained to conformity, by no means always lived up to those principles.[35] None the less some of the blame for tactical errors, to be recounted later, must rest with their admiral.

Beatty can no more be exonerated for one tactical weakness from which the British navy suffered than all the other influential officers of the time – namely acceptance of the rule that 'the British fleet does not fight at night'. Nor does anyone seem to have tried to find out whether the Germans were willing to oblige in that respect, with the result that a very rude awakening came to the Grand Fleet – and to Beatty – on the night of 31st May – 1st June 1916.

Professor Marder argues that many of the Royal Navy's troubles stemmed from 'the ascendancy of the material school' over what he calls the 'historical school'[36] – which is true enough as far as it goes but does not go nearly far enough, since in many respects the Royal Navy's material was greatly inferior to that of the Germans. The explanation for that indubitable fact must in my view be sought in the mistakes made during the Fisher era, when crucial decisions were taken which affected most drastically the offensive fighting efficiency of our ships and their defensive capacity to stand up to punishment. But a detailed study of the cause of those deficiencies lies outside the scope of this biography.

At the beginning of 1914 the fleet carried out a heavy programme of exercises and target practices, and there are certainly no indications that the battle cruisers were at the time less efficient in gunnery than Callaghan's battleships. On the other hand the battleships had been given priority for the fitting of the new and vitally important Director Firing system developed by Admiral Sir Percy Scott, mentioned earlier.

The battle cruisers' exercises were broken off in February 1914 for a round of diplomatic and social visits – which cannot have helped to improve fighting efficiency. Beatty first took the *Lion, Princess Royal, Queen Mary* and *New Zealand* to Brest – chiefly to co-ordinate the activities of the French and British fleets in the event of war; but judging by his letters to Ethel sport and entertainment took a more prominent place in the programme.[37] While those junketings were in progress a crisis arose at home between Lloyd George, the Chancellor of the Exchequer, and Churchill over the 1914–15 Navy Estimates, and the government very nearly split on the issue whether four battleships should be built in order to maintain the accepted 60 per cent standard above German strength. The cost was very heavy and meant that the £50 millions provided under Churchill's original estimates would be quite inadequate. After a heated exchange of letters and many long Cabinet meetings a compromise was reached by Lloyd George accepting a Supplementary Estimate of £2.5 millions for 1913-14 and a total of £51.8 millions for 1914-15, including the four capital ships. In return Churchill optimistically said that he could 'practically guarantee' a saving of £2 millions for 1915-16. On 17th March, in a brilliant if somewhat defensive speech lasting 2½ hours Churchill introduced the last peacetime estimates, calling them 'the largest Estimates for naval expense ever presented to the House'.[38] The programme he proposed, which was actually subject to great changes, was for four battleships, four cruisers, twelve destroyers and 'a large number of submarines'. But probably the greatest contribution to naval strength made by Churchill's Board was the ordering of the five *Queen Elizabeth* class battleships of the 1912 Programme which completed in 1915-16; for their eight 15-inch guns, good protection and high speed (24 knots) made them the most formidable capital ships of the period.

In June Beatty set off for the Baltic ports of Riga, Reval and Kronstadt, where the visit was 'one continuous round of gaiety punctuated by rigid ceremonial'.[39] He was followed by Ethel in the yacht *Sheelah*, and they both lunched with the Tsar and Tsarina at the palace of Tsarskoye Selo, and then entertained the Royal Family on board the *Lion*. To cap the whole series of lavish entertainments Beatty decided to give a ball on an unprecedented scale for over 2,000 guests. The *New Zealand* was brought alongside the *Lion*, one ship providing the ballroom and the other supper rooms – where Beatty's faithful and invaluable steward Woodley set out the 100 dozen bottles of champagne, which he had managed to acquire by assiduous approaches to various embassies and legations, on a large number of small round tables specially made by the ships' craftsmen out of rum casks and wooden planking. The ball was an immense success and the consumption of alcohol fully justified Woodley's anticipations. Then Beatty and some of his officers visited Moscow by special invitation, and were as sumptuously entertained there as in St. Petersburg. Mention

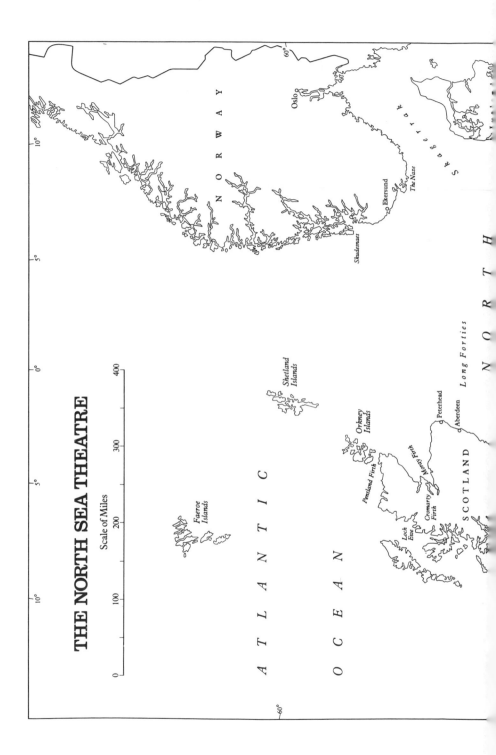

THE NORTH SEA THEATRE

Scale of Miles

0   100   200   300   400

ATLANTIC

OCEAN

NORWAY

Oslo

Skagerrak

Ekersund

The Naze

Skudernaes

Faeroe
Islands

Shetland
Islands

Orkney
Islands

Pentland Firth

Moray Firth

Cromarty
Firth

Loch
Ewe

SCOTLAND

Peterhead

Aberdeen

Long Forties

NORTH

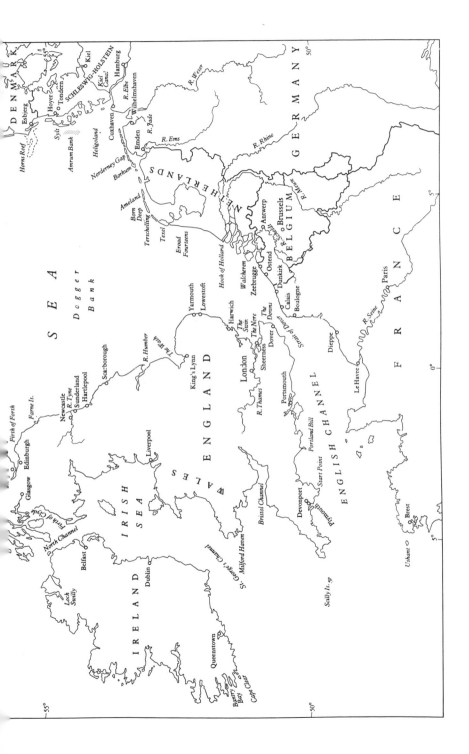

should also be made of the fact that Beatty delivered all the many speeches called for in French, and that Spickernell, who was fluent in that language, gave him vital help in preparing them. Throughout the visit Beatty benefited greatly from the experience and wisdom of Sir George Buchanan, the British ambassador; but the admiral was more than a little surprised to be told that he would be expected to give a substantial tip to the commander of the Russian royal yacht! However, he decided to adhere to local custom and a bag of silver was hastily prepared – and apparently accepted without demur.

When the squadron sailed at the end of the month the Tsar came to sea to witness a demonstration of British naval might provided by the battle cruisers carrying out tactical exercises at high speed. Though the social aspects of the visit were certainly a resounding success one may doubt whether the orgiastic display by both hosts and visitors contributed anything to preparation for war. Rather does it leave the reader unsurprised that collapse and revolution in Russia lay little more than three years ahead.

Beatty was gazetted Knight Commander of the Bath in the birthday honours while in Russia, and on 2nd August he was promoted to the rank of Acting Vice-Admiral. Ethel was no doubt delighted to have a handle to her name. Meanwhile on 28th June, while the festivities in Russia were at their height, the Archduke Ferdinand of Austria was assassinated at Serajevo by a young Bosnian who had received arms and instruction in Serbia. One may doubt whether Beatty or any of his staff appreciated the significance of that early example of what has come to be called urban terrorism.

CHAPTER FIVE

The Test of War, 1914

On 3rd March 1914 Churchill, in answering what was probably an 'arranged' Parliamentary question, informed the House of Commons that a test mobilisation of the Third Fleet, whose principal units consisted of two Battle Squadrons made up from the older ships, would replace the usual summer manoeuvres and exercises.[1] When he introduced the 1914-15 Navy Estimates a short time later he enlarged on the matter, but still spoke on the subject with diplomatic caution – obviously to avoid any appearance of provocation towards the Germans. Though Churchill stressed that a financial saving would accrue from substituting the mobilisation for the 'grand manoeuvres' the change was in fact to have far-reaching strategic consquences.[2] The calling up of Reservists began on 15th July, and on 17th and 18th a review by the King of what Churchill later described as 'incomparably the greatest assemblage of naval power ever witnessed' took place in the historic anchorage of Spithead.[3] Admiral Drax later recalled that a high German official visited the *Lion*, and on his departure Beatty ordered his ship's band to play 'Rule Britannia'.[4] It was the sort of gesture which, though histrionic, made a great appeal to the ships' companies. On 19th the whole fleet put to sea for exercises, and four days later the Third Fleet ships returned to their Home Ports under orders to pay off. But before those orders could be put into effect the news of the Serbian rejection of Austria's arrogant ultimatum was received. On 26th July, when Churchill was absent from the Admiralty, Battenberg courageously ordered the demobilisation to be halted. Two days later Churchill told the King that the navy was 'on a preparatory and precautionary basis', and on 29th the First Fleet, consisting of the Fleet Flagship and four Battle Squadrons, all but one of which were composed of modern 'Dreadnoughts', and Beatty's squadron of four battle cruisers, steamed quietly out of Portland harbour for

Scapa Flow. These ships were in effect the Grand Fleet, whose principal function was to command the North Sea.* The Second Fleet, consisting of a Fleet Flagship and two Battle Squadrons of 'pre-Dreadnoughts', was to form the Channel Fleet. It should here be remarked that in all the principal classes of modern warship the British, who had 20 'Dreadnoughts' and four more building as against Germany's nine plus three building, far outnumbered their adversaries; but that superiority was to a large extent illusory, as events were quickly to show, since whereas the Royal Navy had to protect a world-wide trade and a vast empire, the German navy was saddled with few extraneous responsibilities, and could therefore keep its main strength concentrated in its North Sea bases. By the last day of the fateful month of July 1914 all the principal British ships were at their war stations.

Beatty arrived at Scapa on 31st July. Initially he had with him only the *Lion, Princess Royal, New Zealand* and *Invincible*; and although he was soon reinforced by the *Queen Mary* the *Invincible* was detached to southern Ireland for trade protection purposes. The *Inflexible* (flagship of Sir A. Berkeley Milne), *Indomitable* and *Indefatigable* were in the Mediterranean to keep an eye on the powerful German battle cruiser *Goeben* (22,600 tons, ten 11-inch guns, 25 knots) and protect the transports carrying French troops from North Africa to metropolitan ports; while the *Australia* was in the Pacific to deal with the German Asiatic Squadron, based originally on Tsingtao in northern China, and to help capture the German Pacific island colonies. As to the Captains of Beatty's 1st Battle Cruiser Squadron, Ernle Chatfield (*Lion*), Osmond de B. Brock (*Princess Royal*), Lionel Halsey (*New Zealand*) and Reginald Hall (*Queen Mary*) were all personal friends of their leader and together regarded themselves, not without reason, as 'a Band of Brothers' on the Nelson model. As to the Captains of the other battle cruisers, apart from R. F. Phillimore (*Inflexible*), who reached high flag rank, they were a somewhat mediocre bunch; for the very rapid expansion of the navy had allowed insufficient time to select and train for command a large number of really first class men.

On 4th August Beatty learnt that war had been declared and that the C-in-C, Admiral Sir George A. Callaghan, was to be

---

*The Grand Fleet was not officially formed until September 1914.

Capital ships at Rosyth. Rear line *Ajax, Centurion, Erin, Agincourt.*
Front line *Princess Royal, Tiger, Repulse. (Imperial War Museum)*

Indomitable, Australia and *New Zealand* sailing from Rosyth, probably taken
from the Forth Bridge. (*John Roberts*)

Australia coaling ship. (*Imperial War Museum*)

Princess Royal at sea. (*Paul Popper*)

Tiger at Rosyth. (*Imperial War Museum*)

New Zealand. (*National Maritime Museum*)

relieved by Sir John Jellicoe. The letter he sent to Ethel next day, quoted below, expresses very clearly his feelings on both counts; and he also telegraphed to both Churchill and Battenberg protesting against the change of C-in-C at such a moment.★5

Lion, 5th Aug. 1914.

My darling,

We are at war as you well know. The long talked of and much dreaded has happened and now we are to be put to the test. After all, I can hardly realize that it is so; and it seems as if it was only in a dream that I ever heard of such a thing. It is a cruel war because there never has been any reason for it. We have been forced into it entirely through the rapacity and thirst for power and a large portion of the world by Germany. Never in the history of the world has there been so little reason or so little cause. But there it is. Thank heavens, it's summer months and before the dark nights of winter are on us it ought to be all over. There is not sufficient money in the world to provide such a gigantic struggle to be continued for any great length of time. . . .

We received a royal message from the King and also the terrible news that the C-in-C has been relieved by Jellicoe. I fear he must have been taken ill. It is a terrible handicap to start a war by losing our C-in-C and it will break his heart. Jellicoe is undoubtedly the better man and in the end it will be for the best; but he hasn't the fleet at his finger-tips at present and I do not think is very well either . . . I am not anxious and feel am able to deal with situations as they arise, if I could only have word with Jellicoe and learn his views. I knew poor old Callaghan's, but this is different and one of the curses of changing horses in the middle of the stream. . . .

It is a great relief to me and a weight off my mind to know that you are all well and at Brooksby, peacefully and quietly. I know well, dear heart, what a sore trial it is though for you and how much you would rather be doing something. There will be plenty for you to do later, so reserve your energies and keep well and strong is your principal duty now. . . .

★On 4th Aug. Mrs. Churchill sent her husband a wise letter about what she wittily called 'the Callico-Jellatine crisis' urging him to handle the displaced C-in-C with tact and generosity. 'The league of retired Officers' cats to abuse you' would thus, she urged, be silenced.

> We are making history now, so courage, sweetheart, and
> it shall be a page that will not be behind those of the glorious
> past. All will be well in the end. I have great faith.

Meanwhile Ethel was busying herself over the conversion of
the *Sheelah* to a hospital ship, carrying much of the cost
herself. The Admiralty accepted the gift and the yacht was
stationed at Rosyth; but Ethel seems to have imagined she
could still move her erstwhile property about at will. Early in
August her husband had to check an idea that she herself
should come north in the yacht,[6] and in October he had to
point out that she was not under Ethel's command and could
not be moved 'without the authority of the Senior Naval
Officer present'. At that stage he also discouraged her from
coming to live near his base, which was moved to Cromarty
late in October and to Rosyth at the end of the year, on the
grounds that he had 'set his face against other officers having
their wives come, and I cannot go against my own decisions in
this matter. It would not be right and it would not be fair'.[7]
His family was therefore to remain in Leicestershire which, he
told Ethel, 'mercifully is in the centre of England and you
need fear nothing on their behalf' – in the event of coastal raids
or invasion taking place.[8]
    Very early in the war Beatty started to use money raised by
the sale of his and Ethel's horses and released through the
decline in their lavish style of living to alleviate hardship
among the families of those whom he described as 'the poor,
badly paid sailor, stoker etc.'; and he told Ethel that he was
raising funds in all his ships for that purpose.[9] Though Beatty
had certainly relished the luxuries and high living which his
wife's wealth made possible, he was always mindful, in a
paternalistic way, of the welfare of the men he commanded.
    The first responsibility that fell chiefly though by no means
solely on Jellicoe's fleet was to ensure that the British
Expeditionary Force was carried safely across the Channel to
France. While that great movement was in progress from
ports on the Channel coast the fleet spent 19 out of 26 days at
sea, and on 15th-16th August it swept far to the eastward in
the hope of catching any German force which might try to
attack the transports and supply ships; but the enemy made no
such attempt.
    Also in August Jellicoe drew up the first of the many

editions of the Grand Fleet Battle Orders (GFBOs), and in the following month he expanded and amplified them. These orders were much more detailed than those issued before the war. Although subordinate Flag Officers were accorded discretionary powers in certain circumstances, the use of semi-independent fast divisions of battleships, which Jellicoe himself had proposed earlier, was dropped. The orders now laid down were that 'in all cases the ruling principle is that the fleet keeps together, attempted attacks on a portion of the enemy's line being avoided as being liable to lead to the isolation of that division. . . .' Though it is fair to mention that the idea of using the new and fast *Queen Elizabeths* as a detached division was revived later the principle that 'the whole fleet should form one line of battle' was thus firmly enshrined.[10] In their broad rationale the orders undoubtedly subordinated offensive action to defensive precautions, and centralization of command was heavily emphasised. It is in this rigidity that we find the origins of what Admiral Kenneth Dewar stigmatised as 'corybantic exercises' such as the frequently rehearsed 'equal speed manoeuvres'. Training a fleet on those principles was bound to induce tactical rigidity and discourage initiative, with unfortunate results in battle – as will be seen later.[11] The GFBOs were completely revised later in 1915 and re-issued in the following January – without, however, any significant change in their dominant conception. They comprised 70 pages of close print, and are described by Professor Marder as 'a remarkable achievement by Jellicoe and his staff'.[12] However the same author admits that the GFBOs 'were open to several weighty criticisms that are difficult to refute', such as the assumption that the Germans would prove ready to fight, the almost total lack of any reference to *pursuit* of a fleeing enemy, and the excessive concentration on the concept of a gunnery duel instead of co-operation of all arms[13] – with which criticisms of the GFBOs I am in complete accord and which I have elsewhere stigmatised as 'the fallacy of the dominant weapon'.[14] In passing it should be remarked that the German system of tactical training in 1914 encouraged a far greater degree of tactical flexibility and gave scope for much more initiative than the GFBOs. Also that during Admiral Sir Dudley Pound's tenure of the Mediterranean Fleet Command 1936-39 the tendency for excessively detailed orders and centralized command reappeared. When Sir Andrew Cunningham took over that fleet and led it during the first two years of World War II he scrapped his predecessor's system, insisted on all operation orders being extremely simple, and encouraged flexibility and initiative by his subordinates.[15]

In the autumn of 1914 Jellicoe reviewed the action which his fleet should take in face of a torpedo attack by enemy light forces, and told the Admiralty that his intention was that in such circumstances he would order a turn away in order to avoid the potential threat to his heavy ships. The Board replied that they had 'full confidence' in his decision;[16] but again the lack of offensive spirit on both parts is to be remarked.

Soon after the outbreak of war Beatty set down on paper his 'Remarks on the situation in the North Sea' – presumably for the benefit of the new C-in-C. His chief anxiety lay in the fact that his squadron was numerically only equal with the four battle cruisers which the Germans could send to sea;* and if the *Blücher*, an older and less well armed ship, joined Hipper's 1st Scouting Group and one of Beatty's ships was refitting he would find himself in an inferiority of 3 to 4. Such a state of affairs he considered to be 'courting disaster'. He regarded the retention of three battle cruisers in the Mediterranean as wasteful, since the *Goeben* had, after a lamentable muddle on the British side, escaped to Constantinople on 10th August.[17] He therefore pressed for the *Indomitable* to be brought home at once, because he could not carry out the duties laid on him by way of supporting the cruisers and acting as a fast division of the battle fleet if he was inferior to his probable enemy.[19] This was sound sense, but the Admiralty was well aware of the situation, and measures to reinforce Beatty were in fact in hand.

Meanwhile Roger Keyes (later Admiral of the Fleet Lord Keyes), who was Commodore in command of submarines, and R.Y. (later Admiral of the Fleet Sir Reginald) Tyrwhitt, the commander of the light forces based on Harwich – both of whom were intimates of Beatty – were hatching a plan which might mitigate the increasing impatience of the battle cruiser admiral for action and the growing tendency of the public to asked 'What is the Navy doing?'; for armchair critics had

---

*These were at the time the *Seydlitz* (flag of Admiral von Hipper), *Moltke*, *von der Tann* and *Derfflinger*.

expected another Trafalgar to take place and to be followed by an early peace. Although the responsible newspapers did their best to instil in people's minds some measure of awareness of the silent working of sea power, restlessness became increasingly evident as the weeks passed without a battle.[19] The restlessness was not mitigated by Churchill's constant advocacy of 'offensive measures', and the wildness of some of his ideas caused much concern in responsible naval circles.

The Keyes-Tyrwhitt plan was to intercept the patrols which the Germans were sending into the Heligoland Bight every evening in order to interfere with our submarine and minelaying operations. Two of Tyrwhitt's light cruisers and two flotillas of his destroyers, working with Keyes's submarines, were to lure the enemy ships away from the Bight; and Rear-Admiral Sir Archibald Moore, who commanded the recently formed 2nd Battle Cruiser Squadron (*New Zealand* and *Invincible*) based on the Humber was to act in support of the light forces. Fortunately at the last moment Jellicoe added the three ships of Beatty's 1st Battle Cruiser Squadron and also the 1st Light Cruiser Squadron (Commodore W. E. Goodenough) to the supporting forces; but owing to a regrettable failure in staff work his signal telling the Admiralty of the decision to commit additional forces was not passed to Tyrwhitt and Keyes – who were thus completely unaware that Grand Fleet ships would be on the scene, and were quite likely to mistake them for enemies if an encounter took place in low visibility. By a happy chance at 3.30 a.m. on 28th August Tyrwhitt sighted Goodenough's ships, and learnt for the first time not only that they were acting in support of him but that Beatty's battle cruisers were coming along behind.

The Germans had, however, got wind of the unusual movements taking place, and had sent out reinforcements with the object of turning the tables. The first encounter between the light forces took place at 7.0 a.m. on 28th and a series of confused actions followed. By 10 o'clock Tyrwhitt was entangled in what he described as 'a hornets' nest' of superior forces, while Beatty, to whom he sent an urgent call for help, was still some 40 miles away to the north. On the bridge of the *Lion* the admiral and his Flag Captain (Chatfield) realised that a crisis had arisen, and after a short hesitation about the risk from submarines and mines, Beatty turned east and steamed into the Bight at high speed.[20] At 12.37 p.m. the hard-pressed British light forces sighted the five great ships coming out of the mist – an inspiring spactacle.

The Germans fought well, but lost three light cruisers (*Köln, Mainz* and *Ariadne*) and a destroyer, and had three other cruisers damaged. It was all over in half an hour, and at 1.10 p.m. Beatty gave a general order for all forces to retire, since it was quite probable that German heavy ships were moving out to support their light forces. On the British side only Tyrwhitt's brand new flagship the *Arethusa* suffered serious damage, and she was towed home safely. British killed and wounded totalled no more than 75, while the Germans had 1,162 casualties including 381 taken prisoner. Despite all that had gone wrong, and in particular the failure to co-ordinate the movements of the various British forces, it was a heartening success; and perhaps the most important result was that it strengthened the Kaiser's determination to confine his fleet to defensive operations, and not to risk his most important ships in battle. In the battle cruiser force Beatty's determined leadership raised morale to a new pitch, and his and Tyrwhitt's names were at once blazoned as the Royal Navy's new heroes. Churchill was delighted and, in Tyrwhitt's words 'fairly slobbered' over him.[21]

Beatty wrote to his wife as soon as he got back from the battle. '. . . We got at them yesterday, and got three of their cruisers under the nose of Heligoland, which will give them a bit of a shock . . . Poor devils, they fought their ships like men and went down with colours flying . . . against over-whelming odds. We take no credit for such [? a victory], but it was good work to be able to do it within twenty miles of their main base Heligoland, with the whole High Sea Fleet listening to the boom of our guns'.[22] In the circumstances the exaggeration in the last sentences may be forgiven. He was, however, disappointed at the lack of official recognition accorded him. 'I had thought', he wrote to Ethel, 'I should have received an expression of their appreciation from their Lordships [of the Admiralty], but have been disappointed, or rather not so much disappointed as disgusted; and my real opinion has been confirmed that they would have hung me if there had been a disaster – as there very nearly was owing to the extraordinary neglect of the most ordinary precautions on their part' – by which he doubtless meant the narrow escape from our ships firing on each other.[23] Evidently Beatty, like

Nelson, relished praise and was resentful if he did not receive what he considered to be his due.[24] However on 22nd October Jellicoe did receive a warmly appreciative official letter about Beatty's success, and he sent it on to his subordinate a week later with 'much pleasure' and his full concurrence.[25] It was not unreasonable that the Admiralty should have delayed distribution of praise until they had received and studied the reports of the action.

Unfortunately the success of 28th August in the Heligoland Bight was quickly offset by the sinking of three elderly cruisers (*Cressy, Hogue* and *Aboukir*) by a single enemy submarine (U.9) when they were sauntering along at slow speed off the Dutch coast on 22nd September. Though the loss of life (nearly 1,400 officers and men) and the shock to British public opinion were more important than the loss of the ships themselves it was a very unpleasant disaster. Beatty supposed, wrongly, that 'a large number of submarines' had caused it; but he was correct in writing that 'It was bound to happen; they (our cruisers) had *no* conceivable right to be where they were. It is not being wise after the event, but I had frequently discussed with others that sooner or later they would be caught by submarines or battle cruisers if they continued to occupy that position. It was inevitable and faulty strategy on the part of the Admiralty'. Perhaps it would have been more correct to say 'faulty staff work.'[26]

In the same letter Beatty reviewed the work and prospects of his own force gloomily. 'This roaming about the North Sea day after day', he wrote, 'with no prospect of meeting an enemy vessel I think is the heaviest trial that could be laid on any man, added to which the anxiety of [? about] the mine or submarine always present provides a situation which requires the highest form of philosophy . . . Here I have the finest striking force in the world 6 battle cruisers and 6 light cruisers and for all we can do they might be Thames barges. Under any circumstances we can never do anything because we are never in the right place. Who at the Admiralty is responsible for our movements? I do not know; but it is not the C-in-C, who concurs with me. Not a word of this to a soul. I must not criticize. It is most improper. . . .'[27] Though Beatty's grammar and syntax were, as in this letter, often faulty his *cri de coeur* does express what many officers felt during the early months of the war; and his castigation of the Admiralty's War

Staff was certainly not unjustified.

In late September and early October Churchill's eyes were fixed on the great port of Antwerp, the denial of which to the enemy was essential if the Belgian field army was to be extricated and a threat to the open right flank of the advancing German armies was to be produced. A force of about 3,000 Royal Marines was sent to Ostend and two almost wholly untrained Naval Brigades totalling some 8,000 men were rushed to Antwerp. On 3rd October Churchill, delighting as ever to be in the forefront of battle, took the very unusual step of going there himself – against the advice of his naval colleagues. Despite his intervention the attempt ended in fiasco, the Naval Brigades and Marines had to be hastily withdrawn, and many of the former crossed into Holland and were interned.[28] Antwerp fell to the Germans on 10th October. Beatty's comments were acidulous. After expressing his view that Captain (later Admiral Sir) Horace Hood, the Naval Secretary, had proved 'unable to control Winston' he went on to suggest that the First Lord 'must have been mad to have thought he could relieve . . . one of the most modern fortresses by putting 8,000 half trained troops into it. I cannot think what Kitchener [Secretary of State for War] was up to in permitting him to do it'.[29] Though it can of course be argued that if we had possessed a properly trained and equipped amphibious force it could have been used most effectively in a landing at Ostend, and the arrival of the marines there did cause the German Army Command considerable anxiety, the use of extemporised forces for such an undertaking was foredoomed – as many of the Board of Admiralty understood clearly.[30]

In October Beatty learnt that, as a result of the enquiry into the escape of the *Goeben* and her consort the light cruiser *Breslau* to Constantinople at the beginning of the war, Admiral E. .C. Troubridge, who had been in command of a force of four armoured cruisers at the time but had not engaged the enemy because he had been ordered not to fight 'a superior force',* was to be tried by Court Martial. Beatty, setting

*The actual relative armaments were, on the British side, 22 9.2-inch, 14 7.5-inch and 20 6-inch guns as against the German ships' 10 11-inch and 12 5.9-inch. The relative weights of broadside were 23,980 pounds on the British side against 13,550 if the *Breslau* (which was not with the *Goeben* at the time of contact) is included.

himself up as a one-man jury, told Ethel that he was 'overwhelmed', as was, he claimed, the whole navy by 'the blow which has fallen on us'. 'To think that it's the navy to provide the first and only instance of failure'. It made him 'fear a stain that cannot be wiped out . . . It's too ghastly to think of', he wrote almost hysterically.[31] In fact Troubridge was, in my view somewhat leniently, acquitted; but he was not employed again during the war.

In his next letter Beatty told Ethel that, to his regret Reginald Hall was giving up command of the *Queen Mary* because of poor health, and had been appointed Director of Naval Intelligence in succession to H. F. Oliver, of whom more will be said shortly. This was an inspired appointment; and it is relevant here to mention the story of the recovery of the German naval cypher by the Russians from one of the crew of the light cruiser *Magdeburg* which had been destroyed in the Gulf of Finland on 20th August. On 13th October, just when Hall took over from Oliver, the book arrived in the Admiralty.[32] Thus was born the famous Room 40 OB (Old Building of the Admiralty) and the whole British cryptographic organisation, which contributed so much to victory in both World Wars.* But the establishment of centralised collection, appreciation and dissemination of Intelligence – chiefly done to minimise the risk of compromising the source from which it was derived – held serious dangers, as will be told later.

*Interviews with Admiral of the Fleet Sir Henry Oliver in the 1950s. Though already an old man (he died in 1966 at the age of 101) his memories of World War I were astonishingly clear. He repeatedly told the author how 'We told that boy Churchill [sic] not to go to Antwerp, but he wouldn't listen'. These conversations also elucidated one of the long-standing mysteries of those times – namely the fate of Alexander Szek the Anglo-Austrian who repaired the powerful wireless transmitter in Brussels after the Germans captured the city on 20th Aug. 1914. Szek had access to the German diplomatic cypher, and under pressure from London finally agreed to copy it piece-meal and get the copies to London via Holland. At the last moment, however, Szek refused to hand over the rest of the book. From the British point of view it was then considered far too dangerous to leave him in Brussels, and in order to prevent discovery by the Germans of what he had done he was 'liquidated'. Admiral Oliver, who had been DNI at the beginning of this drama, several times said to me 'I paid £1,000 to have that man shot', which almost certainly provides the answer to the question left open in Barbara Tuchman's brilliant study *The Zimmerman Telegram* (Constable, 1959), pp. 17-19.

When Captain Hall was forced to give up command of the *Queen Mary* Beatty wanted her to be taken over by Captain (later Admiral Sir Rudolf) Bentinck, an officer of high intelligence and great charm. Just when Beatty believed it was all fixed up (as indeed did the *Queen Mary*'s officers)[33] the Admiralty appointed Cecil Prowse to the ship. Beatty was highly indignant about this disregard for his wishes, and told Ethel that when he had been Naval Secretary he had never put forward a name for a command without consulting the admiral concerned. He considered that Hood, his successor in that post, had infringed a wise though unwritten law – and it certainly does seem a very odd thing to have done. Hood was not on good terms with Fisher, who had just replaced Battenberg as First Sea Lord, and in view of the many personal prejudices and the 'low cunning' (Beatty's words) which Fisher so often displayed it is reasonable to suppose that he had a hand in the switch. Beatty was also very sarcastic about Press references to the *Queen Mary* as 'the wonder ship', and told Ethel that 'if they only knew her condition . . . they might be surprised'; but other evidence suggests that such strictures on Hall's ship were very unfair to him.[34] Though Beatty failed to get Bentinck appointed to the *Queen Mary* in replacement of Hall, in the following February, at which time the battle cruiser force was being reorganised, he did succeed in getting him appointed as his Chief of Staff, after Chatfield had been offered the job but had declined to give up command of the *Lion*. In that capacity Bentinck became responsible for almost everything in Beatty's command except fighting efficiency, and proved 'a tower of strength' to the admiral.[35]

Beatty's letters at this time show that he was not only subject to the xenophobia and spy mania which swept Britain at the beginning of the war, but also to the virulent anti-semitism which was a common feature of the British aristocracy and upper class. Thus on 15th October he excoriated 'that German Jew Sir Edgar Speyer', and declared that 'he and his German Frau [who was actually a well-known Austrian violinist Leonora von Stosch] are in all probability German spies and ought to be locked up; there are many like him'.[36] A week later he told Ethel that 'it is a fact that all over Scotland anywhere there is a possibility of there being a naval base, the postmistress (not master) is a German'!; and he complained bitterly that 'the Sir Edgar Speyers, Waechters, Neumanns, Cassels, Oppen-

heimers and all the other Hoggenheimers [are] free to do
as they like, all German Jews; it is inconceivable'.[37]

As the ever-lengthening Army casualty list began to appear
in the Press Beatty constantly deplored the loss of the scions of
his and Ethel's aristocratic friends. It is certainly true that
the losses suffered by such families were tragically heavy, and
in the end possibly deprived Britain of the leadership she was
to need so sorely after the first struggle against Germany was
over. Beatty felt these losses deeply, though perhaps he did
not appreciate adequately that it was by no means only the
upper classes which suffered from the terrible holocausts in the
mud of France and Flanders. At any rate his letters of
sympathy to the bereaved read far more pleasantly than his
anti-semitic tirades.

In mid-October Beatty wrote at length to Churchill
(short-circuiting his C-in-C) from an undefended anchorage
off the Isle of Mull in western Scotland about the strategic
problems facing the fleet. He began by arguing that 'at present
we feel that we are working up for a catastrophe of a very
large character. The feeling is gradually possessing the fleet
that all is not right somewhere'. He went on to urge the
provision of properly defended bases at Scapa, Cromarty and
Rosyth.* As things were, he protested, 'we are driven out of
the North Sea because of the menace of enemy submarines and
mines; and he proposed that Rear-Admiral (later Admiral of
the Fleet Sir) John de Robeck, who was then serving in
command of the forces operating in defence of trade off the
west coast of the Iberian Peninsula, whom Beatty described as
'a born leader of men, of great energy and determination',
should come to the Admiralty to tackle the problem. Beatty
represented that the First Lord knew himself 'well enough to
know that I do not shout without cause', and that although
morale and confidence were high 'we hate running away from
our base, and the effect is appreciable'. He hoped that
Churchill 'with his quick grasp of detail and imagination'
would make something of it. Commander Plunkett, by whose
hand he sent the letter, was fully informed regarding 'all that I
have in my head' and would supply any more information
needed by the First Lord.[38] Though there was a great deal of
truth in Beatty's pleadings he entirely ignored the pre-war

*See Map 1, pages 74-5

warnings regarding the influence which submarines and mines
would have on naval warfare repeatedly proclaimed by 'Jacky'
Fisher, Percy Scott and other far-sighted and unconventional
naval men.[39] A long time was to elapse before the
Grand Fleet's bases were made secure; and in passing it may be
remarked that exactly the same problems arose during the
early months of World War II.[40] Curiously Churchill does not
appear to have acknowledged, let alone answered, Beatty's
letter; but he was of course under very heavy pressure at the
time.

One of the most serious troubles which derived from the
insecurity of the Grand Fleet's bases was the difficulty of
carrying out realistic battle practices at high speeds and long
ranges – in which respect the Grand Fleet's gunnery efficiency
certainly left much to be desired early in the war. The trouble
was aggravated by the paucity of ships fitted with director
firing, mentioned earlier, since ships with that equipment
could carry out what were called 'Throw-off Firings' at a
consort steaming at high speed and with complete freedom of
manoeuvre. In that type of practice the guns were 'thrown off'
from the director, usually by six degrees, so that although the
director was aimed at the target the shots fell at a safe distance
ahead or astern of her (though there were occasions when
human error eliminated the six degree 'throw-off' and so
endangered the target). By a simple system of triangulation
the fall of shot relative to the target could easily be measured,
so giving a good idea of the true accuracy of the firing ship;
but many months were to elapse before such practices became
a regular feature of Grand Fleet gunnery training – because of
the lack of the directors which Percy Scott had designed many
years earlier.

If inefficient fire control systems and lack of realistic
practices were two handicaps under which the British heavy
ships laboured in 1914, unsatisfactory armour-piercing shell
was a third one. This latter had become apparent in trials
against an elderly warship target as early as 1910 when Jellicoe
was Controller of the Navy; but he went to sea shortly
afterwards and I have found no evidence that his successor
(Charles J. Briggs, mentioned earlier) took steps to rectify the
tendency of our shells to break up if they struck armour plate
at an oblique angle, or failed to penetrate it in a fit state to
burst.[41] Though gunnery officers, notably Chatfield and

Dreyer, later blamed all our troubles on defective shells they were interested parties – especially Dreyer – which probably explains why they totally ignored the fire control side of the problem, as does Professor Marder. A few weeks after the Heligoland Bight action Beatty wrote of Admiral F. C. D. (later Sir Doveton) Sturdee, the Chief of the War Staff, that 'he has been one of the curses of the Navy. He was principally responsible for all our disasters afloat, and Fisher showed his acumen by turning him out'.[42] Though history has in the main supported Beatty's view of Sturdee the most weighty reason for his dismissal almost certainly was that he had been a supporter of Lord Charles Beresford at the time when the deadly feud between him and Fisher had split the navy; for on 28th October Prince Louis of Battenberg resigned the office of First Sea Lord – unquestionably at the instigation of the Cabinet – and Fisher, though now in his 74th year, took over in his place. Sturdee's successor as Chief of the War Staff was Admiral Sir Henry Oliver, a far abler man though addicted to the all too common failure among British admirals of over-centralisation. As for Prince Louis, it is undoubtedly the case that his German ancestry produced criticisms of him which were as unjustified as they were malevolent; and those criticisms must have produced great psychological strain. Yet it is true to say that since the outbreak of war he had not shown anything like the vigour and imagination which had been apparent in his earlier appointments at sea and on shore. Among the more irreverent officers in the Admiralty he had earned the nickname of 'Quite concur', since he rarely wrote more than those two words on any paper submitted to him;[43] and it does seem that by the autumn of 1914 he was played out. Beatty's reaction to this change was to write to Ethel that he had heard that 'Prince Louis has resigned owing to his close relationship to Germany.' 'But', he continued, 'that is not the reason why, which is that he did not keep a proper check on Winston and ran the show himself instead of allowing him (W) to do it. Now they have resurrected old Fisher, I am afraid he is too old . . . and of course the service don't trust him. But if he is what he was he has energy, ideas and low cunning, which is what we want . . . I feel [that] provided he is not ga-ga he'll perhaps be alright. But where are the young men? . . .'[44]

With the approach of autumn the usual equinoctial gales

made Beatty's frequent sweeps around the North Sea vastly
more taxing. At the end of September he told Ethel that since
his last letter 'we have been having a most poisonous time.
Blowing very hard with a bad sea Sunday night and Monday
morning [27th and 28th September] it was a full gale and it
was not pleasant. I haven't a dry spot in my cabin. The decks
leak like a sieve and it's like living under a perpetual shower
bath . . . We lost a top-gallant mast with the wireless, and a
gun went overboard . . . this is the fourth day which we have
spent practically hove to. . . .' If conditions were like that in
the quarters of the battle cruiser admiral they were many times
worse on the men's crowded mess decks where nothing was
ever dry; and life on board the small ships almost defies
description. Beatty told Ethel that the conditions reminded
him of Joseph Conrad's novel *Typhoon*.[45]

It was probably the experience of that sweep and similar
operations which caused Beatty to protest vigorously to
Jellicoe over the impossibility of intercepting and bringing in
for examination the very large number of neutral merchant ships
which were certainly carrying contraband cargoes destined for
Germany; and it is a fact that in the early months of the war
our blockade was as leaky as the decks of the *Lion*. Beatty put
forward proposals whereby every ship should be forced to
identify herself, so making it possible to judge whether she
was likely to be carrying contraband. The trouble was of
course that the Foreign Office, and so the Cabinet, were
treading very warily over causing offence to neutral nations –
and especially the USA – by interfering with their shipping.
Memories of the war with America brought about by such
actions in 1812 were still very much alive, and the patrolling
warships therefore had to suffer the constant frustration of
seeing ships which were probably loaded with contraband –
and earning immense profits for their owners and shippers –
slip through the blockade with immunity. The Declarations of
Paris of 1856 and of London 1909 (though the latter had been
rejected by the House of Lords) had in effect deprived
maritime power of its most effective weapon – namely
economic pressure; and many weary months were to pass and
prolonged and difficult negotiations were to be undertaken
before the harm done by those idealistic measures was
nullified.[46]

Ethel evidently complained that she was not told of the

move of the 1st BCS to Cromarty in October, and her husband had to explain to her that he could not have done so because he had not known about the move until just before it took place; and he rapped her knuckles severely by telling her that even had he known earlier he would not have passed the news on 'for reasons which I have always given and which you understand'.[47] Certainly it took a very long time for Ethel to accustom herself to the inevitable restrictions and inconveniences of wartime – if indeed she ever did so.

On the day that Beatty wrote to Ethel about the move to Cromarty the Germans made the first of their 'tip and run' raids on east coast towns. The moment was well chosen by them, though accidentally so, since Jellicoe had been called to London for consultations, the Grand Fleet was at Lough Swilly in northern Ireland, and Beatty's battle cruisers were the only powerful ships which might be able to intervene. Three modern German battle cruisers and the older *Blücher* came out to cover a minelaying operation, and the shelling of Yarmouth was actually incidental to that purpose. 'Room 40' had not yet achieved its full efficiency in providing ample and accurate warning of enemy intentions, and although Beatty hastened to an intercepting position north of Heligoland and the battle squadrons came south in support no action resulted. Beatty's only comment was to tell his wife that 'We had a galop [sic] yesterday and thought we should at last get at the Germans, but they bolted home again. . . .'[48]

A considerable redisposition of our forces did, however, follow on this German foray, with the object of keeping more strength in the southern North Sea and increasing the light forces needed to deal with a raid on the east coast or a serious invasion. In December the 1st Battle Cruiser Squadron moved from Cromarty to Rosyth. Though better placed strategically it suffered from important disadvantages, to be referred to shortly, about which experience was to prove that the misgivings felt by both Jellicoe and Beatty were not without substance.

On 5th November Beatty learnt about the disaster off Coronel on the coast of Chile, where the two weak and ill-manned armoured cruisers *Good Hope* and *Monmouth* under Rear-Admiral Sir Christopher Cradock had been overwhelmed by Admiral von Spee's highly efficient Asiatic Squadron on 1st. We cannot here go into all the details of the

orders and counter-orders which brought about that disaster
But a large share of the blame must rest with the Admiralty,
whose 'confused, unrealistic and, consequently, misleading
instructions'[49] wholly belie Churchill's specious disclaimer
that 'I cannot therefore accept for the Admiralty any share in
the responsibility' for what followed[50] – so placing the whole
blame on Cradock. As the news filtered through Beatty was
puzzled, and ruminated that perhaps Cradock 'saw red and did
not wait for his proper reinforcement, the [old battleship]
Canopus' – which was not far from the truth.[51] As with all his
contemporaries he liked and admired 'Kit' Cradock, a gallant
officer of attractive personality, and mourned his loss deeply.
Then Beatty heard that Sturdee, the recently dismissed Chief
of the War Staff, had been ordered to hoist his flag in the
Invincible, which surprised him as much as he disliked having
Sir Archibald Moore foisted on himself as second-in-
command of the Battle Cruiser Squadron.[52] But bigger events
than Beatty was aware of were in fact in train.

On 4th November the Admiralty ordered the *Invincible* and
Inflexible to complete with coal at once and proceed to
Berehaven 'with all despatch' as they were 'urgently needed
for foreign service'. By way of recompense the recently
completed *Tiger* was ordered to join the C-in-C.[53] Rather
surprisingly Beatty was not at first perturbed about this
diminution of his strength, telling Ethel that 'Moore with the
Invincible and *Inflexible* ought to have gone out there [to South
America] two months ago and then we should have had a very
different story [to Coronel].'[54] Next day he unburdened
himself about the weight of responsibility he had to carry.
'The anxieties of this sea life', he wrote, 'with the valuable
machines and the valuable thousands of lives depending on
you is very, very great and makes a very heavy burden and
responsibility to carry . . .'; and he inveighed against the
three old men – Fisher, A. K. Wilson and Percy Scott – who
had been called back to the Admiralty.[55] He reverted to the
same subject in another letter to Ethel a week later, declaring
that he 'honestly thought' that 'at the Admiralty they are
stark, staring mad, but what can you expect when they
produce two old men over 70 years of age who have no
personal knowledge of the requirements and capabilities of a
modern fleet, [and] working with an ill-balanced individual
like Winston'. He went on to 'thank God the navy afloat is all

right' and that he himself was not at the Admiralty.[56] In passing it may be remarked that criticisms of the Admiralty by sea-going Admirals, such as Beatty expressed so frequently and so freely, have been a common feature throughout Britain's naval history – sometimes with greater justification than there was in 1914. It is perhaps natural for those who carry responsibility for a sea-going fleet or squadron to vent their frustration on the department to which they are responsible; but it none the less remains true that, broadly speaking, in World War I the Admiralty did not distinguish itself. As regards Churchill's recall of Fisher and A. K. Wilson it may be remarked that exactly the same phenomenon recurred in 1939–40, when Churchill as 1st Lord and Admiral Pound as 1st Sea Lord called back elderly officers such as Roger Keyes, Lord Cork and Orrery and Frederic Dreyer to Whitehall, or even to operational commands.[57]

Beatty was not one of the senior officers who appreciated the value, let alone the importance, of publicity conducted by responsible writers and journalists – especially in wartime. In mid-November he told Ethel 'that terrible fellow Filson Young has worked his way and he has been appointed to the *Lion* for special service.' The appointment was undoubtedly made at the instigation of Fisher, who had always been aware of the value of publicity, and had indeed proved himself a master at manipulating the Press in order to further his schemes. Filson Young however proved an able and popular advocate of the navy in general and the battle cruisers in particular, though the full fruits of his time under Beatty were not harvested until after the war – and even then the Admiralty declined to allow him access to official records.[58]

Soon after Beatty had reluctantly accepted the arrival of Filson Young in his squadron the question of forming a women's branch of the naval service was raised. He quickly showed himself to be totally opposed to such an innovation, telling Ethel that he had 'never heard such nonsense' and that there was plenty of work for women which men could not do; while for married women it was enough 'to look after their homes and children'[59] – in other words he supported the German view that '*Kinder, Kirche, Küche*' [children, church and kitchen] were the proper provinces for women. Little could he have foreseen the remarkable work done by the W.R.N.S. or 'Wrens' in both world wars.

Although Beatty accepted without protest, and even commended the detachment of the *Invincible* and *Inflexible* to the South Alantic he did write a strong letter to Jellicoe stressing the possibly serious effects of the weakness of his squadron, which was reduced to three effective battle cruisers (*Lion, Queen Mary* and *New Zealand*) by the despatch of the *Princess Royal* to the West Indies to forestall von Spee bringing his force through the Panama Canal, as he was perfectly entitled to do, and preying on our very valuable shipping in the Caribbean. He also wrote direct to Fisher about the dangers of the situation with which he might be faced, since the Germans had four battle cruisers (plus the older *Blücher*) ready for action, and were in his opinion quite likely to make a challenging sweep in the North Sea or bombard our east coast towns. But as it had largely been Fisher who was responsible for the redispositions brought about by Coronel, Beatty's pleadings – especially for the return of the *Princess Royal* – were not likely to strike a sympathetic chord in Whitehall.[60]

Meanwhile Admiral Sturdee, of whom Beatty as well as Fisher held no very high opinion, had taken command of the two battle cruisers destined for the South Atlantic, which had been diverted to Devonport instead of Berehaven. Fisher and Churchill flatly refused to accept any delay, and the ships were ordered to sail on 11th November.[61] Unfortunately for von Spee the German Intelligence network, though it became aware of the movement of the two powerful ships, failed to pass on a warning to him. Nor did Sturdee press on with all despatch to the Falkland Islands, where the Admiralty expected him to arrive on 3rd December.[63]

While Sturdee was steaming southwards Beatty met Jellicoe with the object of making a thorough survey of the situation and the problems to be faced. He told Ethel that the two of them were 'in perfect agreement' and that on parting he felt 'very much happier than I was before'. He was, however, still resentful of having Admiral Moore as second-in-command, flying his flag in the *New Zealand*; but he took comfort from the fact that the appointment was only temporary and he hoped soon 'to be shot of him altogether'.[64] Unfortunately Beatty's pessimistic prognosis of the result of Moore's appointment to his squadron was to prove well founded.

On the day after Beatty expressed these anxieties to his wife Churchill wrote him an appreciative letter, assuring the

admiral of his complete confidence in his ability to 'give the
enemy's battle cruiser plus *Blücher* a satisfactory trouncing'.
With unjustified optimism he went on to say that 'The Navy
is as far ahead of the German Navy ship for ship, as the Army
has proved itself man for man'.[65] One wonders from what
source the First Lord can have derived such sublime and
excessive confidence, and so great an underestimate of the
enemy – at any rate as regards material. The probability surely
is that such views derived from Fisher, one of whose particular
brain children had been the battle cruisers, whose lack of strong
armour protection he always defended on the grounds that
'speed is armour' – as indeed Beatty had reminded him in his
letter of 15th November quoted above. Beatty, however, was
evidently far from satisfied with the conduct of the fleet's
operations, as well as with the Admiralty's direction of the
navy, despite his recent and successful discussion with Jellicoe.
Churchill's encouraging letter already mentioned had told him
that 'no one has done better than you', and that provided he
steered 'midway between Troubridge and Cradock all will be
well'; but it is noteworthy, and typical, that in the event of a
choice arising Churchill 'preferred Cradock' – that is to say
precipitate gallantry rather than excessive caution such as
Troubridge had shown. At about the time Beatty read those
words he told his wife that 'What we really want is to have
somebody in Command who has the instinct of hunting born
in them, who can lay traps and exercise ingenuity: guile has to
be met by low cunning, a good poacher is the type required
. . . The usual type of honest sailorman is too simple'.[66] This
appears to be the first hint of criticism of Jellicoe recorded by
Beatty.

On the last day of November Churchill wrote again to
Beatty, presumably in answer to his protest about his
weakened squadron. The First Lord hoped that 'it will be
possible to strengthen your squadron in the near future by the
return of the straying cat [*Princess Royal*] and the addition of a
still more formidable feline animal to wit the *Queen Elizabeth*',
which is the first mention of the nameship of that famous class
joining Beatty. He was, however, told that 'for the present
you must just put a bold face on it. The *Derfflinger* is new as
well as the *Tiger*, and of the two I have little doubt the *Tiger*
would win. We are trying also to find you some kittens [i.e.
light cruisers and destroyers] from our not unlimited litter.

You must all get the 60% standard [i.e. the superiority aimed at pre-war] out of your minds. No one has any ground for complaint at fighting on even terms . . .'; and he repeated his earlier assurance that all experience had proved that 'we are their match man for man and gun for gun', to which he added the encouragement that 'no one is more capable of proving that than yourself'.[67]

Early in December Beatty reviewed to Ethel the qualities and failings of his flagship's officers and his personal staff. He was glad that a new Commander, Charles A. ['Carlo'] Fountaine, had joined the *Lion* to replace H. W. Parker, whom Chatfield has described as 'a very able man' but who in Beatty's opinion lacked 'new ideas' and was apparently too much of an autocrat in the wardroom.[68] Surprisingly he described Chatfield as becoming 'more melancholic daily and very taciturn. He is an astoundingly obstinate human being and inclined to be narrow minded . . . and is really of very little assistance; he always sees the bad side of things and never the good . . . I think he must have some secret sorrow and that is a luxury nobody is entitled to in times such as these. . . .' 'The Secretary' [Spickernell], he wrote, 'is my principal standby. I get more assistance out of him than anybody else. . . .' It is only fair to add that Beatty very soon changed his opinion of Chatfield drastically. Rumours that Churchill was to leave the Admiralty had evidently reached Beatty, which was no surprise 'as I cannot see him working in harmony with Jacky Fisher for very long. . . .'[69] Two days later he wrote that 'the situation [in the Admiralty] is curious. Two very strong and clever men, one old, wily and of vast experience, one young, self-assertive with great self-satisfaction but unstable. They cannot work together; they cannot both run the show, the old man can and will, the young man thinks he can and won't: hence one must go and that is Winston. . . .'[70] Though another six months were to elapse before the crisis foreseen by Beatty actually came to pass his shrewd reasoning on the outlook and characters of the two great men at the head of his service was to be proved very near the mark. However, relations between Beatty and Fisher as well as between him and Churchill evidently remained cordial at this time, since a few days later he told his wife that he himself was 'apparently in favour with old Jacky Fisher as he bombards me with letters every mail and always finishes up by saying heavily underlined – "Any mortal thing you want, animate or inanimate, you shall have if you send me a telegram". I have tried him already, and he has played up. . . .'[71]

Late in the evening of 9th December Beatty received 'the glorious news . . . [that] poor old Kit Cradock has been truly avenged' by the destruction of all but one ship of von Spee's squadron off the Falkland Islands on the previous day, and he at once sent Ethel a telegram to that effect. As two of his ships had been the principal instruments involved he took an understandably proprietary interest in their success. Though he reiterated his view that the *Invincible* and *Inflexible* ought to have been sent out to Cradock 'long ago' he roundly declared that 'the victory belongs to old Fisher and nobody else', because he had 'sent them out directly he arrived at the Admiralty, and all credit is due to him'. The good news acted as a tonic not only to the fleet but to the whole nation, and Beatty hoped that it would 'put a stop to a lot of the unpleasant remarks one can detect in a certain portion of the Press that the British Navy *has* been an expensive luxury and is not doing its job'.[72]

In truth luck had been on the British side over the Falkland Islands success, since Sturdee had dallied unnecessarily on his way south, only reached his destination on the morning of 7th December, and was caught coaling ship when von Spee's masts were sighted to the south-west of Port Stanley at about 8 o'clock next day. The junction of Sturdee's battle cruisers with Rear-Admiral A. P. Stoddart's three armoured and one light cruiser gave him an overwhelmingly superior force, and the issue was never in doubt once the British squadron had got to sea and taken up the chase to the south-east of the islands. At about 4.0 p.m. the *Scharnhorst* was sunk, and the *Gneisenau* followed her to the bottom of those icy waters two hours later, at about the same time as the British cruisers finished off the *Nürnberg*, *Leipzig* and two German auxiliaries. The German ships fought to the end most gallantly, and in the opening stages their shooting was excellent; but about 2,000 of their crews, including von Spee were lost. The number of hits scored on the *Scharnhorst* and *Gneisenau* cannot be accurately estimated but was probably about 40 on each ship. The *Invincible* received 22 hits, twelve of which were 8.3 inch, but the *Inflexible* was hit only three times. The two ships had only one man killed and four wounded between them; so Sturdee's policy of fighting at ranges at which he was unlikely to suffer serious damage paid off.[73] Only the light cruiser *Dresden* escaped; but that incident gave Fisher an opportunity to display the vindictive side of his character by demanding an explanation in a series of 'rather rude telegrams' to Sturdee.[74]

The most important lessons of the battle actually concerned the enormous expenditure of 12-inch ammunition (1,174 rounds, of which 285 were armour-piercing shell) and the inefficiency of the fire control system fitted in the British battle cruisers, neither of which was equipped with director firing. The battle was fought at fairly long ranges (generally 12,000 yards or more) and at high speeds – very much on the lines which Beatty had tried out – though with poor results – in 1912. The conditions provided a perfect example of the vital importance of a 'helm-free' fire control system, such as Arthur Pollen had offered to the Admiralty but which they turned down in favour of the simpler, cheaper but less efficient alternative produced by Captain F. C. Dreyer, mentioned earlier.[75]

It was easier to find evidence of the inefficiency of British fire control than of our armour-piercing shells in the Falklands Islands battle. This was because the German ships were not heavily armoured, and as they were sunk it was difficult to establish exactly what damage they suffered. There were no survivors from the *Scharnhorst*, and only 198 from her sister ship; and none of the latter could give evidence of what damage was caused by the various types of shell used (armour-piercing, common pointed and high explosive). On the other hand no enemy ships blew up, as the *Good Hope* had done at Coronel; and the *Gneisenau's* Captain finally gave orders to scuttle his damaged ship. Thus careful analysis and investigation might well have given rise to doubts regarding the efficiency of British shell as well as fire control; but a heavy price was to be exacted before that was done.

Bearing in mind that Sturdee was 14,000 miles from any proper dockyard, and in command of ships which were urgently needed in home waters, no criticism can be levelled at his decision to engage at ranges where he was unlikely to suffer serious damage from his adversaries' 8.3-inch guns; but the enormous ammunition expenditure he incurred now seems to have demanded far more concern than it received. The comparatively little attention given to that subject is made more inexplicable by the fact that after the Heligoland Bight action of 28th August the Admiralty promulgated a warning against excessive expenditure of heavy shells.[76] Captain Macintyre has argued that the Falkland Islands battle brought recognition of the need for improved fire control and more intensive battle practice training, and that the lessons of that battle were obscured by the troubles caused through interference of funnel smoke with the gunlayers – a view which Professor Marder appears to support.[77] It is certainly true that after Jellicoe was able to take his battle squadrons back to Scapa great attention was devoted to target firings; but for Beatty's battle cruisers at Cromarty or Rosyth it was, for geographical and climatic reasons, and because of the threat from mines and submarines, far more difficult to adopt the same policy. Furthermore, apart from fitting more ships with director firing and carrying out quite minor modifications to the fire control system fitted, no study appears to have been made of the technical (as opposed to tactical) problems involved in fighting at long range and high speed.

Early in December Beatty took the unusual step for an officer of his rank and seniority of sending direct to the King an account of his squadron's doings and of the general situation in the North Sea. 'We have now settled down', he wrote, 'to a regular War Routine and might have been at it all our lives. For the first month or two we anticipated a Sea Battle at any moment and the thought of such a possibility carried us over the first strenuous months. As we are great coal eaters we averaged coaling ship every 4 Days and for August, Septr. and Octr. we averaged 5,400 tons and 6,000 miles a month. We have swept the North Sea periodically and only on one occasion 28th August were we fortunate to find any of the enemy Vessels out. Our only menace is the Mine and Submarine'. He concluded by reporting that 'I honestly think that we can claim that your Majesty's Navy still commands the seas', and that it was 'capable of upholding the Traditions of our Great Service'; all of which was probably music in the ears of the 'sailor King', who did in fact regard the navy in a proprietorial way.[78] Moreover as the correspondence continued, though somewhat desultorily, we may assume that such letters, bearing their unmistakable whiff of salt water and sea breezes – mixed with coal dust – gave the Monarch pleasure as well as interest.

In mid-December Admiral Friedrich von Ingenohl, the C-in-C of the High Seas Fleet, decided to take advantage of the absence of three of Beatty's ships by staging a raid by his battle cruisers on British east coast towns, combined with the laying of mines off the Yorkshire coast. The German battle fleet was to support the raiding force from a position in the middle of the North Sea. Admiral Franz von Hipper accordingly sailed from the Jade river in the early hours of 15th December with five battle cruisers, and the supporting force sailed about twelve hours later. Room 40 however, gave warning of the coming operation, but did not foretell participation by the German battle fleet. The Admiralty therefore ordered only part of the Grand Fleet to come south, though Jellicoe wanted to bring his whole force. Beatty's four battle cruisers from Cromarty, together with two cruiser squadrons and a destroyer flotilla, were detailed to trap Hipper's ships. Vice-Admiral Sir George Warrender with the six ships of the powerful 2nd Battle Squadron, who was to command all the British forces, was to be off the south-east corner of the Dogger Bank at dawn on 16th. The first contact took place between his and von Ingenohl's light forces; but the German C-in-C was unaware that the precise opportunity for which he had always striven, namely to catch a detachment of the Grand Fleet with greatly superior strength, had arisen. Believing he was faced by the whole of Jellicoe's force, and inhibited by his orders not to engage in a risky action with his battleships, he broke away to the south-east leaving Hipper to fend for himself. Between 8.0 and 9.15 a.m. Hipper bombarded Scarborough, Hartlepool and Whitby, and the mines were successfully laid.* At 9.30 he turned for home having accomplished his mission with success and unaware that Beatty's battle cruisers and Warrender's six battleships were in a position to trap him. By 11 a.m. the two forces were steaming directly towards each other, and British expectations of a resounding success were high. Then the clear weather gave way to high seas and driving rain, and visibility dropped drastically.

*Only Hartlepool, where there were three 6-inch coast defence guns, could conceivably be said to come within the Hague Convention definition of a defended port. Civilian casualties there totalled 86 killed and 424 wounded.

At 11.25 contact was made between the two sides' light cruisers, but an unfortunately worded signal from Beatty, intended only for the *Nottingham* and *Falmouth*, 'Light cruisers resume your position for look-out. Take station five miles [ahead of the battle cruisers]' was passed on to Admiral Goodenough's 1st Light Cruiser Squadron, causing him to break off contact. Beatty was furious when he learnt what had happened, and it is probable that but for that signal he would have got the battle which he eagerly anticipated. Though he blamed Goodenough for the result a large part of the error must be attributed to the use by the *Lion* of a wrong call sign for the *Nottingham* and by the ambiguous wording of the signal quoted. Beatty's Flag Lieutenant Ralph Seymour should surely have made certain that the signal was addressed only to the two ships which Beatty wanted to rejoin his advanced screen. This was the first of four mistakes made by Seymour at critical moments. At any rate the blunder saved Hipper – just as Warrender had been saved from von Ingenohl's superior force early in the day.

Contact was regained at 12.15 p.m. when Warrender was sighted by the German light forces, so enabling Hipper to disengage by altering to the north before making a wide homeward sweep. At 3.45 p.m. the chase was abandoned. On the British side disappointment and anger were widespread for, as Corbett remarked in the Official History 'Two of the most efficient and powerful British squadrons, with an adequate force of scouting vessels, knowing approximately what to expect, and operating in an area strictly limited by the possibilities of the situation [i.e. the Dogger Bank and the minefields], had failed to bring to action an enemy who was operating in close conformity with our appreciation and with whose advanced screen contact had been established'.[79] Beatty's comment to his wife that 'If we had got them Wednesday, as we ought to have done, we should have finished the war from a naval point of view' though exaggerated is also pertinent;[80] and he wrote to Jellicoe that 'There never was a more bitterly disappointing day . . . We were within an ace of bringing about the complete destruction of the Enemy Cruiser Force – and failed'.[81] Jellicoe endorsed the envelope containing that frustrated letter 'Beatty very severe on Goodenough but forgets that it was his own badly worded signal to the cruisers that led to the Germans being out of touch', a comment which, though true, was probably added later. Shane Leslie in his draft biography described Beatty's unfortunate signal as 'a persistent order to recall the light cruisers', which is surely an overstatement; but Leslie also recorded years later how Beatty still placed a large share of the blame on Goodenough.[82] In his letter to the C-in-C Beatty did suggest that the cruiser admiral should be relieved of his command – preferably by Halsey from the *New Zealand*; but in the end no change was made – a decision which Goodenough's conduct on a later occasion fully justified.

In the Admiralty Fisher expectedly indulged in head-hunting and wanted Warrender sacked; while the bombardment of the east coast towns resurrected the Press questions about what the navy was doing – which had caused Beatty resentment earlier. The final outcome of the *post-mortem* was that although a great deal of anguish was displayed in high places, no heads rolled.[83] In terms of strategy the most important development was the shift of the battle cruisers from Cromarty to Rosyth, where they were certainly better placed to intercept a raiding force. Goodenough's 1st Light Cruiser Squadron now became a permanent part of the Battle Cruiser force, which, however, still remained part of Jellicoe's Grand Fleet.

When the Admiralty analysed the course of events on 16th December they were critical of the 'spread' of the light cruisers at the time when Beatty was seeking his adversary at about 9.15 a.m., and remarked that 'It is not clear whether the battle cruisers were spread or not, or how the 3rd Cruiser Squadron [Pakenham's] was spread. At any rate the front covered in proportion to the number of ships available was very small'. They also considered that on receiving Beatty's signal to resume station ahead of him Goodenough [1st Light Cruiser Squadron] should have reported that he was in action with the enemy before breaking contact. Their conclusion was that 'Throughout the operations the ships were insufficiently spread and there was a want of touch between the battle squadron [Warrender] and cruisers under V.A.C. 1st B.S.C. [Beatty]'.[84] Jellicoe's reaction was to ask 'whether Their Lordships consider that the Battle Cruisers should have been spread', and he 'respectfully submitted' that 'such a course is contrary to the custom which experience of all peace exercises has shown to be desirable'.[85] The Admiralty however refused

to budge from their view that 'in the special circumstances the
1st Battle Cruiser Squadron might have been spread to a small
extent without incurring any risk' – that is to say of loss of
concentration.[86] That riposte caused Beatty to protest that the
conclusions 'appear to be based on data which on many points
disagree with the records kept in *Lion*'; and he argued that to
spread his ships 'in a long line N and S . . . would have been
against all the experience gained and principles evolved during
the past 2 years. . . .'[87] There the argument was apparently
allowed to end. Whether or not a wider spread would have
enabled contact to be regained cannot of course be proved; but
the Admiralty's implication that reconnaissance and enemy
reporting left a good deal to be desired certainly had substance
in it. Perhaps the most enduring results of the Scarborough
Raid were the production of Osbert Sitwell's novel 'Before the
Bombardment' and the description of his father Sir George
sheltering in the cellar of the family's home and his mother
Lady Ida remaining 'resolutely in bed while fragments of shell
struck their home'.[88]

It thus came to pass that 1914 ended on a very distressed
note for Beatty, who felt that failures by colleagues such as
Warrender and subordinates such as Goodenough, as well as
sheer bad luck, had deprived him of the success which was so
nearly within his grasp.

CHAPTER SIX

The Submarine
Comes into its Own. 1915

The early days of 1915 produced the first clear evidence that the strain of Jellicoe's great responsibilities was telling on his health. On 26th January he wrote to Beatty that he was 'not at all well' and was suffering from a 'very bad attack of piles and general run down'. Beatty replied sympathetically saying 'You must take the greatest care of yourself. What we should do without you the Lord knows'.[1] In February Jellicoe was operated on for the piles, and after it was over Beatty assured him that he *was* glad . . . to know that you were going on well, it is a truly poisonous complaint and nothing takes it out of you more. . . .'[2] Jellicoe's illness, coming so soon after his appointment as C-in-C, should surely have raised doubts – even in the mind of Fisher, his chief supporter and admirer – regarding whether he possessed the stamina to carry through the task which had fallen to him. Moreover he provides the first – though by no means the last – example of a man who was not fully fit holding high command in a major war.[3] At any rate Fisher took very good care of his *protégé*, sending famous surgeons from London and Edinburgh to carry out the operation and a trained nurse to look after the patient while he was in a nursing home – disguised as 'Mr. Jessop' to prevent the Germans becoming aware of his absence from the fleet.[4]

Beatty's attitude towards his C-in-C was at this time that of complete loyalty – though he could and did criticise him in his private correspondence; while Jellicoe for his part certainly reciprocated that loyalty towards and confidence in his principal subordinate – as when he sprang to his defence over the mild Admiralty criticism of his conduct during the Scarborough raid operation.

Soon after Fisher returned to the First Sea Lord's desk at the end of October 1914 he started to correspond frequently, and directly, with Beatty. Early in the New Year he described his intention to form a 2nd Battle Cruiser Squadron consisting of

the new fast battleship *Queen Elizabeth,* and the *Inflexible,*
Invincible and *Indomitable.* He proposed that it should be
stationed at Rosyth on the Firth of Forth.[5] In his reply Beatty
described this idea as 'sound' and 'very useful'; but he wanted
it to be called the '2nd Division' instead of '2nd Squadron'
because it would be part of his command and 'imbued with
the same ideas and principles which have governed our
training in the past'; and he wanted both Divisions to work
from the same base. Though he fully recognised the strategic
advantages which derived from the closer proximity of Rosyth
to the waters where his force would probably be needed he
expressed doubts about whether they outweighed the benefits
of using Cromarty Firth or Scapa Flow. His reasons were that
the approach to the Rosyth anchorage was long and narrow,
and therefore vulnerable to enemy minelaying and to submarines lying in ambush; also that the Firth of Forth was liable
at any time to be shrouded in fog. However he considered that
those disadvantages could be overcome if an adequate defence
scheme was created and sufficient small craft were provided for
local defence purposes. Beatty assured Fisher that he was
investigating those matters energetically.[6]

A month later the Admiralty informed Beatty officially that
he was appointed 'Vice-Admiral Commanding the Battle
Cruiser Fleet under the C-in-C, Home Fleets', by which they
meant the forces already referred to collectively as the Grand
Fleet. The 1st Battle Cruiser Squadron (and Beatty's prefer-
ence for 'Division' was evidently disregarded) was to be
commanded by Commodore (later Admiral of the Fleet Sir
Osmond de B.) Brock, an officer for whom Beatty had a high
regard, with his broad pendant in the *Princess Royal,* while
Rear-Admiral Moore, whom Beatty regarded very differently
from Brock, was to take command of the 2nd Battle Cruiser
Squadron with his flag in the *New Zealand.* A 3rd Battle
Cruiser Squadron was to be formed under Vice-Admiral Sir
George Patey with his flag in the *Australia* when the ships sent
overseas had returned.*[7] To Beatty's delight his bellicose

---

*The appointments were later changed. Moore was sent to command a
force of elderly cruisers operating off the west coast of Africa; Patey's
appointment was not confirmed and he went as C-in-C, North America and
West Indies; and Pakenham took over the 2nd BCS. Command of the 3rd
BCS remained temporarily vacant until Admiral Hood took it over. See
page 126.

friend of the hunting field Walter Cowan, who had been eating his heart out in command of an elderly battleship since the beginning of the war, was appointed to the *Princess Royal* as Flag Captain to Brock.[8]

But before the new organisation had been brought fully into effect exciting events took place in the North Sea. On 19th January Beatty took his force out on a reconnaissance sweep to the west of the Heligoland Bight and was sighted by a German aircraft. This report, taken with recent British operations near the Dogger Bank, resulted in Admiral von Ingenohl, the Commander of the High Seas Fleet, sending out Hipper's battle cruisers (*Seydlitz, Moltke, Derfflinger* and *Blücher*) on 23rd January to try and surprise whatever British forces they might encounter in that area. Happily for the British the Admiralty's Room 40 was able to decypher sufficient enemy signals to be sure that they were about to make a reconnaissance in force as far as the Dogger Bank, though the object of the operation, which had actually been postponed several times because of bad weather, was not known in London.

From the German point of view 22nd January, the date when the weather suddenly cleared and there was promise of a fine and calm period ahead, was by no means ideal. In the first place their Third Battle Squadron, comprising the *Kaiser* class and the new and powerful *König* class ships, was working up efficiency in the Baltic. Secondly only three of the four *Ostfriesland* class battleships and four *Nassau* class (1st Squadron) were available in the North Sea; and thirdly the battle cruiser *von der Tann* and several light cruisers were refitting; also the number of destroyers available was well below normal because of damage suffered in recent storms. Hipper, however, argued strongly in favour of a raid on the Dogger Bank area and was strongly supported by Admiral von Eckermann, Chief of Staff to von Ingenohl. The latter had, however, been so influenced by the Kaiser's reluctance to risk his heavy ships that he declined to take the available battle squadrons out in support of Hipper's Scouting Groups. None the less on 23rd January he sent Hipper a cypher signal authorising him to proceed to sea that evening after dark, 'to reconnoitre the Dogger Bank and return to port on the following evening.' This message was picked up by the British interception stations and decyphered in the Admiralty's Room 40.

At 5.45 p.m. on 23rd Hipper accordingly sailed from the Jade estuary – completely unaware that, as his biographer has written, 'the plan was known to the enemy and that every movement and disposition was followed . . . as accurately as if the British themselves were directing them'.[9] An equally serious handicap was Hipper's decision to take with him the armoured cruiser *Blücher*, which was at least three knots slower than his other ships and far weaker in both offence and defence.* Her presence in fact flawed Hipper's plan to make a lightning raid followed by immediate withdrawal at high speed.

On 23rd January Fisher was suffering from a heavy cold which had confined him to his bed. Shortly before noon Admirals Wilson and Oliver marched into Churchill's room at the Admiralty and told him that 'those fellows are coming out again' and that there was just enough time 'to get Beatty there'.[10] Signals were at once sent to Tyrwhitt cancelling current operations and ordering him and Beatty to prepare all available ships for sea. The detailed orders which followed were in fact those already worked out on the chart which Wilson and Oliver had taken to Churchill. The intention was for Beatty and Tyrwhitt to join forces at daylight on 24th in position 55° 13' North 3° 12' East (about 30 miles north of the Dogger Bank and 180 miles west of Heligoland)†. Wilson and Oliver had calculated that this rendezvous would be about ten miles to the east of the position Hipper would by then have reached, so interposing Beatty's and Tyrwhitt's ships between him and his base. Admiral Bradford's Third Battle Squadron (*King Edward VII* pre-Dreadnoughts) and Admiral Pakenham's Third Cruiser Squadron (armoured cruisers) were ordered to a position some 20 miles further north to intercept Hipper if he should be headed off by Beatty and attempt escape in that direction, while Jellicoe's three Grand Fleet battle squadrons were to take up a covering position still further north to deal with the High Seas Fleet if it came out. The trap was well laid, but the successful springing of it depended on all movements taking place as planned or calculated in Whitehall; for the Admiralty had laid down the various rendezvous as well as

*On the *Blücher's* statistics see p 62
†See Map 1, pages 74–5

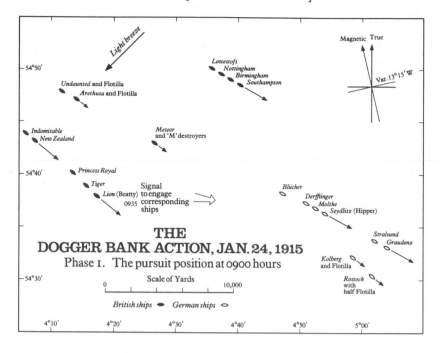

Light breeze

54°50′

Undaunted and Flotilla
Arethusa and Flotilla

Lowestoft
Nottingham
Birmingham
Southampton

Magnetic　True

Var. 13°15′ W

Indomitable
New Zealand

Meteor
and 'M' destroyers

54°40′　　*Princess Royal*

Tiger

Lion (Beatty)
0935

Signal
to engage
corresponding
ships

Blücher

Derfflinger
Moltke
Seydlitz (Hipper)

Stralsund
Graudenz

THE
DOGGER BANK ACTION, JAN. 24, 1915
Phase 1. The pursuit position at 0900 hours

Kolberg
and Flotilla

54°30′　　　　Scale of Yards

0　　　　　　　　　　10,000

Rostock
with
half Flotilla

British ships ● German ships ○

4°10′　　　4°20′　　　4°30′　　　4°40′　　　4°50′　　　5°00′

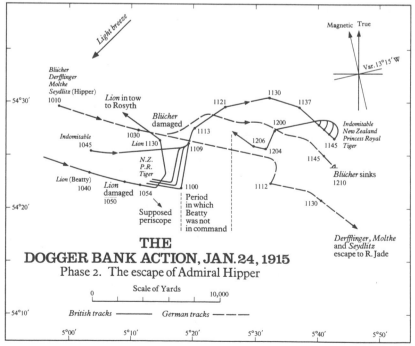

Light breeze

Magnetic　True

Var. 13°15′ W

Blücher
Derfflinger
Moltke
Seydlitz (Hipper)

54°30′　1010

Lion in tow
to Rosyth

1121

1130

1137

Blücher
damaged

1200

Indomitable
New Zealand
Princess Royal
Tiger

Indomitable
1045

1030
Lion 1130

1113

1109

1206

1204

1145

1145

N.Z.
P.R.
Tiger

Lion (Beatty)
1040

Lion
damaged　1054
1050

1100

1112

1130

Blücher sinks
1210

Supposed
periscope

Period
in which
Beatty
was not
in command

THE
DOGGER BANK ACTION, JAN. 24, 1915
Phase 2. The escape of Admiral Hipper

Derfflinger, Moltke
and *Seydlitz*
escape to R. Jade

Scale of Yards

0　　　　　　　　　　10,000

54°10′　　British tracks ———　German tracks — — —

5°00′　　　5°10′　　　5°20′　　　5°30′　　　5°40′　　　5°50′

telling the British admirals what enemy forces were likely to be encountered.

Beatty, with his flag in the *Lion* and accompanied by the *Tiger* and *Princess Royal* (1st Battle Cruiser Squadron)* and Moore in the *New Zealand* with the *Indomitable* (2nd Battle Cruiser Squadron) sailed from Rosyth on the afternoon of 23rd – almost simultaneously with Hipper sailing from the Jade with four light cruisers and 19 destroyers to scout for and screen his big ships. Goodenough's 1st Light Cruiser Squadron, its commander no doubt chastened by the experiences of the Scarborough raid, sailed with Beatty, while Tyrwhitt with three light cruisers and 35 destroyers from Harwich was to join the battle cruisers and place his ships under their commander at 7 a.m. on 24th. Jellicoe with the Grand Fleet sailed from Scapa at 9 p.m. on 23rd to cover the lighter forces. He later expressed the view that he should have been ordered to raise steam earlier if his presence was to be effective – which of course raised the whole question of Admiralty control of operations. As matters developed Jellicoe was 140 miles away when action was joined; and Churchill's defence of the Admiralty's action is unconvincing. [11]

Beatty and Goodenough reached the intercepting position on time by passing over reportedly mined waters, and contact was made punctually with Tyrwhitt's force just before dawn on 24th – which brought a calm and clear day. The conditions appeared perfect to spring the trap laid for Hipper, who was unsupported by the High Seas Fleet's battleships, when contact was made between the opposing light forces at 7.20 a.m.

Beatty at once steered for the sounds of firing on a south-easterly course and increased to full speed of about 27 knots – which resulted in the *New Zealand* and *Indomitable* dropping behind the other three ships. Gradually his three leading ships overhauled the *Blücher*, the rear ship of Hipper's force, which was totally outclassed by her adversaries. Soon after 9 o'clock the leading British ships opened fire on her at about 20,000 yards. The *New Zealand* did not come into action until 43 minutes later; while the *Indomitable* was handicapped not only by being much the slowest of Beatty's ships but by still having obsolete shells for her main armament (2 calibre

---

*The *Queen Mary* was in dock.

radius head instead of 4), which gave her much less range.*
She did not open fire until 113 minutes after the *Lion* and at a
range of 16,250 yards – also at the unfortunate *Blücher*.

The Germans opened fire about 15 minutes after Beatty but
were much hampered by smoke. The *Lion* and *Tiger* became
their principal targets. At 9.35 Beatty signalled 'Engage the
corresponding ships in the enemy's line', intending that each
of his ships should engage her opposite number – *Lion* against
Seydlitz, *Tiger* against *Moltke*, *Princess Royal* against *Derfflinger*
and *New Zealand* against *Blücher*. Unfortunately the *Tiger's*
Captain (H. B. Pelly), believing that the *Indomitable* was in
action with the *Blücher*, concluded that his ship and the *Lion*
were both intended to concentrate on the *Seydlitz*, Hipper's
flagship. This left the *Moltke* free to make undisturbed target
practice on the *Lion*; and she took very good advantage of her
opportunity. Moreover the *Tiger* confused her salvos with the
Lion's – so believing that she was hitting when her initial
salvos actually fell far beyond the *Seydlitz*.

The *Lion* soon began to suffer at the hands of the *Seydlitz*,
Moltke and *Derfflinger,* being hit by seventeen 11 or 12-inch
shells (mostly 11-inch) between 9.28 and 11.0 a.m. She was
put out of action at about 10.18 by two nearly simultaneous
11-inch shells from the *Seydlitz* followed by a 12-inch hit,
probably from the *Derfflinger*. The former put her starboard
engine out of action and the latter her port engine – so
bringing her to a stop. These heavy blows provided the only
occasion 'when the poor side armouring of British battleships
was unequivocally demonstrated in battle'.[12] At 10.47, while
the *Lion* was steadily dropping back, Beatty signalled 'Close
the enemy as rapidly as possible consistent with keeping all
guns bearing', and shortly afterwards ordered the *Indomitable*

---

*The calibre of a gun is its length in units of bore diameter. Thus a
15-inch 42 calibre gun is 15 × 42 = 630 inches or 52½ feet long. Calibre
Radius Head (CRH) is the radius of the pointed nose of a shell. Thus the
point of a 15-inch 4 CRH shell has a radius of 4 × 15 = 60 inches or 5 feet.
As a more sharply pointed shell encounters less air resistance than a blunt
one it will, given the same propellant charge, travel to a longer range. The
Indefatigable, New Zealand and *Australia* were armed with 12-inch 45 calibre
guns, as were the *Invincibles* – not with 12-inch 50 calibre guns as is often
stated. The difference in the range performance of the *New Zealand* and
Indomitable in the Dogger Bank action was solely due to the different CRH
of their shells. See N. J. M. Campbell, 'Persistent Errors in Descriptions of
Ships Armament', *Warship*, Vol. 1, No. 2 (Conway Maritime Press. 1978)
p.62.

to finish off the badly damaged *Blücher*. Then a further misfortune occurred. Beatty believed that the enemy ships were likely to strew the waters through which they passed with mines, and that he was being lured into a submarine trap (he claimed to have actually sighted one himself). He therefore ordered a 90 degree turn to port together. In fact the presumed threat was illusory; and the abrupt turn placed his ships astern of the enemy in their homeward rush. It has been argued that, even if the submarine threat had been real, Beatty should have turned towards and not away from the presumed danger; but a turn away in such circumstances was the manoeuvre accepted by both Jellicoe and him – as the Admiralty was well aware. Almost simultaneously with Beatty's turn to port Hipper ordered his 18 destroyers to relieve the pressure on the *Blücher* by launching a torpedo attack; but on seeing that Beatty's turn had placed the destroyers in an impossible position to attack, Hipper cancelled his order and left the *Blücher* to her fate. She fought to the end against overwhelming odds.

As the *Lion* dropped astern Beatty tried to make clear his intention that his three best ships (*Tiger, Princess Royal* and *New Zealand*) should press on against the fleeing Hipper, leaving the *Blücher* to be dealt with by the *Indomitable*. But his signal to 'Attack the rear of the enemy' made when the one for 'Course North-East' was still flying was certainly open to misunderstanding when they were hauled down (i.e. made executive) together; for the *Blücher* bore about north-east from the three ships now commanded by Moore.* Thus those powerful ships charged off to engage the one enemy which was obviously already doomed, leaving the other three to escape unmolested. Beatty's final signal to 'Keep nearer the enemy' was made at too great a distance to be read. At about 11.50 Beatty, reduced to something approaching despair by what had happened, called a destroyer alongside and endeavoured to catch up with his errant ships. But by the time he had hoisted his flag in the *Princess Royal* at 12.20 p.m. and ordered the pursuit to be resumed Hipper was 12 miles ahead and it was too late. Half an hour later Beatty accepted the inevitable and turned for home – sick at heart. As he wrote to his friend Roger Keyes a few days later 'The disappointment of that day is more than I can bear to think of. Everybody

---

*See Map 2, page 110

thinks it was a great success when in reality it was a terrible failure. I had made up my mind that we were going to get four, the lot, and four we ought to have got. There is no blinking it, we had them beat. Another half hour would have done it, when the old *Lion* was done. My feeling when "the merry hunt went heedless sweeping by" and then swept in the wrong direction was more than words could describe'.[13]

Obviously there were grounds for a thorough inquiry into this disappointing action, and Beatty's wrath was directed chiefly at Admiral Moore and Captain Pelly of the *Tiger*. Moore defended his action by writing that the signal to 'Attack the rear of enemy bearing N.E.' was 'apparently the *Blücher* (she bore approximately N.E. from *New Zealand* at the time)':[14] while Pelly argued that at the time the fire distribution signal was received (9.41 a.m.) he had reason to believe that all five British ships were engaged and that he was therefore correct in adopting the principle laid down in Fleet Orders by concentrating with the *Lion* on the leading enemy ship.[15] Neither excuse proved acceptable to Beatty.

As to Beatty's own actions the turn away from the supposed submarine provides the chief grounds for criticism. Plunkett, who was on the bridge of the *Lion* with Beatty, recorded that he ordered the turn to port without indicating that it was made in order to avoid a submarine, so giving the impression that he was breaking off the action and causing his astonished Staff Officer to voice a protest.[15a] In that case most of the blame must be placed on Beatty himself; but responsibility for the muddles which occurred over the interpretation of his signals must surely rest with his Flag Lieutenant. Beatty certainly held that view when, many years later, he discussed these events with Shane Leslie.[16]

Early in February Beatty wrote to Jellicoe that Churchill 'wanted to have the blood of somebody', and that he and Fisher had settled on Moore.[17] Many years later he told Arthur Pollen in confirmation of the above that he was 'quite sure that Fisher with his fiery nature was bitterly disappointed and wanted to hang, draw and quarter Moore for not going on and completing the destruction of the *Derfflinger* and *Seydlitz*'. He was sure that if there had been a disagreement between Churchill and Fisher after the battle it was not 'of a very serious nature'.[18] As to the conduct of Captain Pelly of the *Tiger* he told Jellicoe that he had 'done very well up to then', but he considered he 'did very badly in not carrying out the orders to "engage his opposite number",' and in 'running a muck [sic] after *Lion* fell out'. Though he disliked changes because they were 'upsetting and inclined to destroy confidence' he felt that Pelly as well as Moore should be relieved.[19]

The Germans also were dissatisfied with the result, and von Ingenohl was replaced by von Pohl, formerly Chief of the Naval Staff. But they gained one very great uncovenanted blessing from the action – namely that a 13.5-inch shell from the *Lion* caused severe cordite fires in the *Seydlitz* which spread to two adjacent turret ammunition handling rooms. Prompt flooding of the magazines saved the ship from blowing up, and action was taken to reduce such risks by limiting the number of cordite charges out of their magazine cases – though later experience (notably in the *Derfflinger* at Jutland) shows that this was not always observed. The crucial lesson that a flash or cordite fire in a gun turret must on no account penetrate to a magazine was not learnt by the Royal Navy until nearly 18 months later – and at great cost in ships and lives.

On the day after the battle Fisher sent Churchill a curiously worded and somewhat incoherent letter. 'We must not say [presumably in the Press release]', he wrote, 'that our wireless [signals] turned back the Germans – the fact is (though I had intended to bury the fact) and it is solely my fault we put the rendezvous for Beatty *in front* instead of *behind* the enemy, *but I beg you not to say a word on this to anyone* and least of all to [Admirals] Oliver and Wilson – as they came over to my room at about 2.30 p.m. [on 23rd] and I deferred to their joint certainty – I mention this as it may recoil upon us that ours was the initial error – though it may truly be said it avoided [enemy] minelaying and a massacre to turn them back but it would have been worth a massacre to have got between them and their home! . . .'[20] In retrospect the old admiral obviously thought that the rendezvous between Beatty and Tyrwhitt should have been further to the east, though the Harwich Force might have suffered more heavily had that been done.

Two days later Fisher wrote to Beatty in terms very similar to his own expressions of disappointment, though both of them were wrong to claim that the *Derfflinger* as well as the *Seydlitz* was 'very heavily on fire'. However, he corrected Beatty about the whereabouts of German submarines, assuring him that 'we know from themselves [i.e. through Room 40] exactly where they were – hours off [i.e. away from] you'; and that of course implied criticism of Beatty's 90 degree turn away at the critical moment described above.[21] On the last day of the month Fisher followed up that 'very hurried line' with a more considered opinion. 'Your conduct', he wrote, 'was glorious. "*Beatty beatus*",' he punned; while Moore 'ought to have gone on' and evidently had not got 'the slightest Nelsonic temperament in him. Any fool can obey orders'.[22] That was the final nail driven into the unfortunate Moore's coffin. In his next letter Fisher accepted Beatty's 'very high opinion' of Admiral Pakenham, the gallant and idiosyncratically attractive commander of the 3rd Cruiser Squadron, which formed part of the Rosyth-based forces, and who was to take command of the 2nd Battle Cruiser Squadron in the following March. Fisher also expressed his regret that Walter Cowan, Beatty's shipmate in the *Alexandra* and his comrade in the Nile expedition of the 1890s, had not been given the *Tiger*. The future of those two officers was plainly assured;[23] while Pelly, possibly thanks to Churchill's intervention, was not replaced in command of the *Tiger*. Churchill has recorded how, when he visited the *Lion* on 3rd February, he found all the senior officers united in their enthusiasm for Beatty's leadership, and how as he was about to leave the ship, the usually phlegmatic Pakenham caught him by the sleeve and said 'First Lord, I wish to speak to you in private'; and how he then said with 'intense conviction in his voice "Nelson has come again".'[24]

Here it will be appropriate to discuss the gunnery performance of the British ships on 24th January. Contrary to what was believed until recently the *Tiger*'s shooting was reasonably effective – with hits on the *Seydlitz* and *Derfflinger*;* while the *Lion* only scored four hits – one each on the *Blücher* and *Derfflinger* and two on the *Seydlitz* – one of which nearly caused her destruction. The table below gives what is believed to be a fair comparison between the British and German ships' shooting, and bearing in mind the smoke handicap from which the latter suffered, the 22 heavy shell hits they scored makes the British performance seem much inferior. Plainly

*On this issue N. J. M. Campbell emphatically corrects Professor Marder's statement that the *Tiger* 'did not register a single hit'. See *Warship Special No. I. Battle Cruisers*, p. 40 and Marder, *Dreadnought*, II, p. 170.

our rangetaking and fire control left a great deal to be desired; yet in the *post-mortem* neither was brought under serious scrutiny.

Despite the poor performance of Beatty's battle cruisers both in offence and in defence in the Dogger Bank action in Fisher's next letter to him he went into typically euphoric raptures about them, claiming that they would 'finish the job if only their gunnery is perfection'. He did not believe that Jellicoe's 'Battle Squadrons will be in this war'.[25] Unfortunately he never realised that their fire control systems and instruments were so defective in design and manufacture that the gunnery perfection he sought was virtually unattainable, that they were supplied with inefficient shell, and that their armour protection was far from adequate.[26]

After the wounded *Lion* had been safely towed to Rosyth by the *Indomitable* temporary repairs, using timber and 150 tons of concrete, were at once put in hand. The Admiralty was anxious that the extent of her damage should be kept secret, and therefore insisted that she should not be brought to one of the major dockyards in the south. Final repairs, which necessitated the removal of many armour plates, were therefore carried out between 9th February and 28th March on the Tyne behind cofferdams with the ship listed to starboard. Close inspection of the damage revealed all too clearly that her 5 and 6-inch armour was inadequate against 11-inch armour piercing shells, and in April Beatty drew the Admiralty's attention to this failure and asked what could be done about it.[27] The reply was not very helpful, telling him that the resistance of armour plate had been improved since the *Lion* was built and that 'the value of armour . . . rests largely on its capability to keep out large capacity shell of all calibres' rather than only armour piercing shell – a somewhat dubious claim.[28] However, action was taken to fit stronger supports behind the armour plates in the new *Renown* class battle cruisers, and various other minor changes were made to improve the standard of British ships' protection; but the *Lion* and her sisters remained seriously vulnerable.[29] We will return later to the complex subject of the thickness of the armour plating fitted in British ships, how it was tested and how it compared in efficiency with German armour; but it is my view that in discussing the causes of the loss of British ships in World War I too much weight has generally been given to

DOGGER BANK ACTION 24th JANUARY 1915

Position in Line	Rounds Fired
I BRITISH SHIPS	(Main Armaments only, APC, CP and HE)★
1. *Lion*	243 (13.5 inch/45 Cal)
2. *Tiger*	355 (13.5 inch/45 Cal)
3. *Princess Royal*	271 (13.5 inch/45 Cal)
4. *New Zealand*	147 (12 inch/45 Cal)
5. *Indomitable*	134 (12 inch/45 Cal)
II GERMAN SHIPS	
1. *Seydlitz*	390 (11 inch/50 Cal)
2. *Moltke*	276 (11 inch/50 Cal)
3. *Derfflinger*	310 (12 inch/50 Cal)
4. *Blücher*	n.k. (8.3 inch(45 Cal)

(Source N.J.M. Campbell, *Battle Cruisers. Warship Special* No.1 (Conway Maritime Press, 1978), and discussions with the author 1978)

★APC = Armour Piercing Capped, CP = Common Pointed, HE = High Explosive

COMPARATIVE PERFORMANCES

Targets and Hits Scored (in brackets)	Hits Received	Casualties
Blücher (1) – *Derfflinger* (1) *Seydlitz* (2)	16–11 or 12 inch 1–8.3 inch	1 killed 20 wounded
Blücher (?) – *Seydlitz* (1) *Derfflinger* (1)	6–11 or 12 inch 1–8.3 inch	10 killed 11 wounded
Blücher (?) – *Derfflinger* (1)	Nil	Nil
Blücher (?)	Nil	Nil
Blücher (?)	1–8.3 inch	Nil
Lion and *Tiger* (At least 8 together)	3 (1 *Tiger*, 2 *Lion*)	159 killed 33 wounded
Tiger–Lion–Tiger (At least 8 together)	Nil	Nil
Lion–Tiger–Princess Royal (5 or 6 together)	3 (1 each from *Lion*, *Tiger* and *Princess Royal*)	Nil
Lion (1)–*Tiger* (1) *Indomitable* (1)	About 70 and 7 torpedoes†	792 killed, 45 wounded and 189 unwounded prisoners

TOTALS OF HITS RECEIVED AND SCORED BY BRITISH
BATTLE CRUISERS
    Hits received – 22
    Hits scored (*omitting Blücher*) – 6 approx

†This figure is taken from the German Official History *Der Krieg in der Nordsee* but is probably much exaggerated.

cordite fires and magazine explosions and too little to inadequate armour protection. This imbalance probably owes a lot to Fisher's sustained readiness to sacrifice armour in favour of speed.

While his normal flagship was undergoing repairs Beatty hoisted his flag in the *Princess Royal* and was evidently well content with Brock's ship. Soon after the battle cruisers moved to Rosyth he rented from the Findlay family Aberdour House, a comfortable old-fashioned mansion overlooking the Firth of Forth about six miles from his base;* but he always slept on board if there was any likelihood of his presence being needed or if his ships were at short notice. Ethel seems to have been less than enthusiastic about his new home and her husband's proximity, since early in March he wrote that he was glad she was going to London and would himself visit the children – a responsibility which should surely have been hers.[30]

The events of 24th January 1915, coming so soon after the muddles which had occurred during the Scarborough raid operations inevitably raise the question whether the advantage of possessing excellent intelligence is best reaped by a centralised operational authority, such as the Admiralty adopted, or whether the intelligence should be given to the sea-going commanders (with its source concealed or disguised) and the ordering of movements and dispositions left in their hands. Though the arguments in favour of both systems are nicely balanced it seems to me that confusion and mistakes are less likely if the delegated system is followed – especially when a fleet has to operate in waters such as the North Sea and Arctic Ocean, where the vagaries of the weather are notorious

---

*The current owner of Aberdour House was Sir John Findlay (1866-1930), Lord Lieutenant of Banffshire and proprietor of the *Scotsman*. A curiosity of naval history is that his sister Dora married the future Admiral of the Fleet and First Sea Lord Sir Roger Backhouse. One wonders whether Beatty, while tenant of Aberdour, realised that an earlier house on the site was the scene of the despatch of the Knight Sir Patrick Spens to 'Noroway' to rescue or ransome the King's captive daughter, as described in the famous Scottish ballad. The loss of Spens in a storm on the way home after the conclusion of his unsuccessful mission is commemorated in the last stanza –

> 'Half owre, half owre to Aberdour
> 'Tis fifty fathoms deep,
> And there lies gude Sir Patrick Spens,
> Wi' the Scots lords at his feet.'

and the central authority cannot possibly be accurately informed regarding conditions hundreds of miles away. For example in the preliminary moves leading to the Dogger Bank action sudden fog delayed the sailing of some of the Harwich Force, and Beatty had to cut across reputedly mined waters in order to reach the rendezvous on time – the Admiralty having over-estimated his probable speed of advance.

At the end of February King George V paid his first visit to the ships based on the Firth of Forth, and from the long description which he wrote in his usually laconic diary he was evidently much impressed by all he saw. He first boarded the *Tiger*, where Beatty had assembled the battle cruiser captains to meet the Monarch, who was then shown the damage suffered in the Dogger Bank action. Then he boarded the *Australia* (Vice-Admiral Patey), *Hibernia* (Rear-Admiral Browning), *Antrim* (Rear-Admiral Pakenham), *Galatea* (Commodore Alexander-Sinclair) and *Southampton* (Commodore Goodenough). After lunching with all the Flag Officers and Commodores he visited Rosyth dockyard where extensions and docks were being constructed as fast as possible. He then viewed the anti-submarine defences from the Forth bridge, and took tea with Beatty on board the *Princess Royal*. 'On board each ship I visited', wrote the King, 'either the officers and men marched past me or I inspected [them] at Divisions . . . They are most efficient and all show the same splendid spirit and are dying to go for the enemy'. In the evening he returned to the royal train at Dalmeny and at once left for London after what must have been a long and tiring day, though excellently organised by Beatty who even managed to get the King onboard the *Sheelah* where he met Ethel and two junior officers who had been wounded on 24th January and were recuperating in her.[31]

Once the dust raised by the events of 24th January 1915 had subsided Beatty, with the help of Chatfield and Plunkett, set about revising and bringing up to date the 1913 and 1914 issues of his Battle Cruiser Orders in the light of recent experience. Under 'General Principles' he reiterated the need for cruiser captains to possess 'in marked degree initiative, resource, determination and fearlessness of responsibility'; and he emphasised that 'War is a perpetual conflict with the unexpected, so that it is impossible to prescribe beforehand for all the circumstances that may arise'. The contrast between the flexibility inherent in Beatty's system and the rigidity of Jellicoe's voluminous Grand Fleet Battle Orders, which sought to prescribe for every possible eventuality, is striking. As regards enemy reporting Beatty doubtless had Goodenough's failure in the Scarborough raid operations in mind when he wrote that 'Signals *must* be brief [and he might have added 'absolutely clear'] . . . and cruisers in sight of the enemy must continue sending off information even though [wireless] interference may prevent them hearing any replies to their signals'. On strategical and tactical issues it is impossible to fault these revised orders, but under 'Training' his 'principal requirement' . . . 'that guns shall be able to shoot effectively when ships are steaming at full speed and perhaps making frequent alterations of course' was to ask the impossible while a 'helm free' fire control system, such as the Admiralty had rejected before the war was lacking.[32]

One deficiency exposed by the Dogger Bank action, namely the lack of signals such as the historic one to 'Engage the enemy more closely', or to indicate that the Admiral had transferred his flag to another ship, was promptly rectified by additions to the signal book.[33] Another lesson which Beatty had evidently taken to heart concerned the advantage of engaging from leeward in order to avoid smoke interference. A month after the battle he wrote to Jellicoe discussing the action to be taken if our fleet was to windward or leeward of the enemy and, thirdly, if the wind was roughly at right angles to his bearing. In those days when most ships were still coal burning and poured forth dense volumes of black smoke from their funnels at high speed this was a highly important consideration. In the same letter Beatty considered the tactical employment of the three squadrons which his force would soon comprise. He assumed that the C-in-C 'would like the Enemy Battle Cruisers to be the objective of 2 Squadrons and the 3rd could perform the duty of a Fast Division on the opposite flank, where they ought to be of the utmost value. . . .' which was an interesting up-to-date version of Nelson's tactics at The Nile and Trafalgar. When Beatty sent Jellicoe his revised order he remarked that 'I have confined myself to principles!!' and modestly added. 'If you think I have said too much or too little I hope you will instruct me';[34] but the C-in-C had no serious criticisms to offer, though he did say he was revising his Cruiser Addendum (to the

GFBOs), and that his primary object would be to gain 'advantage of position before that of getting between the Germans and their base'.[35] He considered it fortunate that what he called his subordinate's recent 'victory' had 'assured a quiet spell', and so enabled him to undergo the operation for piles already mentioned.[36] On 25th February he wrote to congratulate Beatty on his promotion 'to a Vice-Admiral proper'; but the complications produced by Patey being senior to Beatty resulted in the Admiralty not confirming him in his new rank until 9th August.[37]

The interchange between the two admirals about Beatty's revised Battle Cruiser Orders and Jellicoe's Addenda to the GFBOs continued in March, and it is interesting to find the former telling the C-in-C that 'it is very difficult to provide for all cases and therefore necessary to have broad principles to work on'; which explained, he wrote, why he had only 'dealt very roughly' with certain cases of encounter with the enemy.[38] It is a fact that while Jellicoe always tended to produce orders covering every possible contingency Beatty tried to maintain flexibility and to encourage initiative. Another interesting point which emerges from their exchange of views concerns the use of the 'Blue Pendant' to order a squadron to turn so many degrees *together* to port or starboard rather than use the 'White Pendant' ordering a turn *in succession,* which took longer to take effect and could provide an excellent aiming point for the enemy. Beatty evidently favoured the turn together; but he told Jellicoe that it was 'only intended to be used with a Squadron, and not when all squadrons were together which as you say would not be desirable. But with 4 or 5 ships we have found it work very well.'*[39] It will be told later how this matter came up in the battle of Jutland.

Though Jellicoe was to be proved right in his anticipation of a 'quiet spell' from the German surface fleet the months following on the Dogger Bank action were anything but quiet in the field of underwater warfare, and indeed marked the

---

*Vice-Admiral J. W. Carrington, who was Navigating Officer of the *King George V* in 1916, confirms that both Jellicoe and his Master of the Fleet Commander Oliver Leggett were strongly opposed to the use of the 'Turn Together' (Blue Pendant) signal because of the risk it produced of collisions. According to Carrington it was never tried, let alone used, in Grand Fleet exercises and manoeuvres.

beginning of a totally new phase in the war at sea. Up to the beginning of 1915 the Germans had on the whole avoided unrestricted attacks on merchant ships such as plainly contravened the Hague Conventions; but on 1st February the Chancellor, Bethmann Hollweg, yielded to the pressure of the naval staff and Germany proclaimed a 'war zone' around the British Isles within which all merchant ships would be sunk without warning as from 18th. From that date until the end of April U-boats sank 39 merchant ships of 105,000 tons. Then on 7th May the world was deeply shocked by U.20 sinking the great Cunard liner *Lusitania* with the loss of 1,198 lives, including 128 Americans. Though we are not here directly concerned with the ebb and flow of the U-boat campaign against merchant shipping, the under-water threat to our command of the North Sea in general, and to Beatty's operations in particular, come very much within the field of this study.

It must have been at this time that Plunkett, Beatty's Flag Commander (in modern terms Staff Officer Plans would describe his functions better), wrote in his own hand – presumably for his admiral's benefit – a survey of current problems and the future outlook. As regards the latter he prophesied that 'great changes are impending'. 'Our battle squadrons', he continued, 'normally competent (as in the past) to hold any area against all comers, are actually afraid to venture into the waters they wish to command'. The only counter he could propose was to make the North Sea equally perilous to the Germans 'with torpedo craft and submarines, particularly the latter'. With regard to the operations of our heavy ships, and in particular the battle cruisers, he posited that 'the essential need is command of the Air', and foretold that in future reconnaissance work would be chiefly done by aircraft. These thoughts undoubtedly stemmed from the frequent and unhindered flights over the North Sea made by the German Zeppelin rigid airships, which caused great concern at the time though we now know that their navigation was so inaccurate that their reports were far less valuable than we believed. Failing the adoption of such measures as he outlined Plunkett expected 'the North Sea to become untenable' by us. Though there was a certain amount of exaggeration in this pessimistic forecast it did contain the unpalatable truth which had gradually become apparent during the preceding months – namely that the submarine and mine would affect all strategy and tactics, and were capable of inflicting very serious losses unless a counter to them could be quickly produced.[40]

In May Beatty appointed a small committee under Admiral Pakenham to make recommendations on 'Counter Attack against Enemy Submarines', a matter which he said 'deserves the most anxious study'. Officers were invited to forward suggestions and ideas, and three small money prizes (presumably put up by Beatty) were offered for the best of them.[41] Later in the month he expressed his anxiety about 'the attitude of the Admiralty' on this matter in a long letter to Jellicoe, protesting that one enemy submarine was known to have been sitting for a fortnight in a position only some 50 miles outside his anchorage. But in the same letter he claimed that a heartening success had been achieved by a trawler working with a submarine in tow. In fact this attack, which Beatty described as 'a thrilling story and tiger shooting as a sport is not in it', must have been a failure, as we now know that no U-boat was destroyed by such means until the following month.[42] Beatty gave Frank Spickernell, his secretary, all the credit for this idea, and after the first confirmed success had been obtained he tried to get him at least an expression of the Admiralty's appreciation, since the officers who actually sank U.40 on 18th June were all decorated. Though Beatty was no doubt correct in saying that Spickernell had worked the scheme out 'to the smallest detail' it was thanks to the cordial co-operation of Keyes and the submarine service that it was brought to fruition so quickly. This innovation and the introduction of decoy (or Q) ships at about the same time do, however, show that Beatty's frequent strictures about the Admiralty's alleged idleness over countering the submarine menace were, at the very least, exaggerated.

It will be appropriate to mention here that an anti-submarine research establishment was set up a little later at Hawkcraig on the Firth of Forth, with the special object of developing hydrophones for detection purposes. Commander C. P. Ryan was in charge of the naval side, and co-operated closely with Beatty's staff; but relations between him and the scientists recruited by the Board of Inventions and Research were evidently uneasy. Dr. A. B. Wood, a member of Professor (late Lord) Rutherford's brilliant team at Manchester

University, was among the scientists who came to Hawkcraig, and Rutherford himself visited the station several times. In May 1916 W. H. (later Sir William) Bragg, who had recently been awarded the Nobel Prize for Physics jointly with his son W. L. Bragg for their work on crystalline structure, became Resident Director and brought more scientific staff with him; but the truth was that collaboration between naval men and scientists, which was to reach a peak of effort and accomplishment in World War II, was then in its infancy. [43]

In April Beatty learnt from Ethel that his friend and successor as Naval Secretary to the First Lord, Horace Hood, was to give up command of the Dover Patrol and take over a cruiser force working out of Queenstown. He could no more understand the reason for moving Hood than he could the replacement of him by Reginald Bacon, a protégé of Fisher's who had left the navy to join the Coventry Ordnance Works as Managing Director in 1909 and whom Beatty contemptuously referred to as 'the Colonel'. [44] Actually Bacon was an able man, though not an easy one to work with; and it was during his time as Director of Naval Ordnance that unfortunate decisions regarding the fire control equipment of the navy were taken. On receiving Hood's confirmation of what he had learnt from his wife Beatty wrote that he considered he had been 'treated abominably' – which certainly was not an over-statement. However, as he was entitled to another Rear-Admiral when the 3rd Battle Cruiser Squadron, already mentioned, was formed he asked Hood to telegraph if he would like to have the job. [45] The offer was immediately accepted, and Hood moved his family to North Queensferry House on the Firth of Forth, only a few miles from the Beattys' home at Aberdour. Both families had two boys, who now grew up in each other's company. The intimate friendship between their fathers also flourished; but Ethel Beatty appears never to have joined in that family circle. [46]

In the early summer of 1915 the question of shifting the bases of both the Grand Fleet and Battle Cruiser Fleet further south, in order to improve the chances of intercepting the Germans if they made another foray, was resurrected. Churchill and Fisher wanted Jellicoe's battle squadrons to be moved to Rosyth and Beatty's battle cruisers to the Humber. A lengthy interchange on the subject took place, and Beatty told Jellicoe that 'If the BCF were at the Humber then the whole of the rest of the Grand Fleet could be based here [i.e. Rosyth] that would be worth a great deal.' But he was doubtful whether the Humber could accommodate all his own force, and considerable dredging would be necessary if his ships were to be capable of getting in or out at any state of the tide.[47] Jellicoe disliked Rosyth for the same reasons that Beatty had originally disliked it – namely the prevalence of fog and the vulnerability of the long approach to mines and submarines. His preference was for the Battle Cruiser Fleet to return to Cromarty, while his own battle squadrons remained at Scapa, so facilitating gunnery training and, in all probability, improving the chances of co-ordination of movements and concentration of force during a sortie. In the end no major changes were made at this time.

It was in the month of May 1915 that the tension between Fisher and Churchill came to a climax over the despatch of more naval reinforcements to the Dardanelles, resulting in the departure of both of them from the Admiralty. Beatty wrote to his wife that he had 'warned Winston a long time back that if Fisher went to the Admiralty . . . one of them would have to leave'; but he was wrong in believing Fisher would stay on. 'The Navy', he wrote with unjustified acerbity, 'breathes freer now it is rid of the succubus Winston'. He hoped that his successor would be Balfour, who in fact took over as First Lord on 27th May. In the same letter Beatty described his recent visit to Jellicoe at Scapa. He found the C-in-C 'the most cheerful man there', but wished 'he were not *so simple* and charitable' – presumably towards the officers under his command and to the Admiralty.[48] On 19th May he learnt of Fisher's resignation from Jellicoe and at once wrote to the former in almost hysterical language, saying that he could not believe the Government would accept his departure, that it 'would be a worse calamity than a defeat at sea', and that 'Please God it is *not* possible'.[49] What Beatty did not know was that Fisher's manner of resigning, and above all his outrageous letter of 19th May to Asquith setting out the terms on which he was prepared to return to office, had made it out of the question that he should ever do so.[50]

While the new Board of Admiralty under Arthur Balfour and Admiral Sir Henry Jackson was settling down to its task Beatty's chief concern was still with the mine and submarine threat. On the last day of May he wrote in very serious vein

about it to Jellicoe, telling him that he 'hailed with delight' the
idea that the fleet should 'visit or sweep the North Sea or
portions of it . . . more frequently than we have hitherto',
because it would 'meet the Mining Menace in the most
efficacious manner possible'. On the other hand, he continued,
'It is borne in on me that we have not yet found the only way
to meet this very serious offensive' – i.e. from enemy
submarines. He considered that 'Passive Defence will never
succeed', and (in a somewhat mixed metaphor) he did not
think the Admiralty 'have gripped the oldest truism of War
that the only Defence is a vigorous counter offensive'. As
regards his own force's peril submarines had, he declared,
been sighted frequently inside the Firth of Forth; and although
they had so far accomplished nothing (chiefly because their
alleged presence was illusory) he was very anxious that
they would lie in wait outside the boom defences just when
the gates were opened for his ships to enter or leave. In that
connection he believed the Germans must become aware that
our fleet often sailed when some movement by the High Seas
Fleet was in train – in other words they must discover that
their naval cypher was compromised. In fact we now know
that this was not so, and that the Germans attributed our
foreknowledge of their movements chiefly to North Sea
fishing vessels acting as reporting ships – an idea which had
also troubled Beatty about his own movements but which
actually lacked substance in either case. His proposals were,
firstly, 'to elaborate more carefully our system of hunting him
[i.e. a submarine] whenever he is sighted'; and, secondly, that
we should mine the waters leading to the German naval bases
intensively. He realised that large numbers of mines would be
needed for such a purpose, but he could not believe that
provision of them was 'beyond the resources of our great
country'. What neither Beatty nor the Admiralty yet knew
was that our contact mines were grossly inefficient – a state of
affairs which was not remedied until we had copied the
German mine and produced it in quantity some two years
later. In passing Beatty's emphasis on 'hunting' for submarines
and his failure to mention 'convoy' as the decisive strategy
should be noted.[51]

In June Beatty wrote at length and in strong terms to the
Admiralty about the underwater threat, enclosing a chart
showing all submarine reports received within 160 miles of his

base during a recent week; and he remarked that within 40 to 60 miles of May Island at the entrance to the Firth of Forth submarines had been reported almost daily for at least the previous fortnight. Moreover six of his cruisers had been 'vigorously attacked' in that area – though without success. Although many of the reports received were false alarms there were good grounds for his view that 'the situation is deplorable'. Turning to counter-measures he proposed that 'all the forces for hunting submarines' should be placed under the direction of one man, and suggested that Admiral Sir Lewis Bayly should be given the job. As he had been C-in-C Channel Fleet, when the pre-Dreadnought battleship *Formidable* was sunk with heavy loss of life by a U-boat in the early hours of 1st January off Start Point and had 'lost Their Lordships' confidence' because he had failed to provide her with an escort Beatty's choice seems a little odd;[52] but Bayly was to do very well later in the war when he was placed in command of the anti-submarine forces working out of Queenstown. Secondly Beatty proposed that local defence forces should be reduced by 10 to 20 per cent, and the ships so released formed into a 'striking force' which would operate against the U-boats, chiefly at night. Again his emphasis on 'hunting', 'striking' and other allegedly 'offensive' measures and his neglect of 'convoy' is to be remarked.

In Beatty's eyes the improvement of the shooting of his battle cruisers stood second only to the need to counter the submarine threat. He stressed to all his Captains the importance of achieving a high rate of fire from their main armaments, and declared that they should be capable of firing three rounds a minute. Probably his views were influenced by the knowledge that in the Dogger Bank action the Germans were alleged – though on no very firm evidence – to have fired faster than our ships. In truth two rounds per gun per minute was the most that could be expected from heavy gun turrets. Nowhere did Beatty mention the need for improved fire control – though he must have known about Arthur Pollen's inventions since some of his ships were fitted with his gyro-stabilised rangefinders and the *Queen Mary* had the early model (Mark IV) Argo Clock.*[53] Furthermore Beatty's

---

*In 1910 the Admiralty bought 45 Argo gyro mountings for rangefinding and target bearing indication from Pollen. By 1914 six ships had been fitted with the Mark IV Argo clock; but the gyro-controlled Mark V clock, which was an automatic analog computer producing constantly up-to-date range and deflection was never adopted, or even tried, by the Royal Navy.

emphasis on speeding up the rate of fire may well have contributed to the adoption of the highly dangerous habit of stacking cordite charges outside the magazines at the bottom of the main ammunition hoists – which was probably a contributory cause to our ships blowing up at Jutland.

Beatty kept up the pressure about anti-submarine measures in August, and in one of his many letters on the subject he proposed the use of towed Kite Balloons for spotting such enemies. This was far-sighted of him, and in the end aircraft of various types did play a big part in the defeat of the U-boats – though they did so by working with the convoy escorts rather than by the sort of 'hunting' operations on which Beatty was so keen. He also foresaw a great future for the 'hydrophone Detector' which was being developed at Hawk-craig;[54] but in truth that invention was handicapped by inadequate directional sensitivity, and we had to await the Asdic invention of 1917 before such an accomplishment became possible. Balfour told Beatty in reply to his many suggestions that he could not 'doubt that your diagnosis of the situation is absolutely sound', and foresaw a great future for what he called the Magnetophone but which he evidently did not understand.[55]

With regard to Q-ships (or decoy ships) Beatty's experience was not a success – because the vessels provided (one a collier – the other a sailing schooner) were unsuitable; but in the Western Approaches several successes were obtained in 1915. One of them – the sinking of U.27 by the *Baralong* on 19th August off the Scilly Islands – had unfortunate repercussions, since the pursuit and killing by the Q-ship's crew of the survivors from the U-boat who had struggled on board an adjacent steamer were witnessed by Americans who were present in her. Though the Admiralty imposed a strict censorship the *Baralong*'s actions were given publicity in USA, and her captain (Godfrey Herbert) would certainly have been tried as a 'war criminal' had the Germans won the war.[56] Perhaps it was fortunate for the British that another U-boat sank the big liner *Arabic* on 14th August, with the loss of 44 lives, several of which were Americans, as it diverted attention from the *Baralong* incident.

On 8th August Beatty's apprehensions about enemy minelaying in the entrance to British bases were reinforced by a German armed auxiliary the *Meteor*, disguised as a merchant ship, laying a large minefield in the entrance to the Moray Firth. Though she scuttled herself next day when intercepted by British cruisers, and her mines were left in place to strengthen the defences of the harbour, only side channels being swept round them for use by our own ships, the possibility that the battle cruisers might be 'mined into' the Firth of Forth was plainly real.

Fortunately in course of the summer two developments were introduced which greatly lessened the mine danger – namely the Paravane invented by Lieutenant Dennistoun Burney, which ships could tow from their bows to cut the mooring wires by which mines were anchored, and the sweeping device known as the 'A Sweep' which was towed through a mined area to cut the wires and so enabled mines to be sunk or detonated by gun or rifle fire. As the war progressed all major warships and many merchant ships were fitted with Paravanes; while the A Sweep enabled channels to be rapidly cleared through dangerous waters and the safe channels marked with buoys.

By the autumn of 1915 Beatty was still far from satisfied with the gunnery efficiency of his ships – despite practices being carried out at speeds which had been regarded as ridiculous two years earlier.[57] In November he wrote despairingly to Jellicoe about the 'terrible disappointment' he felt over the results achieved by the *Lion* and *Tiger*. Evidently his flagship's control officer had made a hash of things, while the *Tiger*'s rangetaking had again proved bad. On the other hand the *Princess Royal* and *Queen Mary* were, he wrote, 'always good'; while the *Australia* and *New Zealand* were 'distinctly good and improving', the *Inflexible* was 'good always' and the *Invincible* 'sometimes'. As to the *Indomitable* he expected an improvement when her Captain (F. W. Kennedy) was promoted and a successor appointed. However, the principle on which he worked was 'to leave the R.As [Rear-Admirals] to run their own squadrons', and he had found that it 'works well'. He wrote in very warm terms of Admirals Hood, Brock and Pakenham, assured Jellicoe that he had 'a very good lot of Lieutenants', and that he benefited much from Chatfield's gunnery expertise. He was sure that if only he could get to sea once a fortnight for practices the deficiencies would be put right; and he told the C-in-C that he did not 'think you will be let down by the B.Cs when the day comes'.[58] From Jellicoe's next account of the practices carried out by his battleships off the Orkneys it certainly seems clear that their results were far better than those of the battle cruisers; but even in the Grand Fleet disconcerting errors in rangetaking (e.g. the *Benbow* opened fire at 16,000 yards when the true range was 20,000) could vitiate the results seriously. On the other hand he told Beatty that the *Iron Duke* had scored 10–12 hits at 7,500 yards, and that her Director Layer fired nine times in two minutes.[59]

At about the time Beatty was struggling to improve the gunnery of his ships the *Lion* had to go into dock and he turned over to the *Queen Mary*, taking Spickernell and Seymour with him. This meant that the *Lion*'s crew could all be given five days' leave, and he told Ethel that they were 'bubbling over with the joy of it'. Even Chatfield, he wrote, 'was smiling', and his officers and men would 'come back like giants refreshed'. As to his own needs, Ethel was still in London and had evidently been unwell; but Beatty saw a good deal of the boys at Aberdour House (one letter tells of his taking Peter out beagling), and he found it quite impossible to get to London because of the pressure of work to which he was subjected.[60]

A personal problem that troubled him at this time was that the *Sheelah* had cost £400 a month since she was converted to a hospital ship, and the Beattys could no longer afford to carry the whole of the expense. He asked Admiral Sir Frederick Hamilton, the 2nd Sea Lord, if the Admiralty would take her over; but that idea understandably held no appeal for Their Lordships. Beatty therefore suggested that she should be placed at 48 hours instead of immediate notice, and kept fully fuelled and equipped so that she could be made ready quickly if a need arose.[61] The Admiralty, however, refused to countenance Beatty's plan to reduce the drain on his (or rather Ethel's) resources, so in January 1916 he told Hamilton that he was putting into immediate effect his proposal to keep the yacht at longer notice. The officers attached to her 'as shown in the Navy List' were to remain but were to be at the more extended notice; while Sir Alfred Fripp and D. A. (later Sir Douglas) Shields, the two distinguished 'Consulting Surgeons' who had volunteered their services were, wrote Beatty, 'delighted to figure as such'.

Though the year ended without any opportunity for Beatty to demonstrate that the errors revealed in the Dogger Bank action had been rectified there is no doubt that his fleet was in very good heart – even if its gunnery efficiency still left a good deal to be desired. But the most pregnant development of the year had been the dominance of the mine and the submarine, and the fact that no real strategic, tactical or technical antidote to the latter had yet been developed or was even in prospect. Since the beginning of the war the U–boats had sunk the three *Cressy* class armoured cruisers (22nd September 1914), the light cruiser *Hawke* (15th October 1914), the seaplane carrier *Hermes* (31st October 1914) and the pre-Dreadnought *Formidable* (1st January 1915), while a number of other ships had narrow escapes. Mines had sunk the light cruiser *Amphion* (6th August 1914), the Dreadnought battleship *Audacious* (27th October 1914), the pre-Dreadnoughts *Ocean* and *Irresistible* (18th March 1915 off the Dardanelles) and seriously damaged the battle cruiser *Inflexible* on the same day. In addition a large number of smaller warships and auxiliaries had fallen victims to mines; and other more serious losses were to be suffered from the same cause in the following year.* Though the sinkings of major warships did not amount to much in relation to the total strength of the navy, the omnipresent threat was a source of constant and justified anxiety. The most far-reaching influence of the development of underwater weapons lay in their effect on the strategy and tactics of naval warfare – especially in the North Sea. No operation by the surface ships, whether it led to contact with the enemy or not, was uninfluenced by their presence or possible presence; and Fisher's forthright statement of 1904 that 'It's astounding to me, *perfectly astounding*, how the very best amongst us absolutely fail to realize the vast impending revolution in naval warfare and naval strategy that the submarine will accomplish!' was proved extraordinarily accurate ten years later.[62]

As to the defence of Britain's world-wide trade, and the interruption of the enemy's by means of blockade Beatty's interests were more with the latter than the former, and he often protested to Jellicoe and the Admiralty about the transport of contraband destined for Germany in the neutral merchant ships which he encountered every time he went to

*In 1916 the most important losses to mines were the pre-Dreadnought *King Edward VII* (off the Orkneys on 6th Jan.), the elderly battleship *Russell* (off Malta on 27th April) and the cruiser *Hampshire* with Lord Kitchener on board on his way to Russia (off the Orkneys on 5th June).

sea. However, as the defence of shipping was to loom ever larger in the problems which faced the Admiralty and the sea-going commanders it may be useful to review here the situation as it developed during the first 17 months of the war. During the first five months (August to December 1914) 64 British merchant ships totalling 241,201 tons were sunk or captured – the majority of them by the warship raiders which then operated all over the oceans.[63] But the Falkland Islands battle of 8th December 1914 virtually brought that phase to an end, and although disguised merchant raiders re-appeared later their depredations never came near to those inflicted by mines and submarines. During the whole of 1915 British losses were 278 ships totalling 855,721 tons, and it was the under-water weapons which inflicted the great majority of them. Sinkings rose from 11 ships (32,054 tons) in January to 49 (148,464 tons) in August, and although they fell to an average of 23 ships (74,337 tons) during the last 3 months of the year the significance of the threat was not lost on Beatty. His apprehensions would have been magnified had he known that some of his claims to have sunk U-boats were false, that in fact only five had been destroyed in 1914 and 19 in 1915, and that accidents had been one of the greatest causes of those losses.*[64] Moreover as the Germans completed 52 new U-boats in 1915 their capacity to inflict damage on Britain's vital seaborne trade was much greater at the end of the year than it had been at the beginning.

Though Beatty continued to hope and to long for decisive action with the German surface fleet he was never under any illusion regarding the influence of the submarine and mine – not only on his strategy and tactics but on the war as a whole. If 1915 brought him grave anxiety on that score it did see the fruition of much of his desire to bring together in the Battle Cruiser Fleet a 'Band of Brothers' on the Nelson model. With Brock in command of the 1st Battle Cruiser Squadron, Pakenham of the 2nd and Hood of the 3rd he had three men whose character and courage was very much to his liking. As

---

*In 1914 two U-boats were probably sunk by mines, two by ramming and one by unknown cause. In 1915 four were lost through accidents, two were probably sunk by our mines, two by ramming, three by decoy ships and one by trawler-submarine decoy; one fell to a destroyer's explosive sweep, two to our submarines' torpedoes, two to gunfire and the cause of two losses remains unknown.

to the cruisers and light cruisers in his command he had Commodore E. S. (later Admiral Sir Edwyn) Alexander-Sinclair in command of the 1st LCS and Commodore (later Admiral Sir William) Goodenough in command of the 2nd; while Rear-Admiral Sir Robert Arbuthnot, an officer of ardent fighting spirit, had taken over the 1st Cruiser Squadron consisting of four *Defence* class armoured cruisers. With Rudolf Bentinck as his Chief of Staff and Chatfield as Flag Captain his own flagship was in excellent hands. All he needed was the chance to show the mettle of the men he had picked, the quality of their crews, the soundness of their training – and of course the efficiency of the material placed in their hands.

CHAPTER SEVEN

Stalemate,
January–May 1916

We saw earlier how Beatty was by no means wholly satisfied with the gunnery performance of his flagship the *Lion* at the end of 1915; yet at the beginning of the following year he protested strongly to Captain (later Admiral The Hon. Sir Hubert) Brand, then serving as Naval Assistant to the 2nd Sea Lord, who was responsible for all matters concerning personnel, about the Admiralty not having promoted Gerald Longhurst, the ship's gunnery officer, to Commander's rank. Beatty argued that he had been twice in action (obviously in the Heligoland Bight and Dogger Bank battles), had acted as his gunnery adviser ever since the BCF had been formed, and had been recommended 'in the strongest possible language' three times. His conclusion was that the Admiralty was averse 'to promoting officers for actual war service', and was still clinging to peacetime practices such as giving priority to officers serving in appointments like the Royal Yachts.[1] This letter is of interest both because it provides evidence of Beatty's strong sense of loyalty towards his officers, even if he sometimes carried it to excess – notably in the case of Ralph Seymour his Flag Lieutenant – and because it shows that, despite his association with Royalty and the aristocracy, he considered any sign of influence from such quarters irrelevant, if not actually harmful, in time of war.

At the beginning of 1916 Beatty's superstitions were evidently revived, since he wrote to the well-known 'palmist' Edyth Du Bois whom he had consulted before the war, and she replied ecstatically that she had 'long decided to psychologize' a letter in his hand. She wrote to him that she felt that 'more, *much more* must happen before I see the *real fulfilment* of all I foresaw at our first meeting'; and told him that after the Heligoland Bight battle Ethel had written to ask her 'how many times you would be in action'. She had replied 'three times', and described how she saw 'a huge hole in a ship –

water pouring into it' – as indeed had happened in the *Lion* at Dogger Bank. She also told Beatty how she had 'always seen you . . . outside a large town with many white buildings and a curious domed roof to one [which might be taken for the Capitol in Washington] and the great success of your life there'. In general she was confident that success lay ahead for her client, and her 'psychology of the letter' he had written her would soon follow.[2] Though her visions were couched in such general terms that some measure of success could always be claimed for them Beatty and Ethel never lost confidence in people like her and the Mrs. Robinson mentioned earlier; and it is a curious coincidence that later in her life Eugénie Godfrey-Faussett should have become sufficiently a spiritualist to seek contact with Beatty after his death. Perhaps therefore such necromancy had an attraction to the wealthy upper class, to whom orthodox religion held no appeal – even though they conformed to the outward forms of Christianity.

Later in January 1916 Beatty met Jellicoe again – the first time in five months, which says little for the co-operation established between them. They undoubtedly discussed 'Jacky' Fisher's discontent with his work on the Board of Inventions and Research, which he had described contemptuously as 'a chemist's shop in Cockspur Street' (where its offices were situated);[3] but they evidently reviewed a great deal more than the BIR, since Fisher was at that time acting, in Professor Marder's words, as 'a gadfly',[4] writing innumerable letters to his political, naval and journalist friends, and attacking the Admiralty on every conceivable count but particularly about the inferiority of the British fleet's strength in battle cruisers – which was of course a matter which concerned Beatty very intimately. All these complaints Fisher poured out in a stream of letters to Jellicoe, who of course was bound to pass the gist of them, if not the actual letters, on to Beatty.[5] The outcome was that early in February Beatty wrote direct to Asquith (with a copy to Jellicoe), saying that he had found the C-in-C 'perturbed and despondent about the delays in New Construction' – especially of destroyers, light cruisers and battle cruisers. But he much exaggerated the German position regarding the latter class, stating that, as well as the *Derfflinger* and *Lützow*, the *Hindenburg* had joined the High Seas Fleet*;

*Jellicoe wrote that the *Hindenburg* would have 15-inch guns, which was incorrect. Like the *Derfflinger* class her armament was of 12-inch calibre. She did not actually complete until 1917.

and he expected two more 15-inch gun ships to be added 'this year, and possibly at an early date'. Actually they were never completed. Against such formidable augmentation of the enemy's strength we had, so he argued, only completed one battle cruiser, the *Tiger*, since the beginning of the war; while the *Renown* and *Repulse* (six 15-inch guns, laid down in January 1915) were 'becoming delayed indefinitely' owing chiefly to shortage of labour. He stressed that although by the end of the year he would have ten ships, as against eight Germans, the three *Invincibles* were of negligible value because of their slow speed and relatively light armament, while the three *Australias* were little better. Allowing for leave and refits he arrived at the pessimistic conclusion that he might be left with only three ships with 13.5-inch guns; and he still had no destroyers which 'could keep pace with the Battle Cruisers in a sea way'. The views he was representing were, he assured the Prime Minister, 'most certainly those of the Commander-in-Chief', and were supported by 'all Sea Officers'. This dangerous situation could, he wrote, only be rectified if 'immediate action is taken to prevent delays in construction'. This was a highly alarmist letter, and placing it alongside those which the irrepressible Fisher was writing to all and sundry with the object of getting himself recalled to office it is reasonable to detect his hand behind its composition.[6]

While this heart searching was going on in the British high command the Germans were showing signs of adopting a more aggressive strategy. On 24th January Admiral Reinhard Scheer took over command of the High Sea Fleet from von Pohl, who was a dying man, and in the following month the Kaiser gave him a freer hand than he had allowed his predecessor. Scheer at once showed his vigour and determination by making a destroyer sweep east of the Dogger Bank. Though the Grand Fleet and Harwich Force at once put to sea they were too late to catch the striking force, which actually only sank a British sloop engaged on minesweeping.

Towards the end of February Beatty 'respectfully suggested' to Jellicoe that the powerful 5th Battle Squadron composed of the new *Queen Elizabeth* class ships, should be based on Rosyth in substitution for the much weaker and slower 3rd Battle Squadron (*King Edward* class) in order to rectify the possible inferiority in which he might find himself. Jellicoe's reply was a good deal less than enthusiastic. He considered

Beatty over-estimated the *Queen Elizabeths'* speed, which was not much more than 23½ knots; and that would in his view preclude them from giving 'material support to the battle cruisers in an offensive operation'. Moreover Jellicoe pointed out that, even if the *Hindenburg* and *Lützow* were present and one of our battle cruisers was being refitted we would still have the advantage of a total broadside of 66 to 68 guns as against the Germans 52, and that 'as a whole, our guns are the heavier'. Such arguments savour somewhat of waging war by slide rule, because there existed so many imponderables, such as accuracy of rangetaking and fire control, which could influence the result drastically. Jellicoe did, however, agree to forward Beatty's proposals to the Admiralty – with his own, doubtless critical, remarks on them.[7] Evidently Beatty refused to abandon his case, because as soon as he learnt Jellicoe's views he wrote direct to Admiral Jackson, the First Sea Lord, about the enquiry he had made through Plunkett, who had just visited the Admiralty again, regarding the possibility of the 2nd Battle Squadron (Warrender's 6 or 7 *King George V* class ships) being based on Rosyth and the 3rd Battle Squadron being moved to the Humber. Beatty seized the chance to point out 'that most requirements would be fulfilled if the 5th Battle Squadron replaced the 3rd B.S. here'. As it consisted of only five ships berthing problems would not, he argued, prove difficult; and he went on to press strongly, and in the same terms that he had put to Jellicoe, for the *Queen Elizabeths* to join his force. Finally he repeated his earlier opposition to moving the whole BCF to the Humber – because 'we could not get in or out except [during] two hours on each side of high water'.[8] To Jellicoe he represented that if the *Queen Elizabeths* carried less than their full load of fuel he believed they would be capable of 25 knots, the same speed as his *Invincibles*; and he claimed that even if on leaving harbour they could only make 23½ knots 'their value would be enormous'. Experience had, he wrote, shown that 'they would in all cases be able to keep up with us until the moment when we sight the enemy', and that if he himself got to the east of the High Seas Fleet they 'would be invaluable'. He went on to specify various circumstances in which their presence with the BCF could be highly beneficial, and possibly decisive, and he therefore told the C-in-C that he trusted he would 'favourably consider the strategic arrangement I have submitted to you'.

He concluded by saying that as Jellicoe had already sent the Admiralty their earlier exchanges on this issue he had 'ventured to send them a duplicate of this to save time'.[9] This somewhat irregular action by Beatty plainly irritated Jellicoe, who rapped him sharply over the knuckles, saying that he would prefer 'discussion of proposals regarding the strategical distribution of the vessels of the Grand Fleet, other than those under your immediate orders, should be addressed only to the Commander-in-Chief' – except in cases of urgency which 'is clearly not the case in the present instance'.[10] This appears to be the first case of serious disagreement between the two admirals, and to me it seems that even though Beatty acted with less than his usual discretion, he had a strong case. However that may be he evidently wanted to smooth things over and restore the proper harmony between them, since on the day that Jellicoe sent his reprimand he replied with an abject apology, excusing himself on the grounds that the issue *had* appeared to him to be urgent, and that he would not have acted as he did had he 'conceived that you were not in total agreement with the principles of my proposal' – which was surely an extremely equivocal statement.[11]

London was not a happy place at this time. The costly failure of the British offensive at Loos and of the French attack in the Champagne in September 1915, the withdrawal of the Allied forces from Gallipoli at the end of that year after very heavy losses had been suffered, the entry of Bulgaria into the war on the Central Powers' side with the consequential over-running of Serbia, the fall of the pro-Ally Greek government of Venizelos in October, the fierce debate over whether conscription should be introduced in Britain, and the heavy shipping losses inflicted by the U-boats all combined to produce schisms in the Cabinet and public discontent over the conduct of the war. Nor did the formation of the First Coalition Government (still under Asquith) in May 1915 improve matters significantly. In the Admiralty the Balfour-Jackson régime lacked drive and imagination, and was being contrasted unfavourably with that of Churchill and Fisher in some newspapers; while Fisher's intrigues and insinuations about the department's alleged incompetence, and the way he used certain organs of the Press to further his aim to get himself recalled, proved acutely embarrassing to the Board of Admiralty. Early in March 1916 Hamilton (2nd Sea Lord) wrote to Beatty about the old admiral's intrigues, recounting how he hoped to get Fisher to attend War Council or Cabinet meetings and there 'say to our faces what at present he only insinuates through the gutter press';* and he told Beatty how Jackson had recently remarked that 'he could only attend to the war in the intervals of making out answers to Fisher and Co. for the War Council. . . .'[12] Despite its failings it is difficult to withhold sympathy from Balfour's Board over the subterranean campaign conducted against it. That Beatty kept himself clear of such manoeuvres is shown by the fact that few letters appear to have passed between him and Fisher during the first six months of 1916; but Jellicoe was subjected to a steady bombardment from him.[13]

Having failed to persuade Jellicoe to part with the *Queen Elizabeth* class battleships Beatty next turned his attention to the question of who should receive the two *Renown* class battle cruisers (about 26,750 tons, 32 knots, six 15-inch guns) which were due to complete in the summer of 1916. Because the 1912–13 Programme had included the four *Queen Elizabeths* (plus the *Malaya* which was paid for by the Federated Malay States), and neither of the next two Programmes had included any battle cruisers, these were the first ships of that class to be ordered since the *Tiger* (laid down 1912). The *Renown* and her sister were in fact suspended early in the war because it was believed they could not be completed in time to take part in it; but when Fisher returned to the Admiralty he got that decision reversed. In passing it may be remarked that the German navy suffered no comparable break in battle cruiser building, which continued uninterruptedly until 1918 – the *Hindenburg* being laid down in 1913, four *Mackensen* class in 1915, and three *Ersatz Yorck* class (only one of which was begun) in 1916.

Beatty represented to Jellicoe that three alternative allocations for the *Renowns* were possible – namely with the Grand Fleet in the north, with the BCF at Rosyth, or in the south at the Humber or Harwich. The last alternative he dismissed as impracticable, and he argued strongly in favour of them joining his command rather than Jellicoe's 'slow heavy force' on both strategic and tactical grounds because they could then

---

*J. L. Garvin, editor of the *Observer* 1908-42, and C. P. Scott, editor of the *Manchester Guardian* 1872-1929 and its owner from 1905, were Fisher's chief contacts with the Press. It was of course absurd of Hamilton to refer to their papers as 'the gutter press'.

'move quickly to any desired part and could always join the Commander-in-Chief, should he wish it. . . .[14] Jellicoe replied promptly that he fully agreed and had already informed the Admiralty of his views on the matter.[15]

Meanwhile early in March Admiral Scheer took the greater part of the High Seas Fleet to sea on the first of the major offensive operations which he had decided to adopt. They reached a position off the Texel in the hope of catching British light forces; but the results were negligible, and although the main British fleet came out no contact took place. Then it was the turn of the British to try and strike an offensive blow in which the seaplane carrier *Vindex* and her five seaplanes were the chief agents. She sailed with the Harwich Force on 25th March with the object of attacking the Zeppelin base which were believed to exist at Hoyer on the coast of Schleswig.* Beatty took the battle cruisers to sea in the early hours of 24th and reached a position only 45 miles west of Horns Reef to support Tyrwhitt; while Jellicoe came south with the battle-ships to give more distant support in the event of a strong German reaction. Hipper did actually sortie on the night of 25th–26th but never came within 60 miles of Beatty. The weather turned extremely foul, the seaplanes accomplished nothing (there were in fact no Zeppelin sheds at the place they were to attack) and three of them were lost. Beatty's reaction to this fiasco was to tell Jellicoe 'I don't like Air stunts along the lines conceived by us. A tremendous set out, and 5!! are loosed off to bomb a place that does not exist, to support which we (the BCF) were kept hanging about in the vicinity for 15 hours!!. . . .[16]

A week later, in answering a request from Jellicoe for his views, Beatty wrote 'I think the German Fleet will come out only on its own initiative when the right time arrives. Air raids on our part will not bring them out . . . I am not arguing against air raids. Anything that we can do to harass and annoy has great advantages . . . But it is certain that he will not come out in Grand Force when we set the time, i.e. to fight the Great Battle we all are waiting for'. In the same letter he pleaded fervently for better co-ordination 'between the Administrators and those who have to use the instruments which they command', and for 'a proper and personal

*See Map 1, pages 74–5

exchange of views between the Admiralty i.e. the 1st Sea Lord and the C-in-C', which he felt to have been conspicuous by its absence – at any rate since Fisher's resignation. He ended by telling Jellicoe of the progress made by the Hawkcraig anti-submarine team, which had fitted 'Directional Plates' on each side of a submarine's hull in order to obtain some indication of the bearing of a U-boat by the relative strength of the noise picked up by the port and starboard hydrophones. The specially fitted submarine had, he wrote, hunted her target (another submarine) 'all over the Firth of Forth and could not miss him'. He optimistically claimed that this development would revolutionize Submarine Warfare', and he believed it was 'the answer to meet the submarine menace'.[17] Professor Marder claims that this letter 'should once and for all dispose of the legend that Beatty was more offensively minded than Jellicoe'; which seems a very sweeping conclusion to arrive at on somewhat slender evidence, and moreover to ignore the great difference in character and temperament between the two admirals.[18]

Towards the end of April Scheer made a second foray into the North Sea, with the object of making a demonstration off the east coast more or less simultaneously with the German-supported rebellion in Ireland of Easter Sunday (23rd April). The High Seas Fleet sailed from the Jade at noon on 24th, but the Admiralty was as usual forewarned of the movement, though unaware of its precise purpose. Because Hipper was ill the German battle cruisers were commanded by Rear-Admiral Friedrich Boedicker. Late that evening Jellicoe and Beatty put to sea and steamed south against a heavy sea, while Tyrwhitt, with a Harwich Force much depleted by damage suffered in the operation off the Schleswig coast on 25th-26th March and by the detachment of destroyers for operations against the Belgian coast, came north. Meanwhile the *Seydlitz* had struck a mine and been sent back to the Jade with a strong escort; but soon after midnight on 24th-25th the other four of Boedicker's battle cruisers reached a position some 65 miles east of Lowestoft. At 3.50 a.m. his screening ships sighted the Harwich Force, and Tyrwhitt turned south at high speed, in the hope of drawing the enemy away from Lowestoft. Shortly after 4.0 a.m. Boedicker's ships opened fire on the port's coast defences, which were quickly silenced. About 200 houses were destroyed, but casualties were light. Half an hour later they bombarded Yarmouth – but only for a few minutes because Boedicker heard gunfire to the south and turned to support the four light cruisers of the 2nd Scouting Group which were in action with Tyrwhitt's ships. The German admiral thus had a splendid chance to cut off and destroy the Harwich Force; but he failed to seize it, altered course to the east and disappeared. At 5.20 a.m. Scheer also made for home. Meanwhile Jellicoe and Beatty had both been much handicapped by heavy seas, and were still many miles to the north. At 11.10 a.m. the Admiralty ordered them both to return to base. So ended another disappointing operation.

The British counter-blow, which was to bombard the Zeppelin sheds at Tondern on the Friesian island of Sylt, took place early in May.★ In essentials it followed the abortive March attack on Hoyer, except that bombing became a secondary purpose and its real object was to entice the High Seas Fleet out. At dawn on 4th Jellicoe had reached a position off the Skagerrak and Beatty was to the south of him. Mines had been laid and submarines stationed on the enemy's most probable course. The air attack was again a complete failure, only one of the eleven seaplanes being able to take off in the rough sea. Shortly after noon the Admiralty told Jellicoe that the Germans were apparently unaware that he was out, and after waiting in the dangerous waters off Heligoland for some seven hours he and Beatty turned for home. Scheer did actually sail at 3.0 p.m. but came no further north than Sylt, returning to base in the early hours of 5th May. Beatty, evidently unaware that the decision to wait no longer had been taken by Jellicoe, was critical about being deprived of the chance of battle early on 5th. 'We simply cannot go on missing chances like this' he protested to the C-in-C.[19] To Jackson he wrote that he had entertained strong hopes of 'getting at some of their Light Cruisers and Destroyers at Dawn [on 5th] . . . But alas we were ordered to return to our Base'. He assumed, wrongly, that the C-in-C had received orders from the Admiralty to do so, but 'it was with a sad heart that I turned (?) north and felt that a great chance was being missed. . . .'[20] The only concrete gain was the somewhat lucky destruction of the Zeppelin L7 on the morning of 4th by gunfire from two light cruisers which were covering the

★See Map I, pages 74–5

seaplane carriers.[21]

On the German side the Lowestoft raid produced feelings of elation which the actual results certainly did not justify; but it also had the important result of strengthening Bethmann Hollweg's hand in opposing the adoption of unrestricted submarine warfare. On 4th May he yielded to American protests and postponed the start of the campaign.

In Beatty's letter to Jellicoe about the Tondern raid already quoted he reverted to the question of changes in his command. He wrote that in recent practice firings the *Tiger*'s results had been 'as usual unsatisfactory', so he had called for a special report on the matter from Admiral Brock, commander of the 1st BCS. Apparently Commodore (later Admiral Sir Charles) de Bartolomé, the Naval Secretary to the First Lord, had suggested that Keyes should relieve Captain Pelly in the *Tiger*, but Beatty told Jellicoe emphatically that 'this I do *not* want' – because, although Keyes was 'a good fellow' he had 'no experience of Big Ship Command'. Furthermore, he wrote that Keyes 'has not too many brains' – which was certainly true – and he did not want 'more experiments'. His choice for the *Tiger* was therefore Bentinck, though he would 'hate losing him' as his Chief of Staff. If Bentinck went to the *Tiger* he asked for Brand, an officer of charming personality and of far higher mental capacity than Keyes, to take his place; but Brand did not join Beatty's staff until after he became C-in-C, Grand Fleet in November 1916. In retrospect it seems extremely hard to fault Beatty's opinions about the qualities and failings of the Captains and junior Flag Officers of those days. A week after he had opened his heart to Jellicoe about them he wrote to Keyes saying he had recommended him 'for a new galloping ship' – either the *Renown* or *Repulse* – rather than for one of the new *R. Class* battleships 'which are not gallopers'; but that idea also fell through.[22]

After a meeting with Tyrwhitt in mid-May Beatty wrote in strong terms to Jellicoe attacking the Admiralty's War Staff for its lack 'of cohesion and combination between the various units [i.e. ships] or collection of units at the different bases.' 'The system of water-tight compartments [in Whitehall] has', he represented, 'reached its climax'. The Chief of the War Staff, he claimed, 'has priceless information given to him [presumably by Room 40] which he sits on until it is too late for the Sea Forces to take action . . . What it amounts to is the

War Staff has developed into a One Man Show [i.e. Oliver]. The man is not born yet who can run it by himself'. He reinforced his argument by refering to the movements at the time of the Lowestoft raid – when 'there was absolutely no reason why every unit should not have been on the move 3½ hours before it was!!' Moreover Tyrwhitt had received contradictory orders and had no idea where he [Beatty] was on that occasion. 'It amounts to this', he roundly declaimed, 'that we were without general principles and had no plan, no combination and no decision'. He could not, he told Jellicoe, 'put all this in a letter', presumably to the Admiralty, but he urged the C-in-C 'to stop this perfectly hopeless way of muddling on', because 'one of these days we shall be found out'. This was hot stuff to put even in a confidential letter to the C-in-C; but it is undeniable that the staff side of the Admiralty was over-centralised, under-manned and badly organised. Beatty urged that the only solution was to have a conference. He did not want 'a monumental gathering' but only the top sea commanders and the highest authorities from Whitehall to attend it.[23] Though he must have known that we were reading many German cypher signals he did not raise the question of giving the sea commanders the gist of their contents and leaving it to them to act as they thought best. Nor did he raise the issue of how a staff should be organised and work; and those two problems held the key to the troubles about which he complained so stridently. At any rate he promptly got his way about holding a conference at Rosyth – with only Jackson, Jellicoe and himself and their Chiefs of Staff present. The chief decision was to develop Rosyth and the Firth of Forth as the primary base in order to shift the strategic centre of the British naval effort to the south and to concentrate our forces.

Two days after the conference Beatty wrote to Jackson objecting strongly to the proposal to move the seven elderly ships of the 3rd Battle Squadron from Rosyth to the Thames estuary, where Beatty (apparently remembering the fate of the *Cressys*) considered they would be in grave danger. He preferred that they should be based on the Humber. Nor did he like the proposal to move the more powerful 4th Battle Squadron under Sturdee's command from Scapa to the Humber because it would be separated 'from the main Battle Fleet by a distance of 340 miles'; and he harped once again on his favourite theme of 'concentration of force'.[24] This latter proposal was in fact dropped, and a week later Beatty wrote gratefully (and tactfully) to Jackson on the subject, ending with the assurance that 'though I express myself indifferently . . . whatever decision is arrived at you have no-one in command of any unit who will carry out your instructions more loyally or scrupulously than – Yours Sincerely'[25] – which surely expressed a good deal less than his real feelings about the Board of Admiralty in general and Jackson in particular.

Before any important changes in dispositions or strategy could be brought into force the Admiralty became aware that major enemy movements were about to take place in the North Sea. Though it would be premature to try and sum up Beatty's character and accomplishments at this stage it is fair to record that after nearly two years of war he had moulded the Battle Cruiser Fleet into a force possessed of very high morale and inspired by admiration for and confidence in its leader. But a corollary of that achievement was that the BCF had come to consider itself a *corps d'élite*. Its officers, and to a great extent the men too, regarded the Grand Fleet's Battle Squadrons, which had not yet fired a shot in anger against the High Seas Fleet's major warships, with something approaching contempt; and that state of affairs was to produce unfortunate consequences when the need arose for the two forces to work in intimate collaboration.

As regards the personal hold which Beatty had established over the officers and men of his fleet the evidence that he was held in very high regard both as a fighting leader and as a man is overwhelming. In part this must have derived from his good looks, his coolness and bravery in action, and his burning desire to smite his particular adversary – Hipper's 1st Scouting Group. Like most charismatic leaders he deliberately adopted a distinctive style of dress and conduct. We do not know exactly when he first adopted the cap with a specially wide peak, worn with a pronounced tilt over one eye or the other, and also the monkey-jacket (day uniform) with three instead of the regulation four brass buttons down the front; but he was certainly wearing both by 1916. Such histrionic devices are of course commonly adopted by leaders of all fighting services in order to impress their personalities on their subordinates. Nelson and his armless sleeve and eye patch served such purposes; while Montgomery's many-

badged beret of World War II and Churchill's 'romper suit'
and V-sign were their particular brands of distinguishing
marks a century and a half later. If there was more than a
touch of arrogance in Beatty's appearance and conduct it must
surely be excused by the very real need for a leader to impress
his personality on those whom he may at any time take into
battle, and to win the confidence which inspires men to strive
to the utmost limit to deserve the high opinion in which they
feel their leader holds them. In all those respects Beatty's
quirks and oddities certainly achieved their purpose.

As to his character and methods Admiral Chalmers, who
was on his staff and became his first biographer, wrote that
'The first thing that strikes you about him are his keen,
penetrating eyes. They literally flash from one object to
another as each engages his attention; but they never dwelt on
any of them for long 'because he has a phenomenally quick
brain and he can take in all he wants to know in one glance'.
His manner of speaking, 'each sentence is short, clipped and
full of meaning', conveyed the rapidity of his mental proces-
ses; and decisions were given 'without a moment's hesitation'.
Chalmers also attributes to him a great sense of humour, and a
capacity to tease his staff if they 'took themselves too
seriously'.[26] I see no reason to question that description by a
shrewd and intelligent observer, which explains why such a
man established himself so firmly in the regard, and even the
affection of his officers and men.

CHAPTER EIGHT

Jutland,
31st May–1st June 1916

There can be few if any battles fought on land, at sea or latterly in the air which have produced so much controversy and have been re-fought so often on paper as that which took place in the North Sea on the last day of May 1916. Though it is not intended in this chapter to produce a detailed account rivalling or complementing that of Professor Arthur Marder,[1] Beatty's part in the battle was so important that it is essential to describe his actions; and that would be incomprehensible without reference to the actions of his Commander-in-Chief and of the enemy.

The German C-in-C since January 1916 Admiral Reinhard Scheer planned to improve the strength of his fleet relative to Admiral Jellicoe's by making a sortie to the north of the Skagerrak with Admiral Hipper's battle cruisers and light forces and his own battle squadrons in support of them. Submarines were stationed off the British bases and at other strategic points to catch Jellicoe's ships as they came out, and Scheer hoped also to cut off and destroy detached squadrons of the Grand Fleet. Hipper sailed from the Jade at 1.0 a.m. on 31st May and Scheer from the Jade and Elbe two and a half hours later.* Hipper's force consisted of the *Lützow* (flagship) and four other battle cruisers (1st Scouting Group), and four light cruisers (2nd Scouting Group). The destroyers were divided into two groups (1st and 2nd Torpedo Boat Forces) each of which had a light cruiser as Leader. Scheer himself flew his flag in the *Friedrich der Grosse*, which was not attached to any group, and had with him 15 other Dreadnought battleships (1st and 3rd Squadrons), six pre-Dreadnoughts (2nd Squadron) and five light cruisers (4th Scouting Group). The submarine trap was laid by stationing 18 boats off the Orkneys, the Moray Firth, the Firth of Forth and in other favourable positions; but as they accomplished nothing and

*See Map 3, pages 150–1

149

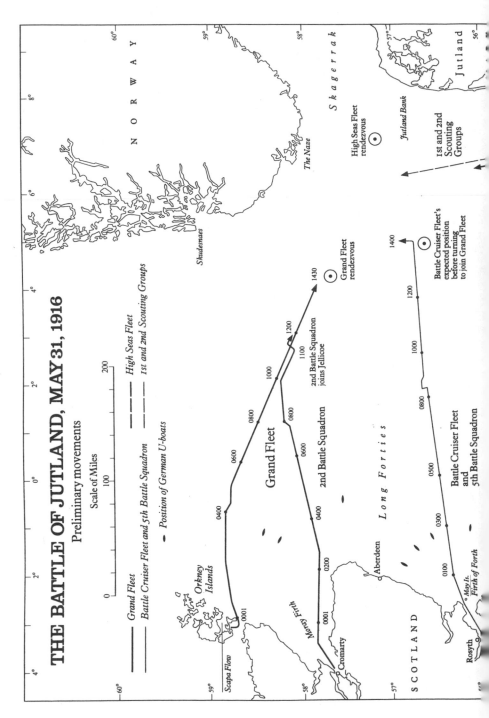

THE BATTLE OF JUTLAND, MAY 31, 1916

Preliminary movements

Scale of Miles

0   100   200

—— Grand Fleet
––– Battle Cruiser Fleet and 5th Battle Squadron   ––– High Seas Fleet
· Position of German U-boats   –––– 1st and 2nd Scouting Groups

N O R W A Y

Skudesnaes

The Naze

S k a g e r r a k

High Seas Fleet
rendezvous

Jutland Bank

Jutland

1st and 2nd Scouting
Groups

Grand Fleet
rendezvous

1430

1200

1100

2nd Battle Squadron
joins Jellicoe

Grand Fleet

0600

0800

1000

0400

0600

0800

1000

1200

0400

0200

Moray Firth

0001

2nd Battle Squadron

L o n g   F o r t i e s

Aberdeen

Cromarty

Orkney
Islands

Scapa Flow

S C O T L A N D

0100

0300

0500

0800

1000

1200

1400

Battle Cruiser Fleet's
expected position
before turning
to join Grand Fleet

Battle Cruiser Fleet
and
5th Battle Squadron

May Is.
Firth of Forth

Rosyth

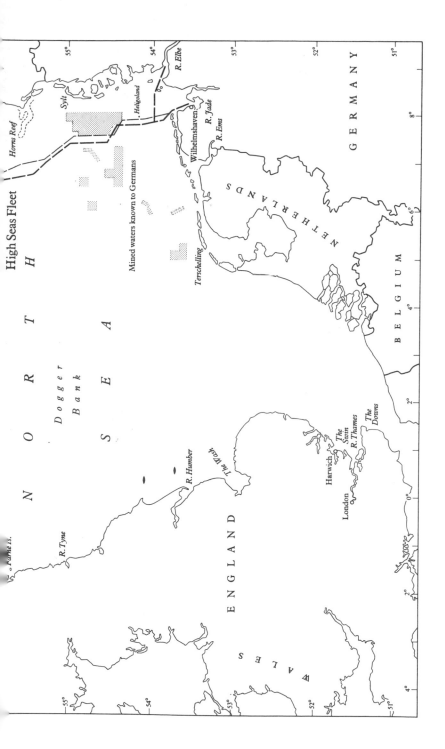

lost one of their number we need take no further account of
their actions.

At noon on 30th the Admiralty, forewarned by Room 40,
ordered Jellicoe and Beatty to prepare for sea, and at 5.40 p.m.
told the former to concentrate his forces in the Long Forties
(about 100 miles east of Aberdeen). The result was that the 1st
and 4th Battle Squadrons (Admirals Burney and Sturdee), the
3rd Battle Cruiser Squadron (Admiral Hood), the 2nd Cruiser
Squadron (Admiral Heath), the 4th Light Cruiser Squadron
(Admiral Le Mesurier) and two and half flotillas of destroyers
had sailed from Scapa for the rendezvous by 10.30 p.m. From
the Moray Firth came the 2nd Battle Squadron (Admiral
Jerram), the 1st Cruiser Squadron (Admiral Arbuthnot) and a
half flotilla of destroyers to join Jellicoe shortly before noon on
31st May. At 11.0 p.m. on 30th Beatty sailed from the Firth of
Forth with the 1st and 2nd Battle Cruiser Squadrons (Admirals Brock and Pakenham) and the four available ships of the
Queen Elizabeth class forming the fast and powerful 5th Battle
Squadron under Admiral Hugh Evan-Thomas, which Jellicoe
had recently detached to Rosyth in replacement of Admiral
Hood's three *Invincibles*, which had just been sent to Scapa to
carry out routine gunnery practices. Beatty thus fortuitously
received the accession of strength for which he had vainly
asked in the previous February – though at too short notice to
integrate it fully with his other forces. Accompanying Beatty's
heavy ships were the 1st, 2nd and 3rd Light Cruiser Squadrons
(Admirals Alexander-Sinclair, Goodenough and Napier
respectively), one seaplane carrier and 27 destroyers. As to the
strength of the High Seas Fleet, the Intelligence given by the
Admiralty to Jellicoe had led him to expect it to consist of 27
or 28 battleships, possibly including the new *Bayern* armed
with 15-inch guns and the ex-Greek *Salamis,* as well as six
battle cruisers including the new *Hindenburg*.[2] In fact this was a
big over-estimate of the ships actually available on 31st May.
The misleading Intelligence given to Jellicoe arose through the
staggeringly bad co-operation of the Admiralty's War Staff
with Room 40. W. F. Clarke, a former barrister who worked
for 30 years in our cryptographic organisation, wrote (almost
certainly to Admiral Chalmers when he was engaged on his
biography of Beatty) that 'In Room 40 we knew the exact
composition and state of readiness of the German fleet from
day to day, but J. R. J. [Jellicoe] was not given this

information and it was only after Jutland, when he raised the question, that we were allowed to tell him . . . we had up till then no means of communicating with the C-in-C, nor did we know what he was being told.'[3] The two sides' relative strengths were in fact as follows, though neither Jellicoe nor Beatty was aware of the extent of the numerical superiority they enjoyed. It is possible that, as Jellicoe later suggested, the faulty intelligence given to him affected his tactics during the battle:[4]

> Battleships – 28 British to 22 German (including 6 pre-Dreadnoughts)
> Battle cruisers – 9 British to 5 German
> Armoured and light cruisers – 34 British to 11 German
> Destroyers – 78 British to 61 German.

When Jellicoe's forces from Scapa and Cromarty had concentrated he steered for the position off the Skagerrak which he had arranged with Beatty for 2.30 p.m.*

Unfortunately for the British a number of things went wrong in the early stages. The first mistake arose through another case of bad co-operation between the Operations Division and Room 40. An officer from the former went to the latter and asked where our Direction-Finding stations placed the German call sign DK – which was that of the flagship of the High Seas Fleet. He was told, quite correctly, that it was in Wilhelmshaven. In fact the Germans had shifted to a shore station both the call sign and the wireless operator who generally worked on Scheer's wavelength – in order to prevent any change of 'touch' being noticed at our listening stations.[5] Room 40 was well aware of this practice, but was not consulted when the Admiralty – to the later fury of the cryptographic team – signalled to Jellicoe at 12.30 p.m. that the German *flagship* was still in harbour. When later in the war Clarke visited Beatty's flagship and was summoned quite unexpectedly to dine with the Admiral he waved a copy of the criminally stupid signal at him and said 'What am I to think of O.D. [Operations Division] when I get that telegram and in three hours' time meet the whole German Fleet well out at sea?'[5] This was the first that Clarke had heard of the signal sent without Room 40's knowledge by Rear-Admiral T. Jackson, the Director of the Operations Division. His horrified

*See Map 3, pages 150–1

reaction can well be understood.* One effect of this blunder was to deprive Jellicoe of a sense of urgency. He proceeded at only 15 knots and delayed to examine various merchant ships encountered on the way to the rendezvous with Beatty, which he therefore reached one hour late. Secondly the Admiralty was anxious about a possible lunge at the cross-Channel shipping routes, and therefore held the 3rd Battle Squadron and 3rd Cruiser Squadron in the Thames estuary, and also kept Tyrwhitt's fine Harwich Force in harbour. Thirdly, through a series of accidents, the seaplane carrier which should have accompanied Jellicoe, and whose aircraft might have been useful for reconnaissance purposes, got left behind and never caught up with the Grand Fleet. Fourthly the Admiralty, perhaps remembering the consequences of their having arranged the rendezvous with Beatty prior to the Dogger Bank action,† left it to Jellicoe this time; and he gave Beatty a position 69 miles SSE of his own expected position for 2.30 p.m. on 31st. Although it is true that in earlier sorties Jellicoe had ordered Beatty to take up a position at least as far ahead of him without unfortunate results it is none the less a fact that the separation between the BCF and the Grand Fleet was too great. Furthermore the errors in the two forces' Dead Reckoning (DR) positions, which were to produce difficulties later, would probably have been eliminated had their light forces been in visual touch with each other. Lastly, Beatty stationed Evan-Thomas's 5th Battle Squadron (four *Queen Elizabeth* class) 5 miles to the north-west of his battle cruisers – which meant they were not in close support of him in the first phase of the battle. The reader will recall

*W. F. Clarke gave the author copies of all his papers on this incident and other matters concerned with cryptography and Jutland. Though it was highly improper of Clarke to have kept those papers historians, including Professor Marder, may be thankful that he did so; since Sir Julian Corbett was forbidden to make any mention of the work of Room 40 in *Naval Operations*, Vol. III. In PRO Cab. 45/269, Part IV, there is a list of the decyphers received by the Admiralty and the Out Signals sent as a result. This is a typescript draft by Jellicoe of what was evidently intended to be published as an Appendix to the Harper Report on Jutland. Admiral John Godfrey's lectures on Jutland in the same file include the decyphers in his 'Summary of the more important British Messages and Signals relating to the Battle of Jutland'. Copies of the Clarke papers are in Churchill College ROSK 3/6, in the Beatty papers and also in SLGF 6/14.
†See pages 109 and 115

Beatty's disappointment over narrowly failing to catch Hipper's 1st Scouting Group in the Scarborough Raid operations of December 1914, and his fury over the same enemy's escape from his clutches in the Dogger Bank action* Though it can hardly be proved with documentary certainty I am convinced that Beatty regarded Hipper as his particular quarry, and on 31st May he was determined that this time he would 'bag the lot' – as he considered his force should have done at Dogger Bank. A clue to Beatty's possible feelings on this matter is provided by a remark made by his intimate friend Walter Cowan of the *Princess Royal*, which has, surprisingly, not been given any weight, and in many cases has not even been noticed by writers on Jutland. Cowan wrote that during the approach to battle he had at first feared that the 'damned 5th Battle Squadron is going to take the bread out of our mouths'.[6] I find it much more reasonable to extend Cowan's thinking to the Admiral whom he so fervently admired than to accept Professor Marder's justification for Beatty's handling of Evan-Thomas's ships.[7] Though it is true that the 5th Battle Squadron had never worked with the Battle Cruiser Fleet before, that its ships' full speed was some three knots slower, and that Evan-Thomas was not a particularly imaginative leader who would sense his senior officer's needs and intentions intuitively, it none the less leaves a sense of unease in my mind that Beatty ignored Nelson's dictum that 'only numbers can annihilate' – despite the fact that he was fond of quoting the national hero's *obiter dicta* when they fitted in with any case he wanted to make.

Many years later when Beatty read Jellicoe's paper on 'Errors made in Jutland Battle', which included criticism of his handling of the 5th Battle Squadron, he defended his actions vigorously, writing that 'If I had waited for 5th BS instead of steaming to get between [the] Enemy and his bases I should never have brought them to action at all . . . and I should have been Court-Martialled for not doing my utmost to destroy the Enemy!! Since when should 6 British Battle Cruisers hesitate to bring to action 5 Enemy Battle Cruisers!!?'[8] But in truth, owing to the incorrect Intelligence sent by the Admiralty mentioned earlier, it was not until about 3.30 p.m. on 31st May that Beatty realised that Hipper had only five ships

*See pages 103–4 and 113–4

instead of the six he had been led to expect; and if he expected
to be only equal in number to his adversary he should surely
have taken action to secure Evan-Thomas's immediate support.

During the forenoon of 31st May Beatty and Hipper were
steering courses nearly at right angles to each other – the
former slightly to the north of East and the latter slightly to
the west of North.* Scheer was about 50 miles astern of
Hipper, with his battleships already disposed in line ahead.
The sea was calm and the visibility fairly good during the early
afternoon, but soon began to deteriorate. The weather had
frustrated the usual German Zeppelin reconnaissance, while
the few seaplanes accompanying Beatty's force were of no use
to him. Thus when Beatty reached the position where he was
to turn to the north towards Jellicoe at 2.15 p.m. he and
Hipper were completely unaware of each other's presence –
though the closest of their screening ships were only some 15
miles apart. Then a Danish merchant ship was sighted in
between the two adversaries, both of whom sent light forces
to investigate her. Thus was contact made at 2.20 p.m.

On receiving the first sighting report from the light cruiser
Galatea Beatty did not, as stated in his despatch, immediately
steer 'for the sound of the guns'. For reasons which have never
been satisfactorily explained he allowed 12 minutes to elapse
before increasing to full speed and altering to the south-east in
order to get between the enemy (whoever it might turn out to
be) and his base.[9] The alteration of course was first signalled to
Evan-Thomas by flags which could not be read at so long a
distance. Not until it was repeated by searchlight did
he turn to conform; and by that time the gap between him and
Beatty had opened to 10 miles. The result was that Evan-
Thomas's ships did not come into action until 20 minutes after
Beatty's – an error for which Beatty himself must carry most
of the responsibility, though Seymour, his Flag Lieutenant,
should have repeated the alter course signal at once by
searchlight. After the war Jellicoe wrote that 'his [Beatty's]
signal officer throughout disobeyed my Battle Instructions
that when in presence of the enemy all signals were to be made
by flags, searchlight and wireless. Had these instructions been
carried out and the 5th Battle Squadron been closed up I think

*See map 3, pages 150-1

Hipper would have been annihilated' – a criticism which certainly has much validity.[10]

Meanwhile Beatty had been left with only one Light Cruiser Squadron (Goodenough's) to serve as his advanced screen, the other two squadrons having steered to the sound of the *Galatea's* guns. Thus it was not until 3.30 that the officers and men straining their eyes to the north-east from the *Lion's* bridge sighted Hipper's ships some 14 miles away. Beatty at once altered to the east and increased to full speed; while Hipper, aware of his inferiority, altered 180 degrees to starboard with the object of drawing Beatty towards Scheer. Both sides opened fire at about 3.48, by which time the 5th Battle Squadron was 'hull down on the horizon'. Both sides at first over-estimated the range, though the German error was much the smaller. Beatty believed it to be 18,000 yards when in fact it was some 2,000 yards less. Unfortunately the British fire distribution signal, made at 3.46 by flags, again led to a misunderstanding – as at Dogger Bank. The admiral meant to utilise his six to five superiority by his two leading ships (*Lion* and *Princess Royal*) concentrating on the leading enemy (*Lützow*, Hipper's flagship), while each of his other ships engaged her opposite number in the German line. The concentration on the *Lützow* was carried out, but the *Queen Mary* (third in Beatty's line) missed or misunderstood the signal and engaged Hipper's third ship the *Seydlitz*. In the rear of Beatty's line the *Tiger* also missed the signal, with the result that both she and the *New Zealand* engaged the *Moltke*. The *Indefatigable*, last in the line, correctly engaged the *von der Tann*; but for some 10 minutes the *Derfflinger*, to her Gunnery Officer's delight, was allowed to make undisturbed target practice, chiefly at her opposite number the *Queen Mary*.[11] The German shooting was extremely accurate, and with the British ships silhouetted against the westering sun the advantage of light and visibility was very much in the Germans' favour.* An interesting point is that the two German ships against which a concentration of fire *was* effected by the British battle cruisers (*Lützow* and *Moltke*) made the best shooting in the opening phase; which supports the view that in those days concentration was unlikely to achieve much, if any benefit – chiefly because of the difficulty of distinguishing each

*See Map 4, pages 158-9

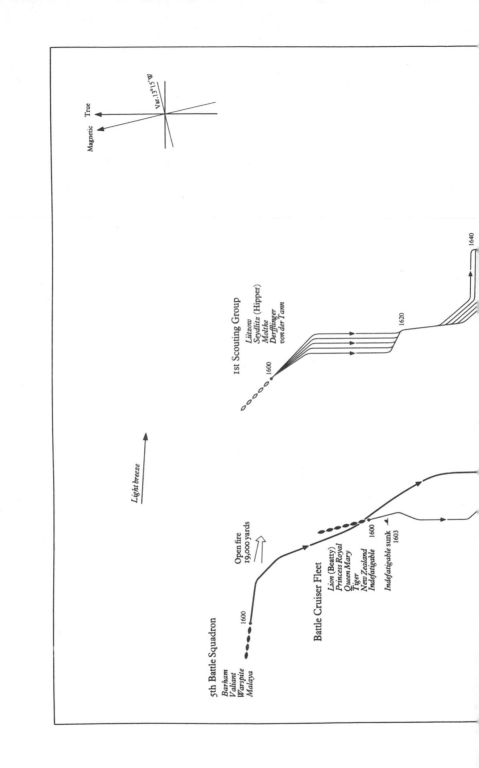

Var.13°15'W

Magnetic   True

1st Scouting Group

Lütžow
Seydlitz (Hipper)
Moltke
Derfflinger
von der Tann

1600

1620

1640

Light breeze

5th Battle Squadron

Barham
Valiant
Warspite
Malaya

1600

Open fire
19,000 yards

Battle Cruiser Fleet

Lion (Beatty)
Princess Royal
Queen Mary
Tiger
New Zealand
Indefatigable

1600

Indefatigable sunk
1603

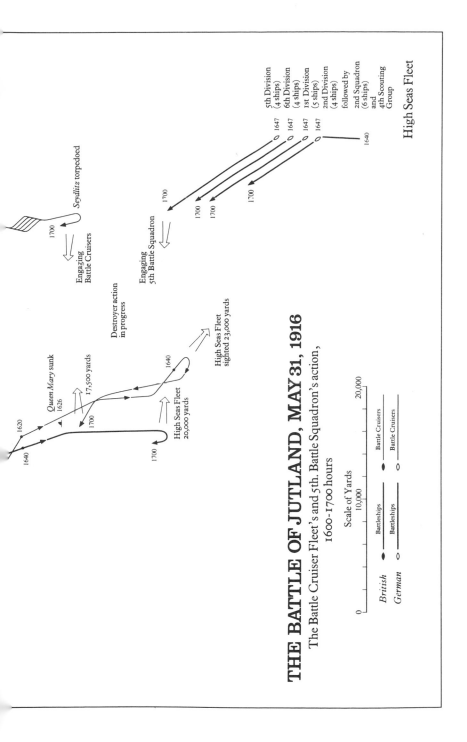

THE BATTLE OF JUTLAND, MAY 31, 1916

The Battle Cruiser Fleet's and 5th. Battle Squadron's action,
1600-1700 hours

ship's fall of shot.

The first hits scored by the Germans were on the *Princess Royal* and *Tiger*, which had received no less than nine by 4.0 p.m. The *Lion* was hit at 3.51 and 3.52, one of which struck the roof of her midship turret and very nearly caused her loss. The best estimate of the results achieved in the first critical minutes is that up to 4.0 p.m. the Germans obtained 15 hits on Beatty's ships (excluding the *Queen Mary* and *Indefatigable*), while the British battle cruisers only obtained four hits. Between 4.02 and 4.05 the *Indefatigable* was hit by about five heavy shells fired by the *von der Tann*, and blew up with the loss of 1,017 officers and men killed. At about the same moment the 5th Battle Squadron opened fire at 19,000 yards, and quickly began to make its weight felt – especially on the *Moltke* and *von der Tann*, the rear ships of the German line. In his report on the battle to his C-in-C Hipper emphasised the ineffectiveness of the British battle cruisers' gunfire and the effectiveness of that of the 5th Battle Squadron.[12]

With such a heavy superiority now in his favour Beatty closed on his adversary, and from 4.15 to 4.35 there ensued what he called in his despatch a duel 'of a very fierce and resolute character'. It was in this phase that the *Queen Mary*, whose shooting had been the best of Beatty's ships, was heavily hit by the concentrated fire of the *Derfflinger* and *Seydlitz*. At 4.26 a salvo struck her amidships and she blew up – with the loss of 1,266 officers and men killed. It was this second horrifying disaster which caused Beatty to remark calmly to Chatfield 'There seems to be something wrong with our bloody ships today'. Chatfield was the only person who heard the remark, and he has since confirmed its correctness.* Churchill's attribution to Beatty of the words "Turn two

---

*I am indebted to Captain A. B. Sainsbury for a copy of his memorandum on this famous incident in which he tells of his 'accidental' discovery that as long ago as 1937 Mr. D. Bonner Smith, the Admiralty Librarian, asked Chatfield if he could verify the reference for use in the Oxford Dictionary of Quotations. In a manuscript note dated 28th Sept. 1937 Chatfield replied that Beatty said no more than is quoted here. See N.M.M. file AGC II. Captain Sainsbury's research should kill once and for all the many incorrect versions which have repeatedly appeared e.g. in Geoffrey Bennett's, *Battle of Jutland* and *Naval Battles of the First World War* (Batsford, 1964 and 1968) and in John Irving's, *The Smoke Screen of Jutland* (Kimber, 1966).

points [45 degrees] to port" i.e. two points nearer the enemy' is total fiction, as is his gloss 'Thus the crisis of the battle was surmounted'.[13]

Despite the losses suffered by Beatty the position in which Hipper found himself was becoming increasingly perilous, and at 4.09 Beatty decided to press him still harder by ordering his destroyers to attack with torpedoes. About five minutes later Hipper tried to relieve the pressure by sending his own destroyers in with the same purpose. The result was that a fierce action between the two sides' light craft developed in the waters between the big ships. Of 20 torpedoes fired by the British only two hit – one on the *Seydlitz*, which did no serious damage, and one on a destroyer. It is unlikely that any German torpedoes scored a hit. Both sides lost two destroyers in this fierce encounter. Hipper and Evan-Thomas both turned *away* from the torpedo threat, and by 4.36 the former was steering almost due east and had broken off the action. To summarise the results achieved in the 'run to the south' the Germans probably obtained 44 hits, including 7 on the *Queen Mary*, 5 on the *Indefatigable* and 2 on Evan-Thomas's flagship the *Barham*. In return Beatty's ships obtained 11 hits and Evan-Thomas's 6. But as the light and visibility were markedly in the German favour too much should not be made of this disparity.*

At about 4.30 Commodore Goodenough's *Southampton* sighted the High Seas Fleet, at once closed to about 6 miles in order to obtain exact information, and at 4.38 signalled to Jellicoe and Beatty 'Have sighted enemy Battle Fleet bearing approximately SE, course of enemy N. . . .'[14] It was a classic example of a light cruiser performing its traditional functions correctly. Beatty altered course to close Goodenough, and quickly sighted the masts and upper works of Scheer's ships about 12 miles away to the SE. Then he turned 16 points (180 degrees) in succession to starboard and steered to the NW and then N so as to fall back on Jellicoe whilst drawing his quarry towards his C-in-C. Evan-Thomas was about 8 miles to the north of Beatty and still heavily engaged with Hipper when the order to turn 16 points was made executive. He did not see Beatty's turning signal – which was again made by flags and not repeated by searchlight. As the 5th Battle Squadron

*See Table on pages 164-5 which gives details of hits scored by both sides in this phase.

approached the battle cruisers on an opposite course one of his staff asked Beatty on which side the former was to pass. He was told on the disengaged side – which in retrospect seems a pity because it was bound to cause a check in the battleships' very effective shooting.[15] At 4.48 Beatty signalled direct to Evan-Thomas to turn 16 points to starboard *in succession*. As Professor Marder remarks there were three things wrong with this signal.[16] It should have been made executive *before* the 5th Battle Squadron came abreast of the *Lion* if the former was to give close support to the latter: it should have been an order to turn *together* if the maximum use was to be made of the battleships; and the turn should have been to *port* instead of starboard if the gap between the forces was not to be widened. As it was the gap had opened to about three miles before Evan-Thomas's ships had completed their turns. The only compensation for these mistakes was that the 5th Battle Squadron, now well astern of Beatty, was able first to engage the leading ships of the High Seas Fleet and then take some of the weight of Hipper's fire off Beatty during 'the run to the north'.

We left Hipper steering a little east of south towards Scheer at 4.50 p.m. Two minutes later he started to reverse course by a turn to starboard in succession (shortly before Evan-Thomas executed his similar turn) and steered again to the north-west, thus closing the range towards Beatty – who was once again handicapped by the poor visibility to the east. Firing was now resumed for about 20 minutes, during which the 5th Battle Squadron, which was on Beatty's port quarter, bore the chief brunt – and inflicted more damage than it received. A curious feature of the Jutland *post-mortem* was Beatty's insistence that the range at this time had been 14,000 when it was certainly two or three thousand yards greater. One can only surmise that he was trying to forestall criticism of himself for not having closed the range – which in fact no one had made and which in the prevailing circumstances would have been a folly.[17] Hipper was still quite unaware that he was steering towards the Grand Fleet, and leading Scheer into Jellicoe's arms.

At 5.40 the action was renewed with the light now for the first time favouring the British, who scored heavily against Hipper, forced him to turn away to starboard (i.e. towards the north) and again order his flotillas to attack Beatty's ships.

Then the totally unexpected appearance of Hood's 3rd Battle Cruiser Squadron made Hipper believe it was the Grand Fleet; so he turned to the south-west and fell back on Scheer. At 6.10 he formed ahead of the High Seas Fleet on a north-easterly course; and the fact that he had been forced steadily away to the east and the south-east prevented him sighting Jellicoe's advance forces. This had the effect of producing the first moment of extreme peril for Scheer – when Jellicoe deployed into battle line right across his line of advance. Meanwhile Hood had encountered the light cruisers of Admiral Boedicker's 2nd Scouting Group, damaged two of its four ships seriously, contributed to forcing Hipper's retreat on Scheer, and diverted his intended destroyer attack from Beatty to himself. Hood thus materially assisted the successful deployment of the Grand Fleet.

In the 'Run to the North' Beatty and Evan-Thomas reversed to a great extent the poor results achieved in the 'Run to the South'. True no German ships were actually sunk to compensate for the loss of the *Indefatigable* and *Queen Mary* – a matter which will be discussed later; but as a fighting force the value of the 1st Scouting Group had been reduced by perhaps 75%, only the *Moltke* having escaped serious damage. Whereas the hits scored by British heavy shell in this phase were 16 on Hipper's ships and 5 on Scheer's – all but one of them by the 5th Battle Squadron – Beatty's ships received only 5 hits and Evan-Thomas's 13.

Beatty, aided by Hood's gallant action, had certainly done very well in leading his adversaries exactly where he wanted them – namely into the hands of the Grand Fleet; but he was later criticised for not making any enemy reports during the 'Run to the North'. Chatfield defended his silence on the grounds that the visibility was often too poor to identify the enemy (which seems a dubious argument), that the light cruisers ahead of the *Lion* should have done the reporting in accordance with their primary function, and that Evan-Thomas's ships were nearer to the enemy and could see better but made no reports. None of those arguments seems entirely to justify Beatty's silence from 4.45 to 6.0 p.m. – a matter about which Jellicoe later complained with some bitterness.[18]

At 5.56 the British battle cruisers gained touch with Jellicoe's advanced forces. The moment for which the whole British Navy had been waiting for nearly two years had

BATTLE OF JUTLAND — 31st MAY 1916
COMPARATIVE PERFORMANCES OF BRITISH AND

Position in Line	Rounds Fired (APC, CP HE)*	Targets & Hits Scored (in brackets)
I BRITISH SHIPS		
Lion (Flagship)	326	Lützow (4), Derfflinger (1)
Princess Royal	230	Lützow (3), Derfflinger (Nil) Seydlitz (2)
Queen Mary	About 150	Seydlitz (4), Derfflinger (Nil)
Tiger	303	Moltke (1), vd Tann (2), Seydlitz (Nil)
New Zealand	420	Moltke (Nil) vd Tann (Nil) Seydlitz (3)
Indefatigable	About 40	vd Tann (Nil)
Invincible	About 110	Lützow (8–mostly by
Inflexible	88	Invincible
Indomitable	175	Derfflinger (3) Seydlitz (1)
II GERMAN SHIPS		
Lützow (Flagship)	About 380	Lion (13), Invincible (?2), Others (4)
Derfflinger	385	P. Royal (6), Q. Mary (?3) Invincible (?3), Others (4)
Seydlitz	376	Q. Mary (4), Tiger (2) Others (4)
Moltke	359	Tiger (13), N. Zealand (Nil)
vd Tann	170	Indefatigable (5), N. Zealand (1)

NOTES *APC = Armour Piercing Capped
　　　　CP = Common Pointed,
　　　　HE = High Explosive
　　　　'OTHERS' includes hits on battleships

GERMAN BATTLE CRUISERS' MAIN ARMAMENTS

Firing Ship & Hits Received (in brackets)	Casualties Suffered
Lützow (13) *Derfflinger* (6), Others (3)	99 killed, 51 wounded 22 killed, 81 wounded
Seydlitz (About 4) *Derfflinger* (About 3) *Moltke* (13), *Seydlitz* (2)	1,266 killed, 6 wounded 2 captured 24 killed, 46 wounded
vd Tann (1)	Nil
vd Tann (About 5) *Lützow* & *Derfflinger* (About 5) ditto (Nil) ?(Nil)	1,017 killed, 2 captured 1,026 killed, 1 wounded Nil Nil
Lion (4), *P. Royal* (3) *Invincible* & *Inflexible* (8), Others (9)	115 killed, 50 wounded
Indomitable (3), *Lion* (1), Others (17)	157 killed, 26 wounded
Q. Mary (4), *Indomitable* (1), *P. Royal* (2), *N. Zealand* (3), Others (4)	98 killed, 55 wounded
Tiger (1 near miss), Others (4)	17 killed, 23 wounded
Tiger (2), Others (3)	11 killed, 15 wounded

Source: N.J.M. Campbell, *Battle Cruisers: Warship Special No. 1* and personal records

plainly come.

Before proceeding to the next phase it will be appropriate to introduce a table compiled from the latest information available to show the comparative results achieved by the British and German battle cruisers, and to discuss the reasons why the Germans scored more hits and suffered fewer losses than the British.

The table shows that the British battle cruisers obtained 32 hits on Hipper's ships and received 52 hits in return from them; a discrepancy which demands explanation – even though allowance must be made for the fact that the visibility and interference from smoke worked strongly in the Germans' favour for most of the time. In the first place the German stereoscopic rangefinders certainly gave better results than the British 'coincidence' type instruments in such conditions. Secondly the error in the BCF's fire distribution, mentioned earlier, brought an uncovenanted benefit to the *Derfflinger* in engaging the *Queen Mary*. Thirdly because Beatty fought almost continuously at a speed near his maximum (25 knots) while Hipper kept his speed as low as 18 knots, British fire control and observation suffered from worse vibration than the German ships experienced. Fourthly the British system of correcting salvos on to the target by 'bracketing' with successive salvos was slower to find the target than the German system, by which two salvos could be in the air together and if the first fell 'Over' or 'Short' correction was made without waiting for the second one to fall.★ Fifthly the German ships were on the whole better protected, their propellant charges were far safer, and their magazine drill and equipment greatly superior (a benefit gained from the *Seyd-*

★There is still some doubt whether at Jutland the Germans did use a 'ladder' system, whereby several salvos were in the air simultaneously and a correction was made as soon as one of them crossed the target. Professor Marder is confident that they did so (*Dreadnought*, III, 2nd Ed. p. 196 *note*), and the Grand Fleet Gunnery and Torpedo Memoranda on Jutland say (p. 29) that some sort of ladder system was used by them to find the range. On the other hand John Campbell's very thorough research into all the surviving German gunnery reports provides no supporting evidence for this. In particular the *Lützow*'s gunnery officer Commander Paschen wrote in the *Marine Rundschau* of May 1926 that he did not use a 'ladder' system. What is beyond doubt is that after Jutland the British, believing the German system was superior, issued new 'Spotting Rules' ordering its adoption. Campbell to Roskill 20th April 1979.

litz's narrow escape in the Dogger Bank action). Sixthly, though the performance of German heavy shells was by no means perfect, it was far better than that of the British lyddite filled AP shells, which too often burst on impact with armour plate instead of penetrating well inside a ship before bursting. Seventhly mention must again be made of the inefficiency of Beatty's signal organisation – for which the responsibility must rest chiefly with the unfortunate Ralph Seymour.

One other failure must be admitted, namely that for all Beatty's efforts to improve the Battle Cruisers' gunnery performance, despite the inevitable difficulties produced by his being based on Rosyth, it was (with the exception of the *Queen Mary* which enjoyed the great benefit of being fitted with Arthur Pollen's 'Argo' fire control system) definitely inferior to that of Jellicoe's battleships, as recorded by Professor Marder;[*] but direct comparison is highly misleading, since the conditions under which the two forces engaged the enemy were totally different. During the battle cruiser action, and especially during the 'Run to the South', the rate of change of range was constantly varying, very high and probably beyond the capacity of the Dreyer Fire Control Tables to cope with. It is noteworthy that the *Tiger* scored her hits when the range was temporarily constant (i.e. nil rate of change). On the other hand when Jellicoe's battleships came into action the rate of change was either low or constant, so greatly simplifying fire control.[†][18a]

We saw earlier how Chatfield retained overall responsibility for the gunnery efficiency of the BCF – even after Bentinck had become Beatty's Chief of Staff. This curious arrangement,

---

[*]The fire control systems fitted in the British battle cruisers were as follows:—

Lion and *Princess Royal* had 'Argo Towers' i.e. the gyro stabilised 9 foot Barr and Stroud rangefinder and bearing indicator mounting, and Mark III Dreyer Fire Control Tables. *Queen Mary* probably also had an 'Argo Tower' and certainly had both the Mark IV Argo Clock and Mark II Dreyer Table. *Tiger* had an 'Argo Tower' and a Mark IV Dreyer Table. *New Zealand* had a Mark I Dreyer Table but it is uncertain whether she had the 'Argo Tower'. *Indefatigable* does not appear to have had a Dreyer Table or Argo Tower. By 1914 the Argo Clock Mark IV was also fitted in the battleships *Orion*, *Audacious* (sunk 27th Oct. 1914), *Ajax*, *Centurion* and *King George V*. I am indebted to Mr. Jon T. Sumida of the University of Chicago for the foregoing information.

[†]See Map 5, page 170

which meant in effect that the Flag Captain also acted as Fleet Gunnery Officer, resulted in Chatfield arguing fiercely against any suggestion that Evan-Thomas's ships, or indeed any Grand Fleet battleships, had shot better than his own ships. He repeatedly insisted that *all* the troubles suffered by the battle cruisers derived from the inefficient shells provided to them, ignoring that the battleships of course had shells of similar design. We will revert later to Chatfield's impassioned defence of the BCF's gunnery.

When Jellicoe received the Galatea's sighting report at 2.55 p.m. he increased speed and altered towards the Horns Reef. On receiving the Lion's report of five enemy battle cruisers he increased to 20 knots – the maximum at which accurate station keeping was possible. His fleet was disposed in six columns each of four ships (a Division) with the flagship *Iron Duke* leading the third column from the port wing. Jellicoe urgently needed reports from which he could deduce the bearing from the *Iron Duke* and course of the High Seas Fleet in order that he might deploy from his cruising formation into the accepted battle formation of single line ahead; but from just before 4.0 p.m. until 4.38 he received no information except that the battle cruisers were in action. The Southampton's report of 4.38 was the first news of Scheer's presence received by Jellicoe, and at 4.51 he told the Admiralty that 'Fleet action [is] imminent'. Unfortunately Beatty's 4.45 report of sighting Scheer, passed through the *Princess Royal* because the Lion's wireless had been put out of action, reached Jellicoe in such mutilated form as to suggest that 26 to 30 enemy battleships were present. Between 4.38 and 5.0 p.m. Jellicoe received five reports, three of them from the *Southampton*; but the value of the latter was reduced by her Dead Reckoning (DR) position being in error. A 'second silence' of 40 minutes followed, during which Jellicoe's anxiety increased, since he was plainly getting uncomfortably close to the enemy with no indication of the best direction in which to deploy. Then at 5.33 came the first visual link with Beatty already mentioned. Unfortunately both he and Jellicoe were subject to errors in Dead Reckoning – Beatty actually being some 7 miles to the west of his DR position and Jellicoe 4½ miles south-east of his. Thus Jellicoe actually sighted Beatty on his starboard bow instead of right ahead as he had expected; and Jellicoe realised that the still invisible enemy was probably to the west of the Grand Fleet and some six miles nearer than anticipated. Shortly after 6 o'clock Jellicoe asked Beatty 'Where is enemy's Battle Fleet?'; but the reply given was merely 'Enemy battle cruisers bearing south-east' – which was not much help to the C-in-C. Ten minutes later Jellicoe repeated his question. Meanwhile Beatty had altered course to the east to pass across the front of the Grand Fleet. At 6.14, on sighting Hipper and Scheer's leading ships he signalled 'have sighted enemy's Battle Fleet bearing SSW' but gave no course. Jellicoe now had to deploy quickly or be caught at a serious disadvantage. After a few moments thought he decided to deploy to the eastward – that is with his port wing column (1st Division under Admiral Jerram) leading and the other divisions executing successive 90 degree turns to port and then to starboard in order to follow in Jerram's wake.* Rivers of ink have been spilt over the question whether this was the best deployment, but nearly all students of the battle – except the brothers Captain A. C. and Vice-Admiral K. G. B. Dewar (of whom more later) and Churchill (who accepted the Dewars' opinion too uncritically) – agree that it was by far the best manoeuvre possible; for it placed the Grand Fleet right across Scheer's line of advance ('crossing his T' in tactical parlance), so enabling an immense concentration of fire to be brought to bear on the German van.

There is some evidence that Beatty expected Jellicoe to deploy on the 4th Division (Admiral Sturdee, who was in fact critical of the decision to deploy on the 1st Division). Not long after the battle Arthur Pollen visited Beatty and in course of their discussion he drew two rough sketches, the upper one showing the deployment actually ordered and the lower one the deployment he had expected.[19] But the upper one is incorrect as it shows the 1st Division turning 90 degrees to port (as did all the other divisions at the start of the deployment) instead of steaming straight ahead as was actually done. The lower sketch shows Beatty himself ahead of the 4th Division (Sturdee) at 6.15, which suggests that he expected to lead Sturdee's ships, while those to port and starboard of them circled around and took station behind them.† Two

*See Map 5, page 170

†The sketch bears Beatty's initials but unfortunately is not dated. My view is that it was produced in late July or early August 1916 (see below pages 192-3)

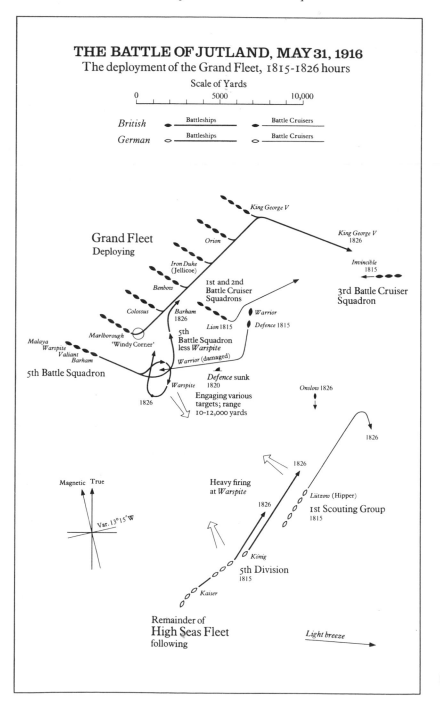

THE BATTLE OF JUTLAND, MAY 31, 1916
The deployment of the Grand Fleet, 1815-1826 hours

Scale of Yards

0   5000   10,000

| | British | Battleships | Battle Cruisers |
| | German | Battleships | Battle Cruisers |

King George V

Grand Fleet
Deploying

Orion

King George V
1826

Iron Duke
(Jellicoe)

Invincible
1815

3rd Battle Cruiser
Squadron

Benbow

1st and 2nd
Battle Cruiser
Squadrons

Colossus

Barham
1826

Warrior

Defence 1815

Lion 1815

5th
Battle Squadron
less *Warspite*

Marlborough

Malaya
Warspite
Valiant
Barham

'Windy Corner'

Warrior (damaged)

5th Battle Squadron

Defence sunk
1820

Onslow 1826

Warspite

1826

Engaging various
targets; range
10-12,000 yards

1826

Magnetic   True

Heavy firing
at *Warspite*

1826

1826

Lützow (Hipper)

1st Scouting Group
1815

Var. 13°15'W

1826

König

5th Division
1815

Kaiser

Remainder of
High Seas Fleet
following

Light breeze

pieces of evidence lend some support to the view that at the time of deployment Beatty was further east than is shown in the plan in Jellicoe's book *The Grand Fleet*. Captain Pound of the *Colossus*, the leading ship of the 5th Division, wrote in his report on the battle '6.4 p.m. First Battle Cruiser Squadron right ahead, 2 miles, firing', and Admiral Burney in the *Marlborough* (commander 6th Division) recorded that 'at about this time [probably 6.9 p.m.] the Battle Cruisers who appeared to be ahead of the leading division, turned to starboard as if to cross the enemy's T'.[20] On the other hand Sir Julian Corbett's track charts, which are probably the most reliable as regards British ships' movements, show the *Lion* ahead of the *Colossus* and on an easterly course at 6.08-6.09 and altering to ESE a minute or two later.[21] The only possible conclusion appears therefore to be that Beatty's memory about his position at the time of deployment cannot be firmly accepted as correct.

What is certain is that at 6.7 Beatty altered to starboard and steered to take up his ordained station in a fleet action ahead of the leading ship of the Battle Fleet. This had the unfortunate effect of his funnel smoke interfering with the battleships' vision, and of forcing Jellicoe to reduce speed in order to allow the battle cruisers to get clear. At 6.15 the 1st Cruiser Squadron (Arbuthnot) suddenly appeared on Beatty's port bow, dashing ahead to find and deal with the enemy's cruisers. This forced Beatty to make a sharp alteration to port to allow them to pass ahead of him. But Arbuthnot came under concentrated fire from the leading German ships, and at 6.20 his flagship the *Defence* blew up with the loss of all 900 of her company. Her consort the *Warrior* narrowly escaped the same fate – for reasons to be explained shortly.

Meanwhile Hood's 3rd Battle Cruiser Squadron had sighted Hipper's ships and turned to a parallel course to the south-east of the deploying Battle Fleet and ahead of Beatty. A sharp engagement ensued at about 9,000 yards range and the *Invincible* and *Inflexible* scored 8 hits (most of them from the *Invincible*) on the *Lützow* and *Derfflinger*. But they too came under concentrated fire, and at 6.33, the moment when Beatty reached his position ahead of the Battle Fleet, the *Invincible* received a number of hits (probably 5) and blew up with the loss of 1,026 of her crew, only six of whom survived.

To shift our gaze from these dramatic events ahead of the

deploying battle fleet to the other end of the British line Evan-Thomas saw that it was quite impossible for him to take up his primary position on the engaged bow of the leading battleship, so steered for the alternative position laid down for him at the rear of the line; and there the most powerful of the battle squadrons remained for the rest of the day – an example of the deadening rigidity imposed by the GFBOs. While manoeuvring to take up this position the *Warspite*'s helm jammed and she described two complete circles, so attracting heavy German fire at the point which came to be known as 'Windy Corner'.[22] The damage suffered by the *Warspite* and her inability to steer properly caused Evan-Thomas to order her to return to base; but her gyrations saved the badly damaged *Warrior* from suffering the fate of the *Defence*, though she had to be sunk by our own forces next day after an effort to tow her home had failed. All her company were saved.

Although Jellicoe's deployment, ordered at 6.15 p.m., was not complete until some 25 minutes later firing became general at a range of about 12,000 yards between 6.30 and 6.40. In this phase of the battle the British ships had the light in their favour for the first time, and the rate of change of range was small; so it is not surprising that they got the best of the encounter. They scored 23 hits on their opponents and received only 20 in return – of which no less than 13 were on the *Warspite*. Fourteen of the hits obtained by the British can confidently be credited to the battle cruisers – 12 of them to Hood's squadron. But at 6.40 p.m., when firing died away only about 2½ hours of daylight remained.

When Scheer discerned the flash of heavy guns to the north and the dim shapes of many battleships barring his path he must have received a very unpleasant shock; for he had no idea that the Grand Fleet had descended on him like an avalanche. At 6.33 he ordered a 'battle turn-away' together of 180 degrees – a manoeuvre which he had practised in order to cope with a critical situation such as had now arisen. He also ordered his destroyers to attack the Grand Fleet with torpedoes and cover his retirement with a smoke screen. Ten minutes later he had disappeared to the south-west and firing ceased. Though some British ships did observe Scheer's about turn none of them reported it to Jellicoe.

In a lecture on the Battle of Jutland I named the 'timidity' of Jellicoe in following up his initial success at this time as the second of the four chief reasons why 'victory slipped through our fingers'.[23] Professor Marder disagrees with that judgment, and I now feel that 'timidity' was too strong a word and would substitute 'centralisation and caution';[24] but broadly speaking I stand by my criticism of the C-in-C. We saw earlier how in the Dogger Bank action Beatty's intentions were frustrated by the discovery that the historic signal to 'Engage the enemy more closely' had been deleted from the signal book, and how it was thereafter reinstated. But there was another historic signal which had also disappeared by 1914, but which had been used to great effect in the past – notably by Anson off Cape Finisterre in 1747 and Hawke at Quiberon Bay twelve years later – namely the 'General Chase'. Ardent pursuit of a retreating enemy is surely axiomatic if a decisive success is to be achieved in war; but such a concept was wholly foreign to the principles enshrined in the GFBOs. Though it must be admitted that a 'General Chase' would have been inappropriate on 31st May 1916, and might well have produced chaos on the British side, a signal ordering something like 'Divisional Commanders act independently in pursuit of the enemy' might surely have reaped a great reward. Sir Julian Corbett evidently considered such a possibility when writing the Official History, but concluded that 'in the prevailing atmospheric conditions and so late in the day, co-ordination between independent squadrons would have been impossible . . . The risk of independent squadrons being overwhelmed individually by a concentrated enemy would have been very great. . . .'[25] In quoting that opinion it is, however, justifiable to remark that Corbett was a personal friend of Jellicoe, who in turn greatly admired his work. To me it seems that the official historian sometimes went too far in his endeavour to shield Jellicoe from criticism – so much so that, as will be told later, his account of the battle infuriated Beatty and Chatfield.

Whatever may have been the arguments for and against an ardent pursuit the issue is academic, because Jellicoe declined any such action. Maintaining a speed of only 17 knots (4 knots less than the maximum) he placed his fleet across the enemy's line of retreat to his bases; altering in two stages (at 6.44 and 6.55) further to the south. His Divisions were now in *échelon* so that they would mask each other's fire – if contact was regained.

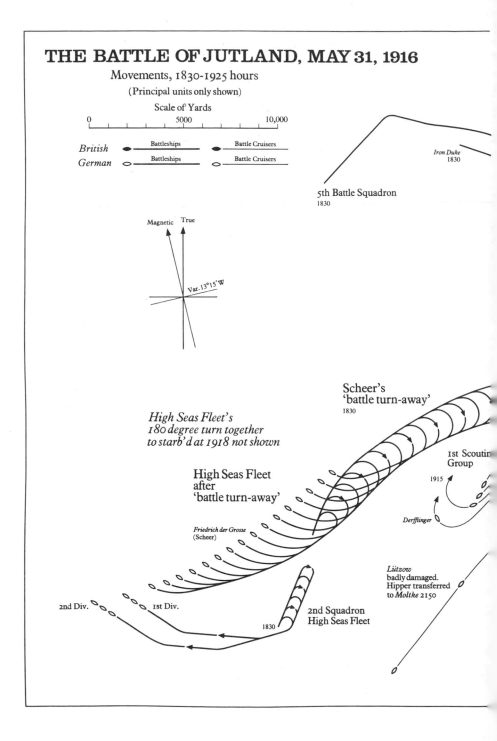

THE BATTLE OF JUTLAND, MAY 31, 1916

Movements, 1830-1925 hours

(Principal units only shown)

Scale of Yards

0   5000   10,000

British   ● ——— Battleships   ● ——— Battle Cruisers
German   ○ ——— Battleships   ○ ——— Battle Cruisers

Iron Duke
1830

5th Battle Squadron
1830

Magnetic   True

Var. 13°15′W

Scheer's
'battle turn-away'
1830

*High Seas Fleet's
180 degree turn together
to starb'd at 1918 not shown*

1st Scoutin
Group

1915

High Seas Fleet
after
'battle turn-away'

Derfflinger

Friedrich der Grosse
(Scheer)

Lützow
badly damaged.
Hipper transferred
to *Moltke* 2150

2nd Div.   1st Div.

2nd Squadron
High Seas Fleet

1830

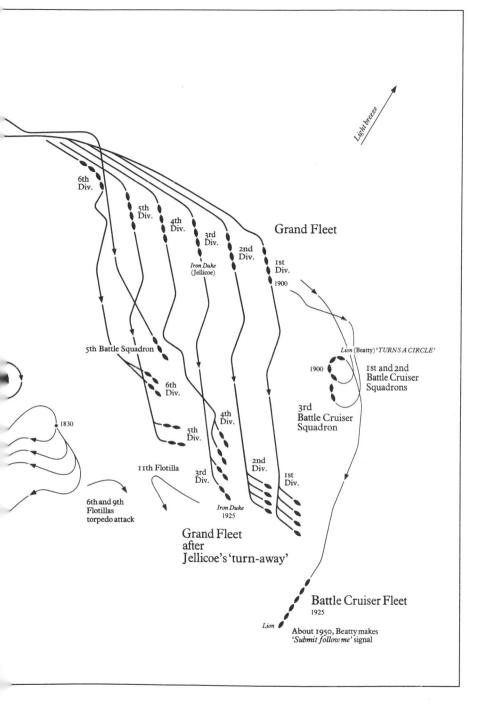

Light breeze

6th Div.

5th Div.

4th Div.

3rd Div.

2nd Div.

Iron Duke (Jellicoe)

1st Div.

1900

Grand Fleet

5th Battle Squadron

6th Div.

4th Div.

5th Div.

1830

11th Flotilla

3rd Div.

2nd Div.

1st Div.

6th and 9th Flotillas torpedo attack

Iron Duke 1925

Grand Fleet after Jellicoe's 'turn-away'

Lion (Beatty) 'TURNS A CIRCLE'

1900

1st and 2nd Battle Cruiser Squadrons

3rd Battle Cruiser Squadron

Battle Cruiser Fleet 1925

Lion

About 1950, Beatty makes 'Submit follow me' signal

At 6.55 Scheer executed another 180 degree turn to the north-east, obviously with the intention of breaking through the barrier of Jellicoe's battle fleet. At that time Beatty was about three miles ahead of the port wing column of the Grand Fleet (Jerram's 1st Division). He has been criticised for not regaining touch after Scheer's first turn-away; and that purpose would certainly have been a proper function for his light cruisers (the four ships of Napier's 3rd Light Cruiser Squadron were in close touch with him). But Beatty gave no such order.

There now took place one of the oddest events of these incident packed hours. At about 7.0 p.m. Beatty unquestionably turned a complete circle to starboard – for reasons which still remain obscure. He later vigorously denied having made any such movement, insisting that his track chart should show two successive 180 degree turns to starboard and port instead of a 360 degree turn.[26] Professor Marder discusses in some detail why Beatty turned a circle and why he insisted he had not done so.[27] I can only offer conjectural reasons why he carried out the manoeuvre and why he refused to admit it. As to the former, he may either have wanted the Battle Fleet to catch up with his weakened force, or at least ascertain how far away it was lest he should need its support; and as to the latter he may have wished to refute any suggestion that he had at this time turned his back on the enemy, or that he was not pursuing Scheer with the utmost vigour – as he wanted Jellicoe to do.*

To digress for a moment, Beatty evidently enjoyed telling Leslie later about the lighter incidents which took place onboard the *Lion* that day; for he reproduced some of them in his draft biography. One told how, during a lull in the fighting Beatty overheard from the bridge a conversation between two stokers who had come up for a breath of air. Their conversation ended by one of them saying 'I did always tell Maria not to 'ave him'; but the action was then resumed, so Beatty never learnt more about Maria's matrimonial troubles. At another time Beatty went briefly down to his sea cabin – to find that the ship's cat had given birth to a fine litter of kittens in his best hat! Presumably the premature *accouchement* was brought on by the ship's gunfire.[28]

---

*See Map 6, pages 174–5

By 7.15 p.m. the leading ships of the High Seas Fleet, and especially the 1st Scouting Group (Hipper) and the 3rd Battle Squadron (Behncke) were again under heavy fire at ranges of 11–14,000 yards. Again the British shooting was the better, 23 hits being scored on Hipper's squadron and 12 on Scheer's battleships. In return 2 hits on the *Colossus* were the only German successes. The situation Scheer now found himself in was desperate, and he ordered Hipper to carry out a suicidal charge ('Battle cruisers, at the enemy. Give them everything!' is Marder's translation of the order, which can hardly be bettered).[29] He also again ordered his destroyers to attack, and to screen his ships with smoke. Hipper ordered his badly battered force to carry out the charge order, but at 7.14 Scheer made a signal which in effect cancelled it. He then carried out another 'battle turn away together' and again disappeared. The arguments about pursuit already put forward on the occasion of his first retreat are perhaps now even more relevant. Jellicoe ordered Le Mesurier's 4th Light Cruiser Squadron and his own destroyers to repel the German destroyer attack; while he himself turned 90 degrees *away* to a south-easterly course – as he had always intended to do in such circumstances, and as the Admiralty had approved. No torpedo hits were obtained. Professor Marder quotes the view of Jellicoe's critics that the turn-away 'came at a very unfortunate moment' and produces five cogent defences for Jellicoe not turning *towards* the expected torpedoes.[30] The best argument in favour of the turn-away perhaps lies, however, in the fact that it resulted in many of the torpedoes running only very slowly by the time they reached the British ships, and so being easy to avoid, whereas if a turn-towards had been made the torpedoes would have arrived at their maximum speed. On the other hand we know that Plunkett, Beatty's Flag Commander, was 'horrified' at seeing the battle fleet turn away; and it is a fair conclusion that Chatfield and Beatty felt the same way.

There now remained about 1½ hours of daylight, with visibility some 6 miles to the west but less to the east. At 7.35 and 7.40 Jellicoe made two big turns (together 180 degrees) in the supposed direction of Scheer, and at 8.00 p.m. he turned a further 90 degrees towards. He also increased speed from 16 to 17 knots 'in order to close the enemy' remarks Marder; which does bring out nicely how slow and cautious his earlier actions had been. Beatty's frustration now came to a boil and at 7.47

he wirelessed to Jellicoe 'Submit van of battleships follows battle cruisers. We can then cut off whole of enemy's battle fleet'. A glance at the charts of the situation at this time shows very clearly how, in Marder's words, Beatty's idea was 'not without substance' – though he claims it was impossible of fulfilment.[31] Jellicoe received Beatty's signal at about 8.0 p.m. and ordered the 2nd Battle Squadron (Jerram), which was the closest to Beatty, to follow the battle cruisers. The charts show that in fact Jerram *was* following Beatty between 7.45 and 8.0 p.m., with their mean courses slightly converging;[32] and as Jerram did not know either Beatty's or the enemy's position he held to the course he was already steering. Chatfield later declared that Jerram could easily have found the battle cruisers had he tried to do so; but with some 5 knots less speed than Beatty's ships it is unlikely that he could have caught up with him – unless of course Beatty reduced speed. At any rate Jerram's inactivity infuriated Beatty. Leslie recorded what he must have learnt from Beatty, that he asked for Jerram to be Court-Martialled, which was very rightly refused; but at their first meeting after Jutland he apparently cut him stone dead.[33]

The final encounter between the two main fleets soon followed on Beatty's abortive attempt to initiate a pursuit. At 7.45 Scheer altered from a south-westerly to a southerly course, and Beatty was converging on the head of the German line. This time he ordered the 3rd Light Cruiser Squadron (Napier) to scout ahead of him, and his flagship soon made contact. Scheer at once turned 90 degrees away. At about 8.23 Beatty sighted his old adversary the 1st Scouting Group again, and opened fire at a range of some 10,000 yards, inflicting still more damage on the *Seydlitz* and *Derfflinger*. Professor Marder remarks that Hipper was saved by the fortuitous appearance of the six old *Deutschland* class battleships of the 2nd Squadron under Admiral Mauve; but the records of the five ships of that squadron which survived the battle show that they did not fire a shot at this time, though they were certainly fired on by Beatty's ships[34] – which makes this encounter perhaps the most confusing of the whole battle. However, one cannot but regret that at this moment Jerram's four powerful ships (*King George V* class) were not with Beatty, since they could probably have wiped out the *Deutschlands*. At 8.40 Beatty ceased fire. There is no doubt that, as Professor Marder has pointed out, several good opportunities were lost in this phase.[35] The most lamentable occurred when two light cruisers scouting ahead of the 2nd BS sighted and reported three battleships – actually belonging to Admiral Schmidt's 1st Squadron. Jerram, believing them to be Beatty's ships, cancelled the intended torpedo attack by the light cruisers. Commodore Hawksley, who commanded the Battle Fleet's destroyers, also sighted these enemies but forebore to attack – for what now appear to be highly inadequate reasons. Lastly these brief encounters turned Scheer away from the Horns Reef, so depriving Jellicoe of his last chance to force a decisive engagement before dark. The leading ships of the two main fleets, both of which were in single line ahead, were then only about 6 miles apart and steering converging courses. So Scheer had another narrow escape. But the tale of opportunities lost through British mistakes was by no means ended.

As Beatty and his battle cruisers played no significant part in the events of the short but portentous night of 31st May-1st June we will here pass over them rapidly. Jellicoe at once rejected the idea of seeking a battle between heavy ships at night as altogether too chancy a business, and moreover one for which the British fleet was neither trained nor equipped. He hoped and intended to renew the engagement at daylight.

One of the points on which Beatty came in later for criticism was the request signalled to the *Princess Royal* from the *Lion* just as it was getting dark asking for the Challenge and Reply for the night, which had got lost in the flagship. For a long time Beatty's critics held that this 'indiscretion' gave away the British secret signals to German ships only a few miles away. We do not know what caused the loss of the secret signal data in the *Lion*, but even allowing for the oft-proven inefficiency of her signal department, it is reasonable to suppose that it occurred through action damage. When Jellicoe learnt about the incident he described the *Lion*'s action as 'idiotic';[36] while someone on Beatty's side (probably Chatfield) sarcastically commented that to read a signal made by shaded lamp from astern was as difficult as to see a man's waistcoat buttons from behind.[37] In any case the argument is fruitless because Professor Marder has found evidence from German sources that they knew the British recognition signals much earlier in the day – though no light is thrown on how they came by this knowledge.[38]

At 9.16 p.m. Beatty received Jellicoe's signal that the course for the fleet during the night was to be south, and he decided that it would be neither 'desirable nor proper' to close the German battle fleet during the dark hours. He was at this time directly ahead of Jellicoe and well placed to prevent Scheer slipping home across his front. At 9.27 Jellicoe ordered his destroyers to mass astern of the battle squadrons as a rearguard and an obstacle to an escape across his stern. Though some doubt exists whether this order became known to the Germans the probability is that it did not.[39]

There were four possible routes by which Scheer might avoid the British minefields and return to his bases. Jellicoe rightly rejected a dash for the Kattegat, which was much the longest, and expected him to try for the route between the Friesian Islands and the southern edge of the minefields – despite it being the second longest. Jellicoe's course covered the approach to this 'Ems route' effectively, but left the two possible routes by the gap in the minefields and round their northern edge by the Horns Reef and Amrun Channel uncovered.[40] Shortly after 9.0 p.m. Scheer altered course direct for Horns Reef, then 85 miles away.

The clearest and most graphic description of the movements which now took place is that by Langhorne Gibson and Admiral Harper. They describe the two fleets as steaming 'down the sides of a very long, very slender V. . . . Tiny factors and no human plans, caused Jellicoe to arrive at the bottom of the V and pass through the junction point [at 11.30 p.m.] minutes before the German ships arrived. The V became an X – the courses of the fleet crossed and . . . from the hour of midnight onward, they began to draw apart'.[41]

Professor Marder's account of the seven phases into which that hectic night's events can be divided, of the lost opportunities for torpedo attacks, of German efficiency in recognition and night fighting, of the many examples of enemies being sighted but not reported to Jellicoe cannot be bettered. His conclusion is that 'The High Seas Fleet had passed through . . . an area occupied by scores of British destroyers without serious opposition. . . .'[42] Nor can his description of the flotilla actions as 'disastrously ineffective' be challenged.[43] What makes the story still sadder is that Room 40 produced conclusive evidence that Scheer *was* making for the Horns

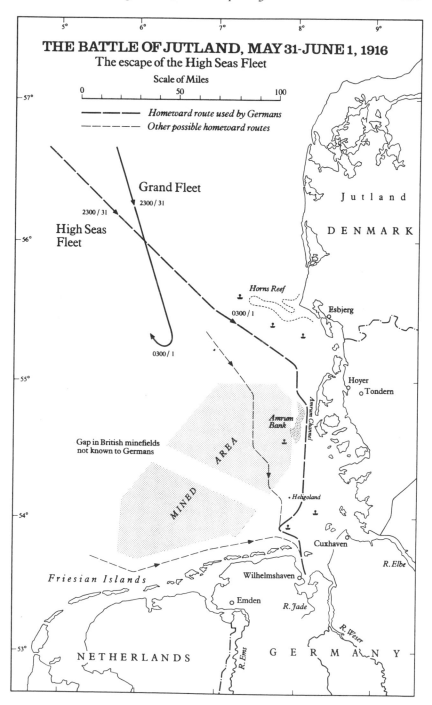

THE BATTLE OF JUTLAND, MAY 31-JUNE 1, 1916
The escape of the High Seas Fleet

Scale of Miles

0   50   100

——— · ——— *Homeward route used by Germans*

— — — — *Other possible homeward routes*

57°

Grand Fleet

2300 / 31

2300 / 31

High Seas
Fleet

56°

J u t l a n d

D E N M A R K

Horns Reef

0300 / 1

Esbjerg

0300 / 1

55°

Hoyer
o Tondern

Amrum
Bank

Amrum Channel

Gap in British minefields
not known to Germans

M I N E D   A R E A

Heligoland

54°

Cuxhaven

R. Elbe

Friesian Islands

Wilhelmshaven

o Emden

R. Jade

R. Weser

53°

N E T H E R L A N D S

R. Ems

G E R M A N Y

Reef channel; but the Admiralty either failed to pass this vital information to Jellicoe or (in one case) passed it on in a form which was neither clear nor emphatic enough. What I called this 'astonishing failure of the Admiralty' and Marder calls 'criminal neglect' by them are certainly not overstatements.[44] One vital message (timed 10.41 p.m.) *was* passed to Jellicoe fairly clearly but was ignored by him because he remembered the earlier blunder about Scheer's flagship being still in port; while a quite recent message (timed 9.58 p.m.) had given an obviously erroneous position for the German battle fleet and so vitiated still more his confidence in the Intelligence signalled by the Admiralty. Though one must admit that the pyrotechnics which flared up repeatedly astern of the Grand Fleet, moving gradually from west to east, could have given Jellicoe a broad hint that he was covering the wrong route he did not interpret them in that manner; and I for one cannot criticise him on that score when such egregious blunders were made in Whitehall.

Professor Marder dismisses the possible effect of fatigue on the senior officers concerned in this night's events. Though obviously impossible to quantify I am inclined to think he underrates its effects. The cumulative effects of long hours of strain, the terrific blast and concussion of ships' gunfire, and the explosions of enemy shells must surely produce numbing shock – even on the strongest mind and body. I think it takes little account of the realities of a long drawn out battle such as we are discussing to admit 'the extreme mental and physical exhaustion of the officers' but to declare it 'risky to make too much of the fatigue aspect'.[45] A fresh, alert and lively mind in a fully fit body (if such a state were possible by 10.0 p.m. on 31st May) might surely have realised what was going on to the north of the Grand Fleet without any signals to prod the recipient into action.

By 2.0 a.m. on 1st June the eastern sky began to lighten. An hour later Scheer reached the Horns Reef – battered and shaken and in no condition to renew the battle, but safe. The badly damaged *Lützow*, Hipper's flagship, was sunk by her own escorting destroyers, after taking off 1,250 survivors, at 2.0 a.m. The sun rose at 3.09 and Beatty's first thought was to sweep to the *south-west* – the direction in which he still believed the enemy to be located. Soon after 11.0 a.m. Jellicoe headed for Scapa Flow, which he reached on the afternoon of

2nd. He refuelled his ships and was soon ready for sea again. Admiral Chalmers has recorded how during the forenoon of 1st June Beatty came wearily into the *Lion*'s charthouse, sat down and closed his eyes. He then repeated the remark made to Chatfield when the *Queen Mary* blew up about there being 'something wrong with our bloody ships', opened his eyes and said 'And there is something wrong with our system'.[46] There was indeed, as will be discussed shortly. At 9.0 a.m. on the 2nd the Battle Cruiser Fleet entered the Firth of Forth. Jellicoe had only learnt of the loss of three battle cruisers on the morning after the battle – which shows how difficult it was for him (or anyone else) to observe what was actually happening – except in his immediate vicinity. Jellicoe was soon on the telephone to get more news from Beatty; but according to Leslie all the latter could say as each of the lost ships' names was mentioned was 'Sunk! Sunk! Sunk!' He left Jellicoe, Leslie remarks, 'to make all comment, which was perhaps contained in one word in his famous despatch – "unpalatable".'[47] Leslie also tells a curious story of how Ethel was rung up several times on 31st May by a person giving the name of Rothschild who asked questions such as 'How is the battle going?' and 'How is your dear husband?' She, however, remembered the way the first news of Waterloo was said to have reached London and refused to give any answers. What Beatty certainly did soon after reaching harbour was to write long and intimate letters about the battle to his sister 'Trot' Courage and to Dean Baillie, the old friend of the family mentioned earlier. When Leslie tried to recover those letters for use in his biography Mrs. Courage replied that 'David and I were like twins and when anything went wrong with either of us we always rushed to each other'; and that was exactly what Beatty had done after Jutland. She could only remember that her brother had written of the battle in terms of 'a famous Hunt where his 2nd horse never came up in time, and so he could not kill his fox – and if he had it would have been the most wonderful Hunt in History. He knew I would understand what he meant'.[48] The metaphor needs no elucidation.

Dean Baillie wrote that Beatty's letter to him was 'one of the tragedies of my life'; for in it Beatty had 'poured out his whole heart to me', and at great length. He felt that 'the letter was so confidential' that he could not 'possibly show it to anyone', not even to his wife. So he locked it away, and did not look for it until he was appointed Dean of Windsor. Then a very thorough search was made, but it was ñever found. The Dean considered that it had been stolen and wondered if the Secret Service had been at work. In the same letter the Dean recalled a visit to the *Lion* a short time before Jutland, and how he had then met 'a large number of Senior Officers of the fleet', almost all of whom 'expressed anxiety because they said that, great sailor as he was, Jellicoe had, as he grew older, become over-cautious. And they were all terrified lest David's Fleet should catch the German Fleet and that then Jellicoe would not come up in time'. He confirmed what other sources remark – that Beatty 'never said a word of criticism about Jellicoe'; but he had remembered and 'read into his letter what these officers had said to me'. Baillie also told Leslie (in confidence) that he 'disliked his [Beatty's] wife very much', and had indeed 'tried to persuade him not to marry her'.[49]

If Beatty's initial reaction was one of depression and of anger over missed opportunities his resilience quickly reasserted itself; for Walter Cowan wrote to Leslie that 'when we got back to Rosyth after the Jutland fighting . . . I was struck by the high-hearted, dauntless way he took it all and was already planning for "next time" and where he could look for reinforcements . . . Lady Beatty did everything to lighten his burden and to help him on his way'.[50] Though Leslie has confirmed that it was to Ethel that he first turned for consolation at this time there is no doubt that their drawing together again proved only temporary. Beatty must also have been cheered to get a congratulatory letter from Lord Fisher, though he knew well enough that the old admiral now had no influence and no future. Fisher wrote that although he knew no more than had appeared in the newspapers that was 'sufficient to make me feel very glorious as to the magnificent courage of all concerned and that when you got them by the throat you didn't let them go. . . .' Beatty replied gratefully, but admitted that 'To be so near and yet so far was gall and wormwood after the losses we had sustained. But they were not in vain and were justifiable. They suffered more than we did. . . .' – he concluded, too optimistically.[51]

The story of the Admiralty's bungling of the initial *communiqué* on Jutland and how Churchill had to be brought in to help draft a more realistic assessment of the results is well known and need not be repeated. The British losses of ships and men were far heavier than those of the Germans – 14 ships (111,000 tons) as against 11 (62,000 tons), and 6,784 casualties (6,097 killed) as against 3,058 (2,551 killed). Yet only 8 British capital ships suffered appreciable damage as against 10 German ships; and on 2nd June Jellicoe had 24 undamaged capital ships to Scheer's 10. Plainly the strategic situation was unchanged and the battle confirmed British dominance in home waters – as Scheer admitted in his despatch to the Kaiser. Though the sense of disappointment was widespread in the Grand Fleet its morale had not suffered at all. The disappointment arose because the British people had been led to expect another Trafalgar, and the Royal Navy had convinced itself that it could and would win such a victory. That there was resentment in the BCF against the Battle Fleet is certainly true, though when I tackled Lord Chatfield on that issue he was evasive.[52] It was not entirely eliminated until the battle squadrons moved to Rosyth; but that runs ahead of the stage now reached in our story.

Professor Marder has analysed the failures and weaknesses in the Royal Navy revealed by Jutland so fully that – with two exceptions – there is no need to go into them in detail here. Communications in the fleet, both visual and wireless, certainly left much to be desired. Admiral Cunninghame Graham has pointed out in his memoirs and lectures the tremendous pressure which the centralized British system of tactical control placed on signal officers and their departments – exemplified by the fact that one flag signal was made every 2.4 minutes in the Battle Cruiser Fleet and one every 1.7 minutes in the Grand Fleet during the daylight action; and he comments that whereas the gunnery branch never expected to get more than 4 or 5% hits the signal staff had to achieve 100% accuracy.[53] Enemy reporting was extremely poor on the British side, with the outstanding exception of Commodore Goodenough; and in the night phase numerous sightings were never reported at all. That failure, together with the inefficiency of the British recognition signals, the lack of training in night fighting, the poor system of searchlight control and the shocking failure of the Admiralty to give Jellicoe all the excellent Intelligence they had, were the principal factors in bringing about Scheer's escape.

Professor Marder comments on the fact that initiative was 'strangely lacking' on the part of senior officers.[54] While I agree with that criticism I do not find it at all strange. As was told earlier the whole system of training junior officers in the *Britannia* and later at Osborne and Dartmouth Colleges was based on unquestioning discipline and absolute subordination to authority. More gold braid, we were taught, necessarily meant more wisdom; and any signs of originality were frowned on if not actively suppressed. This state of affairs lasted into my own time at the naval colleges (1917-20), and indeed until World War II. It is ironical that it was chiefly the impact of air power in that conflict which forced the navy to adopt tactical decentralization and to encourage initiative among quite junior officers. The reason was quite simple – that if officers waited for orders their ships would probably be sunk before they arrived.

The chief point on which I take issue with Professor Marder's 'Comparisons and Reflections' on Jutland lies in his treatment of the relative efficiency of the British and German ships' armour protection, and its possible effects on the loss of three of Beatty's battle cruisers. Marder remarks on the phenomenal 'toughness' of the German ships, and rightly says that their side, deck and turret armour was 'thicker and more extensive' than that fitted in our own ships.[55] So far so good; but he goes on to declare that 'There is at least no firm proof that the German armour was superior to British', and castigates what he calls 'the legend' of our battle cruisers' 'indifferent armour protection' – which ignores Beatty's grave concern over the failure of the *Lion*'s 5-inch side armour against a German 11-inch shell in the Dogger Bank action, referred to earlier. Marder also considers that even if British armour was 'indifferent to moderate' it probably was 'no more than a contributory factor' to the loss of the three ships on 31st May 1916. He also mentions the claim made in 1921 by Sir Eustace Tennyson-d'Eyncourt, the Director of Naval Construction, that armour plate salved from the German battleship *Baden* 'has not stood the test of the actual firing which our own armour is called upon to stand'. Apart from the fact that the evidence of the DNC, who was the official responsible for the design of our ships' protection, can hardly be regarded as impartial, the statements quoted above do not appear to be a fair summary of the trials carried out at Shoeburyness in the early 1920s against the *Baden*'s armour plates. Though the manufacture and testing of armour is a complicated story all the evidence of the 1914–18 war points to the inadequacy of our ships' protection as well as to the inefficiency of our armour-piercing shell; and the latter phenomenon reappeared in the war of 1939-45. The most recent study of the subject, by an officer who served on the Ordnance Board, concludes that it is 'beyond doubt' that we were fighting with inferior armour plate', and that author recalls that, as regards the *Baden* trials, though the plate was 'thickly coated with rust' it proved 'remarkably tough and consistent in its performance, and was more than a match for our new shells'.[56] Thus there is at the very least a possibility that penetration of the weak and inadequate British armour caused an internal explosion (e.g. in a secondary armament magazine) which spread quickly to the highly vulnerable main armament cordite supply system, and so blew up the ships; and that may have happened in the case of the *Hood* in 1941 as well as at Jutland. In sum there is no doubt that Beatty was right to point to the inadequacy of his ships' protection in 1915, and the whole question of ship design, including the manufacture and testing of armour plate, during the Fisher era at the Admiralty (e.g. his claim that 'speed is armour') is open to criticism.

To leave the subject of shell versus armour protection and turn to tactics Professor Marder remarks that he 'finds it extremely difficult to evaluate fairly Beatty's overall performance as a tactician', but declines 'to credit him with the highest grade of tactical excellence' – a conclusion with which I agree. There was too much wrong with Beatty's staff work – especially signalling – to enable posterity to include him among the greatest fleet handlers of the past.

Before leaving the question of Beatty's tactics it is essential to quote a letter which he wrote to Admiral Evan-Thomas, the commander of the 5th Battle Squadron, in very warm terms regarding the support he had given to the hard-pressed battle cruisers – if only because, as we shall see, the movements of that force later became a subject of fierce controversy between the two admirals. 'Just a line to thank you from the bottom of my heart' wrote Beatty in his own hand 'for your gallant and effective support on Wednesday. It was fine to see your squadron sail down as it did. I hope your good ships have not [been] too much knocked about . . . Your coming down in support and poor Bertie Hood's magnificent handling of His Squadron will remain in my mind for ever.

The old spirit is still alive and as bright as ever. I make out the enemy must have lost much more heavily than we are given credit for. Yours ever. . . .'[57] It will be noted that Beatty said no word about the widening of the distance between his and Evan-Thomas's forces, and the failure of the flagship to pass the signal to the *Barham* to alter course to the south-east by searchlight as well as by flags. After the war, when the Admiralty was preparing the various authorised accounts of Jutland Beatty took a very different line about Evan-Thomas's handling of his squadron – as will be told in a later chapter.

As to strategy, there can be no question that, whatever view one takes of Jellicoe's handling of the Battle Fleet on 31st May, he succeeded completely in maintaining British command of the *surface* waters of the North Sea; and his papers and correspondence leave no room for doubt that such was always his primary purpose. Jellicoe's critics have taken too little account of that achievement – though the remarks in Scheer's despatch that 'there can be no doubt that even the most successful outcome of a Fleet action in this war will not *force* England to make peace', and that 'A victorious end to the war within a reasonable time can only be achieved through the defeat of British economic life – that is, by using the U-boats against British trade' – surely justify the conclusion that Jellicoe's strategy cannot be impugned.[58]

A recent commentator on naval policy during the 20th century has described the consequences of producing increasingly large units which seems singularly applicable to the apogee of the Dreadnought battleship and the big gun, and so to the battle of Jutland. 'Military history and nature', writes Admiral J. H. F. Eberle, 'are full of examples of systems and organisations which have, through success, grown in size and power until such time as they have become so large that they have been unwieldy and vulnerable . . . If a single unit is so large and valuable that its loss would, of itself, be a major defeat then it is clearly unsound to place it at risk. Such limitation is a severe restraint on an operational commander's freedom of action. It is likely to limit their ability to take and hold the initiative, both vital ingredients of any offensive posture'.[59] One feels that the shade of John Jellicoe would whole-heartedly applaud such a view as representing the fundamental problem he was faced with on 31st May 1916.

CHAPTER NINE

Investigation and Reappraisal, June–December 1916

On 9th June Beatty wrote to Jellicoe more fully than he had been able to do immediately after the battle. He first offered the C-in-C his 'deepest sympathy in being baulked of your Great Victory which I felt was assured when you hove in sight [on 31st May]. I can well understand your feelings and that of the Battle Fleet, to be so near and miss is worse than anything.' The 'cussed weather', he argued too simply, 'defeats us every time' – in the Scarborough Raid operations, the Dogger Bank action 'and now this time.' 'It is heartbreaking for the fine fellows who have waited so patiently, so cheerfully for so long . . . It was unfortunate that our [DR] positions did not tally sufficiently accurately but that was a small matter if the weather had remained clear. Your sweep to the South [at night] was splendid and I made certain we should have them at daylight. I cannot believe now [how] the enemy got in to the north-eastward of you and feel that they must have tried the S.W. It was perhaps unfortunate that those [ships] who sighted the enemy to the Northward did not make reports, perhaps they did but I did not get them, but the wireless was not very good. It was shot away three times. . . .' All of which was too plainly written to console the C-in-C and defend his own actions. In the second part of this letter Beatty reported the state of his ships and when they would be fully ready again.[1]

A fortnight after Jutland the King spent three very full days visiting the fleet at Rosyth, Cromarty and Scapa Flow. He described to Queen Mary how he had 'been on bd [board] practically all the damaged ships', and confirmed that almost all of them 'would again be ready for sea by the end of the month'. 'The spirit of the fleet', he wrote, 'is even better than it was last year . . . this fight has bucked them all up and made them keener than ever to meet the enemy again.' His impressions of the two Admirals chiefly concerned were that

189

Jellicoe, who had actually just sent the Monarch 14 hand
written pages about Jutland,[2] 'was in excellent spirits', while
'Beatty is a splendid fellow . . . they love him in the fleet'.[3]
Though other evidence indicates that Jellicoe was deeply
disappointed by the outcome of the battle, and indulged in
self-reproach, too much should not be made of this, since it
derives either from Beatty himself or, in later years, from his
eldest son, who always regarded it as his filial duty to defend
the Admiral and propagate his point of view.[4]

Well before the King's visit to the fleet Jellicoe had set up a
number of committees to investigate and report on every
lesson and experience gained from the battle; while Beatty set
up a Battle Cruiser Fleet Gunnery Committee to study and
report on the causes of the weaknesses and failures exposed in
his ships.[5] Towards the end of June Jellicoe and Beatty
attended a conference in the Admiralty at which they pressed
the view, in face of Admiralty opposition, that better armour
protection was needed in the big ships. The final decision was
to fit one or two inches of additional armour over magazines
of existing ships and to strengthen the protection in those
which were building (the *R-class* battleships and the battle
cruisers of the *Renown* class). Beatty, however, considered that
the additional protection was inadequate and did not 'compensate for radical defects in design' which in his opinion the
battle had revealed. Though Beatty probably also had in mind
the damage suffered by the *Lion* in the Dogger Bank action,
when her armour protection had failed against 11- and 12-inch
shells, the loss of three of his battle cruisers at Jutland may
have been attributable to faults in the make-up of cordite
charges and in the drill used to get them from the magazines
to the guns rather than to inadequate armour protection.
British cordite charges were made up in four quarters, each of
which had an unprotected gunpowder 'igniter' at each end – a
highly dangerous practice, the sole justification for which was
that it saved turret crews from bothering about which way
round the charges were loaded into hoists and rammed into
the guns. The German cordite charges were far safer, being
made up in two halves, the front one protected by a light
metal container (which was consumed on the gun being fired),
while the rear one was in a brass case which sealed the breach
and was ejected after the gun had fired. Moreover the
emphasis placed by Beatty among others on achieving the

highest possible rate of fire resulted in thoroughly dangerous practices being adopted in the magazines and handing rooms – such as stacking charges at the bottom of the hoists. After Jutland some of the faults in British ammunition, such as the excessive number of igniters and their lack of protection, were remedied comparatively quickly. Flashtight revolving scuttles were also reintroduced between the handing rooms and magazines, and the latter were thus kept entirely sealed off from the turret hoists and gunhouses. Beatty's signal to Jellicoe of 2nd June recommending reversion to 'the original system of handing room supply scuttles' indicates that those essential safety devices had been removed, presumably in order to expedite ammunition supply and so increase the rate of fire.

Other changes, such as improving the stability of British cordite and the redesign of our armour-piercing shell took far longer to make. The need for new shells, filled with trotyl (TNT) like the German ones, instead of lyddite, was only reluctantly accepted by the Admiralty, and they did not begin to reach the fleet until the spring of 1918. That Britain was far behind Germany in developing and putting into practice the science of the chemistry of explosives, and also suffered from a grievously faulty system of proof-testing armour-piercing shells were defects for which a very heavy price was exacted. It is interesting here to remark how some years after the end of the war Admiral Madden – for all that he had served a long time as Chief of Staff to Jellicoe – wrote very critically to Admiral Dreyer about Jellicoe's responsibility as DNO 1905-7 and Controller of the Navy 1908-10 for the defective AP shell – 'because Lord J. had more to do with the gunnery material we used than any one man'.[6]

But in my view it is necessary to delve deeper in order to ascertain the reason for British inferiority in so many technical aspects. I believe the basic cause is to be found in the excessive dominance of the executive or 'line' officer over the specialist and the scientist, and in the inferior social status accorded to the latter. Though Beatty himself was representative of the type of officer who believed in the inherent superiority of the executive branch, which alone was entitled to take command of one of H.M. ships, he certainly did value greatly the services of his Fleet Engineer Officers, and so presumably those of the subordinate members of that branch.[7] Moreover after the war it was the Board of Admiralty of which he was the Service head which took long overdue action to improve the status of the navy's Engineer Officers.[8] He also appears to have been ahead of the times in appreciating what scientists could do for the navy, notably in the development of anti-submarine devices at Hawkcraig mentioned earlier. But with the Board of Admiralty then, and for many years to come, composed entirely of Executive Officers the apportionment of adequate weight to technical and scientific knowledge and expertise was certainly lacking in the upper ranks of the naval hierarchy before and during the 1914–18 war.

As regards fire control, Professor Marder claims that the German superiority in initial accuracy and rate of hitting on 31st May resulted in the matter being 'carefully investigated';[9] but that statement requires considerable qualification. It is true that the fitting of director firing (including for secondary armaments) was expedited, and that longer base – and so more accurate – rangefinders were introduced, though still of the 'coincidence type' already described. But the fundamental weakness of the Royal Navy's fire control derived from the adoption before the war of the Dreyer Table instead of the more accurate, automatic and stabilised system offered by Arthur Hungerford Pollen, mentioned earlier. As Dreyer was Jellicoe's Flag Captain, and was soon to become Director of Naval Ordnance under him as First Sea Lord, it was highly improbable, especially in the middle of a major war, that any steps would be taken to replace the system for whose introduction he had been responsible and which bore his name.

What the effects on Jutland might have been if most of the British heavy ships had been fitted with the Argo Clock is of course largely conjectural; but its obvious superiority to the system actually installed, together with the fact that the *Queen Mary*, which did the best shooting of Beatty's ships, was fitted with the Argo Clock Mark IV leaves one in little doubt that they would have been substantial.

It has already been told how Pollen visited Beatty at Rosyth soon after Jutland. The visit must have taken place before mid-August because on 20th of that month a paper by him reached the *Lion*. In it he showed considerable knowledge of the inside story of the events of 31st May, and re-stated what he saw to be the fundamental need in order to fight effectively at high speeds and long ranges. Though Pollen's case was clearly and cogently argued, and moderately expressed, Plunkett wrote 'Rubbish' at the bottom of it;* while another member of the staff (initials illegible) minuted that it showed 'there is a very serious leakage of confidential information to a totally unauthorised person', on reading which Plunkett passed the paper to Chatfield. He exploded and proposed that 'Mr. Pollen should be immediately arrested under the Defence of the Realm Act'; and he made some quite unjustifiable insinuations about how Pollen had obtained his information and with what purpose. He wanted him 'to be proceeded against through VABCF' (i.e. Beatty), but admitted that 'his rangefinder probably *is* better than ours [i.e. the Barr and Stroud coincidence instruments] and should be again experimented with'.[10] When the paper reached Beatty he must have smiled, because it is obvious that it was he who had given Pollen the information complained of! There is no record to show whether he told his staff that this was so, but as Pollen was not proceeded against presumably he must have calmed them down. Pollen also wrote a much longer paper on the subject of 'Fire Control' and sent Beatty a copy of it.[11] The admiral replied that he had read it 'with considerable interest', and agreed that 'an efficient Rangefinder is most desirable and the Argo Clock is undoubtedly superior to the Dreyer Table'; but he was wrong to say that 'our system permits us to manoeuvre freely without losing the range'. He considered the difficulty of 'taking ranges with the Rangefinders are so great under present conditions that we must learn to do without them' – a somewhat defeatist attitude. Beatty's letter makes it plain that a copy of Pollen's memorandum had gone to Jellicoe, but I have found no record of any actions being taken on it. However, there is evidence elsewhere that Jellicoe, for all his earlier support of Pollen, became irritated by his persistence.[12] The truth of the matter is that the real opportunity had been lost by the Admiralty before the war.[13]

To turn from Gunnery to Communications, which was certainly one of the weakest chinks in Beatty's armour, Admiral Cunninghame Graham, a very experienced Signal

---

*There is in the Drax papers a lot of evidence of his hostility to Pollen, but there is no indication of the reason for it.

Officer, has emphasised the tremendous pressure which the British system of centralised command placed on signal officers and their departments;[14] and Beatty's Flag Lieutenant Ralph Seymour again showed only too clearly that in battle he was not capable of carrying such a burden efficiently or of interpreting the Admiral's intentions correctly.

Communications leads naturally to Intelligence, which depends on them for collection and promulgation. At Jutland our Intelligence was handled with almost criminal ineptitude; and a vital lesson of the battle was the need for proper co-ordination between Operations and Intelligence. Under Admiral Hall Room 40 now became in effect an Operations Intelligence Centre rather than a cryptographic office, though it was not formally placed within the Naval Intelligence Division until 1917.[15] The stroke of good fortune whereby the German naval signal book came into the Admiralty's hands early in the war* was repeated in September 1916 through the recovery of the new and recently introduced German signal book from Zeppelin L32, after she had been shot down near Billericay, Essex by a British aircraft, with the loss of all her crew.[17]

We have seen how Jellicoe and Beatty had both firmly rejected the concept of night action well before Jutland, and how no training in that form of combat was therefore undertaken. Once the Germans had shown that they had efficient recognition signals, good illumination by star shell and a far superior searchlight control system, so enabling them to open rapid and accurate fire on a ship identified as enemy, we hastened to copy their equipment. But night action was still regarded as too chancy a business to justify acceptance of it, let alone deliberately seek such opportunities. All that was done in the revised orders issued after Jutland was to instruct Light Cruiser Squadrons to keep in touch with the enemy after dark. It was left to officers such as Chatfield, W. W. Fisher and Dudley Pound, all of whom had as Captains witnessed the devastating effect of German gunnery at night, to bring about the revolution which was to yield such great dividends in the many successful night actions fought in World War II.

It was told earlier how at Jutland enemy reporting was, with

*See page 87.

the striking exception of Commodore Goodenough, consistently poor; and how a large number of sightings made after dark were never reported at all. Professor Marder concludes that the fleet was 'badly trained' in reconnaissance work and enemy reporting.[18] But that indictment seems less than fair to Beatty, because ever since the Scarborough Raid of 16th December 1914 he had emphasised the need for constant and accurate enemy reporting; and as Goodenough certainly understood the need – and met it at Jutland – one may well ask why other junior Flag Officers and Captains did not show equal intelligence and initiative. That question inevitably leads one back to the extent to which those qualities were discouraged, if not actively suppressed, in British naval training from cadet time onwards.

The Grand Fleet Battle Orders were, very naturally, reviewed and reconsidered after Jutland, but the principle that a fleet action would be fought in single line ahead remained unchanged, and the amount of decentralisation permitted was small. It amounted to no more than the introduction of a signal which, with heavy qualifications, released Divisional Commanders from their rigid subordination to the C-in-C, and an encouragement to them to 'press on' at 'utmost speed' in pursuit of a retreating enemy . Jellicoe adhered firmly to the 'turn away' in face of a torpedo threat, but Beatty's constant pressure that *attack* by our own destroyers was the best defence did now gain acceptance. A new signal for deployment on a centre column of the Battle Fleet was also introduced, and it is fair to guess that this also owed a good deal to Beatty – since he indicated to Pollen that he had expected Jellicoe to deploy in that manner on 31st May. Not until Beatty became C-in-C, Grand Fleet, were further changes made in the GFBOs, which remained excessively elaborate and all-embracing.[19]

At the Admiralty conference of 25th June it was agreed that our battle cruisers were 'no match' for the corresponding German ships, and that the 5th Battle Squadron was too slow to get away from the powerful German 3rd Battle Squadron (*König* class) – decisions which must have been gall and wormwood to Beatty.[20] The logical solution that the Grand Fleet and Battle Cruiser Fleet should work from the same base was also accepted, and preparations were made for the 1st, 2nd and 5th Battle Squadrons to move to Rosyth, while the 4th BS remained at Scapa with Jellicoe still flying his flag in the *Iron*

Duke. The battle cruisers were now enjoined not to get far
ahead of the battle squadrons and to avoid 'becoming seriously
engaged with superior forces'[21] – which annulled the tactical
principles on which Beatty had always worked, and provoked
him to ask what constituted 'superior forces'.[22] Jellicoe's
dislike of the term 'Battle Cruiser *Fleet*' also became apparent
at this time, because he considered it suggested 'a force distinct
from . . . the battle fleet'; and that again was precisely what
Beatty's methods had tended to make it. As to the 5th Battle
Squadron's future employment the Admiralty conference
came down on Jellicoe's side by declaring it to be a fast wing
of the battle fleet rather than a support for the BCF as Beatty
wanted. However, he did get his way a few weeks later when,
after the next German sortie, the 5th Battle Squadron moved
to Rosyth.

Though there is ample evidence both of Jellicoe's dislike of
the tendency of the BCF to regard themselves as the spearhead
of British striking power and of Beatty's determination to
make his force a *corps d'élite*, after Jutland the C-in-C did make
a strong effort to reduce, if not eliminate, the separatist
tendency between the two forces. Early in August, when
Beatty took the BCF to Scapa for a visit, Jellicoe arranged for
his ships to give Beatty's 'a tremendous reception' – followed
by intensive social interchanges, during which the only banned
subject was the recent battle. Though Beatty told his wife that
he was 'sure that it is all quite sincere' and was 'not being done
to order', the feeling in the Battle Squadrons that, as Admiral
Duff (sub-divisional commander of the 4th BS at Jutland) put
it, 'the BCF were swollen headed and truculent' and desired
'to annihilate the High Seas Fleet' with no more than 'just a
sufficient support of Battleships', certainly was fairly general. [23]
Only the full integration of both forces under one commander
and working from the same base could eliminate the inter-
necine strains; and that was not accomplished until six months
after Jutland.

By August Scheer was ready to make another attempt to
put his cautiously offensive strategy into effect; and he too had
been digesting the lessons of Jutland – the chief of which was
the extent to which he had been surprised by the sudden
appearance of Jellicoe's battle squadrons. For his next operation he therefore placed great emphasis on reconnaissance by
Zeppelins, four of which were to watch the waters between

Scotland and Norway while four more scouted ahead of his fleet. He also disposed two dozen submarines so as to guard his front and flanks, some close to the English coast, some in the southern North Sea and others off the Dogger Bank to cover his withdrawal.

At 9.0 p.m. on 18th August Scheer put to sea with 18 battleships, two battle cruisers and light forces to escort them. The 1st and 2nd Scouting Groups were stationed 20 miles ahead of his battle squadrons, and his intention was that the former should bombard Sunderland while his heavy ships provided close support. As so often before Room 40 was able to give warning of the impending sortie, and during the forenoon of 18th the Admiralty ordered Admiral Burney, who was acting as C-in-C while Jellicoe was trying to recuperate from the recent strains which had left him 'quite played out',[24] to concentrate in the Long Forties. Thus the British Grand Fleet was well out to sea before Scheer had left harbour. Beatty sailed from the Firth of Forth with six battle cruisers that evening, the Harwich Force was also ordered to sea in good time (doubtless another lesson derived from Jutland), and 25 submarines were disposed so as to catch the enemy. Jellicoe was at once recalled to duty, boarded a light cruiser which was waiting off Dundee, and took command of the Grand Fleet when it reached the rendezvous about 100 miles east of the River Tay in the early hours of 19th. This time the battle cruisers were stationed only 30 miles ahead of the C-in-C, and the 5th Battle Squadron was again under his orders. The whole fleet now moved south, but it was the Germans who got in the first blow when a U-boat torpedoed and sank one of Beatty's light cruisers.

At 6.15 a.m. the Admiralty told Jellicoe that the High Seas Fleet had been some 200 miles to the south-east of him an hour earlier; but the sinking of the light cruiser again aroused Jellicoe's fears of a submarine or mine trap, and he turned 180 degrees to the North 'till [the] situation [was] clear'. Four hours were thus lost, and it was 9.0 a.m. before Jellicoe resumed a southerly course. Sir Henry Newbolt, argues in the official history that it is unfair to criticise Jellicoe for his caution, because there was in fact still plenty of time for him to engage the enemy.[25] None the less his about-turn can hardly be described as an endeavour to bring the enemy to battle.

In the early afternoon an Admiralty message made it plain that Beatty and the High Seas Fleet would be only 40 miles apart at 2.0 p.m. The two opponents were now converging on courses at right angles to each other, and Jellicoe therefore increased to full speed. The weather was clear, plenty of time was in hand, and another fleet action appeared certain – in highly favourable conditions for the British. But a Zeppelin's report of the Harwich Force as heavy ships made Scheer believe he was about to achieve his long-held hope of catching part of the Grand Fleet isolated, and at 12.15 he turned to the south-east – away from the rapidly approaching British Fleet. Had Scheer held to his westerly course for another hour Jellicoe would have placed himself between him and his bases. It is highly ironical that an erroneous reconnaissance report should have saved the HSF from probable disaster. Shortly before 4.0 p.m. Jellicoe learnt that his opponent was well on the way home, and turned to the north. During the withdrawal another of Beatty's light cruisers was torpedoed by a submarine, and sank next morning. Although a British submarine torpedoed the battleship *Westfalen* early on 19th she got safely home; so the balance of losses was again in favour of the Germans. In fact the Harwich Force *did* sight the High Seas Fleet late in the evening, but could not gain a position of torpedo advantage. Tyrwhitt, who can certainly not be classed as over-cautious, rejected the idea of a night attack in bright moonlight; and the experiences of 31st May-1st June certainly suggest that to accept action in such circumstances would have been suicidal. Once again Beatty, and indeed all the Grand Fleet, returned to harbour in a state of bitter disappointment; while Scheer had reason to be satisfied with the performance of his U-boats. None the less it should be recorded that this was the last time the High Seas Fleet penetrated so far to the west. On 6th October resumption of attacks on merchant shipping was authorised by the German government, though the 'Prize Rules' were still supposed to be observed.

Caution was not at this time confined to the German surface fleet. On 13th September another conference took place on board Jellicoe's flagship. The events of 19th August had reinforced the C-in-C's chronic pessimism, and he foretold that more losses would be suffered if the Grand Fleet came further south than about 55½° North (the latitude of Horns Reef). Nor did Beatty disagree with that recommendation –

which the Admiralty 'accepted generally'.[26] Thus submarines and mines, rather than the heavy ships, came to dominate the war in the North Sea, on the surface of which a state of stalemate had been reached. On 18th-19th October Scheer made another brief sortie, but the Grand Fleet did not come south; and that was the last foray made by the HSF as a whole until April 1918. Early in November Scheer sent out a small number of his big ships to try and rescue two U-boats which had gone ashore on the coast of Jutland. A British submarine torpedoed two of his battleships on their way home – which caused the Kaiser to be highly critical of his C-in-C for risking so much in so small a cause.

While these events were happening at sea a new wave of mistrust of the Admiralty was generating in London. Two raids by German destroyers into the eastern Channel in late October and November fuelled the flames of criticism – though they actually achieved little. The Admiralty was also in serious trouble with the various high level bodies set up to try and resolve the conflict between that department and the War Office over the manufacture of aircraft and engines and the control of the new arm. It came to a head in October 1916 when Lord Curzon, the President of the Air Board, made a virulent attack on the Admiralty's attitude of non-co-operation and Balfour, for all his dialectical skill, failed to refute it convincingly.[27] These unseemly quarrels in high places did nothing to restore confidence in the competence of the Balfour-Jackson régime; and when U-boat sinkings rose sharply in October and November it became clear that major changes would have to be made. Beatty fully shared the prevailing anxiety about the shipping losses, and in mid-November he told Ethel that he wanted all anti-submarine operations and strategy to be placed under one officer, who would be responsible to the Chief of the Admiralty's War Staff – an idea which he repeated in a letter to the Admiralty a few days later.[28] On the very day that letter was sent Asquith told Balfour that he wanted Jackson replaced, and on 22nd November the First Lord wrote to Jellicoe offering him the post of First Sea Lord. His acceptance was announced a week later. Jellicoe wanted his Chief of Staff Admiral Sir Charles Madden to succeed him in command of the Grand Fleet, and referred, somewhat unkindly to Beatty's 'many mistakes'.[29] The chief difficulty over appointing Beatty was that

he was junior to Burney, Jerram and Sturdee; but no one
wanted either of the first two to be C-in-C, Sturdee was
prepared to waive his seniority and serve under Beatty, and
Madden agreed to replace Burney as second-in-command.[30]
On 10th November Lord Stamfordham, the King's Private
Secretary, sent the Monarch a note reporting that Asquith felt
that Beatty was the right man to succeed Jellicoe,[31] and on
21st Balfour told the King that Jackson had been asked to
resign in favour of Jellicoe and that he proposed to offer
command of the Grand Fleet to Beatty.[32] The King replied
that 'the appointment of Sir David Beatty . . . fills me with
confidence and will be welcomed by the whole country'.[33]
The selection of Beatty and his promotion to Acting Admiral
– at the very early age of 45 – were announced a week later
and received a good Press. On 3rd December the King wrote
to Beatty in his own hand to say 'what pleasure it gave me to
approve this appointment. I have known you for upwards of
thirty years, ever since we were shipmates together in the
Mediterranean; I have watched your career with interest and
admiration and I feel that the splendid fleet which you now
command could not be in better hands . . . . You have my
hearty good wishes and those of the whole Empire . . . .
Believe me, my dear Beatty, very sincerely yours. George
R.I.' [34] This was high praise indeed, to which Beatty replied
begging leave 'to thank you for the Gracious and inspiring
letter', and saying that he was 'profoundly grateful for the
Confidence which Your Majesty places in me . . . .'[35] Few
commanders of large forces can have entered on their
responsibilities with greater good will from royalty, in
political circles and from his own fleet than Beatty did on that
November day. At about the same time he received from
Pakenham a tribute from the Captains of the Battle Cruiser
Fleet in the form of a set of silver trays inscribed with the
signature of all 21 of them. 'You know what we wish you',
wrote Pakenham, 'for you, for ourselves and for the Country
– Long life to use them, a close companionship between
yourself and us and as close a meeting with the enemy as may
be vouchsafed to us'.[36] The recipient must have been deeply
touched to receive so warm and unanimous a compliment
from the officers he had led for more than two years of war.

Beatty's feelings on leaving the Battle Cruisers are best
revealed by the answer he sent to an appreciative letter from

his old friend Walter Cowan. After expressing the hope that he would 'be found worthy' of his new appointment he wrote 'We have been through some odd times together and have had some successes and there is no reason why we shouldn't have more and greater ones. As you well know my heart will always be with the Battle Cruisers who can get some speed, but I'll take good care that when they are next in it up to the neck, this old Battle Fleet shall be in it too . . .' – which was of course an oblique criticism of Jellicoe's relatively late entry into the battle on 31st May.[37]

But the upheaval of the closing weeks of 1916 was not confined to the navy, since on 7th December, after some hectic manoeuvrings behind closed doors which form no part of this study, Asquith resigned and was succeeded by Lloyd George – who made Balfour's removal from the Admiralty a condition of accepting the office of Prime Minister. Though Fisher's supporters campaigned to have him brought back as First Lord – despite his 76th birthday being little more than a month off – Lloyd George would not hear of it. His initial plan was to give the post to Lord Milner and offer Sir Edward Carson a seat in the War Cabinet; but Conservative opposition made him exchange the two appointments. Beatty was sorry to lose Balfour, with whom he had got on well; but he was very much aware of the deficiencies of the First Coalition and welcomed the substitution of a small War Cabinet, initially of only five members, to replace the unwieldy bodies which had endeavoured to conduct the war and govern the country since 1914.[38]

CHAPTER TEN

Crisis for the Navy: Comfort for the C-in-C. January-June 1917

Within a remarkably short time of hoisting his flag in the *Iron Duke* Beatty was able to tell his wife that 'Everything as far as the Fleet is concerned is going like hot cakes and all my admirals are in good humour and I think the Fleet has improved in morale 50 per cent'.[1] That he did not exaggerate the effects of his appointment as C-in-C is confirmed by such disparate characters as Herbert Richmond, the intellectual young Captain then in command of the pre-Dreadnought battleship *Commonwealth* of the 3rd Battle Squadron, and Admiral Tyrwhitt the gallant and resourceful leader of the Harwich Force; for Richmond expressed his delight at finding himself under 'a naval officer who sees so much beyond his own arm',[2] while Tyrwhitt told Keyes that Beatty 'impresses me more and more every time I meet him. He has a wonderful grasp of the situation and absolutely fills me with confidence and hope of the future'.[3] A few months later, after a visit to Rosyth, he wrote that there was 'no doubt that he is the right man in the right place'.[4]

But if Beatty's standing in the navy was very high, and his acceptance as the finest leader it had known for many years virtually unchallenged, his private life was increasingly in a state of turmoil.

We last encountered Bryan and Eugénie Godfrey-Faussett at the time when Beatty was fighting to get Ethel presented at Court in 1909-10. Though it seems very likely that the two families remained in touch, since they moved in the same social circle, and also probably met when the Beattys were entertained at one or other of the aristocracy's stately homes or when he took part in the Royal shoots, no letters between the two families between 1910 and 1916 have survived. By the latter date Beatty's marriage was certainly not going well, though he continued to write regularly to Ethel when they were parted and to take the closest interest in the welfare and education of their two sons. Ethel's promiscuity seems to have been a matter of common knowledge among their intimates, though it was of course never openly referred to. Many years later Beatty told Shane Leslie, to whom he confided his innermost thoughts, how on one occasion he had left Aberdour House to walk back to Rosyth and embark for his flagship but found he had left his cigarette case behind. So he returned to the house to collect it – and found his wife in bed with an officer from his own fleet. Leslie, admittedly a hostile witness so far as Ethel Beatty is concerned, though very much the reverse in the case of her husband, repeated that story to me and gave other examples of Ethel's infidelities when he and I met in the 1950s. Doubtless he had them in mind when, towards the end of his life, he included in his reminiscences the remark that 'she trifled with the laws of marriage and thought nothing of it.'[5]

In one of his letters to Admiral Sir Reginald Drax (formerly Plunkett) Professor Marder asked whether he considered that Beatty's 'most unsatisfactory marital life' had hampered him in performance of his duties, especially as Commander-in-Chief. Drax wrote in the margin '*Not* up to the end of 1916'.[6] Though I have always marvelled at the way Beatty carried his immense responsibilities with unfailing devotion to duty – despite his lack of a stable home background – I have found no indications that the emotional strain to which he must have been subject affected his work during the war. His letters to Ethel were still always affectionate, beginning with a term of endearment such as 'Darling Tata' and ending with assurances such as 'Ever your devoted'. Leslie wrote of those letters that they were 'intensely serious when they deal with his profession, . . . often as intimate and harmonious as Pepys in his home life' – a dubiously accurate description of his domestic affairs. But Leslie added that Beatty's letters to Ethel 'also carry a deeply tragic note which Death alone could close' – which seems a perceptive assessment of the binary nature of their content.[7]

We have no clue as to when Eugénie began to regard the handsome young admiral with more than the interest which such a figurehead would naturally arouse. What we do know is that it was she who initiated the regular correspondence between them, and that she carefully preserved all or nearly all the answers she received. The first of the series is dated

19th June 1916, begins 'Dear Mrs. Godfrey' and ends 'Yours ever'. It makes it plain that Eugénie had sent him a 'charming letter' of understanding and sympathy over the Admiralty's inept handling of the communiqués about the battle of Jutland, since Beatty wrote that 'My poor sailors were terribly upset at first at the injustice . . .'; but he asserted that 'the visit of the King has put that alright'. He also said that he had been 'so glad to see Godfrey', who had evidently been in attendance on the Monarch on that occasion, 'looking so well'. Though he ended by signing himself as 'Yours ever, David Beatty' there is no other hint of incipient affection in either that letter or the next one, written three months later, in which he thanked 'Mrs. Godfrey' for her congratulations on his recently awarded GCB, but expressed himself as 'woefully disappointed at the inadequacy of the rewards meted out to the fine fellows who supported me so gallantly' – that is to say at Jutland.[8]

In October 1916 Beatty wrote again to Eugénie, evidently in answer to a letter in which she had sent him news of happenings in the metropolis. Of greater interest to us is his account of the visit he had recently paid to Scapa, mentioned in the last chapter. 'I never met a more complacent crowd' was his uncomplimentary description of the Grand Fleet's officers. 'The war is a long way off up there and they don't like talking about it'; but the reasons why Jutland was a banned subject on that occasion have already been given. 'They are getting rounder and rounder [i.e. more corpulent]' he wrote 'and have their little personal troubles and joys which seem to satisfy them'; all of which was grossly unfair to Jellicoe and his men but does illuminate the lack of cordiality between the Rosyth and Scapa forces. This time Beatty pressed Eugénie to write again; so he evidently wanted to foster the association. His next letter is only dated 'Satdy' but is obviously a reply to Eugénie's congratulations on his appointment as C-in-C (27th Nov. 1916). It was probably written on 2nd December, and in it Beatty declared rather ponderously that he was 'very sensible of the great honour and the grave responsibilities', but was not 'alarmed' by the latter. He added that ' I *do* hate leaving my beloved "Lion" and Battle Cruisers with whom I have gone thro' so much. . . .' As he was 'exiled now in the North' [i.e. at Scapa] he would 'appreciate your letters more than ever *so* will you write and tell me all the news' was his encouraging ending.[9]

The next letter is the first to show clear affection on Beatty's part, for he dropped the 'Dear Mrs. Godfrey' and plunged straight in with 'Bless you my dear (is that too familiar?) for your delightful letter'; and declared that hers were 'the best I ever get and I *really* do look forward to them.' He again referred disparagingly to Jellicoe, writing 'I think my predecessor loved detail, I hate it!!'; and he therefore intended to use his 'large staff' to avoid being unnecessarily worried. Finally he again encouraged his correspondent by saying 'you will write to me again and I will love you for ever'.[10]

On the last day of the year Beatty sent nine pages in his own hand to the King to convey New Year's greetings from the Grand Fleet and assure him of the 'Loyal Devotion' of 'the Admirals, officers and men', and their hope that 1917 would 'bring success to your Majesty's Navies and Armies which will terminate in a Triumphant and Glorious Peace'. He said that if it pleased HM he would write again 'from time to time to give some account of the doings of Your Grand Fleet, so that you may be kept in touch with all that we do'. He also told the Monarch that 'guarding against an attempt to pass out Raiders' was his 'principal concern', and that 'Unfortunately one got away, sailing it is believed on the 27th [November]' when Beatty had been occupied in taking over from Jellicoe. This remark probably referred to the famous raider *Moewe* which had returned safely from her first successful commerce destroying cruise in March 1916[11] and slipped out again, still commanded by the clever and redoubtable Count zu Dohna, on 22nd November. She was followed a week later by the *Wolf* under Captain Nerger, and on 21st December the *Seeadler*, a full rigged sailing ship commanded by Count von Luckner evaded Beatty's patrols and set course to attack shipping in the Pacific. The *Moewe* again reached home safely on 22nd March 1917, shortly after another raider the *Leopard*, to which we will revert shortly, put to sea.[12] In explanation of his lack of success in catching the raiders Beatty told the King how difficult it was to cover the North Sea and all its exits, especially during the long nights and storms of winter. The escape of the *Wolf* caused Beatty to write direct to Balfour (now Foreign Secretary) protesting that it was impossible for him either to catch raiders using Norwegian territorial waters or to stop leakages in the blockade by neutral ships which took advantage of the same immunity unless he was allowed to visit and search such ships regardless of International Law. But the Admiralty could not allow infringement of neutrality without higher approval, and when the issue was put to the War Cabinet they declined to authorise such a step – despite the escape of the *Seeadler* having provided further support for Beatty's case.[13] It is interesting to remark that exactly the same problem arose early in World War II, when Churchill as First Lord repeatedly pressed for measures identical to those which Beatty had vainly urged nearly 23 years earlier.[14]

As regards fleet training Beatty described to the King how he had brought the battle cruisers (now commanded by Pakenham, in whose performance Beatty was actually by no means wholly satisfied) to Scapa, and had then taken the whole fleet to sea for a week of exercises and firings. He also recounted how, by way of reducing centralisation, he had given each Vice-Admiral the chance to take his squadron to sea and exercise it on his own. One result of these exercises was that he had proposed to the Admiralty and they had approved the transfer of his flag from the *Iron Duke* to the newer and faster *Queen Elizabeth*. Though he told the King that this was because he had found it 'most desirable that the Commander-in-Chief should be in a ship which has a considerable Excess of Speed over The Fleet', in a letter to Eugénie he told her in confidence that 'there was too much Jellicoe about the *Iron Duke*, so I thought a change would be for the best'.[15] After giving the King a graphic account of the collision at night during a North Sea gale between two destroyers (*Negro* and *Hoste*), and the remarkable efforts made to rescue their crews, he concluded with the usual assurance about the excellent health of his officers and men and the 'wonderful spirit permeating the Grand Fleet'.[16]

While Beatty was making his initially cautious approaches to a woman who was obviously greatly attracted to him the Admiralty under Carson and Jellicoe was enjoying a honeymoon period – which was to prove only too brief. Though Beatty feared that, if the new First Lord did not support his principal naval colleague the latter was not a strong enough character to impose his will, in fact the two got on very well indeed.[17] Beatty had little confidence in the other members of the new Board of Admiralty. Admiral Burney (2nd Sea Lord), who had transferred from command of the 1st Battle

Snapshot of Eugénie.
(*Godfrey-Fausset Collection*)

Beatty in Vice-Admiral's uniform,
six weeks after Jutland.
(*Godfrey-Fausset Collection*)

Oil portrait of Beatty by Orpen. (*National Portrait Gallery of Scotland*)

Oil painting of Lady Beatty by Laszlo. (*Earl Beatty*)

Beatty and his aides. Ralph Seymour (Flag Commander), F. T. Spickernell (Secretary), Bryan Godfrey-Fausset (Equerry to George V). (*Godfrey-Fausset Collection*)

The Rangers Lodge, Hyde Park. (*Godfrey-Fausset Collection*)

Squadron, proved as uninspiring in his new capacity as he had
been in his last one. Admiral F. C. T. Tudor (3rd Sea Lord)
was a better appointment as he was capable in technical affairs
and, incidentally, a strong supporter of the recently formed
RN Air Service.[18] Lionel Halsey (4th Sea Lord) carried
responsibility for transport and supplies, and although he was
well liked by some officers Beatty had no high opinion of his
capacity. A 5th Sea Lord was added to the Board on the
recommendation of Lord Curzon's Air Board in January 1917
to carry responsibility for naval aviation, and the incumbent
was Commodore Godfrey Paine – one of the first naval
officers to take up flying.[19] The hard-working Admiral Oliver
stayed on as Chief of the War Staff, but did not modify his
over-centralised methods. Beatty had little use for the Permanent Secretary, Sir William Graham Greene whom he
described, probably too harshly, as 'one of those half-dead
men'; and he was dismissed by Carson's successor Sir Eric
Geddes at the end of July.

Early in the New Year Beatty evidently got so far as to
address Eugénie by her first name because, he wrote, 'Godfrey
told me to' and he always thought of her as such. In return she
was urged to drop the 'Sir' with which she had evidently been
prefixing his first name. Plainly this letter marked a further
step towards real intimacy, especially as in it he wrote that he
had 'reluctantly come to the conclusion that women with their
eyes open and brains like yourself are infinitely more capable
and sensible than men and give one far better advice' – a big
change from the strongly anti-feminist line he had taken about
a Women's Volunteer Reserve some two years earlier.* This
time he closed with 'Bless you, my dear, all good luck go with
you for 1917. May we meet soon, and signed it 'David' with
'Beatty' in brackets.[20] Eugénie had evidently sent the admiral a
mattress for his cabin bed, since in his next letter he assured
her that it was 'most comfortable' and that he would 'dream
all the pleasanter now that I know you tried it'.[21]

At about the time now reached in the story of Eugénie's
interest in Beatty she took a job at the Dorchester House
Hospital for Officers in Park Lane, and when she told her
admirer about it he replied that he was 'sure you look delicious
in your hospital garb. I wish I could see you. Is that asking too

*See page 95.

much?'[22] Plainly the association was rapidly becoming more than a platonic friendship; and the invitation implicit in Beatty's question was soon to be fulfilled.

Early in February 1917 Beatty sent the King another of his long accounts of the doings of his fleet. He again emphasised the heavy demands made on his cruisers and destroyers by the need to try and catch outward or homeward bound disguised commerce raiders. Apart from the 12 ships of the 10th Cruiser Squadron, whose function was to patrol the northern exits to the Atlantic, there had at times been as many as 15 cruisers and 21 destroyers at sea on such duties. He told how in the middle of January he had concentrated the forces from all his three bases (Scapa, Cromarty and Rosyth) in the central North Sea, had carried out exercises and 'swept a very large portion' of those waters but 'with the usual result' – that is to say no enemy sighted. None the less he considered it 'a Good Dress Rehearsal' for the fleet action he still hoped for. The weather had for the most part been kindly, and in consequence he had been able to carry out much tactical training and firing practices – including 'a series of Night Battle Practices', which he described as 'very successful and valuable'. In stressing to the King the need for his fleet to be prepared to continue a day action after dark he obviously had the lessons of 31st May in mind. He next drew the King's attention to the conduct of T.B.D. *Shark* (Commander Loftus Jones) in the battle of Jutland, and of the gallant self-sacrifice of her captain.[23] He was evidently distressed that no recognition had been accorded him in the New Year Honours, as he had sent the whole story to the Admiralty in good time. This prod may have helped to produce the award of a posthumous VC on 6th March – along with other Jutland decorations.[24]

That Easter (5th April) Bryan Godfrey-Faussett noted in his diary that 'Babs' (as he always called Eugénie) had been invited to stay at Windsor Castle, but if it would interfere with her hospital work or with her family duties she 'need not treat it as a command'.[25] When Beatty heard about the invitation he teased Eugénie about 'basking in the smiles of the Monarch and Monarchess'; but he warned her that she would have difficulty in squeezing one [i.e. a smile]' out of the latter. He told his correspondent that the last time he had succeeded in getting a smile out of the Queen 'she thought I was tiddly [i.e. tipsy]'.

Beatty and Eugénie got a lot of slightly malicious fun out of Admiral Brock's courtship of a 'red haired, green-eyed lady' who was evidently known to both of them. Beatty wrote that he feared there was no chance of 'pulling out' his Chief of Staff, though he would 'try if there was a ghost of a chance' as he considered he was 'in for a miserable old age with a very tiresome woman'; but Brock did in fact marry the woman in question.* This letter began 'Eugénie, you are a darling and I love you and your letters more than ever' – words which provided the frank avowal for which his fair correspondent seems to have been waiting. Beatty also described how the raider *Leopard* had been caught and sunk in the far north on 22nd March although it was 'a *dead* secret';[26] but he was confident that 'you don't talk and I cannot resist telling you because you are you and it was a triumph as J. J. [Jellicoe] thought my dispositions were wrong'. In the same letter he told how he was expecting a visit from Lloyd George and Carson next day (14th April) and that it was 'a *secret* visit but I fancy everybody knows'. He asked Eugénie to tell him if she heard of it from other sources.[27] Here one finds support for Kitchener's answer to earlier complaints about his obsessive secrecy – namely that he would only abandon it if persons in high places divorced their wives.[28]

Towards the end of April Beatty wrote again to the King, chiefly about the very serious threat produced by the German declaration of Unrestricted Submarine Warfare on 1st February – which initiated a totally new chapter in the long history of the *guerre de course* against merchant shipping. The 'restricted' campaign of the autumn of 1916 had produced unpleasantly heavy losses (146,000 tons in October, 145,000 in November and 109,000 in December); but these were to prove almost trifling compared with the sinkings of February to June 1917 – to which further reference will be made shortly. In addition to describing his further attempts to reduce centralization by sending his Battle Squadrons on 'independent cruises' and warning the King about the serious effects of the submarine campaign and the Admiralty's apparent inability to produce a solution, Beatty reported the discovery of 'very

*Admiral Brock married Irene Catherine Wake, daughter of Admiral Sir Baldwin Wake-Walker, Bart., and widow of Captain Philip Francklin, who was lost in the *Good Hope* off Coronel on 1st Nov. 1914. Presumably she was the lady apostrophised by Beatty.

serious structural weakness' in the large cruiser *Courage-ous,* which had been completed at the beginning of the year. 'When steaming at 30 knots in a moderate wind of [force] 4 and a very slight sea', he wrote, 'she simply doubled up and cracked right across before the Fore [15-inch] Turret'. As a result she 'very nearly fell to pieces', and he was convinced that the Admiralty had 'carried the margin of Lightness in Build too far'. This experience, combined with the need to increase the armour protection of the *Renown* and *Repulse* made him doubt whether the Admiralty's 'amateur efforts in naval construction are worth anything at all' – which was in effect an indictment of Fisher's whole policy of building fast, lightly protected capital ships.

Beatty also described to the King his visit to Rosyth on 14th-15th April and his meeting with the Prime Minister, the First Lord and other Admiralty officers and officials 'whom I have few opportunities of seeing and discussing things with'. He was strongly of the opinion that such meetings were 'very desirable' in order 'to have constant interchange of ideas and views and avoid working in water tight compartments'.[29] He did not tell the Monarch that at the Rosyth meeting he had strongly criticised the Admiralty for the lack of a properly organised staff and had pressed for the adoption of ocean convoy, about which the Admiralty was still hesitating, as the only antidote to the U-boat campaign. Nor did he mention that his visit to London a few days after the Rosyth conference had convinced him that, as he wrote to Ethel, palliatives were useless and 'nothing but a clean sweep [in the Admiralty] would be of any value' in dealing with the crisis. Lloyd George he described as 'a wonderful man with a mass of energy', but he was very critical of Carson and Jellicoe; and he told his wife that he had no intention of leaving the Grand Fleet in order 'to clean up the mess for them'.[30] Lloyd George brought the convoy issue before the Cabinet shortly after returning to London, and rightly claimed that Beatty had supported its introduction.[30a]

Beatty's flying visit to London on 17th April – made chiefly to discuss the shipping crisis with the Admiralty – evidently brought him little comfort, since he told Eugénie that he found the department in a state of 'chaos and indecision' – which was no exaggeration. He had, he wrote, been worn out 'with their vacillations and hopeless condition of uncertainty about anything and everything'. However, one powerful consolation was derived from the visit, since Bryan Godfrey-Faussett's diary makes it plain that he was 'in waiting' on the King at Windsor on that day and accompanied the Monarch on a visit to the Sopwith Aviation Company's works.[31] He also made a laconic entry in his diary that 'Babs writes that she had David Beatty to lunch';[32] but there must have been more than a quiet lunch à *deux* to that meeting, since on returning to his flagship Beatty wrote a somewhat breathless letter beginning 'Eugénie dear, was it a dream? That one perfectly divine day, I can hardly believe it was a real day, to see you again in such a sudden fashion it was a joy indeed and now it belongs to the blessed past. It is something to think of but the worst is, I find myself thinking of it too much and I don't get on with my work'. He told Eugénie how he had intended to return next day to Ranger's Lodge, the house in Hyde Park just north of the Serpentine where the Godfrey-Faussetts were living at the time; but he was detained at the Foreign Office 'until just on 8 p.m.';[*33] and when he was about to carry out his intention he got a message that he was wanted urgently at the Admiralty. 'I nearly struck [i.e. went on strike] he told Eugénie, 'and wish I had. They kept me there late and I hated sending you the message I couldn't get to you. But I mustn't grumble, you brought so much sunshine into a hectic 36 hours that I am grateful indeed'. As to the business conducted in London, he wrote that 'If it had not been for you I shd have hated it and I did all except about 3 very short hours'. After describing the backlog of troubles he had encountered on returning to Rosyth he thanked Eugénie rapturously for the two letters he found waiting for him, and told her 'That someone believes in one is a thought that helps more than anything else and you dear child with all your 32 years of wisdom are giving intense pleasure'. He told how when he was with her he had forgotten all the questions he wanted to ask because 'with the joy of seeing you everything else went out of my head'. The letter ended with 'Bless you. Yours with love, David'.[34] Though it cannot be said with complete assurance that Beatty and Eugénie first became lovers during

*Lloyd George was in Paris on this date and went on next day to St. Jean de Maurienne in Savoy to meet the Italian Ministers. The discussions in the Foreign Office probably concerned the peace feelers put out by the Emperor of Austria at this time and Italian aspirations in Asia Minor.

those 'three very short hours' in mid-April the opportunity was certainly available to them. At the least relationship obviously moved rapidly from friendship to passion on that day.

Here we must take temporary leave of Beatty's love affair and retrace our steps a few weeks in order to review the progress of the U-boats' onslaught on our merchant shipping, the C-in-C's attitude towards naval policy and strategy in general and the counter to the submarine threat in particular. At the meeting with Carson in February, mentioned earlier, the old question whether it was practicable for the navy to strike offensive blows against the enemy was again raised. Though Beatty always lent a ready ear to a subordinate who could offer ideas about hitting the enemy hard, his officially expressed view was that the only practicable offensive meas-ures were the intensification of the anti-submarine campaign and tightening the blockade of Germany. As regards the latter he had assured Carson that it would ultimately bring Germany to her knees, and that the 10th Cruiser Squadron, which maintained the Northern Patrol of the exits from the North Sea to the Atlantic, was the essential instrument to make it effective. Jellicoe, however, considered he was 'quite wrong in assuming that the blockade will ever cause the enemy to give in', and believed it would do no more than 'cause them a good deal of suffering and discomfort'.[35] He therefore declined to strengthen the Northern Patrol as Beatty had requested.

There had been serious leaks in the blockade ever since the beginning of the war, chiefly because neutral countries (and especially the USA) objected very strongly to any interference with their shipping – and of course with the profits to be made through supplying both sides with scarce commodities. Not until America entered the war in April 1917 was it possible to tighten the blockade until it finally became a stranglehold.[36] Yet, even allowing for the imperfections in the blockade at the time Jellicoe expressed his doubts about its effectiveness, it was well known in London that Germany was already suffering serious shortages; for the winter of 1916-17 was the so-called 'turnip winter' when the food situation was acute. It is therefore difficult to accept Professor Marder's view that '*both* Admirals were right' in the views expressed early in 1917.[37] Nor can I agree that Beatty's 'strategic policy was as cautious as Jellicoe's had been'. Apart from his constant search for offensive measures, to be referred to in greater detail later, his attitude and outlook differed markedly from that of his predecessor – as indeed his Flag Officers and Captains quickly realised; and Professor Marder himself records how he 'itched for action' and hoped, at any rate until the end of 1917, for another major battle.[38] It is true enough that he was still anxious about the structural weaknesses revealed in the British battle cruisers and the inefficient shells supplied to them; also that the Admiralty still exaggerated the number of such ships available to the High Seas Fleet. But with the Grand Fleet's preponderance in battleships, which the Admiralty put at 32 to 21 in March 1917 and which was soon to be augmented by the arrival of the four American ships which formed the 6th Battle Squadron, it is surely inconceivable that Beatty would have declined action – except perhaps in the highly unfavourable conditions which prevailed in the southern North Sea, mentioned earlier. Where he and Jellicoe saw eye to eye was on the issue of maintaining the cross-Channel communications on which the BEF utterly depended, on delivering safely to France essential supplies such as coal, and on defeating the threat to the Atlantic shipping routes by which the entire Allied war effort was sustained and nourished.

In the field of tactics Professor Marder remarks that Beatty did not bring about 'a revolution';[39] but he overlooks the fact that wholesale scrapping of the entire Grand Fleet Battle Orders would hardly have been a tactful act by the C-in-C towards the 1st Sea Lord of the day. Beatty did actually go a long way in that direction, but in such a manner as could not reasonably cause offence in Whitehall. Early in 1917 he added commendably brief Grand Fleet Battle *Instructions* (2 sheets) to the voluminous GFBOs; and it should be noted that whereas in the Royal Navy *Orders* were mandatory, *Instructions* were only a guide to conduct. The general tone of the new Instructions was decentralization of responsibility from the C-in-C to Divisional Commanders; but the concentration of the battle fleet was in general to be preserved. Emphasis was placed on the pursuit of the enemy, even after darkness had fallen, on the offensive rôle of destroyers in carrying out torpedo attacks, on the vital importance of enemy reporting and maintaining contact by light forces, and on junior Flag Officers and Captains anticipating the C-in-C's wishes if possible. The turn *towards* an enemy torpedo attack was accepted, though not without misgivings from the Admiralty; and night action was not to be declined, though it was not to be sought.[40] Concentration of the big ships' gunfire was introduced in order to take advantage of British numerical superiority, harbour tactical exercises were introduced, and frequent conferences took place at which officers were positively invited to express their ideas and opinions. In sum it is certainly the case that, as Professor Marder admits, there was 'a new offensive spirit in Beatty's tactics' – which hardly accords with his denial of a tactical revolution mentioned earlier.[41]

Here it is desirable to say a little about Beatty's attitude towards the use of both lighter- and heavier-than-air craft (i.e. airships and aeroplanes) at sea, which was one of the subjects discussed when Carson visited him early in 1917. The outcome was that Beatty quickly sent two official letters on the matter to the Admiralty. In the first one he stated tersely that 'our present aerial arrangements for the Grand Fleet are inadequate', especially by comparison with those enjoyed by the HSF; and he asked what was being done about it. In the second letter he developed his case more fully, stressing the inadequacies of the seaplane carriers available to him, the need for rigid airships like the Zeppelins, and for large seaplanes. He also insisted that the training of all personnel for the RN Air Service 'should be exclusively naval'.[42] The Admiralty's reply was that the general policy was for the RNAS 'primarily to assist in all operations carried out by the Royal Navy'; but they admitted, somewhat contradictorily, that a large number of aircraft were employed on non-naval operations, including the stationing of a Wing of bombers deep in France. Particulars of a new 'seaplane carrier' (*Argus*) which was due to complete towards the end of the year, of the conversion to aircraft carrier (*Eagle*) of a battleship which had been ordered for the Chilean navy, and of the new flying boats which were in production were given;* and Beatty was assured that

*The *Argus* (15,750 tons) was a converted liner building for Italy (*Conte Rosso*) which was taken over in Aug. 1916. She was the first genuine aircraft carrier with a flight deck covering her whole length. The *Almirante Cochrane* was taken over in July 1917 and launched as the *Eagle* in June 1918 (26,400 tons). She was the first 'island type' carrier with her funnels and superstructure shifted to the starboard side of the flight deck. Neither was completed before the war ended but they both played a valuable part in World War II, especially in flying off RAF fighters to Malta, in 1940–42, until the *Eagle* was sunk in the August 1942 Malta convoy.

training of personnel accorded with his views 'as far as the exigencies of the war permit'. But the long and short of this exchange was that there was little hope of fulfilling the C-in-C's desire for long-range rigid airships and for *ship-borne* aircraft in the near future.* Despite this discouraging reply Beatty went ahead with such measures as he himself could put in hand. The first was to set up a Grand Fleet Aircraft Committee under Admiral Evan-Thomas, which reported early in February 1917 and set out in greater detail the needs which Beatty himself had already adumbrated. He forwarded it to Whitehall with his 'general conclusions', and advocated the sacrifice of part of his light cruisers' gun armaments 'in order to use them as seaplane carriers'. He also asked for 'every effort' to be made to convert the 'freak' battle cruiser *Furious* into 'an effective seaplane carrier' by removing the forward turret, in which a single 18-inch gun was to be mounted, and giving her a flight deck.[43] It should be remarked that although aeroplanes could *take off* from improvised flight decks such as were fitted in these early conversions they could not *land on* them – which was of course a very serious handicap. Though it runs ahead of the period covered by this chapter it is appropriate to mention here that in August 1917 Beatty held a conference with Admiral Halsey, the 3rd Sea Lord, at which they agreed that the large cruisers *Courageous* and *Glorious* 'should be fitted with flying-off decks', and selected one ship from each of four light cruiser squadrons which was to be given 'a flying-off deck for an anti-Zeppelin machine'.[44] Though Beatty was without doubt an enthusiast for the employment of the new arm, and did all in his power to further its progress, it was seriously handicapped by factors wholly outside his control, and by the middle of the year little had been accomplished – except on paper.

On the last day of April Beatty gave Carson his real views on the Board of Admiralty, complaining bitterly about the time taken to introduce his recommendations, some of which he had given to Balfour as long ago as July 1915. 'We are living on top of a volcano', he wrote, 'which will blow the Admiralty and the Navy to hell if we don't pull ourselves

---

*The capture fairly intact of Zeppelin L33 on 23rd–24th Sept. 1916 when she made a forced landing in Essex was an eye-opener about the extent of German superiority in this class of aircraft. The design was copied and the resultant R33 and R34 were the first successful British rigid airships. But they did not complete until after the war.

together'. He considered that we were 'not using the brains and energy of the youth of the Service . . . We dig out old retired officers who are not capable of producing the energy and driving force required . . .'; and he repeated the assertion he had made to Ethel a fortnight earlier that nothing short of 'a clean sweep' in the Admiralty would overcome the crisis. Though his letter was marked 'Personal and Private' Beatty must have hoped that his views would be passed to the highest quarters – namely the War Cabinet. Rarely can such a forthright epistle have landed on a Minister's desk.[45] At about the same time he sent a series of letters expressing his anger and frustration equally strongly to Ethel;[46] and he also vented his wrath with the Admiralty in his letters to Eugénie. Carson having failed to fulfil the high hopes originally entertained for him Beatty first toyed with the idea that Churchill should be called back to his former office; but he soon dropped him in favour of Jacky Fisher – because 'he is a man – unscrupulous but still a man'[47] – an idea which did more credit to Beatty's emotions than to his judgment.

As Beatty saw very clearly things could not be allowed to go on as they were – with public confidence in the Admiralty ebbing fast. Lloyd George was fond of appointing 'thoroughly competent business men' to Ministerial posts, and his solution in the Admiralty's case was to put in Sir Eric Geddes, who had made a name for himself in the field of railway management, as Controller of the Navy with responsibility for production. He was to have a seat on the Board and was given the rank of Honorary Vice-Admiral (whose uniform he had no scruples about wearing) – which was not likely to endear him to the genuine members of the Flag List. Halsey became 3rd Sea Lord in place of Tudor, and was to act as assistant to Geddes; while Rear-Admiral H. D. Tothill, an officer of no great distinction, took over as 4th Sea Lord. Jellicoe became Chief of Naval Staff – which he already was in fact though not in name; while Oliver became DCNS and Duff ACNS. But the chronic naval disease of over-centralization continued, and neither Jellicoe nor Oliver changed their habits. Beatty told Tyrwhitt that the changes were 'the same as before but with new labels . . .'[48] and produced, very probably with some help from Richmond, a long paper on 'Admiralty Organization' – in which he took it to pieces mercilessly.[49]

At the beginning of May Beatty wrote to Eugénie about

what he called 'the fine old rumpus going on about the Admiralty'. He said that although they had accepted his 'principles' – presumably about the introduction of ocean convoy and of a properly organised staff – they would not make them 'effective by using sufficient and efficient weapons'. He described the new Board as 'antiquated old gentlemen' who refused to use 'the masses of really brilliant young fellows' who were available. It is interesting to find this age-old complaint by youth pouring from the pen of the 46-year old admiral. Then, switching abruptly from service matters to the problems and progress of his love affair, he told Eugénie that he read 'the nicest parts' of her letters 'over and over again' – by which he surely meant the parts in which she showed her physical desire for him. He told her that he could only find peace and time to answer her letters in the small hours of the night – when quiet presumably reigned in the *Queen Elizabeth's* vast admiral's suite. At such time his thoughts constantly turned to the woman who brought him so much comfort during these months of acute anxiety. Though it was not strictly true to tell Eugénie that he 'never wrote to anybody else', since the flood of his letters to Ethel had by no means abated at that time, one feels the strength of his longing for his mistress in his assurance that 'I think of you always and the memory of a very short period a fortnight ago is helping me through the weary hours in this cursed region where it is blowing a gale of wind and where the sun never shines'. Again he ended with 'Bless you, dear Eugénie, with Heaps of love'.[50]

While Beatty's frustration over the Admiralty's failure to deal with the submarine campaign was coming to a boil merchant shipping losses were rising catastrophically, reaching a total of 373 merchantmen (869,103 tons), of which 354 ships (834,549 tons) were sunk by U-boats, in April.[51] By way of compensation for those heavy losses only 48 U-boats had been sunk between the beginning of the war and January 1917; and at least six of that number had been victims of accidents.[52] When the Unrestricted Campaign opened the Germans had about 120 operational boats (out of a total of 140); and by the end of 1917 some 220 more were building. Moreover the new boats were much larger than the early ones (displacement increased from about 550 to 850 tons), so giving them longer endurance, and were equipped with better torpedoes.[53]

As regards anti-submarine measures, early in 1917 there were about 280 destroyers available, but neither Beatty nor Jellicoe was prepared to denude the Grand Fleet of its 100 so long as a battle with the High Seas Fleet was possible. A very large number of trawlers and other minor warships were employed in the Auxiliary Patrol, which carried out hunting operations in coastal waters but achieved few successes. The hydrophone development mentioned earlier was not strikingly helpful in locating U-boats because it lacked directional sensitivity; and the production of the Asdic detecting device, which was ultimately to prove enormously valuable, did not begin until mid-1917. The Channel Barrage of nets and mines failed to prevent the egress and ingress of U-boats; and the scheme to lay a vast minefield across the Heligoland Bight, which Beatty had recommended to Carson at their January meeting, required huge quantities of mines (of which no efficient type was yet available), and was not likely to be effective unless the barrage was continuously patrolled. Jellicoe was right to throw cold water on this scheme.[54] Beatty also held exaggerated hopes of success from submarine versus submarine operations.[55]

Though there were some hopeful signs, such as the increasing supply of depth charges and the use of coastal air patrols, by April 1917 the general situation was little short of desperate; and in the paper Jellicoe submitted to the War Cabinet that month he urged the abandonment of overseas commitments such as the Salonika force, which absorbed a large naval effort. In effect Jellicoe joined hands with Generals Haig (C-in-C, British Expeditionary Force) and Robertson (CIGS) in pressing for the concentration of all resources and effort on the western front.[56] Anxiety was increased by a series of raids by German light forces on the Dover Patrol's vessels and shipping in the eastern Channel – though they actually achieved little. The success of the destroyers *Broke* and *Swift* in the 'wild mêlée' of the night of 20th-21st April did, however, put a temporary stop to that threat.[57] But taken as a whole by April there were few glimmers of light on the horizon.

The story of the belated introduction of ocean convoy – the historic defence against any form of the *guerre de course* against merchant shipping – has often been told and need not be repeated here in detail. Professor Marder gives a full account,[58] which tallies in most respects with what I have written elsewhere though his inclusion of me in the flatteringly distinguished company of Lloyd George, Churchill and others who have held that 'the Admiralty persistently and stubbornly fought the introduction of the convoy system' requires qualification;[59] since I have given elsewhere a full description of how Lloyd George's visit to the Admiralty on 30th April 1917 was an anti-climax rather than a climacteric.*[60] In fact the decision had already been taken to run a trial convoy of 17 ships from Gibraltar, which sailed on 10th May and arrived without loss twelve days later.

We are here chiefly concerned with Beatty's attitude to this crucial issue. From the beginning of 1917 he repeatedly urged the adoption of convoy in the Western Approaches, and demonstrated that he had no faith at all in the system of 'patrolled lanes' for shipping then in force, because the U-boats were easily able to find out their location and so make them into what the official historian has correctly and graphically described as 'death traps'.[61] The difficulties Beatty experienced over getting his views on this vital issue accepted arose chiefly from Jellicoe's pessimistic attitude towards the whole problem,[62] and because Admirals Oliver (Chief of the War Staff and then DCNS) and Duff (Director, Anti-Submarine Division and then ACNS) were wedded to the system of patrolled lanes and greatly exaggerated both the number of escorts needed to make ocean convoy effective and the difficulties and alleged disadvantages inherent in such a system. It was Beatty who called the conference at Longhope in the Orkneys on 4th April, which recommended the adoption of convoy for the Scandinavian trade – as he told the King in the letter already quoted; yet the recommendations were coolly received by local Senior Naval Officers. As late as 23rd April the Admiralty still adhered to patrolled lanes, and at that time Jellicoe forwarded papers to the War Cabinet in which he said no more than that convoy was 'under

*Professor Marder's remark is obviously based on the fact that in a lecture which I several times gave at the Imperial Defence College in the 1950s and '60s I said that 'Lloyd George forced the issue . . . and the decision to try convoy was imposed from above'. In my *Hankey: Man of Secrets*, I, pp. 380-4 (1970) I gave a much fuller account, though I still hold that without pressure from outside and above the Admiralty the measures begun in April 1917 would probably have been still further delayed.

consideration'.[63] Such was the 1st Sea Lord's attitude right in the middle of the 'black fortnight' (17th–30th April) when nearly 400,000 tons of shipping were lost.[64] That disaster, combined with the entry of the United States into the war on 6th April, which brought the prospect of naval reinforcements, especially of destroyers, arriving at an early date, and the discovery that convoy was not nearly as difficult as had been made out, produced a complete change of front in Whitehall – and in a very short time.

It would of course be a gross exaggeration – and very unfair to other persons concerned – to represent Beatty as the sole, let alone the chief saviour of the situation which came to a crisis in April 1917; for he had no hand in the discovery that the Admiralty's statistics purporting to compare shipping losses with safe arrivals were colossally misleading. Nor was it he who succeeded in getting the truth infiltrated into the right quarters. The chief credit for that accomplishment belongs to Commander (later Admiral Sir Reginald) Henderson, who risked his career by acting without the knowledge of Admiral Duff, the superior to whom he was responsible. Sir Maurice Hankey, the Secretary of the War Cabinet, also played a vital part – as Lloyd George and Churchill both later admitted – as did Sir Norman Leslie of the Ministry of Shipping.[65] But the credit due to them and to other individuals should not be allowed to detract from that due to Beatty, who was certainly among the first senior naval officers to appreciate the proper remedy for the crisis which he had long foreseen, and to apply his physical and mental energies in the direction needed.

In May, despite the gradual introduction of convoy, shipping losses remained very high, and Beatty again fulminated to Eugénie that the Admiralty 'are now doing what I have been pressing them to do for months, but alas in only a half-hearted way. J. J. [Jellicoe] was always a half-hearted man'. However by 'insulting them once a week' he was hopeful of 'goading them into more determined efforts'. What worried him was that if he went 'the whole length of denunciation of the Adlty and their ways' and was successful it would probably result in him being called to go there – which would mean leaving the Grand Fleet. 'For the life of me', he declared somewhat arrogantly, 'I do not know who to put into the Grand Fleet' if he moved to the Admiralty. Madden was the obvious claimant; but he did not inspire the confidence which always exuded from Beatty – despite his private troubles and heavy responsibilities. 'If we can once get touch with the enemy', he told Eugénie, 'we shall never let him go and I believe . . . we shall destroy him utterly'. As regards Jellicoe, he believed that he 'would do very well [as First Sea Lord] if he had the right sort of men behind him'; but Beatty considered him 'totally incapable of selecting good men to serve under him', and that he 'dislikes men of independence and character and loves sycophants and toadies' – which was altogether too harsh a judgment. Beatty ended this letter by telling Eugénie 'I think of you more than is good for me' – which was no doubt perfectly true.[66]

Beatty devoted most of his next letter to the recent death of his brother Charles, while undergoing an operation made necessary by the wounds he had received in France. He obviously sought to share his distress over the loss of 'the truest and best friend that anyone could wish' with the woman who could best give him the consolation and sympathy he needed.[67]

On the last day of May Beatty wrote lovingly in answer to a letter from Eugénie 'Oh dear, I wish, how I wish that it were possible for you to do all the nice things you said you would like to do. What's the use of wishing, they never come except on the rarest occasions and they are so few and far between . . .'; which surely confirms that they were already lovers. Eugénie evidently retailed a lot of London society gossip about people they both knew; but her account (amplified and confirmed by Bryan's diary) of a terrific row between Lady Meux (wife of Admiral Sir Hedworth Meux, formerly Lambton, who moved a good deal in Court circles) and Lady Derby (wife of the Secretary of State for War) about which side of the Guards' Chapel the King and Queen should sit when they attended the marriage of Derby's son Lord Stanley to The Hon. Sybil Cadogan,[68] does make one feel that the wealthy and aristocracy still lived in a world far removed from the 'carnage incomparable and human squander'[69] then in progress in France and Flanders. As John Pearson has recently remarked in his brilliant study of the Sitwell family 'the rich country house and London life . . . still went on in grotesque contrast with the grim world of the battle fields across the Channel . . . with its complacency and bland acceptance of the slaughter';[70] and it was in that society that Ethel moved and felt at home.

In his letter to Eugénie Beatty recalled that he was writing on the first anniversary of 'the worst day in my life' [i.e. Jutland]. To have been within reach of 'the greatest victory the world had ever seen . . . and then to have missed it . . . rankles terribly', he wrote; 'and Fate is not kind to those that miss opportunities'. He now considered that 'the sacrifices were all but in vain', and that although 'most think it is a day for rejoicing' to him it was 'a day for sackcloth and ashes'. Those sentences undoubtedly represented the view from which Beatty never deviated about 31st May 1916.[71]

A few days later Beatty again expressed his physical longing for his mistress, and for the intimacy she had obviously offered him; for he wrote 'Oh, my dear, how I wish what you wish but what is the use of wishing when it can never come true.' As in all his letters to Eugénie he interspersed expressions of profound love and physical desire with snippets of naval news – such as the alleged sinking of German submarines or enemy minelaying in the Firth of Forth. This time he wrote that Jellicoe was ill and away from the office, and 'that old Mummy [Admiral Sir Cecil] Burney [2nd Sea Lord] is I suppose trying to do something'. He told Eugénie that he might have to come to London, though he doubted it. 'I would if I could, he wrote, '*you* know that'.[72]

In other letters he described his own leisure reading, and recommended books to Eugénie. Thus one finds him, rather surprisingly, commending to her Samuel Johnson's *Rasselas* in order to 'exercise philosophy'. 'It has a wonderfully soothing effect' he wrote. That same letter described another visit by the King to the fleet, this time at Scapa for four days – during most of which a full gale was blowing, causing the King to describe himself to his consort as 'Poor unlucky me' after a dreadful crossing of the Pentland Firth in a destroyer leader accompanied by 'Bertie' (the future King George VI), who was serving in the *Malaya*.[73] On arriving in Scapa Flow he went onboard the *Queen Elizabeth* where he was greeted by Beatty and his Flag Officers. Throughout his visit he was accommodated on board the fleet flagship, which he inspected minutely. Beatty gave up his after cabins to the Monarch, and told Eugénie that he was 'tremendously impressed with the comfort of my little bed', but showed some surprise when the owner of the mattress said 'Oh yes, Mrs. Godfrey had lain on it and selected it for me!!'. 'He is not very quick', remarked Beatty, 'and it required some explanation. Especially as I told him I always had pleasant dreams on it'.[74] One can understand a Royal eyebrow being slightly raised in puzzlement over this description of the C-in-C's periods of repose. Or could some hint of their love affair have reached Royal ears?

Despite the appalling weather the King managed to visit many ships, and on 23rd June he went to sea with the 5th Battle Squadron to witness a practice firing with their big guns. According to the King they 'made excellent shooting'. On his last day he held an investiture at which he gave Beatty the GCVO, Brock the KCVO and Brand the CVO. On 24th June he travelled south again, calling briefly at Invergordon and Rosyth to inspect ships and establishments there. The King certainly showed remarkable stamina and devotion to duty in carrying out such a heavy programme in most unfavourable conditions.[75] Beatty told Eugénie that he had 'not overworked' the Monarch; but he himself could not do his work 'on Barley Water' (which was apparently all the King wanted), but found that he 'must be fortified with something stronger'.[76]

A few days after the King's departure Beatty wrote at greater length to Eugénie about the visit, complaining about the 'hectic time' it had given him and the disruption of his work that it had caused. 'I was never so glad to say Goodbye to anybody as I was to the Monarchial [sic] party', he wrote; but to him the big news was that Eugénie was coming to stay at Aberdour. 'Tata loves having you' he declared with optimism which was not to prove well-founded; while he himself would 'try to get to Rosyth while you are there'. Perhaps there was, for the first and probably the only time, a hint here of love and duty clashing.[77] Eugénie's visit had, however to be postponed, because she was laid low by a sharp attack of pneumonia early in July.[78] In the end, however, her illness brought her lover perhaps the happiest, and certainly the longest period of intimacy throughout the whole of their love affair.

Early in July Beatty wrote again to the King, primarily to acknowledge 'a gracious letter' about his recent visit to the fleet; but he also told the Monarch that the Prime Minister had wanted to talk to him when in Scotland 'about the possibility of more aggressive action on the part of the Grand Fleet'. He surmised 'that Winston Churchill had been filling him up with ideas that we were not doing enough'; but he believed he had been 'able to satisfy' Lloyd George 'that our Naval Strategy was sound'. At the same time he assured the King that 'if any human being could produce a scheme which held any promise of successful issue . . . it would be most gratefully received by myself'. He only insisted that such schemes must be submitted in writing, since 'sketchy references to what could be done and could not be done were of no value . . .'; which was probably an allusion to the rather wild ideas about a 'naval offensive' then circulating in London. To show that his fleet was playing a part in overcoming the shipping crisis he mentioned that some of the Armed Merchant Cruisers of the 10th Cruiser Squadron, which operated the Northern Patrol, were to be employed 'escorting convoy and themselves carrying cargo' – which he considered 'sound for the moment' though it might have to be reconsidered when the long winter nights again produced opportunities for raiders to break out.[79] It will be told in the next chapter how the search for an offensive and the U–boat campaign dominated the second half of 1917.

CHAPTER ELEVEN

A Fleet in Frustration, July–December 1917

At the very beginning of the period covered by this chapter Beatty suffered a most unpleasant shock when on the night of 9th–10th July the battleship *Vanguard* suddenly blew up while at anchor in Scapa Flow, with the loss of about 1,000 lives. Though exhaustive investigations into the cause of the disaster were carried out, and wild rumours about sabotage by German agents circulated, it is virtually certain that the cause was deterioration of some of her cordite to the point of spontaneous combustion, and so to the ignition of the contents of a whole magazine. But coming so soon after the similar explosions which had destroyed the battleship *Bulwark* (a Channel Fleet ship) at Sheerness in November 1914 and the cruiser *Natal* at Cromarty towards the end of the following year it was inevitable that this further catastrophe should affect the morale of the fleet, in which questions such as 'Which of us is to go next?' began to be asked. Beatty of course set himself to counter such dangerous tendencies by diverting attention into other channels, through intensive exercises and, during the hours of relaxation, by organised entertainments; but his letters show that he himself was by no means immune from the anxieties produced.[1]★

A fortnight after the disaster to the *Vanguard* a more pleasant prospect appeared on Beatty's horizon; for he wrote sugges-

★Sir John Wheeler-Bennett is wrong to say in his authorised biography *King George V*, p. 101 that 'more than half [the *Vanguard's* company] were ashore at the time of the explosion'. The numbers of officers and men who were out of the ship were 22 and 71 respectively, not about 500. A. Cecil Hampshire in *They Called it Accident* (Kimber, 1961) postulates more sensational causes of these disasters, but no real evidence of the introduction of explosives by enemy agents was ever produced – at the time or after the war. On the other hand protracted tests did prove that high magazine temperatures and impurities in cordite could produce deterioration to the point of combustion. See John Campbell, *Warship*, No. 6 pp. 138–40

ting to Eugénie that she should come to Aberdour on 25th –
ostensibly as Ethel's guest to convalesce after her recent
illness.[2] Bryan raised no objection and she duly came to stay
for a whole month. In consequence there are no letters to her
until 1st September, when Beatty wrote to thank her for the
present of a seal which 'will always be a souvenir of your visit
and of the fact that for four weeks I was able to see you nearly
every day, also of something more precious, a delicious
memory. Oh, dear, I wonder if I shall ever travel South again'
he wailed; . . . 'I think of you always and wish at times I didn't
but that cannot be helped'.[3] Bryan Godfrey-Faussett's diary
for the month that his wife was in Scotland shows that he was
occupied chiefly working in the Admiralty with the Assistant
Director of Paravanes (ADP) on developments in minesweeping,[4] and he appears to have been entirely confident that
Eugénie's visit had no ulterior motive. Yet Beatty's letters to
her after she had left make it seem very doubtful whether he
was then actually running a *ménage à trois*. The indications are
that Ethel was away a good deal and that Bryan was well and
truly cuckolded.

    Apart from Eugénie's visit to Aberdour the second half of
1917 was a most frustrating period for Beatty; for he
commanded the greatest array of naval might ever assembled,
yet was virtually powerless to defeat the real threat to the
Allied cause. Both he and Jellicoe clung to the concept of
victory by battle, and were reluctant to release appreciable
numbers of the Grand Fleet's destroyers in order to strengthen
the convoy escorts. This was one of the causes which
contributed to the slowness with which a full convoy system
was introduced – despite the fact that the trial homeward
convoys of May 1917 from Gibraltar and Hampton Roads and
in the Mediterranean had been entirely successful. Furthermore the drop in sinkings in May 1917 was not sustained in
the following month, and it was not until late in the year that
the gradual introduction of convoy showed fairly consistent
reduction of losses – to between 3 and 400,000 tons (about 150
ships), compared with the peak of 869,000 tons and 373 ships
in the previous April.[5] Another encouraging sign, though not
fully appreciated at the time, was that sinkings of U-boats,
though still far below the rate of new construction, did rise
during the second half of the year – to 43 compared with only
20 during the first six months.[6]

In the circumstances which prevailed in the middle of the year it is not surprising that criticisms of the Admiralty, which had subsided during the early months of Carson's time as First Lord, should have broken surface again. In May a letter to *The Times* by Admiral Sir Reginald Custance,[7] a retired officer who had been one of the 'Adullamites' or 'Syndicate of Discontent' whose criticisms of Fisher before the war had produced paroxysms of fury on his part,[8] initiated the campaign for a more ardent 'offensive spirit'; and, as Beatty had anticipated, he quickly gained the support of Churchill. In marked contradiction of his earlier arguments he now pressed for steps to 'get at' the German navy by seeking 'a supreme act of naval aggression' instead of 'all this accumulation of deadly war energy [i.e. the Grand Fleet]' lying idle 'on the off-chance of the German Fleet emerging from its harbour to fight a battle. . . .'[9] One here finds a foretaste of the 'offensive' measures for which Churchill pressed so vigorously as First Lord in 1939–40 – at the price of an enormous waste of money and of scarce resources.[10] Beatty was furious with Custance and Churchill, calling the former a 'nebulous old fool' whose nose he would 'like to pull' and castigating the latter for writing 'in a rag of a paper belittling the officers and the Great Service of which he was once the head'.[11] But there was in fact a body of opinion in his own fleet, including Richmond and Drax (formerly Plunkett),* who believed that some form of offensive was possible; and they enjoyed the qualified support of Beatty himself, that of the more thrustful admirals like Keyes and Tyrwhitt, and of the influential Hankey sitting at the centre of the spider's web of authority in Whitehall.[12] Richmond, as spokesman for this group favoured minor combined operations in overseas theatres such as the Syrian coast – on the lines of what Hankey called 'warfare on the littoral'.[13] Such undertakings would, however, have swallowed up a lot of shipping – of which the Allies were still desperately short; and as Jellicoe had no use for Richmond and had refused to bring him into the new Planning Section of the staff set up in mid-July, all such ideas were bound to be stillborn.[14] Beatty's position is made clear from notes prepared by Commander R. M. Bellairs, his War Staff Officer, for a

*In 1916 Plunkett 'assumed by Royal Licence the additional names of Ernle-Erle-Drax'. We will here ignore his four-barrelled patronym and refer to him henceforth as 'Drax'.

conference with Jellicoe late in July – the refrain of which was that the lack of a naval staff and the clumsiness of the Admiralty's administrative machinery stultified all imaginative ideas and plans and positively invited inaction.[15] Beatty considered that the Admiralty 'are riding for a fall and it will be a heavy one' unless they adopted 'the strongest measures' – by which he undoubtedly meant the creation of a properly organised staff and the introduction of a complete and regular cycle of ocean convoys in place of the costly and discredited system of hunting for submarines and routing shipping along patrolled lanes.[16] His view of the futility of hunting operations was probably strengthened by the failure of the destroyer force which at this time he sent to try and catch the U-boats on their transit routes round the north of Scotland.[17]

It is a safe guess that when Lloyd George visited Beatty at Rosyth in mid-April the C-in-C did not pull his punches on the failure of the Admiralty to deal with the U-boat menace and the general inanition in Whitehall of which he so often complained in his private correspondence – thereby lending support to the Prime Minister's increasing lack of confidence in Jellicoe and Carson. Jellicoe was well aware of the movement which was afoot to replace him, and in June Beatty had sent him a letter designed to prop up his morale, which the increasingly vociferous Press campaign was plainly undermining;[18] but reviewing the letters that passed between them at this time, and particularly Beatty's call for 'closer communion between you and I [sic] . . . There can be no question of any difference of opinion between us' one must remember that he had already expressed a determination not to be lured away from the Grand Fleet to take over the First Sea Lord's desk. Towards the end of August Bryan Godfrey-Faussett, who was of course well placed to pick up news of all the plots then in progress, wrote in his diary that 'An underhand sort of campaign is going on against Jellicoe but I do not think it is having much effect now. If Jellicoe went I cannot think who they wd. put in his place; Beatty would be the best man for it (if he would take it) but it is far more important that he should remain C-in-C of the Grand Fleet. . . .'[19] On the other hand Frank Spickernell, Beatty's devoted secretary, considered that he should go to the Admiralty, and Richmond recorded that in Beatty 'we have the makings of a statesman' such as was needed in Whitehall;

but Drax was of the same opinion as Godfrey-Faussett.

In bringing about further, and more drastic changes in the Admiralty's upper hierarchy Lloyd George had to walk like Agag lest he lose the support of his Conservative colleagues. He must have been well aware of Jellicoe's chronic pessimism – to which Beatty as well as the King, Fisher, Generals Robertson and Haig and Hankey have all borne witness;[20] but as Carson was completely loyal to Jellicoe and refused to sack him the only way Lloyd George could achieve his purpose was to promote the First Lord to the War Cabinet – a suggestion which originated from Milner but which held no appeal at all to 'the sacrificial lamb'.[21] After a good deal of vacillation Lloyd George took the plunge, and on 17th July the elevation of Carson and the appointments of Sir Eric Geddes as First Lord and of Churchill as Minister of Munitions were announced.[22] Almost simultaneously the decision was taken that the main Allied effort for 1917 should be in Flanders with the object of capturing the U-boat bases at Ostend and Zeebrugge. On the last day of July the Third Battle of Ypres, which was to develop into the prolonged agony known as Paschendaele in the autumn, was launched.

The shunting of Carson upstairs, soon followed by the replacement of Graham Greene, the Permanent Secretary of the Admiralty, by the far abler Oswyn Murray, boded ill for Jellicoe; and when Lloyd George tried to force him to sack both Burney (2nd Sea Lord) and Oliver (DCNS) he threatened to resign. Jellicoe came north to discuss the situation facing him with Beatty and Madden, both of whom urged him to stay on as 1st Sea Lord, and a compromise was finally reached whereby Burney was relieved by Sir Rosslyn Wemyss early in August; but Oliver stayed on.

In the autumn Geddes introduced a major reorganisation of the Board by dividing its work between Operations and Maintenance Committees,[23] introducing a Deputy First Sea Lord in the person of Wemyss, and bringing Keyes in as Director of the newly formed Plans Division. These measures of decentralisation now seem to have been long overdue, and they broke the monopoly of decision exercised by Jellicoe and Oliver; but Jellicoe certainly disliked Keyes's appointment to an influential position on the Staff. To Beatty, however, the new broom seemed entirely beneficial. Early in September he sent Eugénie a long letter telling her of the visit by 'the

Admiralissimo of the United States Navy' whom he described as 'a dear old cup of tea who never did anything wrong in his life, an impeccable old gentleman – that's no use now is it?'. In fact Beatty's visitor was Admiral Henry T. Mayo, USN who commanded the American Atlantic Fleet from 1916 to the end of the war and had just represented his country at a conference of the Allied nations' leaders in Europe. As he wrote most warmly to thank Beatty for the 'brotherly welcome' accorded to him and his staff, and described his visit as 'most enjoyable and interesting' it was evidently a success. He was touched by Beatty's tactful gesture in hoisting a four star Admiral's flag with his own flag and then presenting him with the former as 'a souvenir . . . of a very pleasant association'.[24] But Beatty found Geddes, the First Lord, 'more my sort'. He told Eugénie how 'For 13 solid hours without stopping we talked. My jaw still aches from the exercise.' He declared that Geddes was 'beginning to find out that he has bitten off more than he can chew and wants me to help in the mastication process' – presumably by coming to the Admiralty in place of Jellicoe. 'Not for me – I am waiting' wrote Beatty, and compared himself to Achilles sulking in his tent.* Moving on to a more personal plane he teased his mistress about the King having evidently paid her a compliment about 'that lovely head and glorious hair'. 'Gosh', he wrote, descending to schoolboy slang, 'I would I were King'. Then, reverting to his last visit to London he repeated that 'Never was there such a divine journey, the memory of it will last for ever'; and he ended with the warmest expressions of love and devotion.[25]

In his next letter he told his 'dearest comrade of Dreamland' a little about the submarine hunting operations on which his and Tyrwhitt's forces were engaged, complained bitterly about the atrocious weather his fleet was having to endure ('a permanent gale of wind'), and then reprimanded her for having destroyed a letter to him written at midnight and burnt the next morning 'because it was not respectable'. 'My dear comrade', he asked, 'why did you do that? There is nothing that could be "not respectable" between us and I should have

---

*A reference to the first book of *The Iliad* where Agamemnon, having been forced to give up Chryseis (daughter of Chryse, priest of Apollo) to her father, threatened to take Briseis away from Achilles who surrendered her but refused to take any further part in the Trojan War, 'sulking in his tent'. It is rather surprising to find a Homeric reference in one of Beatty's letters.

adored it and I don't like respectable things of any sort anywhere, so when you do it again, if you ever do, send it along and make me happy'. He said that he expected to be in London again in mid–October and certainly would be there in December when the *Queen Elizabeth* was due to refit. He sought an assurance that she would then be 'on the premises . . . because you are the most delightful creature in all the world and I just love you all over from your glorious hair to the tips of your toes . . . I wonder if those thoughts will ever come true. No matter, I have had some real joy the last visit I made, and the memory will keep me going for some time';[26] which confirms the supposition that they first became lovers during his brief visit to London in April.

After spending two months with the major part of the Fleet based on Rosyth, which Beatty told the King 'was very valuable in many ways', and had enabled him 'to get through a good many conferences and get into closer touch with the many departments at The Admiralty' – and incidentally to see a good deal of Eugénie – in mid–September he took the fleet back to Scapa, where he was greeted by the succession of gales of which he complained to both his mistress and his Monarch.[27] On 27th September, the day that Beatty had written so longingly and nostalgically to Eugénie, Wemyss took over as Deputy 1st Sea Lord, and Sir Leopold Heath, whom Richmond regarded as a complete bonehead, stepped into Burney's shoes. Beatty expressed pleasure over the former appointment,[28] and with the issue of a new Order in Council making the 1st Sea Lord responsible as Chief of Naval Staff to the First Lord for naval operations a long-standing source of friction and inefficiency was eliminated. Taken together these changes did in theory mark a further step in breaking down the over-centralization which had been the curse of the Admiralty machine for years; but the practical effect could not be as great as Geddes intended as long as Jellicoe and Oliver held the reins; and the fundamental trouble lay, as Hankey remarked, in Lloyd George being 'hot for getting rid of Jellicoe'.[29]

Meanwhile the search for 'a naval offensive' continued, taking many forms. Efficient mines, copied from the German model, had at last become available in quantity and about 16,000 were laid in many different North Sea fields during the second half of 1917. It was in fact mines which proved the

most effective killer of U-boats at this time, probably sinking
no less than 20 of them in all theatres during the year – which
was about three times greater than the corresponding figure
for 1916.[30] An enormous North Sea Mine Barrage, which had
been proposed by Admiral Bacon a year earlier, was also
begun; but we will deal with its accomplishments in the next
chapter.

Other offensive measures considered were the seizure of
Heligoland or of the Friesian Islands of Borkum and Sylt and
the establishment on them of advanced bases for aircraft and
light forces – which was in fact a revival of an idea which
Churchill had enthusiastically supported early in the war; also
the bombardment of U-boat bases from the sea – which
Beatty considered likely to prove quite unprofitable,[31] the
blocking of German estuaries, which Beatty asked Madden to
investigate despite Jellicoe's attitude being entirely negative,
and minor combined operations in the Adriatic or on the
Levant coast, which Richmond had pressed for a year earlier.[32]
The increasing dissolution of the Eastern Front and the
possibility that, after the October Revolution, the Russian fleet
would fall into German hands, produced a scheme to send a
large force under Keyes into the Baltic; but after the Plans
Division had gone into it thoroughly in October it too was
abandoned. An interesting point is that this idea was probably
the genesis of the Baltic operation 'Catherine' which Churchill
so strongly favoured as 1st Lord in 1939.[33] But because Beatty
found little or no merit in the various plans discussed at this
time it should not be assumed that he was satisfied to continue
as before. He was desperately keen to anticipate any move by
the Germans against Denmark or Holland, and wanted to
establish forward bases in the latter country – an infringement
of neutrality which naturally aroused Foreign Office
opposition and provoked him to protest to Geddes against that
department 'dictating Military Policy'.[34] In October Beatty
met Wemyss to discuss the possibilities;[35] but the likelihood of
Dutch resistance combined with the failure of the offensive in
Flanders resulted in no action being taken. At about the same
time the need for a base on the Norwegian coast in order to
stop U-boats using that country's territorial waters was
resurrected – with Jellicoe's support;[36] but again political
considerations were held to outweigh strategic necessities.
One can well understand the feeling of frustration which

Beatty and the officers of the Grand Fleet felt over what they regarded as the unimaginative and obstructive attitude in Whitehall; yet in retrospect, and taking account of the oft-proven hazards of combined operations and the total lack of the specialised equipment essential for success in such undertakings, it is difficult to believe that any of the measures against the northern neutrals discussed at this time would have proved fruitful or would have improved the prospects of victory for the Allies.

Beatty's most favoured project for a naval offensive was for a torpedo-bomber attack by ship-borne aircraft on the High Seas Fleet, which shows that his thinking was often prophetic of much later events, such as the Fleet Air Arm attack on the Italian fleet in Taranto harbour in November 1940 or the Japanese attack on Pearl Harbour in December 1941. At the meeting with Wemyss on board the *Queen Elizabeth* in October, already mentioned, he argued for 'An attack at dawn by torpedo planes on a very large scale, accompanied by aircraft of the larger type carrying 230-lb bombs. . . .'[37] There is no doubt that Richmond and Squadron-Commander F. J. Rutland, a pioneer of naval aviation, had a big hand in propagating this idea, which the former described as 'a most desirable operation'. Beatty, however, knew that Richmond's name 'stinks at the Admiralty', so he gave Jellicoe the plan as 'the suggestions of a committee'![38] At this stage his idea was to carry about 120 'torpedo planes of the new type' (the Sopwith 'Cuckoo') to within an hour's flying of Wilhelmshaven in eight fairly fast merchant ships (a foretaste of the Merchant Aircraft Carriers or MAC ships of World War II), fitted with a flight deck and with blisters and paravanes for protection against torpedoes and mines. These improvised aircraft carriers were to be escorted by destroyers and would fly off their planes to attack in three waves of 40.[39] Though the Admiralty did not actually turn down the idea their reply certainly lacked enthusiasm. They considered that as the ships had to be capable of 20 knots (Beatty had asked for 16-20 knots) they would have to be specially built and could not be ready in less than 18 months; nor could torpedo planes be provided in the required number 'before the latter part of 1918'.[40] Beatty, however, refused to yield, and wrote again pressing for the ships to be 'withdrawn from their present services and fitted to carry at least 17 aeroplanes each'. 'Flying-on and flying-off decks' were, he said 'essential'; and he implied that the Admiralty was exaggerating the difficulty of modifying the ships.[41] This time the reply received was still more discouraging, though the Admiralty did pay lip service to 'the importance of air attacks against the enemy's North Sea bases'.[42] It is difficult not to feel that if the Churchill-Fisher combination had still been in office far greater energy and drive would have been put into forwarding the offensive plan for which Beatty argued so strongly.

On 17th October, just when Beatty's controversy with the Admiralty over the torpedo-bomber attack was at its height, he suffered a nasty shock. So far the daily convoys between Bergen in Norway and the Shetlands had run entirely successfully, even though they were only lightly escorted. Room 40 had obtained warning of a German movement, but the Admiralty appears once again to have failed to give the C-in-C all the Intelligence they possessed. A strong force of light cruisers and destroyers from the Grand Fleet and Harwich was, however, sent to the central North Sea and the waters off south-west Norway; but that was far to the south of the convoy route and beyond supporting distance. Shortly before 6 a.m. on 17th, when the 12 merchant ships with two destroyers and two trawlers as escort were some 70 miles east of the Shetlands, they were caught completely unawares by the German minelaying cruisers *Brummer* and *Bremse*. The destroyers failed to get any enemy reports through but put up a heroic fight against impossible odds. Both were sunk, as was most of the convoy – including nine neutral ships.[43] The news did not reach Beatty until late in the afternoon, and although he at once re-disposed his cruiser squadrons to cut off the German ships they got home safely. Expectedly there was an outcry in some organs of the Press, which was not entirely quelled by Geddes pointing out in Parliament on 1st November that since April over 4,500 ships had been safely escorted to and from Norway.

Beatty was called to London to participate in the post-mortem and at once wrote to Eugénie to warn her. If his wife came with him 'she will want to do what she wants and I shall as usual fall in [with her plans]' he wrote; but if she did not come he would probably go to the Ritz and obviously hoped to see Eugénie.[44] Bryan's diary shows that Beatty lunched at the Ranger's Lodge – apparently alone with Eugénie as he was 'in waiting' at Buckingham Palace at the time. In the evening Beatty gave a small dinner party for her and other friends at Claridge's, and next day he spent about an hour with the King.[45] He then returned north and on 30th wrote to thank Eugénie for 'the great joy you gave me during my short sojourn in the great city'. He complained bitterly about the Press campaign 'villifying [sic] the Admiralty in general and Jellicoe in particular' as being 'against all [?] conception of fair play'. He opined that 'somebody in the Government was at the bottom of it, L.G. probably' – which was not far from the truth. Evidently Eugénie had written to ask if he had told her husband about their lunch together, since in his answer Beatty wrote that he had not mentioned it to Bryan, and enquired of Eugénie 'ought I to have done so?'[46] He may well have begun to realise the truth of Sir Walter Scott's lines

> O what a tangled web we weave,
> When first we practise to deceive![47]

Early in the following month Beatty wrote again – but in a very depressed state of mind over the Russian revolution and the Italian defeat at Caporetto on 24th October. 'The silver lining is very thin just now' he gloomily declared.[48] In his next letter he answered Eugénie's question 'Did anything that happened when you were here make some of your thoughts come true?' 'Dear Comrade', replied Beatty, 'they all came true very much so, the reality was sweeter and more divine than my "thoughts" ever could be. My visit to London was a visit (in parts) to fairyland with a beautiful golden haired Fairy Queen . . . But it has one disadvantage, it makes me hungry for more fairyland, for more Fairy Queen which is not good for me when the chances are so remote. . . .'[49]

In Beatty's next letter he described the foray into the Heligoland Bight of 17th November – though it was a great exaggeration to say that his light cruisers had 'damaged the Hun pretty considerably and frightened him a lot'; but he did also deplore the fact that he had not accomplished 'the success we had a right to expect', and repeated the refrain he had composed after the Dogger Bank action – that 'We should have got the lot'.[50] As the operation illustrated the weaknesses as well as the strengths of Beatty's leadership and command system we will look at it a little more closely.

Because we constantly laid mines in the swept channels used

by the U-boats when passing in and out of the Heligoland Bight, the Germans were repeatedly forced to extend those channels to seaward; and it was their custom to cover the minesweepers with heavy ships of the High Seas Fleet. Having observed the regularity of this practice Beatty and the Admiralty decided to spring a trap on the German sweeping and covering forces. He formed a striking force consisting of the new and very fast (32 knots maximum) but lightly protected large cruisers *Courageous* and *Glorious* of the 1st Cruiser Squadron under Vice-Admiral T. D. W. Napier, the 1st and 6th Light Cruiser Squadrons each of four ships commanded respectively by Rear-Admirals Cowan and Alexander-Sinclair and the 1st Battle Cruiser Squadron of four ships under Vice-Admiral Pakenham, who was put in command of the whole undertaking. A few hours steaming from the striking force he placed the six battleships of the 1st Battle Squadron, lest the High Seas Fleet should come out in strength.

The German minesweeping forces were on this occasion covered by Rear-Admiral von Reuter's 2nd Scouting Group of four light cruisers, with two battleships in support. The British forces sailed from Rosyth on the afternoon of 16th November and by 7.0 a.m. next morning were approaching the Heligoland Bight mine barrier. As Newbolt has remarked, because the striking force was to engage enemies encountered 'on or near the outer edge of the mine barrier it followed that if they found them, the British squadron might be obliged to press on into the mined area in pursuit'.[51] But successful pursuit depended largely on the possession of accurate knowledge regarding the minefields inside the barrier; and it was there that both the Admiralty's and Beatty's staff work proved deficient. Newbolt criticises the 'dangerously haphazard' way in which the location of both sides' minefields was communicated to the fleet, and it certainly seems extraordinary that whereas Pakenham had the latest information Napier did not. Beatty blamed Pakenham for not making sure that senior officers of all squadrons under him were properly informed; but, as will be told shortly, Napier was by no means acquitted of responsibility for the fiasco that followed.

Enemy vessels were sighted by the leading British light cruisers shortly after 7.30 a.m. and were taken completely by surprise. Von Reuter at once ordered his destroyers and minesweepers to lay a smoke screen behind which he retired to the south-west towards his supporting battleships. Though the British ships only glimpsed their targets occasionally they were engaged as opportunity offered, and Napier – to quote his own words – 'settled down into a chase at 15,000 to 10,000 yards'. By 8.35 he had reached a position which, according to the charts in his possession, marked the limit to which he could pursue. At 8.40 he therefore altered 90 degrees to port – to the north-east — and the light cruisers conformed. When the smoke cleared some ten minutes later he again sighted his quarry and therefore turned back 90 degrees to starboard to resume the chase; but by that time he had lost five miles and could only engage at extreme range. At about 9.0 a.m. he was joined by the battle cruiser *Repulse* (flagship of Rear-Admiral Phillimore), which had been detached by Pakenham to support him; but Pakenham, believing that the enemy was out of range, soon ordered the cruiser squadrons to break off the chase and join him at the pre-arranged rendezvous. Napier, however, disregarded this order and held on in pursuit of von Reuter for another 12 miles – until he reached what was marked as 'a dangerous area' on his charts. He then turned his squadron sharply to starboard and signalled that heavy ships 'should not go further through the minefield. Light cruisers use discretion and report movements' – which, on the information available to him can hardly be criticised. The two light cruiser squadrons supported by the *Repulse* continued the pursuit – in high hope of catching von Reuter; while the latter was hoping to trap his pursuers in pincers formed by his own light cruisers and the supporting battleships. Neither side brought off its intended coup, and when at about 9.50 heavy shells began to fall around the light cruisers Alexander-Sinclair turned 180 degrees and fell back on Napier. By the early afternoon all British forces had set course for Rosyth.

Beatty was once again bitterly disappointed at this poor outcome to a promising plan, and was critical of Napier for his turns to the north between 7.30 and 8.0 a.m., for his 90 degree turn away at 8.40 and for not using the full speed of which the two large cruisers were capable. On the other hand Phillimore and the two light cruiser admirals received his commendation. In the Admiralty everyone seems to have decided to make Napier the scapegoat for all the mistakes and lost chances of the day; but Beatty finally decided that 'an error of judgement' was adequate reproof of Napier, and refused his offer that he should be relieved. Yet when all is said and done this action, the last of the war in which heavy ships were engaged, was once again proof of serious deficiencies in staff work and in co-ordination between various forces on the British side. Only one German light cruiser suffered appreciable damage.[52]

Beatty said little more than has already been quoted about the action of 17th November to Eugénie, and in his next letter he told her that his flagship's refit was postponed and so the meeting to which he had been looking forward could not take place.[53] Then something of a tiff evidently occurred between them, since Beatty pleaded to be acquitted of 'any sin of omission or commission' in his hurriedly composed letters, and warmly repudiated the suggestion that 'there could be any such things [as clouds] between us.' He urged that his 'dear comrade of Dreamland' should not 'get cast down or like a broody hen' – a description which can hardly have appealed to the lady.[54] But the disappointment of 17th November did not mark the end of the troubles which beset Beatty during these unhappy months of 1917.

On 12th December an east-bound Scandinavian convoy of five neutral merchant ships escorted by two destroyers and four armed trawlers was attacked shortly before noon in very foul weather by four German destroyers. Since the disaster of 17th October two armoured cruisers had been detailed to patrol the convoy route; but they were some 60 miles to the west when the blow fell. The British destroyers were caught in the leeward position where heavy spray severely handicapped their guns' crews; and there was a muddle over getting an enemy report through to the covering cruisers. All the convoy and its escort except one destroyer, which was saved by a rain squall, were sunk.

On getting the first enemy report at 12.25 p.m. Beatty at once raised steam in most of his ships – believing that the High Seas Fleet might be out; but when it became clear that this was not so he ordered a squadron of three light cruisers which was already at sea off south-west Norway to sweep to the north. Had the German destroyers returned home by the route used on the outward journey they might well have been caught; but they escaped by returning through the Skagerrak.

Three German ships that fought at Jutland. *Derfflinger.* (Drüppel)

Seydlitz. (Drüppel)

Moltke. (Drüppel)

Battle scenes. *Lion* being hit on Q turret. (*Imperial War Museum*)

Queen Mary blowing up. (*Imperial War Museum*)

Seydlitz and *von der Tann* under helm. (*Drüppel*)

Seydlitz on fire.
(*Imperial War Museum*)

The destruction of *Invincible*.
(*Imperial War Museum*)

Nottingham in a heavy sea.
(*Imperial War Museum*)

British ships that fought at Jutland. *Iron Duke*, Jellicoe's flagship. (*Wright & Logan*)

Lion, Beatty's flagship. (*National Maritime Museum*)

Indomitable and *Inflexible* at full speed in the North Sea.
(*National Maritime Museum*)

Once again a Court of Inquiry was convened, the chief results of which were the clarification of responsibility for organising and routing the convoys, which was placed on the Admiralty; the opening out of the convoy cycle to three (later five) days, so reducing the strain of providing continuous escorts and covering forces for daily convoys; the shifting of the western convoy assembly point from the Shetlands to the Firth of Forth, which shortened the convoys' voyages but brought them nearer to the German bases; and the stationing of a more powerful support force in the immediate vicinity of the convoys.[55] In the event these measures were completely successful; but that did not compensate Beatty for what he called 'the most cursed luck'; nor did it still the renewed criticisms voiced in the Press and in Parliament.[56]

Here we must retrace our steps by some months to review Beatty's attitude over one of the most pressing problems of the time – namely the future of the R.N. Air Service and its relations with the conventional navy and with the army. We saw earlier how the Admiralty made itself extremely unpopular in ministerial circles by virtually boycotting the Joint War Air Committee chaired by Lord Derby, and how Balfour as First Lord had clashed with Curzon as President of the Air Board which replaced the JWAC on Derby's resignation. When a new Air Board was appointed under Lord Cowdray in February 1917 it was given the executive powers which had been denied to the Curzon Board; but the Admiralty continued to claim wide powers regarding the ordering of aircraft and engines and the disposition and employment of RNAS squadrons – thereby producing more clashes with the War Office. Towards the end of July Cowdray wrote to General J. C. Smuts, the South African soldier and politician, who had become a member of the War Cabinet in the previous month and was the effective (though not the titular) chairman of the Committee on Air Organisation and Home Defence against Air Raids (generally known as the Smuts Committee), stressing the need to convert the Air Board into a fully fledged Air Ministry. He thus placed the real issue firmly in the forefront of that body's deliberations.[57] Incidentally there was inside the Admiralty at this time a 'Fifth Column' led by Captain Murray Sueter, the Director of the Air Department, and later Superintendent of Aircraft Construction, which was working actively to achieve the same purpose as Cowdray – a schism which certainly weakened the official policy of the department.[58]

On 17th August the Smuts Committee reported strongly in favour of the creation of an Air Ministry and the amalgamation of the RNAS and RFC in a new service.[59] Jellicoe was entirely opposed to this proposal, while Geddes's initial reaction was extremely cautious; but he sent a copy of the report to Beatty for his remarks. He replied that he would 'give it my earnest consideration', and drew the First Lord's attention to the fact that he had 'for some time been clamouring for a definite decision as to the functions of the Naval Air Service' but had received no reply.[60] on 15th August he wrote again, in his own hand, saying that he felt that the Smuts Report was 'a move in the right direction', and he did not 'think there will be any grave difficulties about the provision of adequate assistance to the Navy by the new service if it is adopted'.[61] Nor did the receipt of a paper setting out the Admiralty's reservations on the report cause him to hesitate, let alone change his mind.[62] The result was that when the issue came before the War Cabinet on 24th August Geddes's misgivings were weakly expressed and carried little weight against the views of Curzon and the soldiers. The War Cabinet therefore approved the Smuts Report 'in principle',[63] and on 1st April 1918 the Air Ministry and Royal Air Force came officially into existence.

Beatty's support for the Smuts Report was perhaps the gravest misjudgement of his whole career; for it contributed, perhaps decisively, to the navy losing virtually all its experienced aviators and technicians. Furthermore because the RNAS was absorbed into the much bigger RFC the combined service was predominantly military in training and outlook. Thus co-operating with the Navy or contributing to the maritime side of war quickly became and always remained secondary requirements in the eyes of the RAF. The only explanation of Beatty's strange misjudgment which I can offer is that his criticisms of the Admiralty had been so constantly reiterated that they produced a habit of mind to the effect that the Board was always wrong; and that habit of mind nullified good judgment and the gift of foresight. What is most ironical is that his acceptance of the Smuts Report laid up a rod in pickle for his own back as First Sea Lord – as will be told later.

Far happier than the sacrifice of the RNAS was Beatty's

proposal of 19th November to create the new appointment of 'Flag Officer for Command of Seaplane Carriers etc. of the Grand Fleet' – or Rear-Admiral (A) as it came to be known. The Admiralty quickly approved the proposal, and on 6th January 1918 Rear-Admiral R. F. Phillimore, whom we last encountered with the 1st Battle Cruiser Squadron in the action of 17th November, became the first incumbent.[64]

When Jellicoe visited Beatty at Rosyth on 22nd December he found the C-in-C in a state of fury over a telegram sent by Geddes in a form which the First Sea Lord had not seen and which Beatty regarded as 'insulting'. The reasons for Beatty's wrath were that the telegram usurped his authority over the composition of the Court of Inquiry into the convoy disaster of 17th December, implied that his dispositions had been faulty, and suggested that he might 'pack' the Court. When Beatty met Geddes in Edinburgh on 27th December he evidently did not pull his punches, telling the First Lord that he and his Flag Officers felt deeply insulted by the Admiralty's order – which certainly was tactless in the extreme. Beatty finally extracted a letter of apology from Geddes assuring him that it had not been intended to convey 'any lack of confidence in yourself, or any desire to subject your own dispositions to a Court of Inquiry'; and he read the retractatory letter to his Flag Officers assembled in his cabin on 9th January 1918.[65] Though Beatty perhaps over-reacted the incident does suggest that the trouble between Geddes and the admirals was not entirely the fault of the latter. In the meanwhile cataclysmic events had taken place in Whitehall.

On Christmas Eve, before Beatty had learnt about those events, he sent Eugénie 'a hurried scrawl' conveying his good wishes for 1918 and describing the 'succession of pilgrimages of Adlty. officials' with which he had been beset. He wrote that he had been 'trying to instil a little courage and stout heartedness' into them, but they all seemed to be 'terrified of the Daily Mail' – which, with other Northcliffe organs, was leading the assault on the Admiralty in general and on Jellicoe in particular.

If for Beatty the two Scandinavian convoy disasters and the action of 17th November 1917 were distressing, for Jellicoe they were disastrous, and on Christmas Eve Geddes dismissed him in a manner which can only be described as ungracious, and after he had obtained the agreement of Wemyss to take

Jellicoe's place. On Christmas Day Jellicoe wrote to Beatty
telling him what had happened and why; and he also wrote at
length to the King expressing the hope that he would not
consider 'that I have failed in my duty. If I am assured of this,
I am indifferent to other matters.' There was certainly no lack
of dignity in Jellicoe's acceptance of his downfall. On 27th
Beatty wrote to him that he was 'truly amazed to hear of your
departure from the Admiralty'; but he was still 'completely in
the dark' as to what had happened. He was, however, about to
meet Geddes and Wemyss, and would then doubtless learn
more. He was dubious about Wemyss's capacity 'to run the
complex and great machine' of the Admiralty, and looked to
the future with apprehension; but in view of Beatty's privately
expressed criticisms of Jellicoe one should not perhaps take
this sympathetic letter too literally. As Professor Marder has
dealt in full with Jellicoe's dismissal and its aftermath, and I
have published elsewhere much of the correspondence that
passed there is no need to recapitulate the whole story.[67] As so
often the King put his finger on the real cause, when he wrote
to Beatty that 'The Prime Minister has had his knife into him
[Jellicoe] for some time and wished for a change'.[68] In his
letter of dismissal Geddes offered to submit Jellicoe's name to
the King for conferment of a peerage, and he accepted it as an
honour bestowed on the whole navy before he got a letter
from Beatty in which he expressed the hope that the offer
would be declined. To soften the blow he had administered
Geddes suggested to Jellicoe that he should hoist his flag as
C-in-C, Plymouth; but when the admiral learnt that it would
mean the present incumbent being relieved well before
completion of the usual term he refused the appointment.

Other changes made at this time were the relief of Oliver as
DCNS by Admiral Sir Sydney Fremantle, which Beatty and
Jellicoe had agreed on early in December. Oliver took over the
1st Battle Cruiser Squadron. Admiral Bacon, who had always
been one of Jellicoe's strongest supporters, was replaced at
Dover by his principal critic Roger Keyes – chiefly because of
dissatisfaction over the failure to make the Dover Barrage
impenetrable by U-boats.

Looking back today one must surely feel some sympathy
for Jellicoe; but it must be admitted that he was not a success
as 1st Sea Lord. To give only one example of a critical failure
which should not have occurred, he cannot be acquitted of

some of responsibility for the very tardy introduction of convoy. Secondly I am sure that the mental and physical strain of his 28 months as C-in-C, Grand Fleet had made him a very tired man before he came to the Admiralty;[69] and a tired man could not possibly give of his best in the crisis conditions which prevailed throughout that year. Thus the relief of Jellicoe, though it should have been effected with greater tact and consideration, probably was in the interest of the navy and of the Allied cause. At the end of the year Beatty told Eugénie that 'The changes add horribly to my labours. But I feel as if a great weight had been lifted and am more hopeful for the Future than I have been for a very long time';[70] and those words surely eliminate any doubts which may be felt with regard to his real opinion about Jellicoe's dismissal.

Early in the New Year Beatty summed up the experiences of the preceding months for the benefit of the King.[71] On the subject of the second attack on the Scandinavian convoy he was self-defensive and not entirely convincing; for he wrote that 'under the system in vogue at the time [it] was bound to have happened sooner or later', because with three convoys at sea it was 'manifestly impossible to provide covering or protecting force' for all of them. He blamed 'the Shipping people' for having insisted on getting the maximum use out of their vessels, regardless of the risk entailed; but he was satisfied that with only one convoy at sea under the new organisation the risks had substantially lessened. None the less because enemy agents in neutral ports could easily give warning of the convoys' movements he still expected an attack to be made by a force superior to those escorting and covering them. Thus the Scandinavian traffic remained a 'source of continual and extreme anxiety' to him.

Turning to the battleships of the American squadron, he reported that after six weeks they were 'gradually getting into our way of doing things', that they were 'desperately keen' and had 'worked hard to become acquainted with our methods of signalling, manoeuvring etc.'; but they were handicapped by their 'signalling and wireless being of a very primitive kind'. In their first full calibre firings 'under easy conditions' two ships had done well and two badly. The spread of their broadsides (as much as 1200 yards) was, however, quite excessive; but they were 'trying to improve it'. As regards rate of fire their best ship accomplished about the same as ours but 'the worst was very slow'. Beatty expressed the hope that the King would find time to visit Rear-Admiral Hugh Rodman's ships later on, as he was sure that it would be 'enormously appreciated not only by them but by the whole American Nation'. He offered to bring the squadron to Rosyth specially for the purpose, so saving the King the long and tiring journey to Thurso at the tip of Caithness, and the probably unpleasant crossing of the Pentland Firth in order to reach Scapa Flow. In fact relations between Beatty and Rodman were excellent, and the American admiral and his officers were constant visitors to Aberdour when in Rosyth. Doubtless the presence of an American-born hostess helped to make the visitors feel at home; while in London the Anglophile American Admiral W. S. Sims, who commanded all the U.S. naval forces in Europe, became as intimate a friend of Wemyss as Rodman was of Beatty. Though some British officers probably did cause offence by adopting an overtly patronising attitude, and thereby fuelled the Anglophobia which became so marked in the later phases of World War II when Admiral 'Ernie' King was the American Chief of Naval Operations, many enduring Anglo-American friendships originated in the fogs and blizzards of Scapa Flow in 1917-18. Indeed right to the end of the war it is hard to find a discordant note except in the correspondence of Josephus Daniels, the Secretary of the Navy, and Admiral W. S. Benson his strongly Anglophobe chief adviser.[72]

To revert to Beatty's letter to the King, he went on to describe the appalling storms and blizzards which his fleet had recently encountered, and which had 'taken a heavy toll of our small craft'. He told the King how the destroyers *Opal* and *Narborough* had met 'a terrible end' when they 'ran full tilt' on to the vicious rocks known as the Pentland Skerries at the eastern entrance to the Firth of the same name, while trying to reach shelter during the dark and stormy night of 12th-13th January. Only one of the 180 officers and men in their crews had survived, and Beatty described how, after being thrown on to the rocks he had hauled himself up on to a ledge, whence he had been rescued with great difficulty 36 hours later. 'How he lived through' the blizzard then blowing, wrote Beatty, 'is a marvel'; and as he also described the disaster and the solitary survivor's experiences in a letter to Eugénie he was evidently as distressed by the former as he was astonished by the latter.[73]

To the King Beatty claimed that the action of 16th–17th November in Heligoland Bight had 'harassed the enemy considerably' – an exaggeration which probably concealed his own disappointment at the outcome. With regard to the recent 'upheaval at The Admiralty' he wrote that it 'came as a great surprise'. Tactfully he 'did not find fault' with anyone over Jellicoe's dismissal, which was 'for those who are responsible to decide'; but he did consider 'the manner of his removal' to be 'a matter of regret'. He also quoted Jellicoe's statement that he was 'happy to be released from a thankless task', and expressed confidence that 'Wemyss will do well'. Thus he looked forward to a period of 'mutual confidence between the Fleet and the Admiralty' – which implied that such confidence had formerly been lacking. If this letter glossed over Beatty's frustration at his inability to achieve any striking success, and his disappointment about the setbacks suffered during the period he was reviewing, his remarks on the changes made in Whitehall were as judicious as they were fair.

Although to the officers and men of the Grand Fleet 1917 had been a frustrating year it did produce one result; and that a vital one, for which much of the credit unquestionably belonged to the Commander-in-Chief himself – namely the maintenance of the high morale of the ships' companies despite the tedium of so much of their work and the terrible weather constantly encountered. High morale depended fundamentally on four elements – good relations between officers and men, the maintenance of a sensible and relaxed discipline, the provision of good food and regular mails, and the granting of long leave whenever an opportunity arose; and Beatty himself played a prominent part in fostering all those essential elements.

By the autumn of 1917 the Russian revolution was having considerable impact on the outlook of British industrial workers and Service men; and the latter had become increasingly aware that vastly higher wages were being paid to men and women in industry than to themselves – despite the fact that it was they who had to face the dangers and discomforts of war. Signs were also not lacking in the fleet that the men were beginning to organise themselves on Trades Union lines through Lower Deck Societies – a tendency which was bound to arouse misgivings in the upper hierarchy of the navy. Towards the end of September 1917 a lower deck 'Petition' asking for the removal of certain anomalies and injustices in the pay code and in conditions of service was circulated in the fleet and forwarded to the Admiralty by Beatty.[74] But the government was well aware of what was in the wind, and on 27th September a new Order in Council announced improvements in pay and pensions and the abolition of the much resented 'hospital stoppages'. Lloyd George also published a letter in which he reproached the country for having in other wars been 'willing to avail itself of the services of men who have risked all to serve their country not only without adequate pay, but with no proper provision for dependents or for those who have been disabled'; and he gave a promise that such a state of affairs was to be remedied.[75] Beatty had the new pay code circulated at once to all ships of the fleet, and called for reports on its reception. In almost every case Captains felt able to report that the reception had been favourable; and indeed the Admiralty investigation which had led to it certainly had been very thorough and sympathetic – except with regard to the Lower Deck Societies already mentioned.[76] Thus was the question of pay settled reasonably satisfactorily for the last year of the war. It will be told later how rumbles of discontent rose to an alarming crescendo after it was over.*

As regards discipline it is certainly the case that, although the Board of Admiralty did once consider the reintroduction of flogging for the crime of desertion in time of war, and quickly rejected it, the British system was far more humane than that prevailing in the German Navy. The relaxed disciplinary system was greatly helped by the encouragement given by Beatty and his subordinates, whether the Fleet was stationed at Scapa or Rosyth, to all forms of recreation, in which officers and men took part without regard to rank or status. In addition to the encouragement of games of all kinds, both ashore and afloat, much attention and effort were devoted to theatrical productions, in which an astonishingly high standard of skill and originality was displayed. The store ship *Gourko* was converted to provide a theatre seating 2,000, which enabled such entertainments to be rehearsed and

*For an excellent account of the development of the navy's Welfare Organisation see article 'From Petitions to Reviews' by H. P. (Commander Harry Pursey) in Brassey's Annual for 1937.

produced without interfering with the fighting efficiency or sea readiness of the warships themselves. Admiral Chalmers, who was serving in the fleet flagship at the time, has borne witness to Beatty's part in encouraging such entertainments, and tells how he himself nearly always attended them and would end the evening with an address to the audience which brought them back to the realities of war and the demands which would be made on them;[77] and I have published elsewhere an account of perhaps the most successful theatrical shows of the period – those produced by the famous battleship *Warspite*.[78]

A darker side to the problem of keeping a huge fleet both happy and contented was the increasing trend towards alcoholism among the officers – especially in the smaller ships which experienced the full rigours of North Sea weather. In those days the duty free gin available in all British warships cost about five shillings (25 new pence) per bottle. So an officer of Lieutenant's rank or above, who was allowed a wine bill of £5.00 a month, could if he drank the whole of his quota solo (which was of course unusual though not unknown) consume some two-thirds of a bottle of gin *per day* without breaking any regulation. By the end of the war not a few officers had thus become confirmed alcoholics; and they carried their habits into peace time commissions – which was not conducive to creating happy or successful ships.* The Admiralty became seriously worried over the problem, and finally required Captains to state unequivocally in Confidential Reports that an officer 'was of sober habits' – if he came within that category. The absence of such a statement would be taken as a contrary assertion; but that did not help much if the Captain himself drank too much! It should, however, be made plain that excessive drinking was almost entirely a harbour habit, since most ships closed their wardroom bars on going to sea.

It is thus true to say that the Royal Navy in general and the Grand Fleet under Beatty in particular overcame the social and disciplinary troubles which arose during 1917-18 with skill and

*I served under one such Captain in a sloop on the North America and West Indies station 1925-6, and am thankful that such an experience was not repeated. By a curious coincidence, at the time of writing (1979) the Ministry of Defence has set up a Committee to enquire into alcoholism in all three fighting services.

understanding. In the German Navy a very different state of affairs prevailed, and its consequences first came to the surface in August 1917 – though the British Admiralty could at the time obtain no precise details of what had happened. We now know that the wretchedly bad food, which was of course a result of our blockade, and the harshness of the disciplinary system were the chief causes of the wave of non-violent protest which then struck some of the big ships of the High Seas Fleet; and the reaction of the naval authorities was extremely severe. A series of Courts Martial passed ten death sentences, of which two were carried out on 5th September; while 19 men were sentenced to five to fifteen years' penal servitude and 56 to imprisonment for one to ten years.[79] Though British officers may be justified in indulging in some measure of self-satisfaction over the way such troubles were handled in the closing stages of World War I, it is appropriate to remind them of the serious disturbances which took place in some of the big ships of the Atlantic Fleet in September 1931 – over the issue of pay.[80]

CHAPTER TWELVE

Victory – of a Kind,
January–November 1918

The New Year was only a few days old when Beatty had to make another flying visit to London to discuss current problems with Wemyss and Fremantle, and in particular the possibility of striking offensive blows.[1] This was his first encounter with the new régime in the Admiralty. Rear-Admiral George Hope, an able if not very assertive officer had become Deputy First Sea Lord when Wemyss moved to the 1st Sea Lord's desk, Commodore de Bartolomé had become Controller of the Navy (an office which was merged with that of 3rd Sea Lord in November 1918) *vice* Lionel Halsey, who took command of the 2nd Battle Cruiser Squadron, and Fremantle had replaced Oliver as DCNS. For the first time since the outbreak of war decentralization was the order of the day. Wemyss became Chief of Naval Staff in fact as well as in name, and the staff itself was reorganised and expanded – on the lines which Richmond had long favoured. Beatty found the changes to his liking, and relations between him and Wemyss were, at this stage, far better than his relations with Jellicoe had been. Whenever a serious disagreement loomed on the horizon Wemyss sent Fremantle north to discuss it with Beatty; and the former has recorded how, provided he 'sat quiet for the first hour of an interview and gave him [Beatty] the full chance of declaiming against Admiralty iniquities' their differences were easily resolved.[2]

At the end of January Beatty wrote the first of the long series of letters which passed between him and Wemyss, beginning it 'My dear Rosy' – the nickname by which the new 1st Sea Lord was always known, and ending 'Yours ever'. Though Beatty was opposed to Wemyss's idea that a battle squadron should be stationed in the Thames estuary as a safeguard against raids into the Channel, and wanted the whole of his fleet to be based on Rosyth, there was nothing in the least rancorous in the expression of his views.[3] Before many weeks had passed Beatty was congratulating Wemyss on his success in his new office, while the latter responded by telling the C–in–C that 'co-operation between the Grand Fleet and the Admiralty is excellent',[4] and that 'Geddes is perfectly straight and allright [sic] . . . and will back me up to the last;[5] while Beatty told the First Lord that 'Everything works smoothly between the Admiralty and the Grand Fleet', and that he felt 'in far closer touch' with Whitehall than previously – an obvious dig at Jellicoe.[6] By March Wemyss was addressing Beatty by his first name;[7] but, as will be told later, the cordiality between them soon evaporated.

Much of the credit for this striking change must go to Wemyss, who showed high qualities of statesmanship in an office he had never expected to hold. The only change made at this time among the Grand Fleet's Flag Officers was the translation of Sturdee from the 4th Battle Squadron to the Nore Command. Beatty was glad to see him go, probably because he found his seniority an embarrassment, and disliked his inflated idea of his own capacity.[8]

Beatty's January meeting at the Admiralty produced a fundamental change in his strategic purposes. He first reviewed the heavy demands made on his fleet for convoy escorts, for maintaining the efficiency of the mined area in the Heligoland Bight, and to defend the Scandinavian convoys. Taking account of the proven weaknesses from which his ships suffered, notably the lack of efficient armour piercing shells, he then proposed, no doubt reluctantly, that it would be 'to our general interest to adopt measures which would tend to postpone a Fleet action'. In other words he modified drastically his previously dominant 'Decisive Battle' strategy. On 9th January he forwarded a paper in which he expanded on the reasons for this somewhat startling recommendation, namely the advantages possessed by the enemy in choice of time for an attack, the release of German naval forces from the Baltic consequent on the Russian débâcle, the real British strength in battle cruisers being no more than equal to the six ships of that class believed to be possessed by the Germans, the Grand Fleet's very narrow margin in light cruisers, and the constant calls made on it for destroyers. His conclusion was that 'the correct strategy of the Grand Fleet is no longer to endeavour to bring the enemy to action at any cost, but rather to contain him in his bases until the general situation is more favourable to us'. But he qualified that restrictive statement by adding 'This does not mean that action should be avoided if conditions favour us, or that our role should be passive and purely defensive'.[9] Two remarks on this statement are relevant. Firstly it never had been British policy to engage the High Seas Fleet 'at any cost' – certainly after Jellicoe's memorandum of 30th October 1914 had received Admiralty approval. Secondly the operations postulated by Beatty were to intensify 'offensive minelaying' and to carry out 'offensive operations . . . against the enemy's bases on the Flemish coast' which would, he hoped, 'exert steady pressure, harass the enemy and weaken his morale' until such time as the disabilities from which his fleet suffered had been eliminated. No mention was made of the air torpedo attack for which he had pressed so strenuously in the previous year; but he had certainly not dropped the idea.

On 17th January the Board considered Beatty's paper and Geddes recommended adoption of the policy he had put forward. Next day the War Cabinet gave their approval to the new strategy which, as Professor Marder has remarked, was 'basically identical' to that adopted by Jellicoe.[10] Though the War Cabinet probably did not relish the implications they were at the time beset with so many difficult and urgent problems that the paper seems to have slipped through with little discussion. It does not receive even a mention in Hankey's voluminous and very detailed diary.[11] Before leaving the subject of Beatty's revised strategy it must be recorded that the statement in the German Official History that it was his 'firm intention to avoid a decisive battle' has no substance whatever in it.[12]

After returning from London Beatty wrote to Eugénie that 'It was a joy to see you again, even for so short a time, still I do not grumble, five minutes happiness is not to be sneezed at and I don't believe it was a minute more'.[13] In the same letter Beatty wrote 'I just love your fairy story, and you must certainly send me your real fairy story and I won't show it to a soul and will burn it when I have read it'. What he meant by her 'real fairy story' is obscure, but Eugénie's son found among her papers the drafts (badly disorganised) of two of the 'fairy stories' which she undoubtedly sent Beatty at this time. If one substitutes the real lovers for the imaginary characters in the stories it is plain that they were mildly erotic invitations to

Beatty to persevere. One was the story of a voyage by Oghuz Khan to the Bagh–il–Dilkusha or 'Garden of Heart's Delight' at Shiraz in Persia, and another was the story of Prince Delphinus's journey 'to seek the favour of the stars', during which he visited the Pleiades, which were of course the sailors' stars to the ancient Greeks.* These fantasies of Eugénie's obviously owed a good deal to the story of Shéhérazade and the 'Thousand and One Nights', during which she is alleged to have so beguiled King Shahryar that he spared her life; but to Beatty, wrapped as he was in the northern mists and buffeted by the constant gales and blizzards, they brought great delight – and promise of joys to come. He and Eugénie evidently began to study Arabo-Persian script at this time, and some of his letters are spiced with words or sentences written in it. Some of them cannot be deciphered, but a distinguished orientalist of Cambridge University has identified one frequently repeated calligraph as DĀLN[14] – which requires no elucidation, especially as it is usually addressed to his 'Blue-eyed, golden-haired Hourie' [sic].[15]

In late February and again in early March 1918 Beatty came down to London for talks with Fremantle and Geddes. He then renewed his plea for the air torpedo attack on the High Seas Fleet, though without success. The letters he wrote to Eugénie after these visits suggest that he was unable to arrange an assignation with her on either occasion. On 1st March he wrote to her that he had come to Rosyth 'as there was considerable confusion existing at the base and wanted putting straight' – presumably in connection with the forthcoming move there of the whole Grand Fleet. 'Also', Beatty continued, 'I have to have continual conversations with the new gentlemen at the Admiralty who are attempting [? to direct] the strategy of the war, as it must be that we see eye to eye on the many points at issue . . . However it is something to know that our relations are perfectly harmonious which was never certain under the old régime'.[16] In his next letter, which is undated but from internal evidence can confidently be dated to March 1918, he welcomed Eugénie's latest Fairy Story rapturously, telling her that 'You have acquired the Arabian

---

*In Greek mythology the 'seven sisters' of the Pleiades were the daughters of Atlas by Pleione and were the virgin companions of Artemis, whom the Romans knew as Diana. Castor and Pollux were the sentinels of the Pleiades, who were pursued by the hunter Orion of Boeotia.

lilt in your story-telling which is most effective', and how he longed to join her 'in Sunlit valley land', or to be 'the Astrologer to your Mariana or the Prince Mogireddin to your lovely (?) Feydid'. He assured Eugénie that he could 'administer love potions just as successfully' as those characters.[17] In another letter which can be dated to the same month he wrote that it was still bitterly cold in the far north, but he had 'been maintaining continuous sweeps in the North Sea which is very good for everybody, especially the battleships which haven't done so much [time] at sea as they have done the last 3 months for a very long time'. These sweeps were, however, 'a constant anxiety' to the C-in-C – presumably on account of mines and submarines; and he wrote that he always 'heaved a sigh of relief ' when he saw the ships 'safely back again'.[18]

Meanwhile Carson was continuing his defence of Jellicoe, though he did not raise the matter in the debate on the Navy Estimates early in March as Geddes had expected, and for which he provided himself with briefing 'Notes'.[19] But Beatty was furious with 'that blithering old idiot Carson', who he considered 'is doing no end of mischief '. 'He doesn't believe a word he says', declared Beatty, 'as I have had it from him several times that J. R. J. was an impossible man to do work with and at times he felt he could not go on with him'. He considered that Carson was 'just using Jelly [Jellicoe] to attack L.G. and Geddes with and nothing else' – which probably had more than a soupçon of truth in it about the former First Lord's motives; but Beatty cautiously warned Eugénie that his diatribe against Carson was 'for your dear blue eyes only'.[20]

In March 1918 Beatty fully shared in the grave anxiety produced by the great German offensive on the Western Front, which produced such successes that the vital Channel ports appeared at one time to be in danger. His letters to Wemyss and also those to his wife and to Eugénie make clear the frustration he felt over his own inability to do anything effective towards overcoming the crisis. He even at this time reverted to his old superstition about consulting fortune tellers, telling Ethel that if she could find the famous Mrs. Du Bois in Edinburgh she was to threaten her with dismissal from his staff 'if she does not produce something good for us soon'. He was also much troubled by the thought that the High Seas Fleet might make a sortie in strength to coincide with the land offensive, with the object of attacking another

Scandinavian convoy; and the thought that he would again
have to engage the enemy with inadequate armour protection
in some of his big ships and inefficient heavy shells in all of
them troubled him greatly.[21] As will be told shortly, Admiral
Scheer was about to carry out exactly the plan which Beatty
foresaw.

Towards the end of March in a letter to Eugénie Beatty
exploded on the subject of why the Army had found itself
'fighting against overwhelming odds', why we had been
forced recently to take over more of the French line,[22] and also
send substantial reinforcements to prop up the Italians after
their severe defeat at Caporetto in October 1917 – against the
advice of Generals Robertson and Haig.[23] But it is fair to add
that Beatty was almost certainly unaware of the extent and
seriousness of the mutinies in the French army which followed
the costly failure of General Nivelle's offensive in April 1917,
which produced the need for the British army to take some of
the weight off their allies. After letting off steam about the
causes of the crisis Beatty ended in a lighter vein, telling Eugénie
that 'One gallant old sport who looks after a portion of our
Defences [presumably at Scapa], a Retired Captain confided to
me that he was alright up here but the thing that tried him
most was the Sexual Starvation, as the old gentleman is 65
summers, my heart warmed to him and I nearly gave him the
Fairy Stories to read' – which confirms that their content was
basically erotic.

In his next letter he answered Eugénie's reproach that he had
never replied to her invitation to come to Ranger's Lodge.
'Well, my dear', he wrote, 'you well know the answer, it
would not be a case of a comrade in Dreamland for I would
never let you sleep – unless you swooned and then I would
bring you too [sic] with caresses. In fact you would wish that
you had never been so rash as to run the risk of being squeeze
[sic] to death'. As to his future plans, he wrote that he did not
quite know where he was for the present, since if the ocean
convoy escorts were successful, and his destroyers were
returned to him he would have to alter his plans. But he was
expecting to be in London in April and if Ethel did not
accompany him he would go to Claridge's rather than to
Hanover Lodge, because there were catering difficulties at the
latter. But there may well have been an ulterior motive in his
choice of abode, since he invited Eugénie to join him if he was

unencumbered, but warned her that his plans were fluid. He ended by turning to the question of his leisure reading, about which he had consulted Eugénie before. This time he wrote 'My Literature is confined to the Newspapers for very light reading Morning Post and Pink 'Un they amuse me.* Culled from the latter I can do good work –

> 'Here's to you and here's to Blighty,
> I'm in pyjamas you in a nighty.
> If we are feeling extra flighty
> Why in pyjamas and Why the Nighty?'

'Them's my sentiments' he concluded, which suggests that the Retired Captain was not the only person in the far north to be suffering from sexual starvation. But with a rather sudden switch Beatty asked Eugénie to get him a copy of Plutarch's *Lives* as his own was packed away in one of his houses.[24]

Meanwhile Roger Keyes had taken over the Dover Command, and under the stimulus of his fiery energy the Channel Barrage soon became more effective, four U-boats meeting their end in it between 19th December 1917 and 8th February 1918 – compared with only two from the beginning of the war up to the former date.[25] Though the U-boats in consequence gave up using the Channel to reach their operational areas in the Western Approaches, and changed to the much longer route round the north of Scotland, the Germans reacted powerfully against the patrol vessels on the barrage by making a very successful destroyer attack on the night of 14th-15th February. But Keyes's great plan was the blocking of the entrances to the U-boats' bases at Zeebrugge and Ostend, known for security reasons as 'the 02 Scheme' at the time, which was being organised in the utmost secrecy. Beatty supported it enthusiastically, telling Wemyss in February that 5 officers and 150 Marines, all volunteers to take part in 'a specially hazardous operation', had already left his fleet to join in the training of the assault force, and that he had 8 executive officers and 200 seamen 'ready to go when required' as well as 200 stokers and engineer artificers.[26] As is now well known the attack was carried out on 23rd April after several false starts, and although it was pressed home with the utmost

---

*The *Sporting Times*, or 'Pink 'Un' as it was colloquially called because it was printed on pink paper, dealt chiefly with horse racing but generally included some lighthearted and mildly pornographic material.

gallantry and at heavy cost in life it did not achieve its purpose at Zeebrugge, while the blocking of Ostend was a complete failure; and so it came to pass that, sedulously fostered by Keyes and his formidable wife, the operation was accorded a place in the realm of naval mythology – and was even reproduced with realistic models at the Wembley British Empire Exhibition of 1924-25. What it really accomplished was to give a great boost to the morale of an increasingly anxious and worried nation, and to restore something of the high regard in which it had formerly held the Navy. An interesting side effect of the raid was that when Keyes pressed very hard for bombing attacks on the submarines and destroyers, which he believed to be trapped in Bruges, the recently formed Air Ministry refused all such pleas on the grounds of a prior commitment to 'strategic bombing' of industrial targets in Germany – which was a foretaste of the independent air strategy which was to cause so much heart-burning in World War II. Beatty's first reaction to the Zeebrugge raid was much the same as Keyes's – that it had been 'very successful in some ways and accomplished what it set out to do'; but he deplored the heavy losses suffered. 'I have lost some magnificent officers and men . . . in the enterprise', he told Eugénie; 'they nearly all came from us and we gave of our best which could ill be spared'.[27]

We saw in the last chapter how the huge Northern Mine Barrage was started in 1917. It finally stretched across about 240 miles of the North Sea from the Orkneys to the approaches to the Hardanger Fjord just south of Bergen in Norway. Over 15,000 British and 56,000 American mines were laid in it; but the latter proved as inefficient as our own early mines had been, and in August Beatty complained bitterly to Wemyss on that score.[28] He disliked the whole undertaking – chiefly because of the hampering effect the barrage had on his own movements and operations; and he caused Wemyss some anxiety over his insistence on preserving a ten mile gap at the western end to facilitate support of the Scandinavian convoys. Wemyss feared that this proposal would cause great offence to the Americans in general and to Admiral Sims USN in particular; but Beatty stuck to his guns and preserved his gap. Though he was anxious to obtain the use of a base in Norway for his own vessels he was strongly averse to using strong-arm methods against that country –

which would in truth have been contrary to the principles for which the Allies alleged they were fighting.[29] In the end his patience paid, since in October the Norwegian Government closed its territorial waters to passage by the U-boats and allowed the barrage to be extended to the coast. As to the results accomplished, the latest assessment is that six U-boats were probably sunk by the barrage's mines, which is certainly not a negligible return though hardly proportional to the enormous effort involved in laying them and the amount of material expended.[30] In the other big North Sea minefield, that laid across the Heligoland Bight, 21,000 mines were added in 1918, and although they accounted for few U-boats their presence did force them to use the longer route through the Kattegat in order to reach their operational areas.

In mid-April Beatty told Eugénie that he had moved the whole fleet to Rosyth, 'I could not bear the isolation up North any longer', he wrote, 'with the tragedy going on, on the Western Front'. Though he was now 'in a better strategical situation than away in those Northern mists', he continued, he was still desperately anxious about what would happen if we failed to hold the Germans in the West.[31] In March and April letters passed between Beatty and Wemyss about what should be done if the Germans succeeded in driving a wedge between the British and French armies, so forcing the former to retreat to the Channel ports – which had to be held at all costs.[32] In fact the crisis was overcome in July when the final German offensive was repulsed and the counter-attacks by the Allied armies brought what Basil Liddell Hart aptly called 'the first taste of victory'.[33] But before those happy events had taken place Beatty could only tell his 'Dear Comrade' that his 'promised visit to the Metropolis must be postponed'; he was however enjoying the Plutarch which he had asked for and which Eugénie had evidently got for him very promptly. 'There is no doubt', he wrote, 'that the rascal was much inclined to gossip which makes him more human' – a remark which rated Plutarch somewhat unkindly as an early Creevey. 'I would that I could see you', he concluded, 'and whisper in your ear all that I think of you'.[34] In his next letter he fulminated against the German 'demolition of Rheims', which he described as 'the fairest of all French cathedrals . . . every inch a masterpiece'. The destruction of it, he told Eugénie, made him feel 'quite sick'.

Evidently Beatty urged Eugénie to come to Rosyth at this time, because when he learnt that she refused to do so he replied that 'I am beginning to hate the rectitude that caused you to decline to come North'. 'It was delightful to you', he went on somewhat unfairly, 'but confound it all life is abominably short and it would appear that under the régime ordered by you I shall never see you again' – because he 'simply could not leave the Fleet just now' when 'anything might happen at any time . . . and the chance once slipped will never happen again'. One cannot but wonder whether Eugénie's reluctance to fall in with Beatty's plans arose from the need for extreme discretion rather than from a sense of what her lover called 'rectitude', since discovery would certainly have brought disaster on her and her husband. In the same letter Beatty declared that 'we have been very near bringing off a big thing but the devil was against us' – obviously referring to the operation to be described shortly. 'There is only one thing I want', he continued rather plaintively, 'and that you can't send me . . . well I quite understand, but I am beginning to rebel especially after reading the story of the Delights of Bagh-el-Dilkusha. . . .' The result was that he felt 'restless and unsatisfied', and he hoped that his mistress 'would understand the reasons'.[36]

The 'big thing' to which Beatty referred was the sortie by the High Seas Fleet on 23rd April. The Admiralty had warned him that because the Germans had changed their naval cypher and were using wireless far more sparingly, they could no longer guarantee to give him warning, even of major movements. On this occasion the Admiralty could give no warning at all, and a submarine on patrol which did sight the enemy mistook them for British ships and did not signal a report – a failure which Beatty described as 'incredibly stupid'.[37] Scheer's plan was to use Hipper's 1st and 2nd Scouting Groups to attack the Scandinavian convoys – exactly as Beatty feared[38] – while the Battle Fleet under himself covered the operation from about 60 miles to the SSW. However, just over 24 hours after sailing the battle cruiser *Moltke* suffered a serious breakdown which caused flooding of an engine room. She broke wireless silence to tell the C-in-C of her predicament and fell back on him for support. She was taken in tow by a battleship and finally reached port safely, despite a British submarine putting a torpedo into her. On intercepting the *Moltke's* signal the Admiralty ordered the Grand Fleet to sea. Thick fog enveloped the Firth of Forth at the time – which had always been recognised as one of its potential disadvantages as a base. Beatty told Eugénie that the experience had been 'distinctly unpleasant' but 'thanks to the capabilities and fine qualities of my Flag Officers and Captains we got out 193 ships in shortest time on record without an accident' – which was indeed a remarkable feat of seamanship and pilotage.[39] By the early afternoon of 24th the whole fleet – 31 battleships, four battle cruisers, 24 light cruisers and 85 destroyers – was at sea. It was to prove the last time during the war that Beatty sailed in full fighting array.

Meanwhile despite the accident to the *Moltke* Scheer ordered Hipper to continue with the operation, and he searched the convoy routes up as far as 60° North – without finding his prey. Beatty steered for The Naze, but the charts show that Scheer crossed his track about 100 miles (some five hours steaming) ahead of him during the night of 24th-25th. The failure of a well planned German blow arose partly from the *Moltke's* breakdown and partly from the fact that they had got the sailing of the west-bound convoy wrong by 24 hours. Had Hipper reached the convoy's route a day earlier he might have overwhelmed the 34 merchant ships comprising it and also the escort and covering force – which would have been greatly inferior to the attackers.[40] So although Beatty was once again disappointed the balance of luck was perhaps in his favour.[41]

We saw earlier how, during the first years of the war, the fear of invasion had constantly affected both the allocation of forces and the strategy of their employment. Early in 1917 'Jacky' Fisher (with nothing better to do) had sent Lloyd George an alarmist letter on the subject,[42] with the result that the Cabinet asked for a new review of this hoary problem.[43] Though the Admiralty very reasonably felt that invasion was even less likely than it had been earlier, they did not consider it justifiable to ignore the question of how the Grand Fleet should operate if it did take place. Beatty gathered that their idea was that he should rush south with the maximum strength as quickly as possible – which held no appeal to him, since he considered the High Seas Fleet was, as always, his primary objective. In December 1917 the issue was debated yet again, but Beatty represented that the likelihood of such an operation being launched was negligible. The final resurrection of the invasion bogey took place in April 1918, when a German occupation of Holland appeared to be on the cards. Looking back today it seems hard to justify the effort put into reviewing the likelihood of invasion, and the retention of substantial land forces at home in order to counter it; for the plain truth was that as long as Beatty's fleet held command of the surface waters of the North Sea such an undertaking simply was not a practical operation of war. Yet when the issue arose again in 1940, with far more likelihood of invasion coming off than at any time during World War I, and the C-in-C, Home Fleet represented exactly the same views as Beatty had held more than 20 years earlier, it produced a major clash between him and Churchill as Prime Minister.[44] The truth seems to be that civilian and military minds can never grasp the simple fact that without command of the waters over which an amphibious expedition must pass, to launch such an enterprise is suicidal.

By the summer of 1918 Beatty's problems had been greatly eased by the issue to his fleet of the new armour piercing shells and the return of some destroyers from convoy duty. He rightly gave the chief credit for the provision of efficient shells to Captain F.C. Dreyer, whom he described as 'a most exceptional man';[45] and when he learnt that Dreyer was to return to the fleet in a sea appointment he urged the First Lord to retain him in the Admiralty because 'there is nobody to take his place'.[46] As we have here been critical about Dreyer's actions over fire control equipment it is only fair to pay tribute to his work on the new shell – though it came to fruit too late to affect the war.

The improved equipment and strength of the Grand Fleet gave Beatty the chance he wanted to modify his policy about the conditions in which he would engage the High Seas Fleet. In July he described his more hopeful attitude, and his modification of the cautious policy he had recommended early in the year, in a letter to Ethel. The submarine, he wrote, was 'still a thorn and a very unpleasant one too', but it was no longer 'the danger he was'. Thus the country's food supply was far better than it had been in 1917, although 'the need for patience' still remained. He recalled precedents to that effect from earlier wars, and declared that he would strive 'to tempt the enemy to repeat the earlier mistakes he had made [presumably at Dogger Bank and Jutland]'. He ended his letter in hopeful, even optimistic vein.[47]

Meanwhile Wemyss was thinking on rather similar lines, and in August he wrote to Beatty describing what he regarded as the 'Danger Points' against which a German attack was possible. He named the Atlantic, East Coast and Scandinavian convoys, and the Dover Barrage as coming within that category, and also a raid on some part of the North Sea coast; but he considered an attempt to mine the Grand Fleet's bases or to attack the Northern Barrage minelaying and covering forces more probable contingencies. Beatty replied in general agreement, but pointed out that the forces he could send to cover the Scandinavian convoys could not be adequate to meet a major detachment from the High Seas Fleet, such as Scheer had organised on 24th-25th April; so those convoys still provided him with 'plenty of anxious moments'.[48]

On 11th August Scheer replaced Admiral Henning von Holtzendorff as Chief of the German War Staff, and Hipper took over command of the High Seas Fleet. Though Wemyss told Beatty that in his view it was 'only psychology which will bring the German fleet out', and that he did not believe that 'von Scheer would ever willingly seek an engagement', Beatty was hopeful that the changes in the German high command would produce the opportunity for which he had so long hoped.[49] In other words he had reverted enthusiastically to the 'Decisive Battle' strategic concept – which he had only abandoned temporarily and reluctantly at the beginning of the year; but as 'control of sea communications' in the vital Atlantic theatre had by this time been made far more secure by the decisive success of the convoy strategy, his switch was by no means unreasonable.

Early in June Beatty wrote again to the King, welcoming very warmly his intention to visit the Fleet at Rosyth in the following month. He stressed the advantages which had accrued from the move to that base in April, especially with regard to the maintenance of close relations with the Admiralty; and he described with evident pride how even the fogs which commonly enveloped the Firth of Forth had not proved an insuperable handicap in the sortie of 23rd April. The fleet's visual signalling had, he wrote, so improved that he was able to preserve continuous wireless silence on that occasion – until he wanted the boom gates opened for his return to harbour. 'Wemyss', he wrote, 'is splendid and it is a pleasure to work with him, and from the Grand Fleet point of view I could not wish for a better first Sea Lord'. Again one may note the veiled criticism of the Jackson and Jellicoe régimes. He then went on to describe the latest gunnery development, namely concentration firings – designed to take advantage of his superior strength in battleships – and by 'throw-off firings' which enabled 'far higher speeds to be used than in practices against the towed targets'.* He was also developing air spotting of fall of shot – from seaplanes as well as kite balloons; all of which shows that Beatty's claim that 'we are not standing still' had substance in it.[51]

The King's visit to the fleet duly took place in July, and produced the last of the series of letters Beatty wrote to him. An interesting point is that in this letter he wrote that, although Napoleon's pressure on Villeneuve to go to sea in 1805 might provide a precedent, 'I fear that our chances of bringing the High Seas Fleet to action are small'. Finally he told the King, with pride, that he had just heard that his son David had successfully passed into Osborne College as a cadet.[52]

Between May and August 1918 Beatty kept up his correspondence with Eugénie, with whom he was always striving to arrange a meeting. A hint dropped at the end of May that 'Your plans for July make the mouth water' suggests that something of that nature was in the wind, and the account she had sent him of a 'Divine Bath' produced the thought 'what a delightful experience it would be to be the Gold Fish, provided that you occupied it also and undertook to catch the Gold Fish exactly as did the seductive "*Maia*" ' – presumably one of the characters in her 'Fairy Stories'.[53] In his next letter he described how 'not a day has passed that we have not had some Units prowling round the North Sea in the vicinity of the Enemy and his Bases', and he himself had been out with 'the heavy weights' – though nothing had come of it. He had just returned temporarily to Scapa, where he had been met by 'grey skies, heavy seas, and wind, wind, nothing but wind'; which had made him long for 'a Desert, a Blue Sky and Sun, lots and lots of Sun and *YOU*'.[54] A few days later he wrote that the 'Haven of Rest', which Eugénie had evidently planned for them at some future date, 'sounds delightful, my

*See page 90.

imagination has already rioted over all sorts of possibilities which [it] is not good for me to dwell on too much'. He promised to preserve it 'as a deadly secret between us two'.[55] Unfortunately the destruction of all Eugénie's letters deprives us of any idea of what she had proposed, and in the end Beatty had to be satisfied with far less enjoyment of her love.

Evidently at this time Eugénie sent him a book about the practice of sexual relations, because at the end of June he wrote to her 'My dear, what an amazing book! It fills me with interest to learn that nearly all the troubles in Domestic Life are due to the fact that the man is *too* quick and the Lady too slow. What a tragedy! But the Lady Doctor does not provide the answer as to how this is to be cured . . . I am quite sure that [the] man should do all he could to prolong the thrills, they are so damnably short but how is it to be done? it is no use telling you what is the matter if you don't provide the means of solving the trouble'. In the same letter (continued later) he thanked her for 'the most delicious Golden Curl rich and fragrant', which Eugénie had evidently sent him, and enquired if she was going to visit an 'aged relative in the neighbourhood of Edinburgh', which would necessitate her staying a night at the North British Hotel. If so, he wrote hopefully, 'I'll come and dine with you'.[56] That plan bore fruit, since on 10th July he wrote that Ethel was going south on 14th, and he would expect Eugénie at the hotel on the afternoon of 16th. She was to telephone the Hall Porter of the New Club giving her room number in the form 'The number required is 242 *or whatever it is*', so that he could go 'straight up' without enquiring at the office. They would dine together, and he would 'return after dinner to my ship'; so it was to be a very brief encounter. If he had to postpone or cancel the idea he would wire 'some nonsense' such as 'David goes up for exams 16th, 17th'.[57] The assignation evidently was fulfilled because his next letter tells her a little breathlessly 'What a dream it has been, but just a dream, come and gone . . . No matter, I wouldn't change anything for fear of changing too much . . . and interlaced with some golden moments and one hour that will remain for ever a dream of perfect happiness . . . I thank you from deep down for bringing into my dry and burdensome existence a glimpse of perfect bliss'. At the end he broke into Italian – a language of which he knew but little – with '*Io bacia la tua bocca adorata sempre la vita tua*', which may be freely translated as 'I kiss your adorable lips for ever'.[58]

In the middle of June 1918, before the crisis on the Western Front had been surmounted, Beatty received a delightfully cordial letter from General John J. Pershing, the commander of the U.S. Expeditionary Force. He wrote that his army 'wish you to know from our own lips our admiration for and trust in you. Here in France we are near enough to stretch out a friendly hand and pledge to you our best in the common cause . . . in this struggle for world freedom and peace'. Beatty replied in his own hand that he and his officers and men 'naturally feel the keenest satisfaction for the great and ever growing support accorded by the United States', particularly because of 'our close association with your Countrymen in The United States Battle Squadron who are at once our comrades and our friends. . . .'[59] If the language of this exchange now seems somewhat hyperbolic it does exemplify the extraordinary degree of good will which then prevailed on both sides, and how assiduously Beatty worked to foster it.

In his next letter to Eugénie Beatty indulged in a little self pity, writing that he had told a tiresome and stupid visitor that 'what I really lacked was a sympathetic Emma [Hamilton]!!' to share the heavy burden of his responsibilities. 'You see', he told her, 'I like to talk to somebody who is sympathetic who can look at things from my point of view, and who can help me with a little flattering encouragement'. The same letter suggests that Ethel had seen one of his letters, which produced 'tempestuous scenes followed by reconciliations'. This indiscretion by Eugénie produced a protest that 'it's a bit thick when my letters are handed over to the other side'.[60]

As an example of Beatty's devotion to duty, even while he was longing all the time for Eugénie, we may here quote from an undated letter which was undoubtedly written early in September 1918. 'I had an amusing experience on Monday', he told her, 'all was very quiet and everything had come in, so I thought at least one peaceful night [? lay ahead] so I determined to make the most of it and stepped ashore and said I would return in the morning and would have one peaceful night in the good air of Aberdour. I went to bed early in your bed and helped by divine memories was making the most of it when at 1.10 a.m. I was awakened by the staid Lindsay, "The Secretary wishes to speak to you, Sir David. . . ." Out I shot to listen to the dulcet tones of the Sec. on the telephone that one of my outposts had sent in a bleat fraught with possibilities. I was aboard in under the hour and [a] half and the Fleet was out at 4 a.m. The staff work was excellent but it all petered out and my night of rest was *manqué*. But I did enjoy the 2 hours. Associations, recollections were so heavenly that it was worth it'; all of which confirms that they had been lovers when Eugénie came to Aberdour for a month in July-August 1917. In the same letter he referred to their recent meeting in Edinburgh as '3 weeks ago, one hour of perfect heaven. What a short span of time, but it was worth years of ordinary life and the memory of it is something to treasure' – which enables us to date the letter with a fair degree of certainty to Sunday 8th September. [61]

The tiff which had arisen between Beatty and Eugénie over Ethel seeing one of his letters evidently did not subside quickly, and came near to bringing about a breach. Eugénie had apparently written to him that he 'might say a man can love two women at the same time', but that it 'would be a bitter pill for them [to] swallow and impossible for them to digest'. Beatty did not apply salve to Eugénie's wounded pride; for he told her outright 'I am truly devoted to Tata, so much so that I efface myself in my desire to see her happy. I cannot forget all that she has been to me for the last 20 years (nearly), all that she has done for me, all that she has given me'. None the less during the last four years of war he had 'looked for Love and Sympathy and did not get them' from Ethel. Still, he declared, 'I cared for her so much that I did not want to make her miserable too'; rather had he gone 'without Love and Sympathy until you came along and gave me both, and brought joy into my life'. He even threatened that 'if he [? Bryan] or anybody came between [us] I would shoot him or you or both because you or he or both would be robbing me of that which is doing so much to help me to feel human happiness again . . .' – which was palpably absurd and melodramatic. He went on to say that if 'these terms are too one sided . . . and you will retire from what you call the contest . . . then I must bow to your sweet will . . .' But he was obviously hopeful that such a need would not arise, since he told her that 'my eyes are black and my face pale at the thought of it, and I just long to see you, to kiss you, and to feel you quite close as I once have done, and a repetition of that long divine thrill which you alone in all the world can provide'. The chief burden of this long and rather incoherent letter was his extreme unease over the prospect that he might be going to lose his mistress, and over her having 'tumbled across' an episode in what he called his 'Lurid Past'. He suggested that all such episodes, on both sides, should 'be buried deep down'; and he ended, hopefully 'I just long to –!!. Well I won't say what but you must guess. I should like to kiss you from the tips of your toes upwards, and take some time about it *Adorata Mia*'.[62] Obviously he was trying to keep the best of both worlds.

Here we must take temporary leave of the lovers and return to the war. Whereas the first twelve months of unrestricted U-boat warfare (February 1917–February 1918) had produced the destruction of some 6.2 million tons of shipping (a monthly average of 223 ships totalling 515,361 tons, more than half of which was British) the first months of 1918 showed a marked improvement. Between January and June 1918 the average total of monthly losses was only 122 ships (298,237 tons), and between July and the end of the war it fell to 57 ships (172,932 tons) per month.[63]

Not only did sinkings by submarines show a downward trend which became very marked after April but losses of merchant ships to mines also declined. The reason was that whereas ships which were routed independently might enter mined waters unawares those which were sailed in convoy could be routed along swept channels. Thus the convoy strategy proved as effective an antidote to mines as it was against submarines – a phenomenon which was repeated and reaffirmed in World War II.[64]

Though Allied construction of new merchant ships did not overtake losses from all causes until September 1918 the victory in the first Atlantic Battle actually took place in May of that year – despite German attempts to increase both the rate of building new U-boats and the number of them in operational condition. It is an interesting coincidence that victory in the second Atlantic Battle took place in the same month exactly 25 years later, and was attributable to the same causes, namely the widespread adoption of convoy and the provision of adequate sea and air escorts. The only important difference in the application of the convoy strategy in the two world wars was that whereas in the first one air escorts did no more than force enemy submarines to submerge, in the second one they finally became as effective U-boat killers as the surface escorts. Early in June 1918 the Admiralty told Beatty that a falling off of the morale of U-boat crews had been detected through the interrogation of prisoners, which was perfectly true up to a point;[65] but it should be made clear that U-boat crews never suffered a collapse such as affected the men of the big ships of the High Seas Fleet in 1918.

Two more statistical facts may be quoted here. The first is that in 1918 sinkings of U-boats totalled 69 compared with 63 in the previous year — which was no very great improvement;[66] yet at the end of the year the total strength available to the Germans was little greater than it had been at the beginning of the year. Secondly whereas at the end of 1917 only about half of the active Allied merchant shipping was sailing in convoy, by the autumn of 1918 nearly 90% of it was protected in that manner, and of 16,070 ships sailed in convoy during the war the U-boats only sank 96 or 0.6%. With such a wealth of convincing evidence available regarding the effectiveness of convoy one might have expected that all the early doubts on the matter would have been dissipated; yet that was not the case in the upper hierarchy of both the British and the American navies, as is shown by Geddes advocating hunting rather than convoy in a letter to Beatty as late as September 1918,[67] and by the reservations expressed by Admiral Sims USN to the Secretary of the Navy in April of that year.[68] Nor is there any doubt that the vast majority of British senior naval officers, and also the politicians who controlled and directed their activities, failed to understand the fundamental fact that, although the escort-of-convoy strategy may reasonably be described as basically defensive, it always provides ample opportunities for local or tactical offensives. The reason is simple — that in order to achieve their purpose, commerce raiders, whether surface, submerged or airborne, must approach their quarry; and that provides the escorts with ample opportunities to strike back at enemies which would otherwise have remained elusive.

In the autumn of 1918 lower deck unrest was revived by the men seeing how strikes were bringing industrial workers large increases of pay or bonuses, which the fighting services were powerless to emulate. Signs were not lacking that political action was being canvassed in the fleet, and Lionel Yexley the editor of the influential newspaper *The Fleet*, had been authorised by the men to submit a 'Petition' on their behalf. Early in September Yexley produced a pamphlet setting out sixteen causes of discontent, and sent copies to all persons of influence from the King and Prime Minister downwards. Beatty was, as always, sympathetic towards the men's claims, and welcomed Lloyd George's instruction to Geddes that he should meet Yexley and discuss them. The outcome was that substantial concessions were made; but it was not until after the war had ended that the whole problem of officers' and men's pay and allowances was tackled systematically.[69]

Early in September Wemyss gave Beatty a broad hint that Room 40 had at last broken the new German naval cypher, and that he could therefore expect once more to be given adequate warning of any major movement by the High Seas Fleet. This was indeed welcome news to the C-in-C after the surprise the enemy had achieved on 23rd April.[70] Beatty's hopes of a successful fleet action rose correspondingly; but it was not to be. At about the same time Arthur Balfour (now Foreign Secretary) sent to Lord Robert Cecil (Minister for Blockade) a letter about the possible infringement of Norwegian neutrality in order to close that country's territorial waters to the U-boats and blockade runners. It produced a flurry of letters between Wemyss and Beatty because the former was worried over the apparent disagreement between the Admiralty and the C-in-C on that issue. He accordingly sent Beatty a statement for joint signature by them both, in order to show that there were no differences between them on issues of policy. Beatty was acquiescent, and signed the paper with only slight amendment;[71] so the cordiality of their relations was preserved – for a time.

On the last day of September the first fissure in the alliance of the Central Powers appeared when Bulgaria asked for an armistice, and on 5th October the German government of Prince Max of Baden, who had replaced Bethman Hollweg as Chancellor, sent a Note to President Wilson with a similar request – based on acceptance of Wilson's notorious 'Fourteen Points', which he had enunciated in a message to Congress on 8th January – without consulting the Allied powers. Early in October Wemyss warned Beatty that 'Events are moving rapidly' and that 'the most likely psychological moment . . . has arrived for the High Sea [sic] Fleet to make some demonstration'.[72] At about the same time Beatty wrote to

Eugénie in delight over the good news from the western front but in anger over the 'missed golden opportunities' which made him 'go hot and cold all over with impotent fury'. Presumably he was referring to the discussions then in train over the naval terms of an armistice with Germany. The 'one fly in the ointment' for him was, he wrote, that 'the refit of my good Queen Bess', and so his projected visit to London, had been postponed. This produced a wail that 'I hate above all to disappoint myself of the great joy I was, and have been looking forward to'.[73] In his next letter he told Eugénie that a telegram had just reached him that 'Germany is squealing for a cessation of hostilities'. He considered that 'the utter defeat of the damnable Hun is not likely to be long delayed', and insisted that 'we must *never* return them their colonies'. 'I pray that I step out of Dream Land to Real Land soon', he continued with a rather abrupt switch, 'and have the opportunity of, well, just looking at you soon'. The letter ended with the osculatory Italian endearment already quoted.[74] His next letter reported the glad news that, unless something unforeseen happened, the *Queen Elizabeth's* refit would after all start on 15th October and he would come to London that night. Eugénie had evidently expressed an intention to go to the Carlton Hotel, which Beatty thoroughly approved of 'as it is so near [presumably to the Admiralty] and there would be no waste of time. . . .' He told her to let him know the number of her room and her telephone number to the Turf Club, and passed on the happy news that Ethel was going to the Isle of Wight to visit her son David at the R.N.C. Osborne.[75] However, after an exchange of letters with Wemyss, Beatty agreed once again to postpone the refit of his flagship; but as he came south in the special train put at his disposal for discussions with the Admiralty and the War Cabinet his assignation with Eugénie was not affected.

As regards the naval terms of the armistice which Germany was likely to seek at any moment Beatty argued forcefully about the fate of the High Seas Fleet, and also urged that the island of Heligoland should be taken from the Germans. 'We have got to have the HSF either by surrender or as a result of Fleet action', he insisted. 'There can be no two Naval opinions on this point in the Grand Fleet', he continued; and such opinions must in his view 'carry weight'. He also wrote that he held strong views about the Peace Terms with Germany,

especially with regard to Heligoland and 'the Baltic question' –
by which he meant the opening of that sea to British
warships. [76] Wemyss, however, tactfully pointed out that the
terms could not be regarded solely as a British interest or as
one to be decided by the Admiralty alone, since the Allied
nations and the soldiers had to be consulted. On 21st October
Beatty attended a meeting of the War Cabinet in Downing
Street at which he stated his views. After he had returned
north he sent Wemyss a memorandum setting them out in
detail. We need here quote only a few passages from that
somewhat myopic statement. [77] 'We have built up a great
Military organisation', Beatty declared, 'but the British nation
still exists on Sea Power . . . Therefore, in framing our Naval
Terms . . . we must ensure that no fleet in being is left which
can threaten our supremacy. No compromise on this vital
point is possible . . . To achieve the destruction of German
Sea Power and reduce Germany to the status of a second-rate
Naval Power, it is necessary to lay down . . . conditions
which would be commensurate with the result of a Naval
action. . . .' In consequence the surrender of only the German
submarines, which had been suggested, would not be adequate. 'The Power behind the Submarine warfare of the
enemy', wrote Beatty, 'is the High Seas Fleet. Remove that
power and the Submarine menace would completely collapse
. . . The removal therefore of the High Seas Fleet means the
removal of the one Naval menace – the Submarine'. If on the
other hand we left 'the High Seas Fleet intact, then the
position of affairs, so far as the relative Naval strength is
concerned, is precisely the same as that which obtained at the
commencement of hostilities. . . .'

Beatty's next letter to Wemyss was exceedingly stiff. He
addressed him as 'My dear First Sea Lord' instead of the
familiar 'Rosy' which he had previously used, and vented his
wrath about the Armistice terms having been agreed at
Versailles on 8th October but not communicated to him
until nine days later, which amounted to what he regarded as
the Admiralty ignoring him. 'I request', he continued, 'that
you will inform me by telegram of the date of any further
meetings on this subject so that I can be represented and given
an opportunity of having my views put forward'. This time
Wemyss hit back. The Armistice terms in question were, he
wrote, *not* 'agreed at Versailles', but were only 'prepared for

consideration'; and as the terms put forward by the Admiralty had been sent to Beatty by special messenger the accusation of delay was unwarranted. As to the C–in–C being represented at future meetings, if Beatty was prepared to send an officer 'of rank' and to accept that he would have to wait around until a chance arose to put his chief's views forward, he would raise no objections. [78] Beatty, however, not only refused to retract, but widened the rift by claiming that he had a right to be consulted on 'General Naval Policy' – to which Wemyss replied in sorrow but not in anger that he had 'read it with a great deal of regret'. [79]

On 21st October Beatty attended a meeting of the War Cabinet at which he expressed forcefully his views about the naval terms of the Armistice – though apparently without much effect because the meeting was subject to constant interruptions. He then returned to Rosyth and at once sent a copy of his long statement on the subject to Wemyss, who was still showing great restraint. Beatty also wrote to Hankey in the same vein, enclosing a copy of his paper and asking that it should be brought to the attention of the Prime Minister. [79a] Wemyss replied that he was just off to Paris for a meeting of the Allied Naval Council, which consisted of the Ministerial and Service heads of the navies of Britain, France, Italy, Japan and U.S.A., and hoped to gain from that body acceptance of a unanimous resolution which would be put forward at the next meeting of the Supreme War Council. Wemyss ended his letter by expressing the hope that the war would be ended by the 'glorious and splendid victory which you and the whole of the Grand Fleet so richly deserve'; which shows that late in October the Admiralty still expected the High Seas Fleet to come out and fight. [80] This letter evidently did not reassure Beatty, since on the last day of the month he wrote to Eugénie that he hoped the 'talking party' at Versailles 'won't let us down'; but he was apprehensive that 'the politicians will overcome Naval and Military opinion'. Wemyss, he wrote 'is none too strong . . . and so might easily be talked round'. His anxiety derived chiefly from the question 'are we in the Grand Fleet to be cheated out of our reward of breaking the Sea Power of the Hun for ever?'. 'It would be a very bad thing for the country', he continued, 'if our Great Fleet never has an opportunity of showing its power in a more demonstrative manner than it has'. Meanwhile he had the memories of 'that divine week [? 16th–23rd October] to go on', and he would 'live in it for some time'. He did not expect to come south again until the armistice terms had been settled, so would have 'to exist on dreams of you and your delightfulness' – a diet which he found 'very unsatisfying'.[81]

Meanwhile on 20th October Turkey had asked for an armistice, and on 13th November an Allied fleet, which was predominantly British and under British command, anchored off Constantinople. Also on 20th Prince Max stopped all U-boat attacks on passenger ships – an order which was so restrictive that Scheer at once recalled all his submarines. With the conclusion of an armistice between Italy and Austria on 29th October it was plain that the final collapse of the Central Powers was imminent.

On 22nd October Scheer issued an order to Hipper 'to strike a blow against the English fleet', and the C-in-C, High Seas Fleet accordingly prepared to make a sortie and, presumably remembering the German superiority in night fighting which had been so convincingly demonstrated at Jutland, to fight a battle on the second or third night. Scheer approved Hipper's plan, which was to be put into effect on 30th. Meanwhile the Admiralty had become aware that something was afoot, and on 23rd they gave Beatty, who had just got back from London, a warning – which was amplified by letters to him from Fremantle.[82] However, the mutinies which broke out in the big ships of the High Seas Fleet at the end of the month caused a total miscarriage of Hipper's plan, and on 30th October he cancelled it. By 4th November the Red Flag of revolution had replaced the proud symbol of Imperial Germany in all the enemy's bases.

Beatty's next letter to Eugénie was chiefly concerned with the virtual immobilisation of the fleet by the virulent influenza epidemic which had struck it, and which spread like wildfire in the crowded conditions which prevailed in warships. Though Beatty himself escaped the plague the whole of his staff was struck down, and 'a lot of deaths, especially among the officers', including 'two of my best Captains', had occurred.[83] One cannot but wonder what Beatty would have done if at this moment Hipper had put to sea with all his strength.

Early in November Beatty wrote again to the harassed Wemyss, in language which can be described as aggressive if not positively offensive. He was, he said, 'Very perturbed that the SWC [Supreme War Council] might override the [Allied] Naval Council', and 'there must be no question' of the higher body doing so. He was 'surprised' that Heligoland had been omitted from the Armistice terms, and that 'such an important alteration [was] not communicated to me'. 'I would remind you', he declared, 'that I represent a very large proportion of the best naval opinion in the service . . . History will never acquit us if we miss the present opportunity of reducing effectively the menace to our sea power'; all of which showed that he did not understand the responsibilities and working of the Inter-Allied command organisation, and resented the fact that final authority rested in the hands of the statesmen on the Supreme War Council. Fortunately Wemyss declined to be provoked – at any rate on paper; for he informed Beatty that some ships' companies of the High Seas Fleet had mutinied, but the Admiralty had as yet received no details. He hoped that any 'surrender' of the enemy's warships would take place 'on the quarter-deck of the *Queen Elizabeth*' – exactly as Beatty desired.[84] But the C-in-C refused to be mollified, and he added a postscript to his next letter saying that he hoped 'you will find yourself able to take me a little more into your confidence and consultation in the Future than you have in the Past'.[85]

The realisation that he was not to have his battle distressed Beatty profoundly. 'The Fleet, my Fleet, is broken-hearted', he wailed to Eugénie, 'but are still wonderful, the most wonderful thing in Creation and although it would appear that they can never achieve their hearts' desire, they preserve a cheerfulness which is extraordinary'. It seems more likely that the all-prevailing cheerfulness derived chiefly from the realisation that the war would soon be over; but to Beatty deprivation of the sea fight was a blow which was aggravated by 'the feeling that we are not going to win in the Council all that our great Silent Victory entitles us to'. He continued with an attack on the politicians, such as was a marked feature of the World War I clash between what General Sir Henry Wilson, the CIGS, called 'the Frocks and the Brass'. Beatty ended his letter by thanking his 'golden-haired Comrade . . . ten thousand times for all you have given me'.[85a]

As to the clash between Beatty and Wemyss one cannot but feel that, but for the forbearance of the latter, an explosion like those which occurred between Fisher and Beresford and between Percy Scott and Beresford, such as disfigured the public's image of the Royal Navy before the war, might well have taken place.

Though one can understand the disappointment felt by Beatty and his officers at being baulked of their prey, it was surely right for the politicians to reject the imposition of such severe armistice terms as might prolong the war. In October the Board of Admiralty several times considered whether to insist on the surrender of the German Fleet, as Beatty wanted; but they turned it down. At the War Cabinet meetings already mentioned it became plain that, although General Wilson supported Beatty's hard line General Haig, the C-in-C, British Expeditionary Force, did not; neither did Lloyd George or President Wilson.[86] At the Allied Naval Council's meetings between 28th October and 4th November it was finally decided to recommend that 160 submarines should be surrendered (Beatty's draft terms had asked for *all* submarines), and that Beatty's list of surface ships, except for the High Seas Fleet's flagship, should also be included in the terms which Geddes presented to the Supreme War Council on 1st November.[87] All the surrendered ships were to be held in trust for final disposal at the Peace Conference. The Allied Naval Council's terms were, however, strongly opposed by General Foch, the Supreme Allied Commander on land, and Lloyd George considered them 'rather excessive'. When the issue came again before the Allied Naval Council only the Anglophobe American Admiral W. S. Benson supported the politicians' views; and he was undoubtedly motivated by the fear that Britain would become the chief beneficiary by incorporating the surrendered German ships into her own fleet.[88] Though Beatty pleaded hard with Wemyss not to allow the Allied Naval Council's terms to be whittled away, the decision had in fact already been taken on 4th November.[89] The surrender of the 160 submarines still stood, but the surface ships were to be *interned* 'in neutral ports' or failing them 'in ports to be designated by the Allies'. The blockade was in the meanwhile to continue. When the terms were presented to the Germans at Compiègne on 8th November their naval representative stated that the 160 submarines demanded did not exist – which gave Wemyss the chance to substitute 'all submarines' for the fixed figure, thereby gaining a point Beatty had stressed. Because the *Mackensen* was not near enough completion to be towed across, the number of battle cruisers to be interned was reduced from six to five.[90]

To Beatty all these discussions were gall and wormwood. To be deprived of his decisive battle, taken with the decision to substitute internment for surrender of the German warships, and rejection of his proposal that Heligoland should be handed over, was more than he could bear. But the final appeal he made to Geddes was fruitless, if only because it came too late, since the Armistice terms had already been handed to the German delegates.[91] Moreover Beatty's resentment about Wemyss not having consulted himself over the changes made in the Admiralty's draft terms was not placated by Wemyss's emollient reply to the effect that because the discussions had been virtually continuous and he had been constantly on the move between London and Paris, such consultation had been impossible.[92]

Three days after the signature of the Armistice Wemyss wrote to Beatty expressing his understanding of and sympathy with the Grand Fleet over the 'incompleteness' of the victory. He went on to stress how hard he had fought in the British Navy's interest, and ended by urging that 'Whatever may happen do not let the shadow of a misunderstanding come between you and me'.[93] Beatty at last came off his high horse, and in his reply reverted to the familiar opening of 'My dear Rosy'. He told his colleague and superior that 'You can rest assured there is nothing personal in the whole matter', and so the hatchet was buried – temporarily.

The announcement of the armistice on 11th November was greeted with widespread and sustained jubilation in Britain, amounting at times to hysteria. The best account I know of its reception in Beatty's fleet comes from the pen of a midshipman.

> 'Two tots of rum were issued to the Ship's Company, and as darkness spread over the Fleet the scene was transformed, as all searchlights were switched on and waved up and down the sky in an absurd way, while every ship's siren was sounded continuously and made an unholy din until midnight. All ships also fired rockets and fireworks of various kinds while all the Ships Companies danced and jazzed round the upper deck furiously. After dinner we all went over to the Wardroom and had an

uproarious time. It's been the most wonderful day since the world cooled down!'[94]

The next day Beatty wrote officially to the Admiralty that the magnitude of the British contribution to victory at sea would only be adequately recognised 'if the Sea Power of Germany is surrendered under the eyes of the fleet it dared not encounter, and in the harbours of the Power that swept it from the sea'.[95] The decision of the Allied Naval Council on 13th November that the surface warships were to be interned at Scapa (Spain and Norway having declined to accept them) probably mitigated his wounded pride because it enabled him to treat his erstwhile enemies as having surrendered; and he at once set about organising the transfer of the 'designated warships' to Rosyth. His treatment of Rear-Admiral Hugo Meurer when he came onboard the *Queen Elizabeth* on 15th November, described by Ralph Seymour as 'courteous in the extreme but firm as a rock', makes it plain that such was his intention.[96] On 19th Beatty wrote to Eugénie 'I have been terribly busy with all night sittings with Enemy delegates and I have to carry out all the Terms of the Naval Armistice . . . I am now in the position of commanding the High Seas Fleet as well as the Grand Fleet which is a big business and am now arranging for some Autumn Manoeuvres with the two fleets. . . .'; but he made a cryptic complaint about how 'in the middle of it the Monarch butts in under the auspices of the little ray of sunshine who is such a d . . d fool that he can't be trusted to arrange anything'. As no trace of the King's intervention has been found in the records it must have been conveyed to Beatty by word of mouth. At this hectic time he was greatly troubled by Eugénie becoming a victim of the 'flu epidemic, and by his son David catching measles followed by pneumonia at Osborne College – which he anathematised as that 'cursed spot'.[97]

Here it will be appropriate to reproduce most of the account which Beatty sent to Eugénie of the arrival of the German delegates at Rosyth:*[98]

*The original of this important letter was among those given to me by Sir Shane Leslie in 1959 and, as with all the others, I had typed copies made of it, which I kept when Leslie asked me to let him see the originals again. In 1965 he wrote to me that many of his private papers and mementos had been stolen from Castle Leslie, Glaslough, and it seems probable that this letter was among them. Thus the accuracy of the copy here reproduced cannot be absolutely guaranteed. Letters Leslie to Roskill in SLFG 11/6.

. . . . I hardly leave the ship, 2 hours is the most I've done for a long time and even that has been rare. . . .

I am beginning to wish we were still at war, this Peace business makes me tired, all hopes destroyed, all ideas of glorious achievement gone by the board, nothing but an immense drudgery and masses of problems which there seems to be great difficulty in solving.

It all began with the advent of Admiral Meurer. You wd. have loved that, it was Dramatic and Tragic to a high degree.

He arrived onboard at 7 p.m., pitch dark aided by a thick fog, in which he could see nothing and had no idea he was surrounded by the Greatest Fleet in the World. I arranged a most beautiful setting, my Dramatic Sense was highly developed at the moment. When he marched up the Gangway he was met by a blaze of light from groups of the strongest electric sunlights which lighted the Gangway and the Path to be trod from there to my hatchway, outside the Path everything was inky Black and perfect stillness. Actually on the edge of the Path of Light, half in and half out, was a line of the fattest marine sentries, about 2 paces apart with fixed bayonets upon which the light gleamed, wherever he looked he met a bayonet. He was met by Tommy Brand and Chatfield who were frigidity itself. The wretch nearly collapsed on the Quarter Deck, and his party were led to my cabin where I met him supported by my 2nd-in-Command [Madden] (I wish he hadn't a beard, I nearly asked him to take it off, it spoilt the scene), O. de B. [Brock], Tyrwhitt and several members of my staff.

I wouldn't accept him as being what he said he was until he produced documentary evidence in support of his statement and identified his Staff. Having [requested] "Pray be seated", I read him my prepared instructions and refused to discuss them but said they must be thought over and answered on the morrow. They were greatly depressed, overwhelmingly so, and I kept on feeling sorry for them but kept going on by repeating to myself, Lusitania, Belgian atrocities, Belgian Prince★, British Prisoners, and I won in a trot. So much so that Meurer in a voice like lead, with an ashen grey face, said, "I do not

★This refers to one of the worst atrocities of the U-Boats' Unrestricted Campaign. The SS *Belgian Prince* was torpedoed on 31st July 1917. The U-Boat Captain took her Master prisoner and then tried to murder the rest of her crew. However three men survived and were picked up next day – which accounts for their story becoming known. See A. Hurd, *The Merchant Navy*, III, pp. 18 and 268.

think the Commander-in-Chief is aware of the condition of Germany", and then in dull heavy tones, began to retail the effect of the Blockades. It had brought Revolution in the North which had spread to the South, then to East and finally to the West, that anarchy was rampant, the seed was sown, it remained for the harvest of human lives to be reaped in the interior of Germany as well as on the frontiers. Men, women and children under six were non-existent, that Germany was destroyed utterly, the latter with a wail in his voice. It had no effect, I only said to myself thank God for the British Navy. This is your work, without it no victory on land would have availed or even been possible. I told them to return with their answers in the morning. He then informed me he had 3 delegates of the Sailors & Workmen's Council onboard who were anxious to take part in the conversations. I naturally said I knew them not and did not intend to know them better, which was the one source of relief to the stricken party. And they stepped out into the darkness and fog to do the 12 miles back to their ship.

I retired and was nearly sick.

They returned the next day, still in the thickest fog I've seen in the F. of F., it was a fine achievement on the part of the "Oak" in getting them through but very late, and they brought their replies.

Generally speaking, they would agree to anything, they raised points here and there which were firmly squashed. They prated about the honour of their Submarine Crews being possibly assailed, which nearly lifted me out of my chair. However, I scathingly replied that their personal safety wd. be assured, which wd. doubtless satisfy their Honour. In any case, it was different to ours and we couldn't waste time over it. I had them onboard until after midnight and Woodley overfed them, I fear. When it came to signing the documents, I thought he would collapse, he took two shots at it, putting his pen down twice, but we got him over it and they retired into the Fog in grim silence. If I could draw, I could make a glorious picture but it would require a Leonardo da Vinci to do it well, it was very poignant all the time and rather wearing. It was curious, all the time he was in the Firth of Forth it was the thickest Fog imaginable, he never knew that he passed through lines of the finest ships in the world, they were just out of sight, I think the Bon Dieu was kind to him in that.

The next act in the Drama I must keep for another

letter, you will have read most of it in the papers, there
were rather bad accounts that I saw and it was a
Wonderful Day. . . .

Before dawn on 21st November the light cruiser *Cardiff*
slipped quietly out of the Firth of Forth to meet the German
surface ships about 40 miles out to sea and guide them to the
rendezvous with the Grand Fleet, which left harbour a little
later and formed into two long columns six miles apart
comprising no less than thirteen squadrons of battleships,
battle cruisers, armoured and light cruisers with many
escorting destroyers, totalling in all 370 ships manned by
90,000 men drawn from all the naval Home Commands and
the American and French navies. All the ships flew battle
ensigns as though they were going into action, all guns were
loaded, though kept trained fore and aft, and the crews were at
Action Stations when the two fleets met, since Beatty was in
no mood to trust the Germans. Contact was made at about
9.30 with the nine German battleships, five battle cruisers,
seven light cruisers and 49 destroyers – all the most modern
ships of the once proud High Seas Fleet. After the two Allied
columns had steamed to the end of the German line they
reversed course by turning 180 degrees together and took
station on either side of their erstwhile enemies, whom they
escorted triumphantly back to the Firth of Forth. By noon
they were anchored under guard off Inchkeith, while the
Grand Fleet returned to its normal anchorage above and below
the Forth Bridge. As the stately *Queen Elizabeth* steamed to
her usual moorings the men of the Grand Fleet cheered Beatty
again and again. Otherwise 'the whole thing [was] silent and
almost funereal', Ralph Seymour recorded, though a little
light relief was in fact provided by Ethel Beatty in the hastily
prepared *Sheelah* passing close to the *Seydlitz* and receiving a
derisive demonstration from her crew.

At about 11 a.m. Beatty made the general signal that 'The
German flag will be hauled down at sunset today Thursday
and will not be hoisted again without permission' – an order
which certainly exceeded his authority but met the mood of
the moment perfectly. At sunset the *Queen Elizabeth* 'cleared
lower deck' and after the bugles had sounded the traditional
call and the White Ensigns had been lowered with accustomed
ceremony there were deafening cheers for the C-in-C who, as
he left the quarter deck turned and said with a smile 'I always

told you they would have to come out'. Then followed the order, sanctified by Nelson, to hold a service of thanksgiving that evening, and a final signal by the C-in-C thanking his officers and men for their achievement. So ended a most memorable and historic day which was marred only by the failure to invite Fisher and Jellicoe to be present. The slight was apparently not intentional but came about simply because no one thought of inviting them; but Fisher certainly felt it keenly, and if Jellicoe had been present to share Beatty's triumph later animosities might never have arisen.

On 24th November, shortly before the 1st Battle Cruiser Squadron left to escort the German ships from the Firth of Forth to Scapa Beatty went on board his old flagship the *Lion* and addressed the officers and men of his *élite* squadron. In the circumstances his desire that the battle cruisers should feel themselves to have been the chief means whereby this victory had been won is understandable; yet the contempt with which Beatty spoke of the Germans now seems to have been unfortunate, though others in the fleet certainly felt the same way as him. After all the ships now in his custody had fought well against heavy superiority; and it had been circumstances entirely out of the control of its officers and men – and especially the blockade weapon – which had caused the final collapse of morale. Moreover the submarines, of which 150 had come to Harwich to surrender by March 1919, the destroyers, the minesweepers and many other lesser ships had continued doing their duty to the end. Perhaps therefore Beatty would have been wiser to have shown magnanimity towards his late enemies rather than a desire to humiliate them; since he probably thereby sowed some of the seeds which came to harvest later through the propagation of the 'stab in the back' legend – that the German armed forces had never been defeated but had been betrayed by the civil authorities; and that contributed to the resurgence of German militarism in the 1920s, with consequences which all the world knows.

CHAPTER THIRTEEN

Interlude –
and an Admirals Quarrel, 1919

The end of hostilities and the Armistice negotiations produced a host of new problems for the Board of Admiralty and for Beatty; and the strain on the latter was aggravated by his son David falling seriously ill at Osborne College and by Eugénie being afflicted with kidney trouble, which finally necessitated an operation, in London. Nor were Beatty's anxieties mitigated by Eugénie evidently posing some awkward questions about their relationship; for he seems to have appreciated more clearly than she the fact that it was bound to become more difficult now that he and Ethel would be together much more, and would be expected to present to society the picture of a happily married couple. Moreover Beatty was clearly determined to avoid even a whiff of public scandal – such as could well have ruined his career.

Many years later Leslie visited Eugénie, then a widow living in a 'grace and favour' house at Hampton Court Palace, in order to collect material for his Beatty biography, and she evidently told him that after the 1914–18 war 'there was a chance of the Indian Viceroyalty', being offered [to Beatty], in succession to Lord Chelmsford, 'but the King knew better than anyone that her [i.e. Ethel's] health would not be equal to it'. Eugénie must presumably have learnt of this possibility from her husband, but as there is no mention of it in the King's diary or elsewhere in the Royal Archives it is improbable that the idea ever got further than a tentative suggestion discussed verbally among the courtiers.[1]

Very early in the New Year Beatty began a letter to his 'Golden haired Comrade' saying '*It's alright* that's what you told me to say if it was alright and I say it first to [sic] and at once . . . make it clear that your imaginings are all wrong'. As he went on to describe himself as 'a selfish beast' and to admit that he 'ought to say that I must not trouble you more and ought to retire gracefully out of your life', but could not do so, it seems clear that he was still hoping to get the best of all worlds.[2] Several more letters, written with the object of reassuring his mistress about nothing having changed between them quickly followed.[3] He was touched that Eugénie remembered his birthday (17th January), and promised that what she had evidently called the 'elusive little Flame' was still there, and that it 'burns all day and all night'; so she must not be 'alarmed' but would, he hoped, go to Italy to seek warm weather and better health.[4]

In February Beatty, with Spickernell and Seymour to support him, accompanied the King on a tour of the battlefields of Flanders. They were royally entertained, among others, by the Belgian King and by wartime celebrities such as Cardinal Mercier of Louvain and Burgomaster Max of Brussels; but Beatty admitted to Eugénie that he was 'never any good at sight-seeing of any kind', and that he was bored by the whole enterprise. He was, however, buoyed up by the hope of seeing her on his return – 'if Tata doesn't get the sulks and change her plans'.[5]

We have seen how, at the beginning of Wemyss's time as First Sea Lord relations between him and Beatty had been cordial – despite some disagreements arising over matters of policy such as the completion of the North Sea mine barrage; but the end of hostilities with Germany produced a big change. In Wemyss's words there arose 'a marked disposition on the part of the Commander-in-Chief and his staff to regard the climax [to the war] as unworthy. They had looked for a Trafalgar . . . [but] what they got was a victory more crushing than Trafalgar, but without its losses and without any of the personal glory which would have been attached to the survivors'.[6] A more immediate cause of strife arose over the appointment of officers. For example before the end of the war Beatty wrote a very prickly letter to the Admiralty about Captain F. C. Dreyer's appointment being changed from Director of the Gunnery Division to Director of Naval Artillery and Torpedo. 'It is assumed', he wrote, 'that the Director of Naval Artillery and Torpedo will be at liberty to communicate direct only with the C-in-C'; and again that 'Their Lordships will I am sure recognise the desirability of taking the C-in-C of the Grand Fleet into their confidence before creating a new office and conferring upon it powers and duties which affect very considerably the status and respon-

sibility of the C-in-C in Gunnery and Torpedo questions'[7] –
which came near to arrogating to himself powers which
plainly rested with the Board of Admiralty. It is not surprising
that the Board should have rejected such a claim summarily.
In his memoirs Wemyss admitted that as long as the war lasted
and the fleet might at any time have to fight a battle it was
reasonable that the C-in-C should have a big say in the
selection of his subordinates; but once the possibility of battle
had disappeared the situation was totally changed. He
recorded that ever since he had become 1st Sea Lord he had
'suffered considerable inconvenience and difficulty from the
power which had gradually accrued to the Commander-in-
Chief, Grand Fleet in the matter of appointments'; and that
Beatty 'almost had got into the way of looking upon such
appointments as his prerogative'. As this was constitutionally
wrong he told Geddes, the First Lord, that he 'thought it was
most necessary that the Admiralty should immediately recover
its authority and prerogative'.[8] This purpose led to a clash
over the appointment of Roger Keyes to command the Battle
Cruisers, which Beatty heard about before the Naval Secretary's informative letter had reached him. Beatty 'chose to
regard this as a slight upon himself', wrote Wemyss; and he
considered that it exacerbated 'the bitterness which . . .
without doubt existed in his [Beatty's] mind towards the
Admiralty'.[9] Wemyss also considered, and was sympathetic
about the fears of Grand Fleet officers that the British public
would conclude that the Navy had contributed little to victory
compared with the Army; and he therefore fought strenuously
to ensure that in the matter of honours the Fleet's top officers
should be treated exactly the same as the Army's. The
particularly issue was that if Field-Marshal Haig was given an
Earldom Beatty should be elevated to the same position, and
should not be given only a Viscountcy, as both the Prime
Minister and the King had, according to Wemyss, first
intended. 'Had Sir David Beatty', he wrote, 'been less vain or
had he been a man of more sound judgement he would have
realised the situation; but he never showed it'.[10] Though
Wemyss's attribution of vanity to Beatty was harsh his
conduct at this time certainly substantiates it.

   In March Walter Long, the new First Lord, wrote to Beatty
about the arrangements to be made on the hauling down of his
flag after he had been promoted Admiral of the Fleet. He

suggested a reception in London by the King and a representative of the government, followed by a march through the city at the head of about 1,000 men, and a lunch given by the Lord Mayor at the Guildhall – which one may feel was a pretty handsome acknowledgment of his services. Beatty, however, replied that as 'many of us have been in London during the past three months . . . such a reception would perhaps be inopportune', and suggested a march by 'a very much larger number . . . at a convenient date later on' – a proposal which Long tactfully accepted.[11]

There is no doubt that Geddes discussed Beatty's future with him before he left the Admiralty in December 1918, and that the First Lord then gave him the impression that he would be called to replace Wemyss 'upon the vacation of office', which event he expected to 'take place before very long' as Wemyss 'was to become Commander-in-Chief of the Mediterranean and Governor of Malta'. Long assumed that 'the changes in the office of First Sea Lord had the approval of the Prime Minister' and that 'the appointment of Sir R. Wemyss had been conceded by the War Office';[12]★ but neither assumption was in fact justified. Wemyss was evidently given the same erroneous impression, and when he discussed their future plans with Beatty in London in December 1918, he not only accepted Beatty's desire to become First Sea Lord but gave him to understand that the change would take place 'in the spring of 1919'. Unfortunately Churchill, then Secretary of State for War and Air, objected to a sailor being infiltrated into what the Army had always regarded as one of its perquisites, so the appointment as Governor fell through. To be merely C-in-C, Mediterranean after having held office as First Sea Lord understandably held no attraction for Wemyss, who therefore declined both that proposal and the offer of command of one of the naval Home Ports.

According to Wemyss himself he had always intended to leave the Admiralty soon after the end of the war and 'at the

★It was Wemyss himself who put forward the proposal that the Governor of Malta should be a full Admiral and also naval C-in-C and High Commissioner, Mediterranean instead of a retired soldier being merely Governor. The new appointee was not to fly his flag afloat but was to have a Vice-Admiral under him in command of the Mediterranean Fleet. Had it come off Wemyss would, he wrote 'gladly have gone to the Mediterranean'. Wemyss memoirs.

psychological moment'; but he found it difficult to decide when that moment had arrived.[13] Before it had done so a Press campaign in favour of Beatty replacing Wemyss had started – in the words of the latter 'almost imperceptibly' at first, but gradually increasing in volume, especially in the Northcliffe papers. On 6th January 1919 *The Times* published a statement that 'It is understood that Sir David Beatty will almost immediately come to the Admiralty – an appointment which will help to remove a very widespread anxiety about the control of the Navy during a difficult period of transition'. On reading this Wemyss at once went to see Geoffrey Dawson, the editor, who assured him that he would never have allowed such a statement to be published had he not 'had it on the highest authority'; but he understandably refused to disclose his source.[14] Wemyss at once arranged for the Admiralty to issue a categorical denial. That same day Beatty came to see him, and their talk naturally turned to *The Times* article and the question of the intended change in the holder of his office. Wemyss's account of the interview records that Beatty 'said nothing acid'; but when the Admiralty's denial was mentioned he appeared to be 'nonplussed'. On thinking the matter over Wemyss came to the conclusion that Beatty himself had 'either directly or indirectly' inspired the announcement in *The Times*; and from Beatty's actions a short time later, recorded below, that assumption certainly seems to have had at least some measure of justification in it. Wemyss described this squall as 'an extremely unpleasant incident';[15] while Beatty wrote to Eugénie that 'The Admiralty have annoyed me much lately and it has made me sore about things. . . .'[16] It is a fair guess that the most important of the 'things' which had annoyed him was his encounter with Wemyss.

Early in March Long wrote to Lord Stamfordham saying that the whole *fracas* was 'a most unfortunate legacy' from Geddes's time as First Lord, and he hoped that the Monarch's private secretary would act as '*amicus curiae*' (friend of the court) and persuade Wemyss to retire. He could not, wrote Long, 'just be kicked out'.[17] At about the same time Long wrote to Beatty that as the expected post for Wemyss (i.e. the Malta governorship) had fallen through he was staying on as First Sea Lord 'for the present'; but he hoped that Beatty would come to the Admiralty in due time 'and give the

Empire and the Navy the immense benefit of your abilities and invaluable experience'.[18] A short time later he wrote again, thanking Beatty for a letter in which he had 'put the facts of the past very clearly' and given him 'some fresh information'. 'Of course', continued the First Lord hopefully, 'I must find a *modus vivendi*. That is what I came here for'.[19]

Long's hope was, however, quickly shown to be more easily expressed than achieved, since Beatty was not placated either by his soothing letters or by a long one written by Wemyss at the end of February. In it he said that 'with great regret' he had gathered from Beatty's recent interview with Long that he was 'displeased at the general state of affairs existing between the Admiralty and yourself, and the Admiralty in this case probably means me!' The specific subjects on which Beatty had voiced criticisms were, wrote Wemyss, firstly, that he was being 'constantly ignored'; secondly that he was not coming 'to relieve me immediately'; and thirdly that in the matter of appointments he had not been treated 'with the courtesy to which you [Beatty] are entitled'. He went on to refute all these complaints in measured and moderate terms, described himself and Beatty as 'too old and firm friends to quarrel about anything', and went on to say that he was sure Beatty was 'as determined as I am that the service shall not suffer as it must do if the C-in-C, Grand Fleet and 1st Sea Lord are known to be at loggerheads.' Probably he had in mind the schism produced by the feud between Fisher and Beresford before the war. He invited Beatty 'to come and see me and talk matters over'.[20] Beatty's reply was far less courteous than Wemyss's letter, though he did accept – with rather bad grace – the offer of a meeting to discuss their differences. But if such a meeting took place they reached no solution to their differences.

Meanwhile, far from pouring oil on troubled waters, Beatty had sent the Admiralty the terms on which he would take office as 1st Sea Lord – which included combining that office with the appointment of C-in-C, with power to issue orders to the Navy over *his* signature without reference to the Board. Though a precedent for such powers existed in the case of the Army prior to the changes brought about by the Esher Committee of 1904, no naval precedent for Beatty's proposal existed. Wemyss was strongly opposed to such a constitutional innovation, Oswyn Murray the Permanent Secretary totally demolished it, and the First Lord fully accepted their views.[21] When Beatty learnt about the very unfavourable reaction to his 'terms' he wrote, a little defensively, to Eugénie that 'I daresay the C-in-C 1st Sea Lord idea has caused some commotion and given those who like the well defined paths some food for thought and those evilly disposed a handle to keep me out. But I've given up thinking about it and am not fussing any more'.[22] In truth his proposal is reminiscent of Fisher's outrageous statement of the conditions on which he would return to the Admiralty in May 1915 – which made his downfall final and irrevocable.[23] What Professor Marder calls 'more than a *soupçon* of arrogance and *folie de grandeur*' is surely discernible in Beatty's conduct in this matter.

Walter Long next tried to put a term to the argument by suggesting to Lloyd George that the time had come to carry out his predecessor's intention that Beatty should replace Wemyss; but the Prime Minister would not discuss it until the protracted negotiations in Paris over the Peace Treaty were finished. With Wemyss refusing to go to the Mediterranean unless he was Governor of Malta as well as C-in-C, and also declining either to resign or to carry on with the Peace negotiations except as First Sea Lord, and Beatty turning down flatly a suggestion that he should come to the Admiralty with his whole staff and preside over a far-ranging inquiry into warship design and building programmes, by the middle of March a complete *impasse* had been reached.[24]

With the Northcliffe Press and some other organs campaigning for Wemyss to be replaced Long's position was certainly unenviable,[25] especially as Wemyss was now showing that he too could be obstinate. On 10th March he wrote to Long, in very moderate language, pointing out that although 'the centre of naval interest has lain with the Grand Fleet during the war' it had not been the only naval instrument whereby victory had been achieved. In particular it had 'little or nothing to do with the anti-submarine warfare', and therefore 'is not the only pebble on the beach'. There were, he continued, many other officers besides Beatty, such as Sir Alexander Duff (Director, Anti-Submarine Division) and Sir Roger Keyes (in the Dover Command) to whom a great deal was owed; nor was it fair to ignore the part played by the Admiralty as a whole.[26] In short the letter gently but firmly deflated Beatty's claims. Early in May Walter Long came off the uncomfortable fence on which he had been sitting and replied to a Parliamentary Question to the effect that his predecessor had only told Beatty 'unofficially' about his coming to the Admiralty, that Wemyss enjoyed 'the complete confidence' of the government and that no change in his office was intended;[27] all of which was of course anathema to Beatty.

On 3rd April 1919 Beatty and Jellicoe were both promoted Admirals of the Fleet. As the number of officers authorised to hold that rank was only three, and those places were already filled by Sir William May, Sir Hedworth Meux and Sir George Callaghan, a special Order in Council was necessary. At 48 years of age Beatty was the youngest officer ever to hold that rank, and for four days he flew the symbol of his new status – the Union Flag at the mainmast – in the *Queen Elizabeth*. On 5th April he made his farewell speech to her company and through them to the whole Grand Fleet. It was short and very much to the point. After thanking them for their loyal service 'in success, in disappointment, and in monotony' he touched on the probability of difficult times lying ahead and assured them that, as they well knew, he belonged 'body and soul' to their 'great Service'. They could therefore depend on him for 'sympathising and assisting every man and officer . . . in his just aspirations'.[28] That same day the Board of Admiralty sent him perhaps the most warm-hearted letter ever issued in their august name; for the Lords Commissioners paid tribute to 'those qualities of resolute leadership, unerring insight, and quick decision' exemplified by his 'achievements in battle', described him as 'a beloved and well trusted leader', and declared that 'Posterity will always associate with your name the chapter of the Royal Navy's history now drawing to a close'.[29] If we now feel that there were some exaggeration in those plaudits few if any of the Grand Fleet's officers and men would at the time have considered them other than fully merited.

The hauling down of the Union Flag on 7th April marked the end of the Grand Fleet, and of an era. Under the new organisation the main strength of the navy was divided between the Atlantic and Home Fleets, both commanded by Beatty's former second-in-command Sir Charles Madden, and the Mediterranean Fleet. Smaller squadrons, composed mainly of cruisers and sloops, were soon distributed all over the world in the accustomed foreign stations. Beatty recorded his feelings about the termination of his command by telling Eugénie 'The Grand Fleet is dead and safely put to rest. It was a harrowing experience which I don't want to repeat but it had to be done. There's nothing like departing with a little dignity and they [presumably his officers and men] were all so kind and seemed truly sorry to see the last of me that in some ways it repaid. However, most of my Staff have received a soothing draught in the shape of an honour to help them on their way and to remind them [that] their services to me had been appreciated'. Rather surprisingly he added that 'The Admiralty were very good in that respect [i.e. about the honours] and met my rather large demands in the right spirit.'[30]

While the argument over his future and other matters was in progress Beatty sent Eugénie 'a few typewritten facts that you might keep to yourself as to their origin and at the same time place before [her brother Charles] Dudley Ward in your own language as pertinent queries which give food for thought', because it had struck him 'that the General Public would be likely to be disturbed if they knew the actual facts'. They were, firstly, 'That up to the Cessation of Hostilities the C-in-C G.F. was consulted upon, and actually governed every operation against the Enemy'; and, secondly, 'That immediately hostilities ceased he ceased to be consulted or to have anything to do with the decisions arrd. at which in reality became more vital but less dangerous than when the war was on'. In addition he claimed 'that the advisers to the P.M. are not those who actually conducted the War and who have not the experience to enable them to give the best advice'. He also asked whether 'even if they had the experience or were the best advisers is it reasonable to suppose that those who bore the actual responsibility under War Conditions should not be capable of giving Valuable assistance in solving some of the many problems which have to be decided under Peace Conditions?' This letter certainly produces a sense of distaste; for it was not only a covert attack on Wemyss but a disguised attempt to enlist the services of Eugénie's brother, who had written a number of books and articles, to further Beatty's purposes.[31]*

*Eugénie's son George considered that the Dudley Ward referred to was her younger brother Charles and not her elder brother who had been a Liberal MP before the war but held no official post after it; nor did he ever write anything that was published. Endorsement by George Godfrey-Faussett on typed copy of the letter.

On 21st April Beatty set out on a visit to Paris and the former front line – apparently as one of the guests invited by the French Army. Verdun and particularly the 'Tranchée des Bayonettes' (which is still preserved) made a deep impression on him; but he took offence because, although Paris was full of British politicians and service men, 'No member of the British Adty. . . . made any attempt to receive or pay any respect or salute to any part of their representatives of the British Navy recd. by France'. He asked Eugénie to tell her brother the foregoing 'and see what he says', as in his view 'it was obviously done deliberately and of set purpose' – an accusation which continued his covert attack on Wemyss and Long, and was almost certainly groundless.

Having thus worked up another grievance Beatty went on to Cannes where he embarked in the *Sheelah* which had steamed out from England, still under the command of the faithful Captain Grint. We do not know the size of the *Sheelah's* crew, but as she was a coal fired vessel and could carry about half a score of passengers in comfort, it is a fair guess that it must have been at least a dozen men; but as with other very rich Americans the Marshall Field's enormous wealth had certainly not diminished because of the war, and the standard of living kept up by the Beattys continued to be as luxurious as before. Beatty had evidently seen *The Times* leader of 24th April, which had declared that while 'there was, and is, no disposition anywhere to minimize his [Wemyss's] services', it was 'felt universally that one man and one man only can fill a particular post to universal satisfaction. . . .' He told Eugénie that although the leader was 'pretty strong' he doubted 'if it will do much good unless it is continued' – to which end he was evidently offering assistance.[32] He asked her to continue writing to him at Hanover Lodge, the big London house in Regent's Park which they rented, whence her letters would be forwarded. He and Ethel then set off on a two month cruise starting at Monte Carlo, where they gambled successfully in the Casino and took money off the Duke of Westminster 'and his harem' at tennis.[33]* Then they went on to Elba, Naples, Corfu and Patras, whence they passed

*This was the 2nd Duke of Westminster (1879-1953), known to his intimates as 'Bendor'. The *locus classicus* of this enormously wealthy but unattractive character is Christopher Sykes's brilliant study of him in his *Evelyn Waugh* esp. pp. 164-6 in Penguin Ed. (1977).

through the Corinth Canal to Athens. After being royally entertained there they visited some of the Greek islands and then returned to Cannes via Taormina and Naples, where the yacht replenished her bunkers.

But despite what should have been an idyllic cruise, with Ethel as always at her best at sea, Beatty managed to work up another complaint – this time over the Admiralty having refused to issue railway warrants for Ethel and her maid to travel to Boulogne, despite the former having been invited to Paris as a guest of the French Government. He told Eugénie how, in marked contrast to what he regarded as the Admiralty's stinginess, the French had laid on a special train to take them all to Cannes free of charge; while Lady Jellicoe had been 'sent round the world in a British Man of War at Government expense' during her husband's Empire tour. But Beatty warned Eugénie to keep quiet about the latter arrangement 'as nobody else knows of it and it could hardly have come from any other source' than himself.

Then he worked up yet another grievance about articles in the *Morning Post* and *Daily Telegraph* of 3rd May having implied that the reception to the officers and men of the Grand Fleet in London had been postponed 'to suit my convenience and [that] consequently I was depriving the men of the G.F. from [sic] a Public reception'. 'Dirty dogs aren't they' was his comment; and he again invited Eugénie to tell her brother about it. In the same letter he told her that he had heard that at a Royal Academy dinner Wemyss had 'stated that the Navy was full of Bolshevism' – but he could not believe it. He went on to declare, most libellously, that Wemyss and 'his Hun wife' were 'the only Bolshys [i.e. Bolsheviks]' he knew.[34] In fact Wemyss had married Victoria, elder daughter of the 'eminent diplomat' Sir Robert B. D. Morier.[35]*

In Athens Beatty's equanimity was further disturbed by reading Walter Long's statement in Parliament about himself, already referred to, and he at once dashed off a letter telling Eugénie that it was 'one unadulterated lie from end to end'. Firstly because, contrary to Long's statement, he '*was* offered and accepted' the post of 1st Sea Lord; secondly that Geddes not only asked him to come but told him that Wemyss was

*Lady Wemyss was, however, brought up in Germany and according to the memory of a contemporary always spoke with a strong German accent. Presumably Beatty had this in mind when he described her as quoted.

leaving; thirdly that, again contrary to Long's statement, a
date *was* mentioned – namely the date of the signing of the
Peace Treaty; fourthly that it was untrue to say he had been
consulted 'on Naval Policy since the Armistice'; and lastly that
he had not refused to undertake the inquiry Long had
suggested 'for personal reasons' but 'on Public Grounds and
very good ones'. 'What', he asked, 'are you to do with a lying
old hand like that?'; but at least he was glad that Ethel was far
distant from London, since otherwise 'in her wrath [she]
would surely be indiscreet', because she was incapable of
understanding that 'the wisest thing is to preserve a dignified
silence'.[36] Though Beatty's polemic against Long was not
without some measure of justification, he seems never to have
grasped the simple fact that the verbal offer made by Geddes
could hardly be held to be binding on his successor when the
circumstances affecting Wemyss's future had altered fundamentally. It was Churchill who put his finger on the basic
problem of the time by writing to Lloyd George that 'Wemyss
is a very good First Sea Lord . . . At the same time he is in a
weak position in his own profession and far overshadowed by
Beatty. Beatty is very anxious to become First Sea Lord and
was I believe encouraged by Eric Geddes to believe that his
appointment was imminent. At any rate, it seems to me that
sooner or later Beatty will have to replace Wemyss, and in a
reasonable time I think this would be the right thing to do. On
the other hand, you must remember, once Beatty is
enthroned, he will be in a position to champion the particular
interest of the Admiralty to an extent which it would be quite
impossible for Wemyss to do'. His conclusion was therefore
that it was 'extremely important that no change should take
place at the present time'.[37]

Beatty had to get home again by 10th June to receive
various honours. He told Eugénie that he was sad that the
cruise was coming to an end, 'but it has the consolation that I
shall see you again, and if that is to be [?] removed [then] I am
done . . . You know what I mean'.[38] The last sentence can
hardly be misunderstood.

Meanwhile Wemyss had, in Long's view, strengthened his
position by 'the dignified way in which he has borne these
most undeserved attacks', and by the fact that the naval
conditions of the Peace terms were 'absolutely satisfactory'.
All in all Long found him 'a most excellent First Sea Lord',

and he was therefore not prepared to put him 'on the beach'. Beatty on the other hand had, in Long's view, 'behaved very foolishly'; while Ethel had been very rude and had 'openly cut' the First Lord on two occasions.[39]

Soon after Beatty returned home from the Mediterranean he received the Freedom of the City of London and of at least ten other cities. On 12th June he and Lord Haig received from the King's hands the rare and very distinguished Order of Merit, and ten days later the Monarch enjoyed what he described as 'a very pleasant dinner' with Beatty and about 20 Admirals, among whom he found 'many old friends', at the First Sea Lord's official residence Mall House.[40] In addition to the many honours heaped on Beatty by Royalty and the cities of Britain he received honorary degrees from several universities. Such ceremonies involved him in a heavy burden of speech making; but, with Spickernell's help in preparing the speeches, he carried the load lightly and with complete success. On 6th August he received his Earldom and took the additional title of Baron Beatty of the North Sea and of Brooksby, so combining the scene of his war service with his favourite peacetime home.[41] For his eldest son he took the courtesy title of Viscount Borodale – so bringing in his Irish ancestry.

When the Cabinet considered money awards for the top naval and military leaders Churchill proposed £100,000 for Beatty, but added the sour comment 'if he wants it'.[42] However, on 7th August Parliament voted him that sum, while Jellicoe only got half as much.[43] As for Wemyss's rewards, he had been told the he was to receive a Viscountcy and a money grant, and when neither materialised it was his turn to be piqued and he sent Long his resignation – which the First Lord refused to accept.[44] Wemyss was finally persuaded to hold his hand on the grounds that resignation at such a time and on such an issue was almost certain to lay him open to serious criticism; but on 28th August he formally handed in his resignation, to take effect two months later. On leaving the Admiralty Wemyss was promoted Admiral of the Fleet; but when he learnt that he was only to be offered a Barony he stood out for the higher honour which Long had unwisely foretold for him, and wanted it to be dated to Armistice Day. However, in the end he accepted what was offered him. If his conduct in this matter was ill-advised he surely comes out of the unsavoury squabble of the time better than Beatty.

The long awaited Peace celebrations took place on 19th July and Beatty led the large naval contingent representing all branches of the service. The procession moved off from Hyde Park's Albert Gate at 10.0 a.m., the King took the salute standing on the steps of the Queen Victoria memorial in The Mall, and the march ended at Hyde Park Corner about 2½ hours later. Beatty told Eugénie 'It was a wonderful day, wonderful in many ways but most of all in the extraordinary reception accorded to the Navy. Surely no one can misunderstand the place that the Navy holds in the hearts of the people. I don't care what anybody says I am certain that none really touched the hearts of the people like the Sailors did. I who know them so well was filled with admiration and pride at their bearing and appearance, how much more then must it have appealed to those who had never seen them before. They [? The Press] complain that I never smiled. I never felt less like smiling and am not good at camouflaging. I was more nearly weeping than [?] smiling and that's the truth. . . .'[45] The events of that day suggest that Beatty had good reasons for throwing cold water on Long's earlier suggestion about a reception and parade in London.

At the end of the letter quoted above Beatty dropped a hint about meeting Eugénie in London when she returned from her convalescence abroad; but nothing seems to have come of it. His next letter was written from Brooksby where his whole family had foregathered to produce an atmosphere which he described as 'peaceful and warm'. Eugénie had gone to stay with the Eshers in Perthshire, and Beatty suggested to her that as he was going to Scotland for the grouse shooting in the near future and she was likely to be coming south they might meet at their old place of assignation the North British Hotel in Edinburgh; but he warned her that if she sent him a letter to that address she should 'disguise' her 'flowing hand' – presumably to prevent Ethel recognising it.[46] We do not know whether the assignation came off. After helping to kill 'only 190 brace' of grouse Beatty went briefly to Aberdour and then to London in order to see 'poor little David' go back to Osborne in September. Soon afterwards the Beattys gave up their tenancy of that house – because his appointment as 1st Sea Lord was about to take effect. 'We hated leaving dear little Aberdour', he wrote, 'it was a great wrench for poor Tata who had got very fond of it, and the associations of 5 very strenuous years could not be wiped out at one blow'.[47] for Eugénie too the house must have held golden memories.

Of all the avalanche of honours showered on Beatty in 1919 probably none gave him greater satisfaction than the dinner given to him by the Lower Deck of the navy in Portsmouth Guildhall on 22nd September. His car was first hauled through densely crowded streets by a seamen's gun's crew, and his reception was rapturous. At the dinner he sat between a Chief Writer and a Seaman Petty Officer, his speech struck just the right note, and at the evening's end sixteen bells were struck as a hopeful sign of the dawn of a new era in the relations between officers and men.* One may feel that all these quite sincere outbursts of hero-worship were enough to turn the head of a far less vain man than Beatty; and they must surely have contributed to the less attractive features of his conduct here described.

On 1st November Beatty was 'read in' as 1st Sea Lord, and so began the last phase of his naval career. Among the many letters of congratulations and good wishes he received he probably appreciated the one from 'Jacky' Fisher as much as any; and in it the old Admiral made one of his many astonishingly accurate prophecies. 'It is a momentous time', he wrote, 'when the whole aspect of Sea War is so utterly changed by the prodigious and daily development of Aircraft'.[48]

At the time Beatty took office Ethel seems to have been in a comparatively stable condition; but, as will be told shortly, serious mental and nervous deterioration soon set in. Plainly Beatty still wanted to keep up his love affair with Eugénie; but with both married couples living in London the prospects can hardly have seemed favourable. Moreover his letters suggest that he was slowly changing from passionate lover to devoted and intimate friend. As to his conduct after leaving the Grand Fleet, Professor Marder refers to the period having revealed 'the new Beatty'[49]; but I am inclined to think that the vanity and arrogance he exhibited in the period covered by this chapter had been there for a long time – certainly since he became C-in-C, Grand Fleet – but that those defects had not

---

*At one minute to midnight on New Year's Eve sixteen bells are traditionally struck in R.N. ships by the youngest rating on board to herald the New Year.

become so offensively prominent until peace brought him a torrent of adulation. And the defects became more pronounced when for the first time since he began his extremely rapid climb up the naval ladder, he found that he was not going to be allowed to have his way on an important issue – namely his early accession to the office of First Sea Lord.

CHAPTER FOURTEEN

First Sea Lord.
Phase I, 1919–1923

The reader who has persevered thus far will not be surprised
to learn that, at the beginning of his term of office, Beatty
inveighed against the Admiralty and all its works. After only a
week in Whitehall he wrote to Eugénie from Brooksby that
'My 1st week in the Sink of Iniquity has gone and has left me
Cold. From 10.30 to 7.30 every day in that spot is not my idea
of life for the future. But it was necessary to become
acquainted with the personelle [sic] and what they were doing.
I just itch to blast the whole place and begin afresh. . . .' He
had just enjoyed a day's hunting in Leicestershire, and told
Eugénie how 'some thousand farmers' of that county had
presented him with a cup and given him 'the right to ride
over' the whole of their lands. This gesture Beatty described as
'the best freedom I have received'. But he was still longing for
Eugénie and told her 'I must see you some time and it has got
to be managed somehow . . . Anyway you know well what
my desires are. . . .'; which leaves no room for doubt that he
hoped they would remain lovers.[1] That hope is confirmed by
a letter written just before Christmas in which he told Eugénie
'Times are changed, circumstances have altered, and will alter
again and again, but nothing can destroy the memories of the
times we have had or change the friendship between us. . . .'
He 'prayed' fervently that in years to come nothing would
'permit any extraneous or petty happenings to interfere with
what has been to me "All Joy" '.[2] On Christmas Day he
wrote again from Brooksby that he had enjoyed a good day's
hunting with all his family mounted, and was thankful that he
could still 'take pleasure in riding a good horse across
Country';[3] and it is a fact that during the next few years it was
in the hunting field or on the grouse moors of Perthshire that
he found the relaxation he needed. But neither his home life
nor the course of his love for Eugénie ran smoothly at this
time. Early in 1920 Ethel was prostrated at Hanover Lodge by

what her husband called a 'general collapse' – a precursor of
the very severe mental illness now looming over her; while
Eugénie was also far from well.[4]

Inside the Admiralty Beatty soon arranged that the principal
appointments should be held by officers who had served under
him in the Grand Fleet. With himself as a very active Chief of
Naval Staff as well as 1st Sea Lord and Sir James Fergusson as
his Deputy (vice Fremantle) he had the nucleus he wanted, and
in March 1920 he further strengthened it by persuading
Chatfield to change over from 4th Sea Lord to Assistant Chief
of Naval Staff. The activities of the Staff Divisions were
divided between those two; and they were given sufficient
powers to ensure that only matters of real importance were
passed upwards to Beatty.[5] But although he was successful in
recruiting the officers he wanted at the top he had at the same
time to resist insistent demands for reductions in the number
of officers serving on the staff – which had increased to twelve
divisions and 336 officers by the end of the war. By a process
of amalgamation and rationalisation the divisions were
reduced to eight and the number of officers by 97;[6] but the
pressure for cuts continued, and in 1922 Beatty, no doubt with
the repeated failures of the war time staff organisation in
mind, laid down the limits beyond which he was not prepared
to go. 'No departure can be contemplated', he told Keyes who
was chairman of a committee appointed to investigate the
matter, 'from the fundamental principle on which the work of
the Admiralty is at present organised'.[7] Unfortunately pressure for economies forced further reductions on the Board
later, and by 1939 the staff was but a shadow of what it had
been in 1918.

The principal international issue in which Beatty was
involved at the beginning of his time as 1st Sea Lord was the
War of Intervention in Russia, which necessitated keeping a
large number of warships in the Baltic, at Archangel in the far
north, in the Black Sea and Caspian, and in the Far East,
where there were enormous stores of ammunition near
Vladivostok which the government was anxious to prevent
falling into Bolshevik hands. We cannot here deal in detail
with each of those campaigns about which I have written at
some length elsewhere.[8] But from Beatty's point of view the
unpopularity of the intervention in British left wing circles,
combined with the fact that it was delaying the demobilisation

of officers and men, produced a conflict between his strong
dislike of the Bolshevik régime and the promise he had made
to the men to look after their interests. The naval forces in the
Baltic were commanded by Beatty's friend Walter Cowan,
whose bellicosity was not always tempered by consideration
for the feelings of men who were required to fight a war
which in the politicians' eyes was not a war.[9] It is not
surprising that serious trouble should only have been experienced in Cowan's ships; and Beatty was probably referring to
them when he told Eugénie that 'the unrest in the Navy . . .
nearly breaks my heart'.[10] Apart from such disciplinary
troubles his chief anxiety lay in the possibility that the
expansionist aims of the USSR would lead to their domination
of the Middle East, the source of most of the oil fuel needed
by the navy.[11]

The British government was anxious to restore normal
relations with the USSR in order to foster a revival of trade,
and towards the end of May 1920 Beatty circulated a paper on
the 'naval conditions' he considered essential to an economic
agreement. But as his 'conditions' amounted to the virtual
confinement of Soviet naval forces to the Baltic, Black Sea and
Caspian they were most unlikely to be acceptable to their
government.[12] Walter Long sent this paper on to Lloyd
George with a supporting minute; but in fact the issue had
already been settled by the British government's decision to
bring intervention to an end as quickly as possible. By the
autumn of 1920 virtually all our commitments had been
liquidated, and the White Russian forces in the various theatres
had disintegrated; but in Soviet minds the War of Intervention
left a legacy of mistrust which has not yet been dispelled.

Before Beatty had taken office the Admiralty had set up two
important committees designed to take full advantage of the
experiences of the recent war, and to plan the composition of
the post-war fleet and the design of its ships. These were the
Post War Questions Committee, the chairman of which was
Admiral Sir Richard Phillimore, and the Reconstruction
Committee, of which the effective though not the titular
chairman was Admiral of the Fleet Sir William May.[13]
Both bodies rendered voluminous reports containing a
host of recommendations, some of which bore fruit during
Beatty's term of office while others became submerged in the
insistent pressure for disarmament propagated by bodies such as

the League of Nations Union.

What has been called the Era of Conferences now opened with the politicians gathering in stately homes or moving from one attractive continental spa to another. Between the beginning of 1920 and the end of 1922 no less than twenty-three separate international conferences were held in accordance with the new principle of 'open diplomacy'; but the system had many grave disadvantages, the chief one being that, as a shrewd diplomat who attended some of them has put it, 'they exposed democratic diplomacy to those temptations which it was least able to resist'.[14] Beatty never attended the conferences as one of the British delegates, but he often had to produce memoranda setting out the Admiralty's position on some involved and difficult question; and on some occasions he was called to give evidence to the Cabinet or CID when one or other of those bodies was considering the policy to be adopted at a conference. For example when early in April 1920 Beatty told Eugénie that he was being 'harassed . . . by Foreign Office meetings' the probability is that the department was preparing for the First Lympne Conference which took place in Sir Philip Sassoon's luxurious house 'Belcaire' in mid-May with the object of repairing Anglo-French relations, which had recently deteriorated badly, and of arriving at an agreement on the money to be extracted from Germany by way of Reparations.[15] In Beatty's next letter to Eugénie written just after the conference broke up, he enlarged on the luxury of the setting in which it was held but described Sassoon as no more than 'a superior flunkey' with no real influence.[16] Incidentally Beatty's reference to Sassoon as 'the Jew boy' suggests that his anti-semitism, which was commented on earlier, had not abated with his experience of war.[17]

We saw earlier how the 1917 increases in naval pay and the elimination of some Lower Deck grievances had stilled the rising tide of unrest on those issues; but the lull proved no more than temporary, and by the middle of the following year it was obvious that pay was going to be one of the most important problems which the post-war Board would have to face. Before he left the Grand Fleet Beatty had set up a Naval Pay Committee to frame recommendations, and Geddes as First Lord had begun to put pressure on the Chancellor of the Exchequer. Early in 1919 the Admiralty set up committees under Admirals Halsey and Jerram to review officers' and men's pay respectively, and the views of Beatty's committee were placed before them. In the main the recommendations of the two Admiralty committees were accepted by the Government, which must have been a considerable relief to Beatty. The chief exception was the rejection of the Grand Fleet Committee's proposal for a Marriage Allowance for officers, the lack of which was an extraordinary anomaly and was not eliminated until 1938. The weakness of the new pay codes lay in the fact that the Treasury considered, though without any legal authority, that they were 'index-linked'. This claim produced serious difficulties later for Beatty's Board when the cost of living fell and the Treasury tried to reduce pay proportionately. None the less the accomplishments of the 1919 committees were both substantial and timely; and the chief credit undoubtedly belongs to the Long-Wemyss Board.[18]

The Admiralty's endeavours to restrict the activities of the Lower Deck Benefit Societies to what they regarded as their legitimate functions by introducing a Welfare Committee to review and recommend action on representations regarding conditions of service were far less successful than the review of pay. The new body was virtually boycotted by the Lower Deck, and in consequence it was 'suspended' in 1920 and a biennial Welfare Conference was substituted;[19] but that innovation was no more successful than its predecessor. The problem of how representations by the men should be handled thus remain unresolved throughout Beatty's time as First Sea Lord. Not until the Invergordon Mutiny of 1931 brought about a complete overhaul of the welfare machinery was any real advance made – notably by the substitution of a 'Review of Service Conditions' for the Welfare Conferences.[20] Beatty's attitude on the men's welfare may be described as benevolently paternalistic; but as with all senior officers of the period he was very much opposed to allowing anything that savoured of Trades Union practices to develop on the Lower Deck.

In August 1919 Long had sought a ruling from the Cabinet 'as regards the supremacy of the seas over the United States and over any probable combination [of naval powers]';[21] and that led directly to the enunciation of the notorious 'Ten Year Rule' laying down that the estimates of the service depart-

ments were to be based on the assumption that there would be
no major war for ten years.[22] At about the same time a very
drastic cut was imposed on the naval estimates for 1919-20,
which Long presented to Parliament at £157½ millions
(compared with £334 millions actually spent in the previous
Financial Year) exactly a month after Beatty had taken office.
Beatty thus found himself immediately involved in the
perennial struggle for funds – just when he was hoping to
restart capital ship building in order that the Royal Navy's
strength should not fall below that of the United States, whose
enormous 1916 programme was beginning to bear fruit and
which had another very large building programme under
consideration. As regards modern capital ships the United
States had no less than 12 building under the 1916 programme,
while Japan had eight of the same class under construction. As
Britain had only one post-Jutland capital ship (the battle
cruiser *Hood*) on the stocks it was obvious to Beatty and his
colleagues that, according to the accepted measure of naval
strength, namely the number of modern capital ships possessed, Britain would very soon fall far behind the two other
principal powers. In July 1920 Long told the House of
Commons that the government's firm policy was that 'our
Navy should not be inferior in strength to the Navy of other
powers', which in effect meant the establishment of a One
Power Standard – a far more modest yardstick than the
famous Two Power Standard of 1889.[23] To implement such a
policy Long put forward Beatty's proposal to lay down four
capital ships in 1921 and four more in the following year.[24]
But the reaction of the Press and of many Ministers and MPs
to the whole concept of capital ship building was so hostile
that in December 1920 the Chancellor of the Exchequer
(Austen Chamberlain) assured the House of Commons that
such a programme would not be initiated until 'an exhaustive
investigation' had been carried out by a sub-committee of the
CID under the chairmanship of Bonar Law (Lord Privy Seal),
generally referred to as the 'Bonar Law Enquiry'.[25] Thus was
the stage set for Beatty's first struggle with the government on
behalf of what he regarded as essential for the navy.

An entry in Bryan Godfrey-Faussett's diary made some
months before the Bonar Law Enquiry set to work states that
Beatty was determined 'to resign rather than go down to
posterity as the First Sea Lord in office at the time such a

shameful decision' as to surrender 'supremacy of the sea to America' was taken.[26] In mid-December he accordingly submitted two strongly-worded papers stating the Admiralty's case. In the first one his chief point was that the skilled labour necessary for making armour plate and big guns was being rapidly dispersed, and if no orders were placed in the near future with the few firms capable of undertaking such work the result 'would be nothing less than disastrous to our chance of retaining our equality with the strongest naval power'. Lest it be thought that Beatty was exaggerating it may be remarked that when rearmament was belatedly started fifteen years later, orders for the armour plate for some of the new warships had to be placed with the Skoda works in Czechoslovakia. In his second paper Beatty argued with some passion that 'the latest type of capital ship is so well protected that she can be hit by a considerable number of the most effective torpedoes now existing without being sunk', and that there was 'nothing in the present offensive qualities of aircraft which render them a menace to the capital ship' – construction of which must therefore 'inevitably ensue'.[27] This argument became the theme song of the Admiralty throughout Beatty's time in office – and long afterwards. It was not resolved until World War II demonstrated its fallaciousness. Though the Bonar Law Committee took evidence from the leading protagonists of air power, and a number of naval men of middle rank such as Rear-Admirals de Bartolomé (a former Third Sea Lord), S. S. Hall (an experienced submarine commander) and H. W. Richmond (then President of the RN College, Greenwich) supported them, Churchill came down in favour of the capital ship and wanted to build four such ships yearly for the next four or five years – a truly gargantuan meal. In the end the committee split. The chairman and two others signed a report which Churchill and Beatty refused to accept; while Walter Long, who had been absent ill during most of the investigation, was dragooned by Beatty into signing the alternative report.[28] Thus the first round in what was to prove a very protracted debate ended in a draw. The case against the capital ship was rejected, but authority to start building new ones immediately was not forthcoming.

Meanwhile such stability and happiness as had existed for Beatty in his home life had been utterly destroyed. At the end of August 1920 he wrote from Grantully Castle – the estate in

Perthshire to which he always tried to return for the grouse shooting season – to tell Eugénie that Ethel had suffered a severe nervous breakdown. 'Such depression you never saw', he told her, 'and [it] does not seem to get any better'.[29] In his next letter he asked her to find for him 'the very best nerve specialist in London'. By early October the Beattys were back at Hanover Lodge, but 'the situation is much the same', he wrote, 'signs of improvement one day relapsing back to the old condition the next'. 'It is a heart breaking business', he told Eugénie, 'and I don't know how long it will or can go on'.[30] Ethel's tragedy evidently strengthened the bond between Beatty and Eugénie, on whom he now came to rely for mental comfort rather than physical love. On New Year's Eve he again opened his heart about the 'perpetual black despair' which had engulfed Ethel. She was talking of going abroad, and Beatty wanted her 'to get into the sun' but could not find anyone suitable to accompany her; while the 'row about the Naval Programme and the [Bonar Law] Enquiry' made it impossible for him to join her for long. He was therefore 'thinking now of resigning the 1st Sea Lord job' in order to 'go away with her for 3 months and see what that will do', as 'this present dog's life is not worth living'.[31] Those extracts from his letters make plain the severity of the psychological strain on Beatty, just at the time when his first major tussle with the government was taking place. Yet despite the strain to which he was subject, when he was elected Lord Rector of Edinburgh University in October he produced in his address a comprehensive survey of the achievements of sea power from the earliest times, and foretold the certain disaster which would befall a nation dependent on seaborne trade and traffic which failed to provide the means to defend it. Admiral Chalmers has testified to Beatty's gifts as a public speaker, and there is no doubt that on this occasion what he said, with its reference to his fleet's dependence on the deep water Scottish bases and his concluding quotation from Robert Burns, was perfectly attuned to the audience and to the occasion.[32]

Meanwhile Walter Long, whose physical health and mental capacity had never been really adequate to cope with the responsibilities of the office of First Lord, had resigned and on 18th February 1921 Lord Lee of Fareham, whose name was to become connected chiefly with his gift of the Chequers estate to the nation for use by its Prime Ministers, took over the office.

The first post-war clash between the recently created Air Ministry and the Admiralty had taken place while Wemyss was still First Sea Lord, and concerned the organisation of RAF units working with the Navy and the secondment of naval officers to the new service to fly some of the aircraft needed by the older service. By October 1919 an *impasse* had been reached and Wemyss, being about to leave office, washed his hands of the whole issue and left it to his successor to cope with it.[33] He did, however, warn his colleagues that if they took the case for re-creating the RN Air Service to the Cabinet 'the decision would go against the Admiralty'.[34] In uttering that warning Wemyss showed greater prescience than Beatty, who very soon lent his authority to achieving precisely that purpose – in marked contradiction to the support he had given to the Smuts Committee's proposals about the future of the Air Service in 1917. In December 1919 Beatty did, however, agree to the request made by Sir Hugh Trenchard, the CAS, for a twelve-month truce to enable him to get the Royal Air Force firmly organised;[35] but by the spring of the following year relations had become very strained and an appeal by the Admiralty to the Cabinet was only dropped because Oswyn Murray, the Permanent Secretary, was sure it would fail.[36] Chatfield, who had recently become ACNS, was the chief advocate of 'a fight to the finish' in the matter of regaining for the Admiralty full control of naval aviation; and his views of course carried great weight with Beatty. By September 1921 the latter had come down in support of a full-scale attack through the agency of the recently appointed Committee on National Expenditure, to which we will revert shortly.

Early in 1921 Beatty told Eugénie that he had got Ethel safely off to Pau, though she had 'hated it terribly'. He was going to try and join her in February, but in the meanwhile he was enjoying the company of his two boys and the fox hunting of the Shires. This letter contains the first intimation of a love affair between Beatty's Flag Lieutenant Ralph Seymour and Ethel's niece Gwendolen ('Gwenny') Field, which was to end in tragedy – due to Ethel's jealousy. Beatty seems to have regarded it as a *mésalliance* and had a hand in rusticating the girl to Rome and sending Seymour back to sea – a forced separation which was not likely to achieve its purpose.[37] His next letter was written from Paris on the way to join Ethel at Biarritz for about ten days. He recorded with glee how he had 'defeated the attack on the Capital Ship with great Slaughter', and congratulated himself on having 'handled the situation [before the Bonar Law Committee] with considerable tact and skill'. Ethel was, he reported, better and he expected her to return to England fairly soon – a prospect he evidently viewed with misgivings.[38] Meanwhile his troubles were aggravated by Eugénie injuring her spine as a result of a skiing accident in Switzerland. Beatty met her in Paris on his way back from Biarritz, but he was for some time unaware of how serious her injury was.[39] A number of hastily written, anxious and undated letters next reached Eugénie, who was encased in plaster, from various addresses. They were probably composed while Beatty was preparing the Naval Estimates for 1922-23, which showed a drop from £82½ millions to slightly under £65 millions – despite the concentration of naval forces in the eastern Mediterranean consequent on the crisis which nearly brought war with Kemal Atatürk's resurgent Nationalist Turkey.[40] It was probably the likelihood of conflict on that issue which caused Beatty to write that 'War is a wonderful thing, far more so than is ever credited to so sombre and baneful a set of circumstances. It is responsible for crediting many of us with qualities of which we have no real claim, and stirs the emotions to such an extent that it creates an atmosphere among human beings which in the cold and calculating periods of peace are so often shown to be false or at least over estimated. I feel I am one of those that have reached a pinnacle in the minds of some to which I have no real claim'. He went on, most uncharacteristically, to express considerable self-doubt regarding his qualifications to hold his present position, and to hanker after 'the firm convictions one possesses in time of war'.[41]

Beatty and Eugénie must have seen a good deal of each other during the first half of 1921, as Ethel was apparently still abroad and Eugénie was immobilised; but his letters contain no hint of a renewal of their love affair. On or near the fifth anniversary of the Battle of Jutland he thanked her for having remembered it, and wrote 'I often sigh for the peaceful war days' when 'one knew where one stood . . . and looked ahead accordingly'; which was surely viewing the experiences of 1914-18 through rose-tinted spectacles.[42] Probably in August, when he was back at Grantully Castle for the shooting, he wrote to thank her very warmly for her letters, which he greatly appreciated; but as he added 'we are and can be always Comrades can't we, and that is a great deal to me and of lasting value' it seems clear that, at any rate on Beatty's part all passion was now spent.[43]

While the letters quoted above were being exchanged Beatty was deeply engaged in getting approval to start construction of a great naval base at Singapore, and in June 1921 Arthur Balfour, the Foreign Secretary, announced to the Imperial Conference that, although no appreciable financial liability was to be incurred for the time being, the scheme had received Cabinet approval.[44] Beatty himself gave the conference a statement about Admiralty intentions in the event of war with Japan, which included the despatch to the Far East of a large proportion of the navy's strength, including eight battleships and 16 cruisers.[45]

Meanwhile preliminary negotiations were in train between the principal powers for a conference on naval limitation, the chief object of which would be to forestall the renewal of a capital ship building race, such as was then held to have contributed greatly to the disaster of August 1914. In July 1921 President Warren Harding instructed the American ambassadors in London, Paris, Rome and Tokyo to propose such a conference, and on 11th he issued firm invitations. In the Admiralty a flurry of activity followed with the object of preparing proposals which would be acceptable to the department – a process in which Chatfield played the leading part. The British Delegation to the conference was led by Balfour. Lord Lee, the First Lord, and Sir Auckland Geddes, the ambassador in Washington, were the other members. In view of the American desire to keep control of the conference strictly in civilian hands no admirals were nominated as delegates (except by Japan). Beatty and Chatfield therefore were relegated to being merely the two chief members of the 'British Naval Section, Washington', whose function was limited to giving expert advice to the full delegates.

Beatty, accompanied by Ethel, sailed for America about a month before the delegates, as he had been invited to tour the country as the guest of the American Legion. He received a rapturous welcome wherever he went, starting in Washington where cavalry escorted him and Ethel from the station to the Field mansion, followed by an official call on the President in the White House. Ethel stayed in Washington when Beatty went to New York to receive the Freedom of the City and attend receptions or dinners given in his honour and that of Marshal Foch by many public bodies, including the Pilgrims and the officers of the US Navy who had served in the Grand Fleet. From New York he went to Chicago and then to Kansas City to attend the Convention of the American Legion. After visiting Philadelphia he returned to Washington in time for the opening of the conference.

In October someone in London conceived the idea that a Victoria Cross should be laid on the tomb of the American Unknown Soldier in the Arlington National Cemetery in Virginia, and on 20th Lord Stamfordham wrote to Lloyd George that the King 'feels strongly that the proper person' to carry out the ceremony was Beatty because 'he commanded the greatest Fleet that has ever taken part in War' and as an Admiral of the Fleet was 'to all intents and purposes an Aide-de-Camp to the Sovereign'.[46] Cabinet approval was obtained, and a telegram was accordingly sent to Beatty at the end of the month.[47] On 12th he wrote to the King to tell him that his instructions had been carried out. He also gave the Monarch an account of his 'very busy time, mostly taken up with travelling and eating Dinners and making Speeches'. 'The welcome accorded to me as the Representative of Your Majesty's Navy', he continued, 'has indeed been very warm and sincere and the further west we went the more they appeared to appreciate the work of the Navy during the War and the fact that it was not only the British Empire but the World in general [that] was greatly indebted to it. . . .'[48] But if Beatty's reception showed a great deal of good will on behalf of the rather limited section of the American public whom he met it made no difference at all to the intentions of the President and the Administration regarding naval disarmament – as became plain at the very first Plenary Session of the conference, which took place on the day Beatty wrote to the King about the V.C. ceremony. In Beatty's words the proposals then put forward by Mr. Hughes, the Secretary of State 'certainly caused considerable surprise in many quarters not excluding the American Naval clique'; but they had, he continued 'caused much satisfaction in the minds of many'. He considered that the principles enunciated by Hughes 'can be accepted but the difficulty will be in carrying out the proposed

10 years Naval Holiday' in building new capital ships, because in so far as Britain was concerned 'we have already . . . had a holiday of 5 years the result of which has almost broke[n] the armament firms of the Country'. Thus 'another 10 years would', he argued, 'require a large subsidy from the government which would defeat the Economical object'. 'Ten years of no construction would', he claimed, inevitably 'be followed by a hectic period of feverish building of the Navies of the World', which would 'on the whole be greatly more expensive than a steady but very small building programme'.[49] Such arguments became the constant refrain of the British delegation throughout the early phase of the conference.

While Beatty was in America Ethel's insensate jealousy of any attractive woman to whom she thought her husband was paying attention was aroused by her reading a letter from Eugénie to him in which she expressed regret about Ethel's recent attitude, sometimes amounting to plain rudeness, towards herself. Eugénie very sensibly wrote direct to Ethel saying that as she had read the letter there was no point in recapitulating its contents; but she gave her view of Ethel's conduct with tact but frankness. Eugénie told her how, by chance, her husband had been present when the storm blew up and, probably because he was well aware of Ethel's capacity for picking quarrels, he had described this one as no more than 'a storm in a teacup'. Eugénie therefore wrote that she hoped that, on reconsideration, Ethel would take the same line, and ended her letter 'Yours affectly'. Ethel replied penitently saying 'how sorry I am if my manner ever seemed rude or in any way cold', that she 'always had a great affection' for Eugénie but had been 'hurt that you should have written to David instead of coming direct to me'; but she agreed to regard the squall in the same light as Bryan, and there the matter ended.[50] Beatty seems never to have known about this tiff between the two women who shared his favours; at any rate it is not mentioned in any of his surviving letters to Eugénie.

Later in the same month Beatty wrote to Eugénie that his trip around America had been 'entirely spoilt by the health of poor Tata who has had another breakdown and has caused me much anxiety and complicated matters terribly'. He would be glad to get her back to England and was 'dreading the future months but must stick it out somehow'. As regards the

Conference he believed he had 'steered clear'- of all the pitfalls and had got agreement for 'a complete plan of policy to be pursued by us'. Consequently he was leaving for a strenuous four day visit to Canada, whence he would return to New York and sail for home on the last day of November.[51]

So much has been published about the Washington Conference that it is unnecessary here to do more than summarise the principal decisions incorporated in the Treaty, which was finally signed on 6th February 1922. Britain, the USA and Japan were to maintain a ratio in capital ships of 5:5:3, and the total tonnage permitted to them was reduced to a figure which would ultimately allow the retention of 18 ships by Britain and USA and 10 by Japan. France and Italy were also allowed to keep 10 ships, but of much smaller total tonnage than that allowed to Japan. Future capital ships were not to exceed 35,000 tons displacement or to be armed with heavier guns than 16-inch. Aircraft carriers were limited to 27,000 tons, and a total of 135,000 tons each for Britain and USA and 81,000 for Japan was agreed. Cruisers and destroyers were not restricted as regards total tonnage, but future cruisers were not to exceed 10,000 tons displacement or to be armed with heavier guns than 8-inch. No agreement was reached on limitation of submarine tonnage, but a subsidiary treaty signed on 6th February 1922 prohibited their use in a commerce destroying role – which was one of the British desiderata. Capital ships and aircraft carriers were allotted a life span of 20 years, and complicated rules were devised to control their replacement.

For Britain the Naval Treaty meant the scrapping of 20 pre-Jutland capital ships and cancellation of the four projected 'super-*Hood*' battle cruisers – on which hardly any work had in fact been done. As the USA was to scrap 15 pre-Jutland ships and 11 uncompleted ships of the 1916 programme a fair balance was maintained, and British apprehensions about the effects of the Americans completing their huge war time construction programme were to a great extent allayed.[52]

Among the British ships to be scrapped was Beatty's dearly loved *Lion*, and Maurice Baring, who was an admirer of him and a lover of the Royal Navy, penned a threnody for her:

> 'For all the pomp and power of black and gold
> Drenched in story
> Scarred with glory
> Must now be broken up and sold

And broken up and sold or thrown away
And *Lion* shall not live to fight another day
For *Lion* once the flagship of Lord Beatty
Must now be scrapped forthwith, so says the Treaty.'[53]

One of the problems which the Washington Conference set itself to resolve was the future of the Anglo-Japanese Alliance of 1911, which fell due for renewal in 1921 and towards which both the USA and Canada showed marked hostility. The solution reached was to replace the Alliance by the 'Four Power Pact' signed by Britain, USA, Japan and France on 13th December 1921. This Pact included a 'non-fortification' clause regarding islands in the Pacific; but Britain deliberately excluded Singapore from its provisions, and Japan did the same regarding certain islands north of the equator. In the long term the Four Power Pact had far more weighty strategic consequences than the Naval Treaty; but at the time attention was concentrated on saving money by reducing the size of fleets rather than on seemingly remote strategic considerations.

Beatty was on firm ground in telling Eugénie that he would be 'more use soothing Lloyd George and keeping him straight' over the current Navy Estimates than by remaining in Washington;[54] but on his return he stepped straight into a minor storm over a telegram drafted by Churchill and sent by Lloyd George to Balfour on 9th December to the effect that the Naval Section in Washington was showing too much independence by pressing its own views on their American opposite numbers. Beatty at once penned an angry memorandum to the Cabinet and also made a verbal protest to the CID. But when Churchill offered an olive branch denying any 'intention of making insidious reflections' on the officers concerned (i.e. Beatty and Chatfield) he accepted it, and the antagonists buried their hatchets good humouredly.[55]

Far more serious than the above squall was the major assault made by the Committee on National Expenditure, generally known as the Geddes Committee after its chairman the former First Lord, on the Naval Estimates for the next Financial Year (1922-23), which they proposed to cut from £81 to £60 millions. Beatty was in the forefront of the battle over the First Interim Report of the committee,[56] and was well pleased when the government referred it for review by a new committee under Churchill – with whom Beatty always remained on good terms. The Geddes Committee rubbed salt into the Admiralty's wounds by rejecting the claim that a considerable economy would be achieved by the return of the Naval Air Service to its own full control – thereby prolonging the exchange of acerbities between the two departments concerned and the unsatisfactory condition of that branch of the naval service.

Another of the Geddes Committee's recommendations was that a Minister of Defence should be appointed to replace the civilian heads of the three service departments, which Geddes considered would both improve inter-service co-ordination and produce economies. The three Chiefs of Staff discussed the proposal informally and Sir Henry Wilson, the CIGS, wrote to Lloyd George that he had found Beatty 'almost as keen about it as I am', though the admiral anticipated opposition from his own Board of Admiralty who, according to Wilson, Beatty considered to be 'relapsing into its pre-war condition . . . [and] will become unable either to consider war intelligently or conduct it efficiently'. Nor was Trenchard, the CAS, opposed to the idea.[57] However, departmental opposition was so severe that the proposal was dropped – for a time. Beatty's reaction when it came up again will be recounted later.

The main burden of negotiating with the Churchill Committee of 1922 fell on Beatty's shoulders – because Lord Lee was, to the Admiral's evident satisfaction, still in Washington. Though Churchill originally looked like taking a very tough line, Beatty was able to tell Ethel in February that 'the battle rages on . . . Winston and Birkenhead have supported us nobly . . . I think we shall win in the end and defeat the Geddes Committee side. . . '; and by the following month he confidently told her that 'the Navy is coming out of the struggle satisfactorily'.[58] Bearing in mind that he was telling Eugénie at about the same time that 'Poor Ethel has been very miserable, nothing seems to bring any comfort to her tortuous [? tortured] mind. . . .', and again that 'I am nearly off my head with worry and anxiety' one cannot but marvel at his resilience,[59] especially as he was involved in a motor accident in 1922 and suffered a broken breast bone.[60] Though Churchill finally recommended a cut in the estimates to £62 millions he refused to accept the Geddes Committee's drastic reduction in naval personnel, and recorded that he had been 'deeply impressed' by Beatty's evidence on the Japanese threat and the need for a proper fleet base at Singapore.[61] Finally the Estimates were presented to Parliament on 10th March at just under £65 millions – which adequately explains Beatty's satisfaction at the outcome of his long struggle.

Throughout 1921 and the following year Ethel's bouts of melancholia continued with few breaks in the clouds. She consulted many Harley Street specialists, and when on the Continent travelled the round of spas and sanatoriums where specialists – some no doubt genuine though others were certainly charlatans – prescribed treatment for the wealthy, neurotic wrecks of Europe who allowed themselves to be relieved of vast sums of money in search of a cure for what in nearly every case must have been psychosis. Perhaps the best known of all the doctors whose consulting rooms Ethel frequented was Doctor Coué of Nancy, whose theme song 'Every day and in every way I am getting better and better' became a joke of the period; but in fairness to the doctor it should be recorded that not only did Ethel declare that she had benefited from his treatment but he refused to accept any payment from her. A curious by-product of Ethel consulting Coué was that Beatty recommended him to King Albert of Belgium, who wrote gratefully that 'Following his method' he did not 'suffer any more' from the trouble in one of his arms which had been causing him pain.[62] But even if Coué, and perhaps other doctors as well, brought Ethel some relief it never proved to be to be more than transitory, and the black clouds of depression soon returned.

Though Beatty generally showed remarkable patience with Ethel, only opening his heart about her troubles to Eugénie, he did sometimes reprimand her for the handicap she imposed on him in his fight to preserve British naval strength. For example early in 1922 he told her 'I am a public man, and I have a right to ask you to do all you can to make yourself well, so that you can be of assistance to me in my life';[64] but such admonishments had as little effect as the doctors' prescriptions and treatment.

A leaf from Shane Leslie's manuscript notes, written at the end of that year, gives perhaps the most vivid, and the most painful description of her condition:

> 'I was staying with the Beattys in Scotland at Grantully Castle', he wrote. 'To his [Beatty's] relief I eloped [with]

her when on the edge of breakdown. We went to
Edinburgh whence we took sleepers to London. I held
her arm with mine for fear she would leap from the train.
She needed my deep devotion and support. I could not
betray the Admiral though I knew he no longer cared. I
could not make love to a mad woman, beautiful and
caressing though she was. We were in different forms of
agony when we came to London. I took her to Tyburn
Convent and sank her knees under the BS [Blessed
Sacrament]. Under the Nuns she became limp and I took
her home to Hanover Lodge'.[65]

As a result of this experience Beatty wrote to Leslie ' . . .
Ethel was so much better for her visit to the little Chapel it
(the Spirit) entered into her and she has been more at peace
than she has been for a long time. Please drag her out of
herself and take her again. She is lacking in Back Ground – has
nothing to fall back on when in trouble. She is groping in the
dark and does not know where to go for comfort. You have
helped her and I am more than grateful if you can find the
time and opportunity [to] take her again. She listens to you
and is more reasonable in consequence and less enamoured of
herself and her ills. Yours very gratefully'.[65a] That letter
probably expresses the only genuine religious experience
gained by Beatty and Ethel.

The fall of the Lloyd George coalition government after the
famous Carlton Club meeting of 19th October 1922 and the
return of the Conservatives to power for the first time since
1905 made no very great difference to Beatty except that he
considered Leo Amery much superior to Lord Lee as his
Minister, and worked in intimate harmony with him until the
fall of Baldwin at the end of 1923.

The signature of the Washington Treaties produced great
activity among both the naval staff and the Admiralty's
technical departments, since neither had previously had to
consider the design of major warships (battleships, aircraft
carriers and cruisers) from the point of view of getting the best
possible results on a strictly limited displacement, while taking
full account of war experience. The 'legend' or broad
particulars of the two new battleships which Britain was
allowed to build by the Treaty was actually approved by the
Board on the day it was signed, sketch designs were produced
for 10,000 ton cruisers armed with 8-inch guns, and plans

were made to convert the light but fast 'large cruisers' *Glorious*
and *Courageous* into aircraft carriers. Preparations were also
made to add 3,000 tons of additional armour to existing capital
ships – as was permitted by the Treaty. It is ironical that the
'Treaty for the Limitation of Armament' thus led to greater
activity in the field of warship building and naval armaments
manufacture than at any time since the Armistice; and the
same state of affairs prevailed in the other signatory countries.
Moreover all the nations concerned decided, with scarcely any
hesitation, to build right up to the limits permitted by the
Treaty. One of the voices raised in Britain against building
monster battleships was that of Admiral Sir Herbert Richmond, whose intellectual capacity Beatty had always held in
high regard; but by 1922 his influence on naval policy was
declining, and the chief result of his advocacy of 10,000 ton
capital ships was that it earned him the lasting enmity of
Chatfield – who was already marked as a man who would
eventually occupy the First Sea Lord's desk.

All warship design is of course a matter of compromise
between the requirements for speed, armour protection and
gun calibre; and when displacement is limited the achievement
of the best compromise is inevitably made more difficult. The
naval staff, doubtless with the lessons of Jutland in mind,
decided to give priority to armour protection and armaments
at the expense of speed in the *Nelson* class battleships. They
were therefore given a main armour belt of 14 inches and deck
armour of 3-6 inches, which was about double the thickness of
the *Lion*'s protection and more than was fitted in the *Queen
Elizabeths*; but the great increase in protection and the
adoption of 16-inch guns in triple turrets meant that their
speed was in reality little more than 20 knots, though they
were theoretically capable of 23. Furthermore the requirement
that all armaments should have a high-angle as well as a
low-angle capability produced very serious difficulties
for the design engineers; and many years elapsed before
the new armaments had been made really efficient. Only in the
field of surface fire control was the *Nelson* class really superior
to any previous British capital ships, and the supersession of
the Dreyer Table by the Admiralty Fire Control Table did at
last give the degree of 'helm free' gunnery which Arthur
Pollen had offered and the Admiralty had several times turned
down before the war. Finally the treaty limitations resulted in

the *Nelsons* being the most ugly ships ever to join the Royal
Navy; and every sailor will confirm the importance of
aesthetics in the design of the ship which is to become his
home for long periods. Much the same arguments affected the
design of the new 'Washington Treaty' cruisers; but as the first
of them did not appear until the 1924 Programme they will be
considered later. Though the Board of which Beatty was the
service head cannot escape responsibility for the weaknesses of
the major warships ordered in the 1920s it is only fair to stress
the unprecedented problems and difficulties which had to be
faced.

In the autumn of 1922 Beatty suffered a shock which,
according to Leslie, he felt far more deeply than he openly
admitted. In October he was paying a ceremonial visit to
Brighton, where the family of his former Flag Lieutenant
Ralph Seymour were living. We have seen how, in Leslie's
words, Ethel Beatty 'rose in all Hell's fury' to break
Seymour's engagement to her niece 'Gwennie' Field. In 1921
Seymour had suffered a nervous breakdown, probably
brought on by Ethel's behaviour towards him, and had been
invalided from the Navy. His intention then became to study
agriculture at Cirencester, and he was staying with his family
at the time of Beatty's visit before joining the College.
Apparently he could not bear to meet the Admiral again, and
on 5th October he flung himself over the steep cliff known as
Black Rock near Brighton. The verdict of the Inquest was
'suicide during temporary insanity';[65b] but his family always
blamed the Beattys, and especially Ethel, for the tragedy.[66]
His mother wrote what Leslie called 'an atrocious letter to
Beatty which should have been sent to Lady Beatty', and in
1926 Lady Seymour published a memoir of her son, including
some of his wartime letters, with the object of neutralising
Ethel's calumnies about him.[67] As to Gwennie Field's fate,
after Ethel had frustrated two engagements she married
Charles Edmonstone, and Leslie recalled that she 'set up life in
a castle with a Scotch Laird'.[68]

In March 1923 the government set up a sub-committee of
the CID under Lord Salisbury (Lord President of the Council)
'to enquire into the co-operation and co-relation' between the
three services 'from the point of view of National and Imperial
Defence generally', including the possible introduction of a
Ministry of Defence, and 'to deal with the relations of the

Navy and Air Force as regards Fleet air work';[69] and the latter issue was at once referred to a special sub-committee under Balfour. Beatty of course became deeply involved in the deliberations of both bodies. Before the Balfour Committee had been formally set up he evidently discussed with Bonar Law the case for the Admiralty assuming complete control of the Fleet Air Arm, since in mid-February he wrote direct to him to try and clear up the 'misapprehensions' which he considered the Prime Minister was labouring under with regard to 'what the withdrawal of machines and personnel meant to the Air Service'. He stressed that, far from that service being 'left with nothing', the Navy would only take 4½ squadrons away, leaving the RAF 'with 32½ Service Squadrons, not including Reserve Squadrons or [?shore] Establishments'. As regards personnel under 5% would, he wrote, be taken over, so his proposal could 'hardly be considered as wrecking the Air Service' – which was perfectly true. Bonar Law was, however, careful to avoid committing himself. Though he admitted in his reply that 'the numbers are smaller than I imagined' he considered that 'the difficulties are still there', and he 'sincerely trusted that it may be possible for a compromise to be arranged' – which must have brought cold comfort to Beatty. [70]

When the Balfour Committee called on Beatty to give evidence he was emphatic that a fleet could defend itself effectively against any probable scale of air attack – whether it was protected by aircraft carried in its own ships or not, a view which placed very high confidence in the A-A weapons and control systems then being developed. With greater justification Beatty argued in favour of the convoy system for the protection of merchant shipping against submarine attack; but his chief case was his forcible argument in favour of recreating a genuine Naval Air Service. [71] Despite Beatty's able presentation of the Admiralty's views, in the final report of the Balfour Committee that body declined to grasp the nettle, and only proposed the adoption of a number of palliatives. Nor was Amery any more successful when he put forward the same arguments to the Salisbury Committee, which merely accepted the recommendations proposed by Balfour. [72]

While the controversy over the Naval Air Service was in progress Beatty was involved in an alleged 'leak' by the Admiralty to the Press. One of the arguments they had used

to the bodies then deliberating the matter was that under the
Letters Patent appointing members of the Board they alone
were responsible for the fighting efficiency of the navy, and
that their responsibility was infringed by the naval air element
being in part under Air Ministry control. To the fury of the
Air Lobby that argument was reproduced *verbatim* in an article
by Lord Rothermere published in the *Daily Mail* of 30th July
1923. Though Beatty certainly had no hand in the alleged
leakage of confidential information, for which Rear-Admiral
C. T. M. Fuller the 3rd Sea Lord was in fact responsible,
when the Prime Minister demanded an explanation it naturally
fell to him to provide it. [72a]

The Sea Lords described the Balfour report as 'most
unsatisfactory', but the suggestion that they wished to resign
en bloc on the issue, made by Sir Samuel Hoare, the Secretary
of State for Air and repeated by Lord Trenchard's biographer,
finds no support in the records of the debate of 1923 or in
Beatty's voluminous papers and correspondence. [73] Stanley
Baldwin, who had replaced the ailing Bonar Law as Prime
Minister on 22nd May, was well aware of the Admiralty's
disappointment and anger over the Balfour Committee's
recommendations; but he brought heavy pressure to bear on
the Board 'to do everything in their power to work the
[Balfour] scheme' – a request which obviously had to be
heeded. So there the issue of the future of the Fleet Air Arm
rested – for a time.

Many years later Chatfield, who as First Sea Lord was
fighting the last battle to regain control of naval aviation for
the Admiralty, wrote to Roger Keyes, who although then
retired was an MP and was taking a lively interest in all naval
matters, surveying the whole history of the struggle. As to
Beatty's part in it Chatfield wrote that despite his 'admiration
of him after 13 years' comradeship' his 'one bad mistake was
over the FAA'. Presumably Chatfield was referring to Beatty's
recommendation of 1917 that the Smuts Committee's report
should be accepted by the Admiralty, referred to earlier. More
surprising is his statement that Beatty 'never had his heart in it
or he would have got the FAA for us. . . .'[74] Though
Chatfield was of course admirably placed to observe and
remark on Beatty's actions in the 1920s, and he may well have
felt that he should have pressed the Admiralty's case harder,
the records do not confirm that there was anything half-

hearted in the efforts he made before the various bodies appointed to consider the matter.

As regards the Salisbury Committee's proposals, the most fruitful were the formation of the Chiefs of Staff Sub-Committee of the CID, which Beatty welcomed, and the subsequent creation of the Imperial Defence College – with Beatty's friend Herbert Richmond as its first Commandant. The question of forming a Ministry of Defence to replace the three service departments, to which Beatty had no objections – subject to certain reservations – was again shelved. [75]

In preparing the 1923-24 Naval Estimates and their subsequent presentation to Parliament Beatty had an invaluable ally in Amery, whose warning that 'a great Navy, once let down, cannot be improvised in an emergency' echoed very precisely the words used by Beatty in his Rectorial address at Edinburgh University. [76] Actually at £58 millions the estimates showed a reduction on almost every Vote except for Contract Shipbuilding and Naval Armaments, for which a £2 million increase was sought for the new battleships. Though the House voted the sums asked for with little opposition, except from the Labour Party, there followed a heavy attack by the Treasury on the 1919 pay code on the grounds that the cost of living had fallen since it was introduced. This demand touched Beatty on the raw, since he had repeatedly promised to look after the men's interests. Strong protests passed between the Admiralty and Treasury Chambers, and the very real anxiety felt in the former was only partially allayed by the Chancellor's promise that reductions 'would not apply to men now in Service' – which forecast the introduction of lower rates of pay for new entrants. [77]

In May 1923 another Imperial Conference took place in London, but Beatty's desire to form an Imperial Naval Staff was frustrated by Dominion susceptibilities, and all he could get was the creation by each country of a staff on British lines and the frequent interchange of officers between them; and even that modest measure aroused no enthusiasm at all in Canada and South Africa. [78] The chief fruits of the conference were the general acceptance of the need fully to maintain the One Power Standard, and the strong support given by Australia, New Zealand and India to the Singapore Base. But the delegates also paid lip service to 'further limitation of armaments', provided that 'the safety and integrity of all parts of the Empire' were not threatened – a condition which showed little logic.[79] With his wartime experience of Dominion ships and seamen in the Grand Fleet in mind Beatty always wanted to achieve closer integration of the various naval services – even to the point of having an Imperial Navy; but such an idea never stood a chance of acceptance by the Dominions.

While the Imperial Conference was still in session Beatty and his colleagues were working on a replacement programme for the elderly cruisers and destroyers of the fleet; and in the autumn they sent to the Treasury a request for funds to start work on eight 'Washington Treaty' cruisers, as well as a new aircraft carrier and a number of destroyers and submarines. This was the 'small but steady programme' for which Beatty had argued at Washington and later; but the total cost of £23½ millions over five years was accorded a chilly reception by Neville Chamberlain, the Chancellor of the Exchequer, though he did apparently tell Amery that he would accept total estimates for 1924–25 at £62¼ millions, of which £5 millions were to be used to start the new programme.[80] However, before any money had been actually voted the Conservative Government was defeated on the issue of Tariff Reform, and on 23rd January 1924 Ramsay MacDonald became the first Labour Prime Minister of a minority government.

From the foregoing brief account of the conferences and discussions which took place in 1923 the reader will readily appreciate the strain under which Beatty worked. That it was made very much heavier by Ethel's condition and behaviour is certainly true, for that subject is the *leitmotif* in almost all his letters to Eugénie at this time. To give only one example, at the beginning of 1924 he wrote to her 'I simply cannot go on contending with Ethel [and] her moods and illnesses, more than ¾ of which could be prevented if only she would exercise Control and not be so damnably selfish'.[81] Though his letters to Eugénie continued to be couched in affectionate terms he did from time to time hint that, although they were good friends and would he hoped always remain so, their friendship could not again develop into a love affair. Thus Beatty often suggested a meeting for lunch or dinner, but nearly always with others present; and in his letters of 1923–24 there is not a single hint of surreptitious assignations such as he quite often proposed in those of 1917-19. Eugénie's son George and her maid and confidante Mrs. Doris Taylor are both certain that in about 1924 Beatty dropped her in favour of another mistress – to whose identity a clue will appear later.[82] Moreover that Beatty's infidelities were known fairly widely is suggested by a quatrain allegedly by Hilaire Belloc which was circulating at this time:

> 'I am informed by David's wife
> That David's always true to life.
> But still I'm sure she would prefer
> That David should be true to her'.[83]

Whoever may have been the author of those lines he or she was plainly unaware of Ethel's promiscuities – as exemplified by Leslie's manuscript account quoted above. There is moreover evidence that Ethel was not much more lavish than her husband in bestowing her favours. After the admiral's death his elder son and his wife (later Lady Brownlow) were going through his huge collection of papers and found several bundles of letters from his lady friends, all neatly tied with ribbon with an appropriate memorandum and in some cases a photograph on top. Among them were Eugénie's letters to Beatty. They threw the whole lot into the fire.[84]

Yet when all has been said about the mores and manners of this pair of 'rapid falcons in a snare' Beatty's capacity to handle a vast load of paper work, prepare memoranda (often in his own hand) for high level conferences, expound the views of his department at Cabinet or CID meetings, and inspire confidence in his entourage remains an astonishing accomplishment. Although at times he certainly toyed with the idea of resigning his responsibilities in order to devote more time to Ethel and to provide a more stable home life for his sons, it seems unlikely that he was ever in earnest about doing so;[85] and a day in the hunting field in Leicestershire or a good bag of grouse on the moors of Perthshire usually revived his spirits and his stamina.

CHAPTER FIFTEEN

The Jutland Controversy,
1919-1927

The purpose of this chapter is to try and present a fair and balanced account of the controversy which began in the early 1920s and has continued to this day about the involvement of Beatty, and to a lesser extent Jellicoe and other admirals, over the extent to which they endeavoured to get their own points of view incorporated in the various published accounts of the battle.

Even the short account of Jutland given earlier will make it plain to the reader that there was vast scope for post-war controversy on its conduct and outcome. But before we turn to the part played by Beatty and others it is essential to emphasise that many perfectly genuine uncertainties existed regarding the movements of ships and what the combatants saw – or thought they saw. By modern standards the plotting of ships' movements was then archaic. Dead reckoning positions were calculated by the courses and speeds of a ship, obtained from the bridge compasses and a towed log respectively, since the last observed position; and on 31st May 1916 weather conditions were such that few if any opportunities existed for navigating officers to establish observed positions from celestial bodies, and so give plotting officers new and accurate data from which they could carry on the plotting of courses and DR positions. Nor did the discovery by Commander Oswald Frewen, about whom more will be said shortly, of the exact position of the wreck of the *Invincible* contribute significantly to the construction of charts and diagrams, since it merely established a datum point to which all other ships' movements could, with all their inherent uncertainties, be related. Thus when it came to drawing maps of the various phases of the battle historians had inevitably to rely chiefly on the deck and signal logs of ships and on the diaries kept on their bridges or at their plots. It was therefore by no means unreasonable that wide disagreements should have existed between those charged with analysing events for historical purposes and those who had been present on that fateful day.

The controversy began with the publication in 1919 of Jellicoe's account and the riposte made to it, with considerable prejudice against the former C-in-C, by Commander Carlyon Bellairs in the following year.[1] Nor did the publication as a government Blue Book in December 1920 of the official (though emasculated) admirals' despatches, signals and other documents related to the battle help matters because it consisted of an indigestible, unanalysed and in some important respects incomplete mass of material from which it was difficult for the expert and impossible for the layman, to form a fair opinion regarding what had happened and why.[2]

Beatty never wrote an account of the battle, but his private correspondence and officially recorded opinions in Admiralty papers such as Board Minutes leave no room for doubt regarding his profound chagrin over what he called 'that terrible day when we might have accomplished so much and our failure to do so has cost us dear'.[3] That his feelings were shared by virtually all the senior officers of the Battle Cruiser Fleet is also beyond doubt.[4] What concerns us is his actions regarding the controversy while he was First Sea Lord. Although on some occasions he took steps to deter the publication of views which were antagonistic to Jellicoe – for example in Captain A. C. Dewar's review of Volume III of Sir Julian Corbett's Official History[5] – he did repeatedly show his dislike of that account, and he used his influential position to get the Admiralty's 'Record' of the battle, to which further reference will be made shortly, amended to present a more favourable view of the Battle Cruiser Fleet's actions and so of his own.[6] He also initiated the preparation of a Confidential Book entitled the *Naval Staff Appreciation* of the events of 31st May-1st June 1916 in which the authors came down heavily on Beatty's side and so provoked Jellicoe to protest vigorously. Yet the persistence of the legend of Beatty's impartiality and of his alleged self-denying ordinance regarding participation in the controversy was very enduring. For example when, after his death, Stanley Baldwin as Prime Minister introduced a proposal in the House of Commons that a monument should be erected to his memory he stated that Beatty had 'kept himself aloof' from the controversies which 'have raged since the war'; and that, as we shall see, was very far from the truth.[7]

The appointment of Sir Julian Corbett to write the Official History had been made long before Beatty took office in Whitehall, and it was Wemyss who early in 1919 directed that a *Record* of the events of 31st May-1st June 1916 was to be prepared by Captain J. E. T. Harper, the Director of Navigation, with the help of a small body of research assistants using the reports and logs of the ship as the primary source.[8] Harper's Terms of Reference were 'to prepare a Record, with Plans, showing in chronological order what actually occurred in the battle'. No comment or criticism was to be included and no oral evidence was to be accepted. All statements made in the *Record* were to be in accordance with evidence obtainable from Admiralty records.[9] On 29th October 1919 Walter Long, the First Lord, told the House of Commons that the *Record* 'will be published when printed',[10] and about a month later he told members that 'it is hoped to publish shortly' – a promise which was repeated in the following February.[11] In his answer to a Parliamentary Question on that occasion (18th February 1920) Long stated that 'a narrative of the Battle of Jutland', by which he obviously meant the Harper *Record*, was then being prepared; but he did not commit his department to publication in advance of the completion of Corbett's official history.[12] The extent of Parliamentary and public interest in the publication of the *Record* is shown by the fact that it was raised on at least 22 occasions between 1919 and 1927.[13]

Apart from publishing an account of his involvement in the controversy Harper deposited in the Royal United Service Institution a collection of papers giving his version of the controversy which raged around the preparation and publication of the *Record*. After lengthy correspondence the Council of the RUSI allowed me access to most of the Harper papers in 1963, so enabling me to compare the version of the *Record* as finally published with the original typescript and printed proof;[14] but they withheld Harper's own narrative of the controversy until after the death of Lord Chatfield in 1967 at the age of 9½, because it was severely critical of his attitude and actions. When it was finally released the Council of the Navy Records Society decided to publish it as an Appendix to Volume 2 of Professor A. Temple Patterson's selection from the Jellicoe papers.[15]

So much for the background to the Harper *Record*. His

standpoint is however made entirely clear by the introduction to his book which he added in 1928, in which he described 'the unfair manoeuvring resorted to by the First Sea Lord [Beatty] to mislead the public as to the share he took in the Battle of Jutland . . . It was transparent from the day Lord Beatty assumed office as First Sea Lord that attempts were being made to neutralise the effect of the plain, unvarnished, chronological Record of facts. . . .'[16] These were very serious charges to lay against any man, especially the officer who had played a distinguished part in the recent war and who had only recently relinquished the position of naval head of his service; and it is only fair to state that by the time he penned the words quoted above Harper was not only embittered by what he regarded as his unjustified retirement but had reached a state of neurosis over the whole protracted story of the delay in publishing the *Record*.

As regards Harper's career, on completion of the *Record* the minute of a Board meeting of March 1923, at which Beatty was in the chair, records that he 'should be retained as a Flag Officer only provided that he is well reported on by his C-in-C'.[17] None the less when he was promoted Rear-Admiral in August 1924 he was retained for further service, and in June 1926 he was told that his name had been 'noted as suitable for employment . . . [and] in all probability [he would] be appointed to a Dockyard'.[18] That recommendation was, however, rescinded by Chatfield, who had by that time become Controller of the Navy and so was responsible for the Royal Dockyards, and Harper was placed on the Retired List on 1st February 1927. This change probably increased the neurosis produced by his treatment over the publication of the *Record*.

Within a short time of Beatty taking over the office of First Sea Lord he studied Harper's original typescript and the associated plans and diagrams, and at the end of 1919 he employed Ralph Seymour, his former Flag Lieutenant who was now his Naval Assistant, as go-between with Harper. It is here that the extent of Beatty's attempted interference becomes disturbing; for he *ordered* the addition to the *Record* of the despatches of Jellicoe, Scheer and himself, and also a complete schedule of the signals sent during the battle. As the depatches were about to be published the addition of them contributed nothing to the authority of the *Record*; while the signals could only be of interest to the student of the minutiae of naval history. Far more justifiable was Beatty's deletion of a long paragraph in the *Record* dealing with the Battle Cruiser action which, no matter what its merits or accuracy may have been, was a flagrant breach of the instructions to Harper to exclude 'all comment and criticism'. Otherwise the alterations demanded were described by Harper as 'minor' – though one may still feel that Beatty would have been wiser to have had no hand in demanding that they should be made. His point of view is best demonstrated by a manuscript note (unsigned and undated) which he left with his other papers. In it he wrote 'Harper compiled his report from the Logs of all the ships engaged. These logs, kept under conditions of action, were very inaccurate and did not agree, indeed it was difficult to reconcile the statements they contained, and consequently Harper had per force [sic] to arrive at a happy mean and produce plans etc. as nearly accurate as possible. Those plans and diagrams when reviewed by those who were present were found in some instances to be entirely inaccurate and not in accordance with the facts as known to them; and consequently were discarded, which caused Harper to be disgruntled. Further later information received from sources which were not available to Harper showed that in many cases the deductions drawn by Harper were inaccurate and misleading, and consequently it was considered premature to issue an official record until all data and information were available'.

The chief conflict between Beatty and Harper arose over the 360 degree turn by the *Lion* at about 7.0 p.m. on 31st May, which Beatty insisted had never been made but which the evidence of Admiral Chalmers has, as mentioned earlier, proved conclusively to have been carried out. We need not here repeat the possible reasons why Beatty was so anxious that his flagship's track chart should not show that she had turned a complete circle; but his insistence on the point did enhance Harper's suspicions about his motives. In the Official Despatches (Plate 10) the turn is shown as a circle, as it is in Corbett's official history (Diagram 55). The former is signed 'David Beatty' – as it had to be in order to make it an official document. But the Official Despatches contain another chart (Plate 8a) which according to Harper was not an original document and so was unsigned. It showed the turn as a reversed S i.e. 180 degrees to starboard and then 180 degrees to port. For some reason Beatty wanted this chart to be included, and to make it official he had to sign it. That he apparently did late in 1920, and added the date '17th July 1916'. Harper traced and compared the genuine 1916 signature on Plate 10 with that which he considered Beatty to have added some four years later; and it must be admitted that the signatures are markedly different, the latter apparently being (Lord) 'Beatty' with the 'David' added. Harper calls this 'a stupid deception which could serve no useful purpose', and if his conclusion is correct Beatty was surely unwise to lay himself open to a charge of having pre-dated his own signature – and for so trivial a reason.[19]

To go back a year, towards the end of 1919 Harper asked Chatfield, then Assistant Chief of Naval Staff, for definite instructions regarding the alterations to be made to the *Record*, and in the following February Beatty ordered them to be included 'in accordance with Board decision'.[20] Harper's account tells us that at about this time Walter Long sent for him and asked 'what was actually causing the delay in the publication of the Record', and that he replied that it was because of the large number of changes demanded by Beatty; on hearing which Long is alleged to have said that Beatty 'should not have read the Record and that he intended telling him so'.[21] Though we have only Harper's evidence of this conversation it is reasonable to accept it, as the cause of the delay in publication is beyond dispute. At any rate Beatty did tell Harper shortly afterwards to go ahead with printing the amended *Record*. On 20th February he accordingly submitted it to Chatfield and approval was given.[22]

In February 1920 Long apparently saw Harper again and told him 'that he was particularly anxious that no alterations, which could in any way affect Lord Jellicoe's position in the future, should be made to the Record by any member of the Board of which he was the head'.[23] Again we have only Harper's evidence, but presumably Long had in mind the effect on Jellicoe as Governor-General Designate of New Zealand. He also told Harper that he was 'taking steps to have all orders, previously given to me by the First Sea Lord, cancelled'; and as Beatty did precisely that on 11th March Long was evidently as good as his word.[24] This retreat by Beatty enhances one's regret that he ever embarked on tampering with the *Record*. Harper accordingly submitted a

fresh draft with some of the changes cancelled though the two
180 degree turns alleged by Beatty to have been made by his
flagship at about 7 p.m. on 31st May were still shown.[25] Long
approved this revision for publication on 13th March, and on
14th May Harper submitted the final proof to him, with a
copy to Beatty.[26] It was in this form that the *Record* was finally
published in 1927. It should, however, be remarked that
Harper did not reinsert the long paragraph about the battle
cruisers' gunnery to which Beatty had taken exception – even
though Beatty's cancellation of his orders about his amendments presumably entitled him to do so.

   Despite the apparent progress towards publication made by
the spring of 1920 Beatty had not abandoned his view that the
Record was in some respects inaccurate, and he next sent Long
a large number of 'notes' on it, about which the harassed First
Lord sought the advice of Admirals Brock, Chatfield and
Browning (DCNS, ACNS and 2nd Sea Lord respectively).
They all made their observations in writing, and on 21st June
the Board discussed them at length, seeking Harper's view in
each case. On Beatty's initiative the Board decided to add a
Preface; and it is a fair assumption that Beatty and Chatfield
were its principal authors. Harper summarised the fresh
changes in the *Record* for Long's benefit on the day after the
Board meeting. Scanning them today they do not appear to
amount to a great deal, and they were all included in the 1927
published version of the document.

   So far Jellicoe had been waiting quietly on the sidelines,
holding the view that he ought not to read the *Record*. A point
should, however, here be made which historians have generally overlooked – namely that Jellicoe was a close friend and a
fervent admirer of Corbett, he was acquainted with Harper
and was on very intimate terms with Oswald Frewen, a
member of Harper's committee who was a specialist navigator
and, incidentally, a first cousin of both Winston Churchill and
Shane Leslie. Jellicoe corresponded freely and frequently with
both Corbett and Frewen about Jutland,[26a] and also with his
former Flag Captain F. C. Dreyer, who was then considered
to be marked out for the highest ranks.[26b] Thus Jellicoe had
good reason to believe that his point of view would be fairly
represented both in Corbett's history and in the Harper *Record*.
As long as Beatty and Chatfield did not use their current
positions to influence those works he could therefore leave for

New Zealand with an easy mind; but once that condition was removed by the changes made and the addition of the Preface to the *Record* the position was entirely changed. Jellicoe therefore got into touch with Long, who on 29th June 1920 asked him to study the *Record* and the 'alterations, additions and deletions' which, so the First Lord told him, 'the Board of Admiralty desired to make' to it.[27] Jellicoe took such strong exception to some of the changes that he told both Long and Lord Milner, the Colonial Secretary, that he could not take up the New Zealand appointment unless he was given an assurance about what was to be published in the *Record*. He wrote in carefully considered and moderate terms to Long setting out the type of amendment which he regarded as acceptable, even desirable, and the type which did not come within that category. The latter included 'Alterations or suppressions which result in impressions being given to the reader which differ from those which would be gathered from a perusal of the original version'. He also confessed 'to a feeling of surprise' at the intention to include the Beatty Preface, and criticised it severely paragraph by paragraph. Apart from factual inaccuracies, the impression given was, he wrote 'that the British Battle Fleet and attendant vessels arrived late on the scene of action, and that their arrival had little or no effect upon the course and result of the action'; and it must be admitted that perusal of the Preface today does lend support to Jellicoe's strictures.[28]

According to Harper the Board discussed Jellicoe's criticisms on 14th July 1920.[29] Though we only have Harper's word for it, and the Board Minutes do not actually record a meeting on that day, it is certainly not improbable that such a discussion did take place – informally. One point which arose concerned a statement in the draft *Record* that the Grand Fleet battleship *Hercules* was straddled at 6.15 p.m., which Beatty wanted largely if not wholly deleted. When Harper demurred Beatty is alleged to have remarked that he supposed that 'there was no harm in the public knowing that someone in the Battle Fleet got wet, as that is about all they had to do with Jutland'.[30] Again we have no evidence except Harper's regarding the remark attributed to Beatty, but he must surely have intended it to be taken as 'off the record'. None the less if Beatty did express his views on the relative importance of the parts played by the Battle Cruiser and Grand Fleets so crudely one cannot but regret it.

On 6th August 1920 Long pressed the Board for 'a definite conclusion' about publication, and the decision was taken that the Naval Staff 'should be asked to settle with Captain Harper the redrafting of the plans', since an important one had allegedly been shown to be incorrect. They also decided that Corbett should be asked to write a Foreword, which should be shown to Jellicoe before he left for New Zealand.[31] The former decision held no appeal for Harper, because in his view Beatty as Chief of Naval Staff would be able to tamper as much as he liked with the *Record*; but the latter decision was entirely agreeable to Jellicoe. On receiving an assurance from Long that no changes would be made without his concurrence he sailed to take up his new appointment.

As Harper had foretold more trouble soon cropped up, especially over the plans showing the relative positions of the Battle Cruiser Fleet and the Battle Fleet, which had resulted from the substitution, on Beatty's insistence, of the two 180 degree turns for the circle turned by the *Lion* at about 7.0 p.m. The reader who desires detailed information of the squabble over the two forces' tracks may be referred to Harper's account of the discussions held in late July and early August;[32] but that version does give the impression that his nerves were badly frayed, and that his animosity towards Beatty and Chatfield had reached obsessive proportions. Some years later Oswald Frewen wrote to Admiral Evan-Thomas that at this stage Harper 'went off to Devonshire suffering from a nervous breakdown'.[33] As Frewen was personally involved in Harper's work, and this story fits in with other aspects of his conduct, it seems probable that it is correct.

Harper's account of the controversy makes it abundantly clear that he had come to the conclusion that Beatty was determined to delay publication of the *Record* for as long as possible, if not stop it altogether. In fact the decision to abandon the *Record* was taken by Long and not Beatty, on the grounds that Messrs. Longman, the publishers of Corbett's history, had protested that it would do serious damage to sales of the latter. One can sense Long's relief over the discovery of this escape route in his remark that it rescued his department from 'a not inconsiderable difficulty';[34] but Beatty correctly foretold that this 'would look like a rather transparent effort to avoid publication', which remark contradicts strikingly the attitude attributed to him by Harper. Beatty much preferred that all the available material, including Harper's proofs, should be given to Corbett, and that the Admiralty should only publish the despatches of Jellicoe, Scheer and himself, the full record of signals and the plans and diagrams of the battle.[35] The final Board decision was, however, to arrange with Corbett that his volume should include an Appendix containing part of the text of the *Record* and the diagrams.[36]

If, as seems likely, Long believed that the decision not to publish Harper's work but to hand it over to Corbett for use in the official history would put a term to the controversy he was quickly disabused. Sir James Craig, the Parliamentary Secretary to the Admiralty, told the House of Commons what was intended on 27th October 1920, but it was raised again twice within the next few days. The subject was evidently regarded as important enough for the Prime Minister to answer the questions; and as he was unfamiliar with all the intricacies of the issue his reply was by no means unambiguous.[37] Nor was the feeling in some quarters that the Admiralty wished to suppress something allayed by Craig's later statement that 'All the material, including Captain Harper's record, will be placed at Sir Julian Corbett's disposal, and this undertaking will be interpreted in the widest possible way'.[38]

In the autumn of 1920 Moreton Frewen, Oswald's father,*entered the fray by writing to Admiral Sims, USN, the former Commander of the US Naval Forces in European waters, to try and induce him to publish a letter about Jutland favourable to Jellicoe; but Sims tactfully declined to get involved.[39] At about the same time Walter Long had a long correspondence with Moreton Frewen in which he made it abundantly clear that he stood on Jellicoe's side, and attacked the Northcliffe Press for the campaign it was conducting against the admiral.[40] Though we have no clues to show

---

*Moreton Frewen's nickname was 'Mortal Ruin', and the fact that he indulged in reckless speculations is well illustrated by his involvement in the extraordinary story of the creation of the Cheyenne Club as 'an oasis of urban luxury in nineteenth century Wyoming' – to which the scions of wealthy English families were sent to make their fortunes from cattle ranching. The object of the club was to provide amenities comparable to those found in the West End of London; but the savage winter of 1887-88 destroyed both the hopes of the ranchers and the club. See article by Samuel Stanley, *The Cheyenne Club, History Today*, Vol. XXIX (July 1979).

whether Beatty became aware of these behind-the-scenes manoeuvres his encounters with Long must have left him in no doubt regarding the First Lord's views on publication of the Harper *Record*. One can therefore feel some sympathy for his conviction that his own side of the story was not going to be fairly represented unless he took some counter-action.

Beatty's riposte took the form of the brothers A.C. and K. G. B. Dewar being selected by Brock (DCNS), probably on Beatty's initiative and certainly with his knowledge, 'to write a full appreciation of the Battle of Jutland, to serve as a groundwork for a further Staff appreciation'.[41] Jellicoe considered the selection of the Dewars a bad choice, because as he put it, the older one was 'a retired Lieutenant of but little sea experience', while the younger one was 'a recently promoted Captain [who] had never as yet commanded a ship at sea'.[42] It was true that A. C. Dewar had retired as a Lieutenant in 1910, had been given the War Service rank of Commander in 1916, and retired for a second time as a Captain shortly after the Armistice; but as K. G. B. Dewar had been promoted Captain on the Active List in June 1918 it was hardly correct to describe his promotion as 'recent' some four years later. The truth seems to have been that both brothers belonged to the 'intellectual' or 'historical' school of officers known in the fleet as the 'Young Turks', whose capacity for original thinking and literary talents always held an appeal for Beatty but whom Jellicoe thoroughly mistrusted. It should, however, be remarked that when K. G. B. Dewar was given an important command he certainly did not prove a success in it.[43] As he never flew his flag afloat and finally became a Vice-Admiral on the Retired List the ranks by which he and his brother are generally known do give a somewhat inflated impression of their standing in the service.

Admiral Brock's instruction to the Dewars, which Beatty must have approved, were that they were 'to include any operation orders issued prior to the battle and a full analysis of the movements of the British Fleet'. They were to be given all necessary papers, including Harper's work, but were 'to avoid any reference to the fact that it [i.e. the *Staff Appreciation*] was being compiled'.[44] Despite the Admiralty's edict on publicity the fact that it was being prepared was leaked to the London *Evening News* only a fortnight after Brock gave the Dewars their remit.[45] In his autobiography K. G. B. Dewar exculpated Beatty of any attempt to influence his work, and stated that he only had one interview about it with the First Sea Lord; but he was then told to 'endeavour to bring out the lessons' – which obviously widened his terms of reference.[46]

The first draft of the *Staff Appreciation* was completed in about September 1921, and Beatty and Chatfield both then read it, and required certain changes to be made particularly regarding the harsh criticisms of Jellicoe. Revision was accordingly undertaken, but when Chatfield read that version he commented that it was 'written in a somewhat severe style', which 'might be considered undesirable.' He also wanted the Dewars to emphasise that the reason why three British battle cruisers blew up on 31st May while the equivalent German ships had withstood severe hammering was solely 'because the British shell was of inferior make' – which was a considerable over-simplication.[47]

Towards the end of 1921 the Admiralty decided to print about 100 copies of the *Staff Appreciation*, which was given the number CB 0938 and classified 'Secret'. The distribution was to be strictly limited. It seems clear that Beatty was delighted with the Dewar brothers' work, since Shane Leslie recalled him reading passages from it out loud at one of their meetings; but he refused to leave the copy he was reading from in Leslie's hands.[48] Some ten years later, after his retirement, Beatty also allowed the American journalist J. Langhorne Gibson to read the book, with the result that he asked Harper to get him a copy – which of course was quite impossible except, as Harper told Gibson, 'by burglary'.[49]

The criticisms of Jellicoe and other Grand Fleet admirals in the *Staff Appreciation* plainly produced uneasiness among senior officers in the Admiralty, including Beatty's intimates – probably because they remembered the way the navy had been split by the feud between Admirals Fisher and Lord Charles Beresford before the war. At any rate it was on the initiative of Roger Keyes, who succeeded Brock as DCNS in November 1921, that the Board decided to produce an abridged version for wider circulation.[50] In March 1922 that 'de-venomised' version (as it was later described) was approved by the Board as the *Narrative of the Battle of Jutland*, and a copy was sent to Jellicoe in New Zealand. His reaction was to describe it as 'very full of inaccurate statements and misleading statements'.[51] After careful examination of the text he forwarded a large number of corrections – some of which were accepted and others rejected.[52] Meanwhile the Board had become more cautious about the probable effects of allowing the Dewars' work to be widely known, and early in 1922 it was decided not to issue it. Corbett, Richmond and K. G. B. Dewar were allowed to retain their proof copies, Beatty kept his in his private papers, while the one preserved by his secretary Sir Frank Spickernell came into my hands shortly before his death in 1956.[53] All other copies were ordered to be destroyed in 1930, apparently on the order of Sir Charles Madden, Beatty's successor as First Sea Lord and Jellicoe's former Chief of Staff in the Grand Fleet.

That a more cautious attitude towards the *Staff Appreciation* and Admiralty *Narrative* was gaining ground in the Admiralty in 1922 is shown by a memorandum which Keyes and Chatfield sent to Beatty in August. Though they remained critical of Jellicoe's actions at Jutland they wrote that they could see no 'sufficient cause . . . to justify the issue to the Fleet of a book that would rend the Service to its foundations'.[54]

Jellicoe's chief criticisms of the *Narrative* concerned the actions of Admiral Hugh Evan-Thomas, commander of the 5th Battle Squadron at Jutland, and the deductions which the C-in-C, Grand Fleet (i.e. himself) could justifiably have made from the Intelligence available to him.[55] In the autumn of 1923 the Admiralty sent Evan-Thomas, who was then C-in-C, The Nore, the extracts from the *Narrative* which dealt with his own actions, and especially the opening of the distance between his squadron and Beatty's ships during the approach to battle. The result was a strong protest from Evan-Thomas, emphasising in particular that the order to alter course to the SSE at 2.38 p.m. was not repeated to him by searchlight in case the flag signal could not be read, and the fact that the 180 degree turn to the north by the 5th Battle Squadron at 4.48 p.m. was not made executive until some time after his flagship the *Barham* had passed Beatty's *Lion* on an opposite course.[56] Early in December Evan-Thomas asked to see the First Lord (now Leo Amery) to represent his views; but he had hardly begun to do so when Beatty came into the room and 'bundled me out'. The result was that Evan-Thomas suffered a severe heart attack that night, and in the following March he was placed on the retired list.[57] The contrast between Beatty's treatment of his former comrade on this occasion and the very warm letter of thanks for his support written a few days after Jutland, quoted earlier, gives an unpleasant impression of the lengths to which Beatty as First Sea Lord went to get *his* version of events accepted as gospel.

Jellicoe asked for his principal criticisms of the *Narrative* to be printed as an Appendix, and his defence of his own actions certainly reads convincingly today. He also wrote an Appendix for insertion in a new edition of his book *The Grand Fleet*; but as his publisher would not reprint the book it did not see the light of day until it was printed in the second volume of the Navy Records Society's edition of *The Jellicoe Papers* in 1968.

Jellicoe's correspondence with Oswald Frewen shows that he considered that Beatty and his associates had exerted improper influence in the preparation of the *Staff Appreciation* and the *Admiralty Narrative*;[58] but that correspondence can also be said to show that Jellicoe himself did not hesitate to give both Harper's assistant and the official historian the benefit of his own views and purposes. To adjudge which of the two admirals endeavoured to bring the greater influence to bear on the authors of the various accounts is a nice point; but to me it seems clear that Beatty, supported by Chatfield, was the more guilty in that respect. None the less the fact that Corbett's account appeared to the Naval Staff to be 'written entirely from the point of view of the Commander-in-Chief'[59] caused further trouble, including a very hostile reaction from Chatfield, who had by that time gone to sea in command of a cruiser squadron. He produced a passionate defence of the accuracy of the battle cruisers' gunnery, which more recent research has by no means confirmed, and again blamed the poor results it achieved solely on the inefficiency of the British shells.[60]

Beatty's remarks and other annotations are to be found on the set of proofs sent to him, and he obviously did not like the account. Corbett died suddenly on 21st September 1922, and it fell to the Secretary of the CID's Historical Section to try and resolve this new conflict. The solution arrived at was that the Admiralty inserted a 'strengthened disclaimer' in the book which not only impugned its accuracy but stated that 'some of the principles advocated', notably 'the tendency to minimise the importance of seeking battle and of forcing it to

a conclusion' were 'directly in conflict with their views'.★
Perhaps more justifiably the Admiralty insisted that no
mention should be made of the decyphered German signals
which were in the Admiralty's hands during the night after the
battle, but on which the Admiralty's action left a great deal to
be desired. That important omission from the official history
was only partially rectified by the addition of a note and
Appendix when a second edition was published in 1938; but at
that time the British people had more urgent defence issues to
occupy their minds and it aroused negligible interest.

Publication of the Admiralty *Narrative* in 1924 with its
pro-Beatty bias was soon followed by that of Sir Reginald
Bacon's book *The Jutland Scandal*,[61] which showed strong
prejudice in Jellicoe's favour. Two years later the third volume
of Churchill's memoirs revived the controversy,[62] and internal
evidence makes it plain that he had been given access to the
Staff Appreciation, possibly by Beatty to whom he had written
in 1924 '. . . I am one of your greatest admirers, and I never
cease to proclaim you as an inheritor of the grand tradition of
Nelson. How I wish I could have guided events a little better
and a little longer. Jutland would have had a different ring if
the plans already formed in my mind after the Dogger Bank
for securing you the chief command had grown to their
natural fruition. I live a good deal in those tremendous past
days. . . .'[63]

The appearance of Churchill's account provoked Evan-
Thomas, the commander of the 5th Battle Squadron, to
publish a letter of protest in *The Times*;[64] while an article in
Truth (23rd Feb. 1927) and a review by Harper of Churchill's
book in the *Morning Post* the following month produced
strong reactions from Beatty's disciples, including another long
letter from Chatfield defending the gunnery efficiency of the
battle cruisers.[65]

Early in May 1927 questions were again asked in Parliament

★As a curiosity in the story of the preparation of 'Official Naval Histories'
and an example of the Admiralty's long memory it may here be mentioned
that the Permanent Secretary of the Admiralty threatened to take exactly the
same action over the first volume of my *War at Sea 1939-45* when the proofs
reached the department in 1953. However, in that case my knowledge of the
treatment of Corbett over his *Naval Operations*, Vol. III and the firmness of
the editor of the Military History Series (Professor Sir James Butler)
resulted in the threat being quickly withdrawn.

about publication of the Harper *Record* — to which an affirmative answer was now given.[66] In that same month Beatty proposed that in order 'to clear up the supposed mystery' the typescript submitted by Harper in October 1919 should be published with an appropriate preface; but as the original typescript could not be found (it had actually been retained by Harper) the proof copy which had suffered the least amendment should, he suggested, be used. The First Lord (now W. C. Bridgeman) approved, and the long delayed *Record* thus appeared – and produced hardly any interest.[67] After his retirement Harper published his version in *The Truth about Jutland*, and also collaborated with the American author Langhorne Gibson in another account of the battle. Contrary to the expectation of the pro-Beatty faction the tone of the former work, though it championed Jellicoe, was so moderate that Beatty declined to allow the riposte which some of his supporters had drafted to be published.

After he had left the Admiralty for good in July 1927 Beatty's interest in Jutland did not flag; nor did he ever modify his views on his own conduct or that of other participants. He gave all the help he could to Shane Leslie in the writing of his stupendous *Epic of Jutland* in 5,200 lines of Alexandrine heroic couplets, which he produced with Oswald Frewen's help and to which Captain Augustus Agar VC, a warm admirer of Beatty, contributed a Preface. Its publication in 1930 produced what now seems to be a surprising amount of interest, although some of the lines plumb the depths of banality, e.g.

> 'The mind of Jellicoe with searching strain
> Judiciously decided to refrain
> Deployment to the Starboard, lest his wing
> Should take a concentrated hammering.'[68]

But despite its obvious defects, such as false rhymes and invented words, this poetic *tour de force* gave Beatty and his friends much satisfaction.

In 1933 Beatty was delighted by the appearance of a small book entitled *New Light on Jutland* by The Rev. J. J. Pastfield, a former teacher of science at Winchester College and member of the Professorial Staff at the RNC Dartmouth.[69] That author made a valiant attempt to compare British and German gunnery, and the record of hits obtained by both sides; and he strongly defended the battle cruisers against 'the old superstition' that their shooting had been bad. The loss of the three ships he attributed entirely to what he called 'the cordite danger'. This work, though now known to be erroneous in many respects, produced more correspondence between Beatty and Leslie. [70]

The last mention of the controversy prior to World War II which I have found is an Admiralty memorandum addressed to Lord Chatfield in March 1938, to which was attached an account, written by the Deputy Secretary of the Admiralty in 1921, of the history of the Harper *Record*. This memorandum mentions that no 'correspondence or material concerning the Harper Committee can be found', and that in 1927 Beatty 'ordered the destruction of all the Harper charts'. It also stated that 'no trace of the correspondence concerning this Staff Appreciation, since it was handed to Sir Oswyn Murray by the DCNS (Admiral Dreyer) in 1932 can be found'. [71] The solution to the disappearance of the papers referred to was that they had, to a large extent, been retained by Lord Beatty himself. Why Chatfield should suddenly have shown renewed interest in the documents concerned with the Jutland controversy at so late a date is obscure.

In conclusion it is difficult not to feel that Beatty was unwise ever to involve himself in the production of historical accounts of Jutland – especially when he was First Sea Lord; also that Chatfield should have restrained himself from producing his repeated and heated defence of the battle cruisers' gunnery. As to Harper, though one can sympathise with his resentment over the interference in an account which he obviously believed to be as accurate as it could be made, it was a pity that he allowed his animosity towards Beatty to become so obsessive in the exchanges over the production and publication of the *Record*.

The Dewars' *Staff Appreciation* still seems to have merit, but it was surely regrettable that they allowed themselves to indulge in such far-ranging and astringent criticism of Jellicoe's strategic, tactical and technical organisation and methods. Finally, lest the reader should feel that Beatty's interference in the production of the Harper *Record* and his dislike of Corbett's account were wholly unjustified, it is fair to remark that had he done nothing at all the versions of Jutland published in the 1920s would have shown considerable bias in favour of Jellicoe. Thus a generous view of his actions would be that the support he gave to the *Staff Appreciation* and the Admiralty *Narrative* should be regarded as no more than an attempt to preserve a fair balance.

One final point may be made in mitigation, if not in full explanation, of Beatty's actions on the Jutland controversy – namely that he retained virtually all the correspondence, copies of minutes and other relevant documents in his private papers. Had he wished to ensure permanent suppression of his part in the controversy he would surely have destroyed those records, since there could be no sense in preserving what was bound to come to light some day.[72] Thus although Beatty must stand convicted of highly injudicious, even reprehensible, interference in the preparation of the various accounts of the battle, a generous verdict would be to acquit him of the most damaging charges made against him by Harper, Frewen and others in the opposite camp.

CHAPTER SIXTEEN

First Sea Lord.
The Second Phase, 1924–1927

The General Election of 6th December 1923 produced such a large increase in Liberal and Labour MPs that the Conservative Party was left in a minority. Baldwin therefore resigned and the King invited Ramsay MacDonald, as leader of the next largest party, to form a government. In the Admiralty there was intense interest about who would become the first Labour First Lord, and the appointment of Lord Chelmsford, who had recently been Viceroy of India, was totally unexpected. Rumour had it that the appointment had been instigated by the King but the fact that Lord Stamfordham, the monarch's Private Secretary, wrote to Lord Rosebery that 'Chelmsford was a surprise. I believe he accepted on the condition that the Navy was adequately maintained . . .' refutes such an idea.[1] Later evidence shows that the real reason why MacDonald nominated Chelmsford was that, unless a Peer could be found to provide the necessary quota of Secretaries of State in the House of Lords, he could not form a government. Chelmsford apparently accepted on condition that the Admiralty's cruiser programme was carried out, that the construction of the Singapore base should continue, and that he should never be involved in questions of party politics in the Cabinet.[2]

Beatty regretted Amery's departure after a tenure of only 15 months and was at first rather contemptuous of Chelmsford's acceptance of office, telling Ethel that he would have 'preferred to have had a real Labour man'; but he soon modified that view, declaring that his new master was 'a gentleman and straight as a die'.[3] He quickly made friends with Frank Hodges, the former miners' leader who had become Civil Lord, and also told Ethel that he thought he would 'get on all right' with C. G. Ammon the Parliamentary Secretary 'when once we get to work'; but he found Philip Snowden, the Chancellor of the Exchequer, 'the thorn in our side'; while with some members of the Cabinet it was necessary 'to teach them Imperialism', which was perhaps unsurprising.[4] Though he told Eugénie that the change of government meant that his Board 'had a pretty tough job' before them before many weeks had passed he was writing quite warmly to both Ethel and Eugénie about his new colleagues and associates – except for Snowden.

It was just as well for Beatty that things should have run fairly smoothly in the Admiralty because at the beginning of 1924 he was having a wretchedly difficult time with Ethel. On 10th January he wrote to Eugénie from Brooksby that she 'ballyrags me so all the time that I don't want to go anywhere with her myself'; but if Eugénie was prepared to go to the French Riviera with her it would, he said, 'make all the difference'. She responded most nobly and set out to Hyères with Ethel towards the end of the month, taking her son George, then aged 15, with her. Many years later George recalled how Ethel's behaviour had been 'quite impossible', and Eugénie finally moved to Cap Ferrat to join her sister-in-law Freda Dudley Ward, whose long love affair with Edward, Prince of Wales was then at its height.[5] Beatty sent his faithful naval steward Woodley with Ethel, and so obtained first hand news of the way this oddly assorted party worked out. 'You have no idea', he told Eugénie towards the end of January in the letter already quoted 'what a relief it is after the last 4 months to come home and sit down and do exactly what I like . . . and I enjoy every minute of it and do not budge until I want to and then to the Admiralty'. Knowing Ethel's jealousy he evidently concealed the fact that he was corresponding with Eugénie by sending his letters in envelopes of 'peculiar shape which I acquired to avoid remarks at your end'.[6]

A few days later he wrote that he was 'afraid Ethel is in a very contrary mood and her letters are full of woe'; but his reaction to her complaints was that the only alternatives were that she should either go 'into a Nursing Home or bring a life of hell at Hanover Lodge, which is unthinkable'. However, Eugénie's report that 'an interesting young man is available to wait on her' he considered a promising diversion – evidently being beyond caring about his wife's infidelities. His gratitude to Eugénie for 'handling the situation' so skilfully was profound; but he warned her not to 'let it get on your mind or we shall crack together'.[7] But despite Eugénie's efforts his troubles continued, with Eugénie writing that Ethel hated her and was pressing to come home again – to which Beatty replied 'begging her to remain out' and saying that 'it is for my sake as well as her own', because he was having 'a hectic time with the Government', whom he described as being 'very like Ethel, obstinate as mules'; but he was determined that 'they must and shall give in' – presumably on the cruiser building programme. He told Eugénie that his doctor had warned him that 'the strain of looking after her [Ethel] the last 4 months and contending with the difficulties of my office were such that if they went on I should bust up, which is quite true . . .'; so he besought Eugénie 'to make friends with her' and to continue her efforts on his behalf.

Beatty's next letter told how the latest reports received from Eugénie 'fill me with terror more especially when taken in conjunction with those I have received from Ethel' – because her doctor had apparently put her on to morphia in order to give her sleep. He told Eugénie that Ethel's mother had become a drug addict and 'to start [Ethel] on morphia is a fatal thing and will lead to the craving which always ends in disaster'. From recent research into the causes and effects of drug addiction it seems that he was probably right; so he urged Eugénie 'to see the d – d doctor and tell him on no account whatever to make use of it'. He told her 'to hide' this letter and write again, as he was planning to come to the south of France on his way to visit the combined Mediterranean and Atlantic Fleets in March during the usual spring exercises.[8]

In the letter just quoted Beatty also wrote that, as regards naval affairs, 'we are having a very troublous time with the Estimates', over which he would 'come to grips' with the Chancellor that week; and in the following week the future of the Singapore base was to be tackled. Thus it will be appropriate here to turn to the problems which arose during the first months of the Labour Government's term of office. In the first place the controversy with the Air Ministry over the control and manning of the Fleet Air Arm and of the shore-based aircraft of what was then known as the Coastal Area Command (later renamed Coastal Command) continued unabated; and Chelmsford was quickly as much at odds with Lord Thomson, the new Secretary of State for Air, as their predecessors Amery and Hoare had been.[9] In consequence early in March the Cabinet appointed a new committee under Haldane, the Lord Chancellor, to adjudicate on the issue. As Beatty was absent on the Mediterranean trip just mentioned it was Keyes, the DCNS, who presented the department's case; and in a long exchange of letters he and Trenchard hammered out the complicated compromise which came to be known as the Trenchard-Keyes Agreement. Haldane accepted it, and recommended it to the CID which forwarded it to the Cabinet.[10] In July it received formal approval, and it was under this compromise that naval aviation struggled to develop during the next 13 years. Beatty accepted the agreement, though he certainly never liked it – chiefly because it failed to alter the principle that the Fleet Air Arm formed a constituent part of the Royal Air Force and was not the independent Naval Air Service which he had helped to sacrifice in 1917 but had endeavoured to revive since he had come to the Admiralty.[11] In working to achieve that purpose the prime movers were Chatfield, who became Third Sea Lord and Controller of the Navy in April 1925, and Dreyer who was ACNS from 1924–27.

To turn to ship building, the change of government made no difference to the Admiralty's plan to get approval for a modest programme spread over ten years. Capital ships (except of course the two *Nelson* class) were excluded by the Washington Treaty; but British cruiser needs were assessed at 70, of which not more than ten should be over 15 years old by 1929. This figure was arrived at partly on the requirement for 31 cruisers for fleet duties and 39 for trade defence, and partly on the principle of maintaining a 25% superiority over Japan. This meant the construction of 17 ships, all of which were to be 'Treaty Type' of 10,000 tons armed with 8-inch guns, between 1924 and 34.[12] Similar arguments applied to destroyer and submarine building; and four new aircraft carriers were included in the programme as well as a large number of lesser vessels. The total cost of the Ten Year Programme was estimated to be £262½ millions – a sum which the Labour Cabinet, bent as it was on improvements in social welfare and education and on cutting down the fighting services, was not likely to view sympathetically.[13] In February they accordingly appointed a committee under J. R. Clynes (Lord Privy Seal) to review the policy to be adopted and to make recommendations to the Cabinet on the future of the Singapore base as well;[14] and Beatty was obviously referring to the deliberations of this body when he told Eugénie about his difficulties in the letters already mentioned.

At the first two meetings of the Clynes Committee Beatty gave a long and impassioned review of the historical and diplomatic background to the termination of the Anglo-Japanese alliance in 1922, and so to the initiation of the Singapore base scheme. He emphasised the economic aspects of the question, and claimed that abandonment of the base would imperil overseas trade to the value of nearly £900 millions a year, and would also destroy Britain's position in the Far East. Furthermore he argued that the signs of the revival of German naval power since 1918 and the strategic changes wrought by the Washington treaties increased still further the need for Britain to be able to deploy strong naval forces in the south-west Pacific. He summed up the issue by stating that 'the security of the enormous British interests' depended entirely 'on the sufferance of another power (i.e. Japan)', and that no less than three Cabinets and two Imperial Conferences had accepted the need for the Singapore base.[15] Until that was done, and adequate forces were provided to work from it, Japan could, he argued, 'exercise complete control of the sea communications in the Indian Ocean for 42 days and [for] at least a year in the Pacific'[15a] – which was a remarkably accurate prophecy of what actually happened between 1942 and '44. Early in March Beatty wrote to Eugénie, who was still trying to cope with Ethel at Hyères, that 'This is an awful life, the struggle this end has been Very acute with a good deal of bitterness and I am accused of all sorts of things Nobbling Cabinets etc which is all too foolish, and [I] fear that the Cabinet in this case refuses to be nobbled and will turn down the Singapore scheme. However it will depend upon how they do it and their phraseology etc as to whether we are to take serious notice of it at the Admiralty'.[16] Beatty's prophecy about the Cabinet's decision over the Singapore base was quickly proved accurate. Despite J. H. Thomas (Colonial Secretary) supporting the Admiralty on 17th March MacDonald told the House of Commons that, after consulting the Dominions, the government had decided that they 'could not ask Parliament to go on with this scheme'[17] – a statement which produced anger and dismay in the Admiralty and caused Beatty to draft a memorandum which in effect was a threat of resignation. As, however, it was never forwarded to the CID or Cabinet he must have had second thoughts – or perhaps the other members of the Board dissuaded him.[18]

The Admiralty fared much better over the cruiser programme than over the Singapore base – probably because Chelmsford had, as we saw earlier, made its continuation a condition of his accepting office. In January he told the Chancellor that he would accept a reduction of the eight ships originally proposed for each of the next three years to four in 1924-25 and five in the following year 'provided that the deficiency was made up in the following years'.[19] The Cabinet, however, went one better, and decided that the first slice of the programme should consist of five ships – chiefly in order to relieve unemployment in the shipyards. On 25th February Ammon informed the House of Commons accordingly.[20] Then followed the tussle over the Estimates referred to by Beatty, and on 18th March Ammon introduced them at a total of £55.8 millions, which was £2.2 millions less than the preceding year's but included £1.8 millions to start building five cruisers and two destroyers.[21] According to Admiral Oliver (2nd Sea Lord) the success over the cruiser programme 'was achieved by Beatty tackling MacDonald about them after dinner' at Admiralty House;[22] but it seems more likely that it was the unemployment problem which swung the Cabinet round. Thus was born the *Kent* class of 10,000 ton cruisers, armed with eight 8-inch guns with an A-A as well as a low-angle capability. They had long endurance – for trade defence purposes – but were ugly ships with a very high freeboard, and it was a long time before their armaments worked with reasonable efficiency.

Beatty had good reason to be satisfied by the outcome of the debate on the Estimates, and told Eugénie that 'We had a tremendous victory the day before yesterday [21st March] when all the Pacifists, Communists and Socialists that go to make up the Labour Party voted solid for The Admiralty View and for money to build cruisers with', and that only a fraction of the Liberal Party (73 out of 152) had opposed the motion. 'It is a feather in the cap of the Admiralty', he gleefully declared, 'and we are duly elated'.[23] Except for Ethel's condition he must have had an easier mind than for many months when he left London to embark at Toulon in the *Bryony*, the 'despatch vessel' used as a yacht by the C-in-C, Mediterranean, on 18th March to join the Combined Fleets at Pollenza Bay, Majorca, on the following day. He accepted the risk of taking Ethel

with him, and his belief that a sea change would do her good
was evidently justified. From 18th to 22nd March Beatty was
happy to be back among 'old friends', and it made him feel
'like old times'.[24] After witnessing some of the Combined
Exercises and holding conferences with the senior officers he
went on to Malta, 'inspected the whole place and made myself
acquainted with the various problems'. He even managed to
get in 'a little Polo' at which, to his great pleasure, the Navy
defeated the Army. On 28th he left for home calling at Taormina, Naples and Elba on the way, and spending a few days at
Nice. On 4th April he was back at his desk, and told Eugénie
that the trip had done them both a lot of good, though Ethel
continued to complain about life 'holding nothing of interest
or pleasure' for her. He urged Eugénie to write to her at
Hanover Lodge assuring Ethel of her friendship but concealing
the knowledge 'about her and her movements' which he had
given.[25] There is then a gap of six months in the Beatty-
Eugénie correspondence, presumably because she had returned
to London from the Riviera. One cannot but admire the
devotion she showed in trying to relieve her former lover of the
strain and burden of his matrimonial troubles.

The first major problem Beatty had to deal with on his
return was the government's plan to achieve a further measure
of disarmament – probably in the form of a codicil or exten-
sion to the Washington Treaty. In April he told the Board that
they were required to prepare a memorandum on the subject.
He himself was ready to accept a reduction in the size of new
capital ships from 35,000 to 25,000 tons, and to extend their
effective life from 20 to 25 years. Cruisers could, he considered, be reduced from 10,000 to 7,000 tons and their armament from 8-inch to 6-inch guns.[26] The technical departments
accordingly produced sketch designs for such ships; but they
and the staff were worried by the fact that they would be
greatly inferior to the comparable ships being built by the
other naval powers. None the less in May Ammon assured the
House of Commons that 'nothing will be left undone . . . to
assist in the direction of a further conference on naval limitation'.[27]

In August Beatty got the yacht *Sheelah* recommissioned
under the faithful Captain Grint and sent her out to the
Mediterranean, where he and Ethel and their son David and a
large party of aristocratic friends joined her for a protracted

cruise.*[28] After visiting Venice the party went on to the Dardanelles, where they visited the war cemeteries on Gallipoli, and then went through the Straits to Constantinople. In his draft biography Leslie wrote that Beatty insisted on flying the White Ensign and refused the Turkish request that he should 'obey the custom of flying the Turkish flag at the fore' when in their territorial waters. Though hardly well mannered towards his host country this attitude was certainly characteristic of Beatty. Apparently the Turks finally agreed to make an exception for the *Sheelah*, and after spending the best part of a week at Constantinople she passed through the Bosphorus to Galatz – still flying the White Ensign.[29] From Galatz the whole party went to Bucharest by invitation of Beatty's girl friend of adolescence, now Queen Marie of Roumania. Beatty carried out the usual formality of laying a wreath on the tomb of the Roumanian Unknown Soldier, and then they were 'lavishly entertained' and 'dashed about the country in high powered cars' – apparently with little consideration for any peasants who got in their way.[30] After these jollifications the yacht returned through the Straits and called at Athens, after which the party split up in Italy and Beatty returned home while Ethel and others motored 'through the Lakes and Swiss mountains.' His first letter from London to Eugénie told her that they had 'a wonderful trip . . . everything went well, no untoward occurrences and everybody the best of friends'. So Ethel must have made a substantial recovery since March, though it was to prove only temporary.

Beatty's absence for nearly two months meant of course that on his return he was 'frightfully busy picking up the threads of a multitude of important questions which they kindly kept from coming to a head until my return. . . .'[31] Among those questions was the line the Admiralty should take with regard to the draft Treaty of Mutual Assistance which the League of Nations was considering, and the 'Protocol for the Settlement of International Disputes', generally known as the Geneva Protocol. At the end of July 1924 Beatty warned the CID of the

*In *The Times* the Duke and Duchess of Sutherland, Lord and Lady Ednam and Lord Caledon are named as guests on board the *Sheelah* in late August. Lady Ednam was a daughter of Millicent, Duchess of Sutherland. In the early 1920s, before his liaison with Freda Dudley Ward began, Edward, Prince of Wales had wanted to marry her, but King George V disapproved of marriage to 'a commoner'.

dangers inherent in the proposal, because it would impose on
Britain obligations such as defending the sea communications
of a country which had been attacked or threatened, and so
might involve her in conflicts in which she had no interest,
and the Royal Navy in actual combat without a declaration of
war having been made.[32] Two months later Chelmsford circulated a memorandum to the Cabinet stating the Admiralty's
objections to the Protocol in very similar terms to Beatty's;[33]
but in October the League Assembly accepted the document –
to the consternation of the Admiralty, which had enjoyed the
strong support of Maurice Hankey throughout the campaign
against it. However, before the Protocol could be brought
before Parliament the Labour Government had fallen, and it
was actually the next Conservative Government which finally
rejected it in March 1925 – for the very reasons which Beatty
and Chelmsford had put forward some six months earlier.[34]

On 8th October 1924 the Labour government sustained a
heavy defeat on a comparatively trivial issue and MacDonald
asked for the dissolution of Parliament. At the October General Election the Conservatives, aided by publication of the
notorious 'Zinoviev Letter', were returned with a huge majority, and on 7th November Baldwin appointed W. C. Bridgeman, who had been Home Secretary in his previous administration, to the Admiralty. A rumour circulated at that time that
Beatty was about to resign office, but on 20th November it
was officially denied.[35]

Before Bridgeman had really settled into his new job Beatty
had to rush off to the south of France with his two boys –
much against his wishes – in order to be with Ethel for
Christmas.[36] He was back again before the end of the year and
sent Eugénie a depressing report on Ethel's condition – which
he described as 'not as bad as last year but bad enough.'[37]
Early in the New Year he wrote from Brooksby to thank the
ever-loyal Eugénie for remembering his birthday, but told her
how the strains to which he had been subjected had resulted in
his losing his capacity to sleep which, he wrote, 'frightens me
as I am generally good for 10 hours and thought a hunt would
put me right'; but even his favourite sport was evidently now
failing to bring him mental and spiritual tranquillity.[38] His
next letter, which cannot be dated exactly, told Eugénie how,
contrary to all his expectations, Ethel's 'continued attacks of
neurasthenia' had 'at last been getting a hold on me'. Though

he had never admitted it 'to a human soul' he could not conceal from her the fact that 'I get frightful waves of depression'. Moreover a nasty fall out hunting in which he had 'got badly squashed' had renewed the trouble in his chest caused by the motor accident mentioned earlier, and had kept him immobilised for some days. This was the most depressed letter in the whole Beatty-Eugénie correspondence, and by 1925 it must have been plain to him that no human being could carry simultaneously the psychological strains to which he was subject and the heavy responsibilities of the First Sea Lord's office.[39]

In February, on Ethel's insistence, Beatty sold the lease of Hanover Lodge, the London house which he had always liked best, and they moved to Mall House, which she had always abhorred because of the noise of the traffic.[40] Typically of her as soon as the sale contract was signed she wrote that she had changed her mind, so Beatty had to tell her that she was too late and that they had to give possession towards the end of March.[41] To Eugénie he wrote 'What a fool I was to sell Hanover Lodge but I succumbed to the perpetual abuse of the House after 3 years and could do no less'.[42] In the following July he bought the lease of 17 Grosvenor Square, and so had to endure all the inconvenience and disturbance of another move.

A minor annoyance to Beatty at this time was the publication of what he called 'Bacon's bl--dy book' *The Jutland Scandal*; but it is interesting to find that K. G. B. Dewar sent him the draft of the notice about it which he had written for the *Naval Review*, and that Beatty recommended omitting the reference to the *Naval Staff Appreciation*, of which Dewar had of course been co-author, on the grounds that as it had never been issued and 'in so far as the World in general is concerned [it] does not exist'.[43] This exchange suggests that the influence of Beatty on the preparation of the suppressed book was greater than Dewar later admitted.

We have one of the best descriptions of Bridgeman and of Beatty at this time from the pen of J. C. C. (later Lord) Davidson, who became Parliamentary and Financial Secretary of the Admiralty and so had excellent opportunities to observe them both. Of Bridgeman he wrote that he 'appeared to be the bluff country gentleman and was consistently underrated by those who failed to penetrate behind his modesty and engaging humour. In reality, he was a good scholar and a very experienced politician. He had abilities of a very high order and was a tireless administrator who mastered patiently every question with which he had to deal ' – an opinion which my own study of the principal characters of the period, spread over many years, fully confirms. Davidson also wrote that 'The dominant figure when I joined the Admiralty was the First Sea Lord, Lord Beatty. His hat was worn at a rakish angle over one eye, he was a devoted friend of all horseflesh, and he had that rather attractive Irish horseman's face. He was a very good–looking man and had a most attractive personality, could be very witty, and was beloved by all those who were of the same making as himself; but not so by those who were a little more cautious and careful. He had immense energy and was prepared to take risks, but he had that genius for running risks which turned out to be [so] successful that they appeared not to be risks at all . . . He spoke well and forcibly, and wrote much as he spoke. His powerful mind and immense concentration enabled him to master a case and put it so confidently and with such ability that he carried great conviction. He could stand up to the toughest Cabinet – several times during the discussion of the Estimates the Admiralty case was left entirely to him. . . .'[44] Though Davidson obviously knew little or nothing about the stresses and strains of his home life it is plain that Bridgeman, Beatty and he, with Oswyn Murray's clear mind and long experience always at hand to advise, and sometimes to steady them constituted a strong team.

Naturally it took a little time for Beatty and Bridgeman to appreciate each other's qualities, and the Admiral seems at first to have under-estimated those of his political chief; for in January 1925 he sent him two letters from Malta stressing the importance of resisting 'the Chancellor [Churchill] supported by Sir George Barstow [a Controller of the Treasury]' in their attempts to dictate Cabinet policy.[45]

Though Beatty probably welcomed the return to power of the Conservatives he was soon to find that, with Churchill at the Treasury, his problems and difficulties, especially over getting money for the ships he wanted to build, were in no way diminished. He quickly found that Bridgeman, whom he soon described to Ethel rather patronisingly as 'a dear little man', was a whole-hearted and invaluable ally in the battles with the formidable Chancellor[46] – the first of which was of course

After the battle. *Seydlitz* at Wilhelmshaven after the Battle of Jutland. The extent of the damage is very clear. (*Drüppel*)

Wreck of the *Invincible*. (*Imperial War Museum*)

'917.   *George R. J.*

King George V and Beatty. In a letter to Queen Mary the King described him
as '...a splendid fellow...they love him in the fleet.' (*Godfrey-Fausset
Collection*)

Photograph of Beatty in uniform
but without cap.
(*Godfrey-Fausset Collection*)

Relaxing with his son in Guardsman uniform. c.1910.
(*Sport & General*)

Encaenia at Oxford, 1919. Curzon, the Chancellor of the University is in the
centre of the front row, Beatty third from right, Wemyss extreme left.

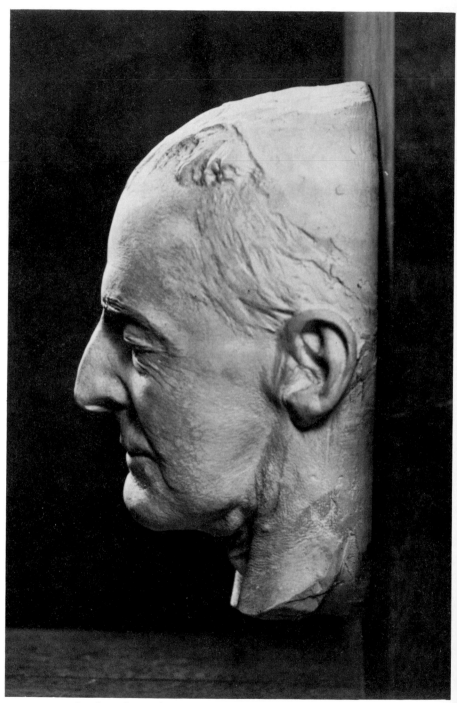

Death mask. (*Earl Beatty*)

over the 1925–26 Estimates. The Board asked initially for nearly £65 millions, an increase of some £9 millions over the previous year's estimates; but the increase was in part due to the inclusion for the first time of a sum for the Fleet Air Arm – formerly financed out of the Air Vote – and also a little money for the Singapore base.[47] Churchill's counter-attack was immediate – and severe. He asked for a new review of the likelihood of a major war within the next decade, and described the Admiralty's proposals in terms very similar to those in which Lloyd George had attacked his own Navy Estimates in 1913.[48] The poacher of those days had indeed become the most astringent gamekeeper of the 1920s.[49]

Bridgeman and Beatty produced strong counter arguments, but rejected Churchill's proposal to accept 'a constant figure' of £60 millions during the next few years, and refused at first to go below £62½ millions. Beatty told his wife that he had been involved in 'some bitter struggles in the past but never so bitter as this',[50] though he and Churchill always remained on friendly terms; while Bridgeman described the final stage of the dispute as 'two days in the last ditch'.[51] In the end the estimates were presented to Parliament at only £60½ millions but excluded any appropriation for new construction, which was to be provided for later by a Supplementary Estimate when the report had been received from a new Cabinet Committee under Lord Birkenhead, the Secretary of State for India, who was of course an intimate friend of Churchill's, which had been set up to consider all aspects of the problem.[52] At this time Beatty initiated another attempt to get naval officers a Marriage Allowance; but the conditions of the time were hardly favourable to such a proposal, and Churchill rejected it summarily.[53]

Having gained acceptance of the 1925–26 Estimates, in March 1925 Beatty set off again to join the Combined Atlantic and Mediterranean Fleets in Majorca, and on 15th he wrote to Eugénie that he was 'resting in the bosom of my [sic] Fleets and am feeling consequently happier and more at home than I have been for some time'. He quickly found himself free of the cold which had been troubling him, and was 'an entirely different human being . . . 20 years younger'.* In his next letter

---

*The letters 'To a friend' dated 15th and 19th March and 17th June 1925 reproduced in part in *Chalmers*, pp. 407–8 were certainly to Eugénie, but the originals have not survived. Either Chalmers forgot to return them or Leslie, who undoubtedly lent them to him, subsequently lost them.

he foretold the redistribution of British naval strength with the object of making the Mediterranean rather than the Atlantic Fleet the principal one – which was gradually carried out over the next few years. The reasons were that naval strength in the Far East could be reinforced much more quickly from the Mediterranean than from home waters, and that it provided a far better training ground than the North Sea and eastern Atlantic.

After about a fortnight with the fleets Beatty was back at his desk before the end of March. As there are not many letters to Eugénie in 1925 but Beatty wrote a large number to Ethel it is safe to assume that, while the latter was abroad, he was seeing a good deal of the former. Thus it was to Ethel that he described a dinner given to him and Jellicoe ('we were like brothers') on 30th June by the officers of the Grand Fleet; and to her that, in July, he described the deadlock reached over cruiser building.[54] But it was Eugénie who received a description of the reinforcement of the China Squadron to protect British interests and nationals in the Treaty Ports, where there were many cases of strikes and violence.[55]

The Birkenhead Committee, to which Beatty gave evidence for a whole day on the need for cruisers, reported in May and when it came before the CID Bridgeman and Beatty strongly contested the claim of the Foreign Office to predict the date of another war under the Ten Year Rule; but they did modify the building programme and proposed to build four 'Treaty' cruisers in 1925-26 and three in each of the following years until the programme was completed. Churchill, however rejected this compromise out of hand. In July the issue came before the Cabinet, but only Lord Cave, Amery and Balfour supported the Admiralty whole-heartedly, though Hankey gave the department his unobtrusive but influential support behind the scenes.[56] That month Bridgeman twice visited Baldwin at Chequers to try and induce him to get Churchill to modify his attitude; but he was unsuccessful. The resignation of the entire Board of Admiralty was now a distinct possibility;*[57] but on the night before the fateful Cabinet meeting the Conservative Whips and managers brought such heavy pres-

*Lord Bridgeman's unpublished memoir of his father pp. 582-96 is the best source on these protracted negotiations as it quotes *in extenso* the First Lord's diary and private correspondence with Baldwin. Copy in Churchill College.

sure to bear on Baldwin that he gave way. On 23rd July he told the House that in addition to the seven cruisers to be laid down in 1925-26 and the following year (two of them for Australia) a flotilla of destroyers and six submarines were to be added.[58] The necessary Supplementary Estimate was introduced a week later. This was perhaps the greatest administrative victory of Beatty's time as First Sea Lord, though he did of course owe a very great deal to Bridgeman's steadfast support. Churchill took his defeat magnanimously, though he came in for some barbed criticism from Lloyd George and MacDonald and for a good deal of satire in the Press.*[59] In the Admiralty and among naval men generally the feeling of relief and gratitude was profound.

But if the victory over the cruiser programme brought a wave of euphoria to the Bridgeman and Beatty Board they were quickly disillusioned; for the Treasury returned to the attack by setting up in August a Fighting Services Economy Committee under the chairmanship of Lord Colwyn, a businessman with much experience of government committees but little or none of the defence services;† and as it was established by virtue of a Treasury Minute, and not by Cabinet authority, this most unusual step gave that department a completely free hand regarding its constitution and terms of reference. Though Bridgeman's Board had for some time been scrutinising every nook and cranny of the Admiralty's finance in order to effect sufficient savings to offset the expenditure on new construction, this did not save them from a steady bombardment of letters from the Colwyn Committee and the sub-committee which it set up under Mr. John Biles, a naval architect, to scrutinise the organisation and work of the Royal Dockyards.[59a] It naturally fell to Chatfield as Controller to deal with that body; but Beatty took little part in the Colwyn Committee's deliberations, as he was either abroad or absent from the Admiralty a good deal due to ill health at this time.

*The cleverest satirical comment was Strube's cartoon in the *Daily Express* of 24th July captioned 'The Half-Nelson' and showing Bridgeman applying that grip on Churchill on top of the Nelson Column.

†The other members were Sir Holberry Mensforth, formerly Director General of War Factories, and Sir James Lithgow, chairman of the Clyde shipbuilding firm, who was replaced later by Mr. W. L. H. Hichens, chairman of Cammell Laird, the Birkenhead shipbuilders.

Bridgeman, abetted by Dreyer (ACNS), made a bad tactical mistake by reopening to the Colwyn Committee the question of the control of the Fleet Air Arm, arguing that transfer to the Admiralty would achieve substantial savings. We cannot here go into the prolonged battle of words produced by the Committee's report of 23rd December 1925, but it must be mentioned that it castigated the alleged lack of co-ordination in the Service departments, favoured the creation of a Ministry of Defence, rejected the Admiralty's claim to take over complete control of the Fleet Air Arm, and proposed a cut in the Navy Vote of £7½ millions. This attack on his department's outlook and activities produced a strong protest from Bridgeman to Neville Chamberlain, in which he wrote that he had 'seldom seen a more offensive document from our point of view', and complained that although the Colwyn Committee had heard Trenchard on the Fleet Air Arm issue 'they would not see Beatty'.[60] Chamberlain replied sympathetically, but as Minister of Health there was little he could do to counteract the influence of the all-powerful Treasury. However, the combined efforts of Bridgeman, Beatty and Chatfield did defeat the Biles Committee's proposal to transfer responsibility for the Royal Dockyards from naval to civilian hands; and it was probably on Bridgeman's suggestion that Baldwin sent for Beatty a few days later and expressed his appreciation of the Admiralty's efforts to achieve economies. In sum all that this Treasury investigation achieved was to produce a large mass of paper, and cause a great deal of work to the Naval staff and Supply Departments which would have been better devoted to more constructive purposes.

On the question of creating a Ministry of Defence, resurrected by Colwyn, Beatty seems to have had a fairly open mind. Early in 1926 he told Ethel that he was 'all for a Ministry of Defence' – provided that the civilian heads of all three Service Departments were abolished and the Chiefs of Staff had only one Minister to deal with. That, he considered, would produce 'a real working machine and certainly economy'; but he did not believe that such a drastic reorganisation would be accepted.[61] Ethel, who was abroad at various spas most of this time, underwent an operation in March 1926, and in June Beatty was operated on for appendicitis – which kept him away from the Admiralty for the best part of a month.[62]

Meanwhile the Naval Estimates for 1926-27 had a comparatively easy passage, and by skimping on such items as oil reserves and new aircraft for the Fleet Air Arm, and extending the period between ships' refits they were finally approved at just over £58 millions.[63] The building programme was maintained and the Board aimed to bring the navy up to its full authorised strength in the classes which were not subject to quantitative treaty limitations (70 cruisers, 144 destroyers, 72 submarines and 110 minesweepers) by 1st April 1936. It was no fault of the Bridgeman-Beatty Board that such hopes were only fulfilled after rearament began in 1937.

As the normal term of office of any member of the Board of Admiralty was limited to seven years it was natural that in 1926 there should have been speculation both about Beatty's successor and his own future. In February Amery reviewed possible candidates for the post of Governor-General of Canada, which Field-Marshal Lord Byng was about to relinquish. Among the possible candidates was Beatty, but Amery wrote him off because he 'has no manners and an impossible American wife'.[64] If the second epithet was justified the first was certainly unfair, as Beatty had convincingly shown during his American tour of 1921 and on many other occasions. The choice finally fell on Lord Willingdon. Early in November *The Times* carried an Admiralty announcement that Beatty, having been First Sea Lord and CNS since November 1919, 'has expressed a desire to be allowed to resign office on completing the period of seven years named in Article 243 of the King's Regulations as the maximum for which an officer will be retained on the Board of Admiralty, except in special circumstances. He has, however, consented at the request of the First Lord, to defer his resignation'.[65] Bridgeman's 'Political Notes' and his son's unpublished memoir confirm his reluctance to lose Beatty's services;[66] but Leslie recorded, presumably on Beatty's authority, that the King had a big hand in persuading him to stay on, and that he remarked, obviously in jest, that he was thereby deprived of his one remaining ambition – to become Master of the Quorn Hunt.[67]

From time to time Beatty was involved in dealing with the industrial unrest which was so marked a feature of the 1920s, and which culminated in the General Strike of May 1926. Lord Davidson has recorded how submarines were used to provide power for the docks during that conflict, and also how Beatty used tugs flying the White Ensign to carry food from the docks to the London wharves, so defeating the attempted blockade of London.[68] Another improvisation was, however, evidently less successful, since the same authority tells how, when the civilians who worked the Admiralty's heating system downed tools a short time later Beatty brought in naval stokers. They raised the pressure in the system to such unprecedented heights that when Davidson turned on a hot tap the place was filled with scalding steam![69] Though that attempt at strike-breaking had to be dropped Davidson evidently developed a strong admiration for Beatty and for the measures organised by the Admiralty on behalf of the very secret Supply and Transport Committee to keep essential services in the seaports running. The crews of the warships which were sent to all the major ports at the time of the emergency acquitted themselves very well, and showed such great restraint that there was hardly any serious trouble, and the sailors were soon even playing football against teams drawn from the strikers! Davidson's admiration for Beatty was evidently heartily reciprocated,[70] since when the Parliamentary Secretary left to become Chairman of the Conservative Party in 1926 Beatty wrote to Ethel saying how sorry he was to lose him and how 'very helpful' he had been, especially in his dealings with the Prime Minister.[71]

It was in late 1925 and early 1926 that the question of the censorship of the quarterly journal *The Naval Review* again came before the Board. The journal had been launched in 1913 when Richmond, K. G. B. Dewar, Plunkett and other 'intellectuals' of the 'Young Turk' group of officers founded the Naval Society 'to encourage thought and discussion on such subjects as strategy, tactics, naval operations, staff work, administration, organisation, command, discipline, education, naval history and any other topic affecting the fighting efficiency of the Navy, but excluding the material aspects of the technical sciences'.[72] Initially the Society had enjoyed the strong support of Prince Louis of Battenberg as 1st Sea Lord, but during the war it ran into rough waters, and in July 1915 it was suppressed by Admiral Jackson, the successor to Battenberg at one remove. Shortly after the Armistice its rivival was approved, though not without misgivings on the part of the Long-Wemyss Board; but the Honorary Editor (Admiral Sir William Henderson) soon found himself in trouble with the authorities again, and in March 1919 the journal was again 'suspended' – for reasons which today seem totally inadequate. However, in the following August the ban was lifted, subject to the Editor obtaining Admiralty approval of what he proposed to publish.[73] In 1925 Admiral Henderson tried to get the power of censorship lifted, and received strong support from the Naval Staff except for Admiral Field, the DCNS. Rather surprisingly the Permanent Secretary, Oswyn Murray, also opposed relaxing the rules – on the same grounds as had caused the 1915 suspension. Fortunately at this point Beatty's 'more enlightened influence broke through'. Posing the rather obvious questions 'Is the Review of value to the Service?' and 'Does the censorship adversely affect the Review?' he concluded that the answers to both questions were a resounding 'Yes', and recommended the removal of all restrictions. A 'Committee of Naval Officers' would in future be charged with responsibility for acting sensibly with regard to what was published; and from that day to this the journal has continued to flourish under a succession of devoted and highly responsible Editors – without any serious difficulties with or interference by the Admiralty. This is surely an outstanding example of Beatty's breadth of vision, and of his sympathy with officers who were prepared to risk their careers in order to identify, and if possible cure the faults in the British naval 'system' of which he became so aware after Jutland.[74]

To turn to Beatty's extra-marital entanglements a letter from him to Eugénie, apparently written late in 1926, gives the only clue we have regarding the transfer of his affections elsewhere at about this time. Eugénie evidently wrote in protest about what she had heard from 'Audrey' – who was almost certainly Audrey James, the daughter of an American industrialist. She was married three times – to Dudley Coats of the cotton family, to Marshal Field Jr., a nephew of Ethel's and brother of 'Gwennie' Field, and to Peter Pleydell-Bouverie, Lord Radnor's brother. She therefore moved in the same circle as the Beattys.*[75] Eugénie's letter evidently distressed Beatty greatly, for he wrote 'I do not know why you have jumped to the conclusions you have as to the relations

*Audrey Pleydell-Bouverie died in February 1968, leaving an estate of nearly £½ million including what *The Times* called 'one of the most valuable collections of French Impressionist paintings in England'. The Queen Mother was represented at her Memorial Service.

between Audrey and myself', and blamed it on 'the evil tongues of others'.[76] He asked her to come and see him, and as in his next letter he wrote that 'old sores are healed', that in his 'heart and mind' there existed only 'the remembrance of a wonderful friendship which lasted a very long time', and that 'between us the hatchet is buried' the reconciliation was evidently successful.[77] But in view of Eugénie's loyalty and the way she had eased Beatty's burdens by trying to cope with Ethel one cannot but feel sympathetic towards her protest against her erstwhile lover seeking consolation elsewhere.

For the 1927-28 Financial Year the Admiralty was able to ask for slightly less money, and there was no serious battle with the Chancellor and the Treasury; but when the 1928-29 Estimates came before the Cabinet in October 1927 Churchill returned to the charge over the cruiser programme – on the grounds that we should wait and see what the Americans were going to do.[78] This renewed assault on what Bridgeman and Beatty had regarded as long settled produced an angry response from the former to Baldwin, and Leo Amery, a former First Lord, wrote in his autobiography that Beatty made it clear to the Prime Minister 'that the Board of Admiralty could not be overridden without breaking up the government'.[79] It was probably at this time that Beatty, so Leslie recorded, 'sought Mrs. Baldwin at a London party and told her privately that in less than a month she would no longer be sleeping with the Prime Minister of England'.[80] Though it is impossible to say precisely what influences were decisive it is a fact that, despite Churchill's intervention, the Estimates were accepted by the Cabinet at only a slightly lower figure than the previous year's.

In 1927 a great deal of time and effort was expended over the so-called 'Coolidge Conference' at Geneva which the American President had called with the object of reaching an agreement on the number and tonnage of cruisers to be allowed to the three principal naval powers; but as Bridgeman himself lead the British Delegation with Admiral Field (DCNS) as his chief naval adviser Beatty was not directly involved. A letter to Ethel states that 'The PM says he could not spare me to go to Geneva with all these very real troubles on hand'[81] – by which he meant the despatch of reinforcements to China to cope with the renewed and widespread anti-foreign outbreaks in the Treaty Ports and at Shanghai,

and unrest in Egypt where, in Beatty's words, 'the National-
ists have taken the bit between their teeth', necessitating the
despatch of battleships to Alexandria and Port Said.[82] As
regards China he told Ethel that he had 'a squadron of cruisers
all ready to leave Malta' and was 'collecting 1,000 Marines'
for immediate departure'.[83] Meanwhile at Geneva a state of
deadlock was reached, and at the beginning of August the conference broke down. Beatty, though he had left office by that
time, wrote thankfully to Bridgeman that the Americans had
failed to accomplish their purpose – which he described as
being 'to achieve command of the sea at any cost.'[84]

On 7th July 1927 Beatty entertained the King and senior
naval officers to dinner at Mall House – to mark the approaching end of the long and close association between himself and
the Monarch.[85] For him it must have been a sad and nostalgic
occasion – especially as Ethel was still abroad moving from
spa to spa and doctor to doctor. On 30th July, his last day in
office, he attended a Cabinet at which Bridgeman reported the
causes of the breakdown at Geneva – the chief one being the
refusal of the Americans to accept any gun smaller than 8-inch
for their new cruisers.

There can be no greater tribute to the strength of the position Beatty built up during his period as First Sea Lord than
the attention given to his retirement in the Press. As long ago
as 30th April *The Times* had reviewed his work at length, and
followed it with a leading article a few days later.[86] Reports of
his entertainment at a number of complimentary dinners followed, and on 25th July he was sworn as Privy Counsellor – by
his old friend and associate in so many struggles on behalf of
the navy Maurice Hankey, then Clerk to the Privy Council as
well as Secretary to the CID and Cabinet. On the actual day of
his retirement *The Times* published a long biography of his
service, accompanied by photographs. Plainly in Fleet Street as
well as in Whitehall everyone was aware that his departure
from the stage of public affairs marked the end of an era – for
the country as well as for the service to which he had devoted
his life. Though today it may seem that his character and
actions were flawed by defects such as his snobbery and arrogance, and that his Imperialism is wholly outdated, there can be
no doubt that the comparative readiness for war of the navy in
1939 owed a great deal to him and to his principal disciple
Chatfield, who was to succeed him in the office as First Sea

Lord at two removes at a most difficult time early in 1933. But perhaps Beatty's greatest accomplishment as First Sea Lord was his maintenance of the morale of the navy's officers and men throughout a period when many influences, such as constant cuts and reductions, were at work which might, but for his strength of character and powerful personality, have had most deleterious effects – as the disaster of the Invergordon mutiny of 1931 was to show only too clearly.

It will be appropriate to end this chapter with the letter he wrote to Eugénie in answer to her 'sweet, sympathetic and altogether delightful letter' about his retirement. 'Your understanding', he wrote, 'is great and you put your finger on the spot. It will be a wrench to sever my connection with the Service I have spent my life in. But I have never admitted this to anybody, [and] hardly to myself. The great days of the past were and are unforgettable, the latter days since 1919 at times appear like a nightmare, but they had their compensations. However the everlasting struggle is over and my task is done'. Turning to his relations with Eugénie he wrote that 'I shall never forget your sweetness and love for me in the past, and you can believe me when I say that . . . there *is* as you say deep down a very tender place for you in my heart which nothing which you can say or do will ever eradicate . . . and no time can obliterate the gratitude and affection which is steeped in lovely memories of all that you have given me and been to me. Bless you Eugénie, with love. David'.[87]

CHAPTER SEVENTEEN

Last Years, 1928-1936

As Beatty was only in his 56th year when he left the Admiralty he might have enjoyed many years of happy, tranquil and occasionally useful retirement – if his home life had been stable and he had been prepared to moderate his addiction to his favourite sport of foxhunting. It is interesting to recall that two of his close associates, Sir Henry Oliver and Lord Chatfield, both of whom became Admirals of the Fleet, lived to the age of 100 and 94 respectively; but Beatty was temperamentally totally different from those two. During the first months after his retirement it seemed that Ethel's melancholia was improving, and she even accompanied him in the hunting field on a few occasions; but the amelioration of her condition soon proved evanescent, and in 1928 he again tried the cure of taking her on a cruise in the *Sheelah* to the Mediterranean, where his old friend Roger Keyes was in command of the fleet and his son David was serving as a sub-lieutenant in his flagship. At Keyes's request they met at Gibraltar after the Combined Exercises. Beatty there gave a fine speech to the massed officers and men of the fleets – to many of whom he was of course still the chief naval hero of the war. From Gibraltar the Beattys went on to Seville and then to Madrid as the guests of King Alfonso; but Ethel's old trouble soon made their travels an ordeal for her husband. A letter from Sir Frederick Ponsonby (1867-1935, later Lord Sysonby), who had long been associated with the Royal family, to Bryan Godfrey-Faussett gives a harrowing description of how Ethel destroyed the pleasure of the tour by being 'often quite impossible', accusing her husband of heartlessness and selfishness and often behaving 'like a lunatic'.[1] It is not surprising that, early in March Beatty wrote to Eugénie 'I am not sure I am able to continue to compete with what is obviously an impossible task', and told her that the sale of his beloved Brooksby was on the cards.[1a] Fortunately for his peace of mind it did not take place at that time.

His other favourite sport was of course shooting, and each summer he and and as many of his family as could accompany him migrated to Grantully Castle for the grouse season. A letter to Peter tells of the slaughter of 1,300 brace at this time; but Beatty was never in the least perturbed by participation in such *battues*. Apart from sport his chief interest lay in the work and progress of his sons, and it must have been a disappointment to him when in 1930 David decided to leave the navy and enter Parliament. He won the Camberwell constituency for the Conservative Party in the General Election of the following year. Peter, whose health had never been robust, turned to breeding race horses – a risky speculation in which his father also participated. He followed the successes of his own and Peter's horses with enormous interest, regularly attended many race meetings and placed many bets. To quote many of his letters about his race horses would be tedious, and probably incomprehensible to most readers; but extracts from two will show how absorbed he became in the arcana of the turf. In 1930 he wrote to David from The Priory, Reigate 'Epsom is over and as far as I can judge a pretty disastrous one for most of the Backers. What with *Blenheim* winning the Derby and *Rose of England* the Oaks the heavy punters were (?) bust. Wragg rode a very good race on *Blenheim* and won exactly the same way as he did on *Fristead* 2 years ago. *Diolite* and *Rustom Pasha* raced together in front and were then done . . . We were lucky to win the last two races yesterday with *Tagra* who ran real well and won easily. The result was never in doubt from the top of the hill and she had a good deal in hand. She has improved enormously and will win again. *Blatmire* ran and won easily by 2 lengths a very fast race and the little chap looked very well. I put you a sovereign each way *Tagra* and enclose you £25 the proceeds. . . .'[2]

In the same year he told his son how he had put five of his horses 'in the small paddocks so that they should not galop [sic] about too much.' '*Camelia*', he continued, 'was not fast enough for the Point to Point. They ran it at a very fast pace and ran her off her legs [in] the first mile and [a] half . . . she would never have caught them but did well considering she is wrong in the wind. . . .' The letter ends 'Mummy's eyes have given a lot of trouble . . . very unhappy I've been with her since you left and read to her every afternoon and evening'.[3]

That remark recalls a story Beatty told Leslie and he recorded
– that when the Admiral was reading to his wife she used
sometimes to stuff her ears with cotton wool so as not to hear
him – which for some reason Leslie found amusing.

The best horse ever owned by Beatty was undoubtedly *Gold
Bridge* a very handsome chestnut and a fast sprinter. His por-
trait by Nina Colmore still hangs at Chicheley Hall, the
Beatty family home of recent times in Buckinghamshire. After
Gold Bridge went to stud at Newmarket his progeny won huge
sums in prize money; but Beatty did not live to enjoy either
their success or the occasion when in 1938 Peter led in *Bois
Roussel*, the Derby winner.

Beatty's proneness to accidents, most of which arose
through his hard riding, has already been mentioned. In 1930
he broke an arm; but a much worse accident soon followed.
Leslie tells us that at that time a number of really bad, even
vicious horses were exported from Germany to Ireland, and
then resold as Irish hunters. Though it is surprising that anyone as knowledgeable on horseflesh as Beatty, and with many
experienced friends to advise him, should have fallen into such
a trap that is apparently what happened. At any rate the ex-
German horse gave him a very bad fall and he received a kick
which shattered his jaw in several places. For some three
months he was immobilised and had to be fed through a tube.
In the following year another fall broke three ribs. All those
accidents sapped his strength and vitality, though Leslie considered that the final break-up was attributable chiefly to the
breast bone damage received in the car accident mentioned earlier.[4]

Though much of his time in retirement was spent on sport
Beatty did not fail to give support to charitable and educa-
tional causes. Before leaving the Admiralty he accepted the
Presidency of the Society for Nautical Research, which still
carries out very valuable work in fields such as maritime
archaeology and publishes its quarterly journal *The Mariner's
Mirror*.[5] He often spoke on naval issues at dinners given to
distinguished people and, less commonly, on the same subject
in the House of Lords – notably on cruiser strength shortly
before the 1930 London Conference was convened.[6] He
became Vice-President of the Royal British Legion, chairman
of the Appeals and Propaganda Committee of the National
Playing Fields Association,[7] President of the Coastal

Development Council[8] and of King's College Hospital, London, Vice-President of the Navy League,[9] President of the International Horse Show,[10] President of Dockland League and of the Empire Day Movement;[11] and he lent his name and authority to many appeals for money to help provide playing fields and to support ex-Service men. But the strain of all these activities and of looking after Ethel, combined with his recurrent accidents soon began to produce signs of heart trouble, and his physician Sir Alfred Fripp recommended a complete rest abroad. Accordingly he went to Aix-les-Bains, but one may doubt whether the 'cure' produced any real improvement.

Then came what Leslie described as 'a fearful few months in which her [Ethel's] melancholy seized her fiercer than before. The inevitable quiet period followed but this time there was no revival'.[12] On 15th July 1932 Beatty wrote to Eugénie 'Poor Ethel is very ill and we can do very little for her . . . It is very sad to see her wasting away, and I know that you who knew her so well for so long in the days of long ago will be sorry for her and for us all in our trouble'.[13] Ethel died at Dingley Hall two days later, on 17th July, and was buried in the local cemetery. Captain Grint was present at the funeral, and recalled that it was the only time he had seen tears in the admiral's eyes. So was the ever-devoted Walter Cowan, to whom Beatty wrote thanking him for his support 'on the worst day of my life'.[14] Leslie found in Catullus's work an appropriate epitaph, but it was not used –

> *Odi et amo, Quare id faciam, fortasse requiris*
> *Nescio; sed fieri sentio, et excrucior*

(I hate and love at the same time. Why I do so you may want to know. I cannot tell, but I feel that it is so, and I am tormented).

What is certain is that, despite all Ethel's infidelities and her frequently impossible behaviour Beatty would never consider divorce or even separation from her. Although among the hundreds of letters which they exchanged there are occasional notes of exasperation on his side, the dominant tone is genuine love and appreciation. But, as we have seen, Beatty did tell a few intimate friends about the strain to which she subjected him, and the state of near despair to which she could sometimes reduce him. That she was utterly spoilt by the wealth which came to her from her father is beyond doubt, as is the fact that she was chronically jealous of any women who appeared to her as a possible rival for her husband's affection. Yet it is probably true that her wealth helped Beatty to move in the highest social circles, and so to get to know the individuals in whose hands power rested, or to whom it might come with a turn of the political wheel.

On Beatty's retirement from the Admiralty Maurice Hankey, who had probably seen his work at closer quarters and over a longer period than anyone else, wrote to him that he was 'the only First Sea Lord I have known in twenty-six years' experience who could really talk on even terms with the highest Cabinet Ministers and stand up to them in argument';[15] and it is not fanciful to suggest that Ethel's wealth helped him to acquire and exploit his natural gift for clear and forceful expression of his views, regardless of who might be present. In her wrath too Ethel could be devastatingly effective. Leslie tells a story of how Sir Henry Deterding, the oil magnate, persuaded her to invest a large proportion of her Jutland Fund's money, collected to support the widows and dependants of those who lost their lives, in Shell Oil. When the share price dropped heavily in the 1920s Ethel bearded Deterding when out hunting, and berated him so severely that he immediately signed a huge cheque to make up the loss.[16] Regarding Ethel's manic jealousy of any woman who she suspected of setting her cap at her husband, Leslie recounts that Lady Lavery was not allowed to paint his portrait, and Clare Sheridan was deemed too attractive to be allowed to sculpt a bust of him.[17] As to her attitude towards Eugénie, it seems that she never knew that she and her husband had been lovers, though her quarrels with Eugénie suggest that she suspected it.

Beatty's attraction for women evidently did not abate with Ethel's death, since there is in the Leslie papers an undated letter in French endorsed by him that the writer was Lady Cameron and that she was 'hopeful to marry him and sailing thereto when he died'. As it begins 'Mon adoré', and is all written in the second person singular of familiarity, it seems that there is truth in Leslie's view about the purpose of this rather mysterious 'Marie-Anne'.[18]

By 1935 it was plain to Beatty's medical advisers that he was suffering from serious weakening of the heart; but it was very

difficult, if not impossible to induce him to take life more easily. In November of that year he was suffering from influenza
and had a high temperature when he learnt of Jellicoe's death.
Leslie records him as saying 'So Jellicoe has gone! Well, I feel I
shall be the next to be summoned. I do not think the call will
be long. I am tired. I am tired'. His doctors forbade him to
face the cold weather when the funeral took place on 26th; but
his answer was 'What will the Navy say if I fail to attend
Jellicoe's funeral?'. So he insisted on walking as a pall bearer in
the procession to St. Paul's cathedral. When it was passing
along Fleet Street an observant spectator thought he looked so
ill that he sent a glass of brandy out to him. When King
George V, for so many years both Monarch and friend to
Beatty, died on 20th January 1936 he again insisted on taking
part in the funeral. There is no doubt that these two typically
courageous acts hastened his own end.[19]

Beatty's last letter to Eugénie is dated 8th February 1934
from Dingley Hall near Market Harborough (Brooksby was
about to be put up for sale). He invited the lady whom he now
placidly addressed as 'Eugénie my dear' to come and stay the
weekend with him in order to benefit from the good air and
the peaceful countryside. We do not know whether she went,
and their long and sometimes passionate correspondence ends
on this tranquil note – just over two years before Beatty's death.
In 1947–48 when Leslie was working on his biography of the
admiral he wrote several times to Eugénie to ask for her
memories of him and to borrow Beatty's letters to her. In one
letter he asked whether he could mention her by name in the
book. Her reply was both firm and witty. 'No, for Heaven's
sake don't mention my name' she wrote. 'It would be very
embarrassing and as a matter of fact I should imagine much
more intriguing if [quotations from Beatty's letters are] left
anonymous don't you think? David was the type who have so
many *affaires galantes* that to mention one name would make
about 20 others snigger, so I should imagine [it is] far, far
better to leave them wondering than to make them chortle'.[20]
That is obviously how it came to pass that the extracts from
the letters printed by Admiral Chalmers are merely headed
'To a friend'; and when I told him the truth about their love
affair he admitted that he had never had any idea that Eugénie
had ever been more than a close friend of the admiral's.

As we shall now be taking leave of the 17-year Beatty-

Eugénie correspondence, and of the 158 letters by him which have so far been discovered, it will be appropriate to summarise the impression it makes on me. I am strongly reminded of the French saying about love affairs that '*Il y a toujours un qui aime et un qui tourne la joue*' (There is always one who truly loves and one who merely offers a cheek). In the story here told I am convinced that the one who really loved was Eugénie; for she showed unfailing devotion to Beatty, always remembered his birthday and other anniversaries, sent him many presents, and wrote (including her 'Fairy Stories') far more fully than he did. According to Leslie her love for Beatty was so enduring that after his death she even tried to get in touch with him through a spiritualist medium.[21] On Beatty's side I think he was motivated chiefly by physical desire for a very attractive woman, which became stronger after his love for Ethel had been destroyed by her own follies. He exploited Eugénie's devotion ruthlessly; and whereas she was faithful in her love for him, Beatty had no scruples about transferring his attentions to other women. I am therefore left with a great admiration for Eugénie's character, and a feeling of distaste for her lover's selfishness and the inconsiderate way he not seldom treated her. None the less it is possible that, just as Nelson remarked that 'if there were more Emmas there would be more Nelsons', but for Eugénie's love and support Beatty could not have overcome his matrimonial difficulties and carried so successfully the great responsibilities which fell to his lot.

September 1935 produced Beatty's last letter to Leslie, in which he discussed Pastfield's little book on Jutland, declined the suggestion that he should write his own memoirs, and considered whether Keyes should attempt a biography of himself. He wrote that 'Roger Keyes as a writer is rotten [but] as a critic and faithful historian [he] is excellent. In view of his reputation, rank and experience it will and must Carry much weight and remove some of the stigmas that have been made on me personally and my gallant Command generally. For instance it [Pastfield's book] brings to light the fact that the oft repeated allegation that the Battle Cruisers Couldn't shoot was a myth and an injustice'.[22] Chatfield also wrote at about the same time suggesting how Pastfield's work might be brought to wider notice – perhaps by Beatty himself.[23] Though none of these proposals bore fruit it is interesting to see how deeply

Jutland and the question of the Battle Cruisers' shooting still rankled with those two nearly twenty years after the battle.

Early in 1936, when the doctors insisted that Beatty should stay very quietly in bed for three weeks, he said he was reminded of the condition of the wounded *Lion* after the Dogger Bank action. Though he never gave up hope of recovery his heart was in fact failing. On the evening of 11th March he was allowed a small whisky and soda, and when at about 11 p.m. his son David looked in on him he seemed much brighter. 'In fact', he remarked, 'I could ride from the Prince of Wales's to Coplow' – two famous coverts in the Quorn country where he had enjoyed so many good hunts. He slept peacefully until 1 a.m. when the final heart attack came and by the time young David reached his bed he had died. Leslie recalls how the admiral kept his colour after death, and attributes this unusual feature to an inheritance from his Longfield grandmother, of whom the same phenomenon was remarked.[24]

On 16th March 1936 Beatty was borne through the streets of London to St. Paul's cathedral, by the route along which he had so painfully followed Jellicoe eighteen months earlier. His coffin was draped in the Union Flag which he had proudly flown from the *Queen Elizabeth* in 1919. The address before a huge congregation was given by the Archbishop of Canterbury, Cosmo Gordon Lang, who quoted the words of Walter Cowan that Beatty had been 'the very embodiment of the fighting spirit of the Navy. In him something of the spirit of Nelson seemed to have come back. As with Nelson – to use the words of the old psalm – his was the ministry of flaming fire'.

The obituary notices were very naturally long and wholly laudatory of Beatty's life and work – though they left out a great deal which has been told in this book. On 5th May Baldwin, the Prime Minister, moved in the House of Commons that 'an humble address' should be communicated to the King 'praying that His Majesty will give direction that a Monument be erected at the public charge to the memory of the late Admiral of the Fleet Earl Beatty'; and he went on to recapitulate 'his illustrious career'.[25] But owing to the onset of World War II, no action was taken on Baldwin's motion until 21st October (Trafalgar Day) 1948 when memorial busts of Jellicoe and Beatty were unveiled in Trafalgar Square in the presence of the Duke of Edinburgh and the Duke of Gloucester, and were dedicated by Dr. Fisher, Archbishop of Canterbury, in the presence of a huge assembly which included the survivors of both admirals' closest friends.[26] Today their bodies lie close to Nelson's in the crypt of St. Paul's, and their memorials, though far more modest than Nelson's, stand close together on the site associated forever with the prowess of the Royal Navy and its leaders; but one may doubt whether many of the thousands of young tourists who throng that site in the 1970s, pause to give a thought to the endurance and sacrifice symbolised by those memorials, or to the men to whom in a large part they owe the freedom which they so evidently relish.

EPILOGUE

The Last Naval Hero

Of all the leaders of World War I on the Allied side none impressed his personality more on the British people than David Beatty. It was chiefly his conduct in the Heligoland Bight and Dogger Bank actions which caught the public imagination; and it was certainly not diminished by his handling of the Battle Cruisers at Jutland. There can have been few British subjects who could not at that time have produced the name of the commander of the Battle Cruisers, and later the Grand Fleet; and there can also have been few who did not know who was First Sea Lord from 1919 to 1927. The contrast with World War II and its aftermath is in that respect striking; for today it would not be easy to find anyone outside the navy, or those who write about its work who could give the names of the commanders of our principal fleets in that conflict – with the possible exception of Mountbatten, who is the only other candidate for the title of this Epilogue. As however his purely *naval* commands never rose higher than a Destroyer Flotilla I feel that he must be excluded from that Valhalla – despite his great services in other fields and responsibilities. The change which has come to pass reflects not only the decline in the influence of the Royal Navy, but also suggests that leadership of the type practised by Beatty has gone out of fashion. In short the hero of warfare and hero-worship have become outmoded, and a totally different type of leader has emerged in all the defence services of democratically governed countries. To me the new type can best be described, firstly, as being immensely competent in the specialised tasks which may fall to the lot of his service; he is far better educated and more intellectual than were most of the officers of Beatty's generation; he is international rather than nationalistic in outlook, skilled in negotiating with the civilian and service leaders of the countries with whom his forces may have to work, and far more understanding of the outlook and purposes, as well as the limitations, of his own and the sister services. His relations with junior officers and ratings have also changed from the paternalism, backed by enforced discipline which could be very harshly applied, to a far more relaxed relationship based on mutual respect and accepted discipline. The personalities of these modern leaders are certainly impressive – once the extreme reserve which many of them exhibit has been penetrated. They are totally lacking in the arrogance which was one of the less attractive sides of Beatty's character, and are I believe inspired and guided by deep awareness of the meaning of *integrity*, a quality which was by no means always exhibited by senior officers of the previous generation – including Beatty on such issues as the Jutland controversy. If they lack the charisma which was so obviously a prime source of his influence, and show no wish or tendency to cultivate it, they have gained in stature in many other respects. Moral and physical courage, with which Beatty was of course liberally endowed, is of course still there; but it is often shrouded by a laudable modesty and tolerance – especially of the views and opinions of juniors. Though Beatty often showed readiness to invite and to listen to the ideas of subordinates, and his interest in and support of the small group of 'intellectuals' such as Herbert Richmond, Reginald Drax and the Dewar brothers must stand to his credit, modesty was certainly not one of the most prominent traits of his character. Stephen King-Hall (Lord King-Hall 1966), who served in Commodore Goodenough's flagship during the war and at Jutland, and saw a good deal of Beatty after it was over, and who was moreover no uncritical admirer of all things naval, described the admiral in his autobiography as 'a tremendous and impressive personality . . . who had in him some elements of a bounder'; but he qualified the criticism by writing 'I use this word in no uncomplimentary sense. If you prefer the word "thug" or "condottieri" you can have them'. Though one can understand what King-Hall was trying to convey, none of his descriptive nouns seems apposite to me. Later on the same writer compared Beatty with Nelson, whom he also called 'a great personality, somewhat of a bounder'; so if one accepts that writer's view Beatty was placed in august company![1]

In the practice of religion Beatty certainly accepted the Anglican Church's rites, and followed them in his ships as was then laid down in King's Regulations; and he attended the village churches of his country homes. He seems to have accepted the existence of a Supreme Being who guided and decided the destinies of mankind. Leslie considered that his religion was the same as Nelson's;[2] but one can hardly imagine Beatty on his knees composing a prayer such as Nelson wrote before Trafalgar. On the other hand Leslie was probably right to say that 'he [Beatty] believed that God would use him as an instrument to protect his beloved country', and that 'he simply trusted in God and kept his powder dry'.[3] It is of course impossible to reconcile even such a mild form of religous faith with the superstitions and pagan practices indulged in by Beatty, as was told earlier.

It will perhaps be appropriate here briefly to review the history of the rise and decline of heroes and hero-worship. Though heroes a-plenty can be found in the history of warfare from ancient times onwards it was I am sure Thomas Carlyle, 'the Sage of Chelsea' (1795-1881), who gave birth to hero worship in the form which was so evident in the British Empire in the 19th and early 20th centuries. In May 1840 he gave a series of six lectures 'On Heroes and Hero-Worship' in London, and they were published in book form (initially in America) in the following year. The lectures and book attracted enormous interest, and the latter was still in print in the World Classics Series in the 1890s.[4] Though Carlyle by no means confined himself to the heroes of warfare, his admiration for Cromwell, Marlborough and the young Buonaparte, taken with his description of Shakespeare's scenes describing Agincourt[5] as 'one of the most perfect things, in its sort, we have of Shakespere's' [sic], and as containing 'a noble Patriotism . . . A true English heart breathes, calm and strong, through the whole business',[6] leave one in little doubt regarding whom he admired and why. His gargantuan biography of Frederick the Great[7] and his espousal of the German cause in the 1870 war against France make his outlook even clearer.

At the end of his brilliant account of the final collapse of the Nazi dictatorship in 1945 Professor Trevor-Roper (now Lord Dacre) remarks that Carlyle 'supposed that power should be entrusted unconditionally to great men, heroes who were laws to themselves, not responsible to the institutions or the prejudices of inferior men', and that 'This doctrine rang musically in German ears in a time of gloom and defeat [i.e. in the 1920s]. . . .' His conclusion is that in the utterly ruthless autocracy of Adolf Hitler 'we see the last, logical consequences of Carlyle's dream.'[8] Another very percipient historian and biographer of that period, Iris Origo, has written in the same vein on that theme, and postulates that Carlyle ended up by accepting uncritically 'adoration of the individual and of the event, power [and] success'.[9] I find myself in complete agreement with those two authoritative students of the influence of Carlyle on the development of the tragedy of the two World Wars. It is true enough that hero worship on the Carlyle model war carried on by Thomas Babington Macaulay, Lord Tennyson and (as regards the Navy) by Sir Henry Newbolt in quite recent times;[10] but their prose and poetry no longer have the old appeal.

To Beatty's generation, and to officers of those which followed him, Nelson was of course the chief naval hero – first last and all the time. It is astonishing that, as far as I have been able to make out, there have been twenty-eight biographies of Nelson, not including a great many books about his comrades and contemporaries. In the present century the young officers of the navy were suckled on a course of undiluted naval hero-worship based chiefly on Sir Geoffrey Callender's three volumes titled *Sea Kings of Britain*[11] – which all cadets (or rather their parents) were required to buy. It certainly took me many years of wider reading, as well as the better teaching given at the R.N.C. Greenwich, notably by Professor Michael Lewis, to realise that Callender had applied buckets of whitewash in order to make his heroes truly heroic, and that there was a great deal more to naval (or as I prefer to call it) maritime history than the battles they fought.

During his lifetime, and for many years afterwards, Beatty was often compared to Nelson; and he himself by no means discouraged the analogy by hanging Nelson prints and texts in his cabin. Shane Leslie in his draft biography of Beatty emphasises the comparison – and especially the fact that they both fell in love with other men's wives; but he also compared Beatty to the great French Admiral the Bailli de Suffren. Yet the truth is that, as with most historical analogies, there are as many differences as resemblances between Beatty and Nelson. Though the hold which Beatty established over the officers and men he commanded may reasonably be compared to the adoration with which Nelson was regarded in his fleets, the former never won a battle comparable in its completeness to the most famous sea fights of the latter; nor did the influence exerted on the 1914–18 war by Beatty's fleet in any way compare to that exercised by Nelson's in the wars against Republican and Napoleonic France.

It can of course be argued that success in war demands that top leaders should possess charisma; and one may well ask whether the 8th Army's victories of World War II would have been accomplished if Montgomery had not possessed that gift, or whether the British Mediterranean Fleet would have come through the ordeal of Greece–Crete 1941 if Andrew Cunningham had lacked it, or whether, on the other side, the German Afrika Korps would have fought as it did under a less charismatic leader than Erwin Rommel. Though no answer to such questions can of course be given, and Professor Marder has argued that what he calls 'charismatic qualities can be very important *where they exist*' (italics supplied)[12], I remain of the opinion that, even though advantage can of course be taken of such gifts 'where they exist', in modern times leadership depends far more on subtle qualities – such as complete professional competence, adequate education, resolution and physical and moral courage – than on the creation of heroes and the inculcation of hero-worship on the Carlyle and Callender model. For all my, possibly pardonable, affection for the Royal Navy and my admiration for its leaders of recent times I am therefore not at all concerned that Heroes have markedly diminished in the fighting services of democratic countries, and that leadership of a new type has been slowly but visibly developing. There has even been published a (not very good) book about the modern British Navy titled 'No More Heroes';[13] and my generation has surely seen too much of the evils perpetrated through hero-worship degrading into autocracy not to welcome the disappearance of the earlier class of leader.

To return to David Beatty, he certainly did possess Marder's 'charismatic qualities', as his contemporaries admitted virtually unanimously, and as I hope this biography has adequately emphasised. The strength and endurance of Beatty's hold on the officers and men who served under him in the 1914–18 war is perhaps best illustrated by the fact that when in 1962 the 17th British warship to be named *Lion* (a cruiser) recommissioned at Devonport her Captain arranged for the survivors of Beatty's flagship to attend the ceremony. Over 70 of them came, headed by Chatfield who, though nearly 90 years old 'stood like a ramrod on the Quarter Deck while members of the 1916 ship's company filed past'.[14]

In conclusion Beatty's philosophy of life is perhaps best summed up by the words he wrote in the Duchess of Sutherland's 'Treasure Book' – 'To achieve great happiness, work hard, fight hard, play hard, love hard'.[15] What appears certain in this year of grace is that we shall not see his like again, and that, for better or for worse, he was The Last Naval Hero.

Source References

CHAPTER 1
Early Years
Pages 19-29

[1] *Titles and Forms of Address. A Guide to their Correct Use* (A. and C. Black, 13th Ed., 1969).

[2] Quoted by Sir Shane Leslie in article 'Memories of Beatty', *The Quarterly Review*, Vol. 290, No. 593 (July 1952).

[3] Beatty to Miss Sally Lunn, age 15, of 17th Feb. 1915. Quoted in typescript of Leslie's draft biography. SLGF 12/2.

[4] Quoted in Ch. II of Leslie's draft biography, *ibid.*

[5] Letter to the author from Charles Beatty, son of the steeplechaser of the same name, of 9th Aug. 1979.

[6] Extracts from records of H.M.S. *Britannia* supplied to Sir Shane Leslie.

[7] See for example Oswald Frewen *A Sailor's Soliloquy*, Ed. G. P. Griggs (Hutchinson, 1961) pp. 40-1. Frewen (1887-1958) joined the navy from Eton College, on a 'First Lord's Nomination', of which a small number were then permitted, obtained by his redoubtable mother. She was born Clare Jerome, a sister of Winston Churchill's mother Jennie and of Shane Leslie's mother Leonie; so Frewen, Churchill and Leslie were all first cousins. Oswald Frewen appears later in this narrative in connection with the Jutland controversy. See Ch. 15.

[8] Admiral Sir Frank Twiss in conversation with the author, 1978.

[9] Quoted in Ch. III of Leslie's draft biography. SLGF 12/2.

[10] *Ibid.* But as Leslie drew a ring round this remark in his typescript and wrote '? Omit' in the margin its authenticity may be dubious.

[11] This was Captain W. A. Piggott.

[12] Richard Hough, *Admirals in Collision* (Hamish Hamilton, 1959) gives a full account of this disaster. Peter Padfield, *The Battleship Era* (Hart-Davis, 1972) has a valuable account of the condition of the navy and the characters of the principal personalities involved.

[13] In Beatty papers.

[14] *The River War* (Eyre and Spottiswoode, 1899), pp. 196-7. Beatty's journal does not record that the Second Engineer and a stoker were rescued through the bottom of the capsized vessel, an experience which Churchill described as 'sufficiently remarkable'.

[15] Churchill, *My Early Life* (Macmillan, 1930), p. 210.

CHAPTER 2
China 1899 and Marriage, 1901
Pages 30-39

[1] Ronald Tree, *When the Moon was High* (Macmillan, 1975) p. 16.

[2] In Beatty papers.

[3] Quoted Admiral W. S. Chalmers *The Life and Letters of David, Earl Beatty* (Hodder and Stoughton, 1951) pp. 69-70 and 71. Henceforth cited as *Chalmers*.

[4] Leslie's draft biography Ch. 2. SLGF 12/2.

[5] Quoted Leslie *op. cit.*

[6] Quoted in Leslie SLGF 12/1.

[7] Edyth Du Bois 6th Jan. 1916. SLGF 12/2.

[8] Hardy, *The Well-Beloved* (Macmillan paperback Ed., 1975), p. 156. The character of Jocelyn Pierston in that book is, certainly in part, autobiographical. Hardy tells how he 'bowed the knee three times to this sisterly divinity' – the new moon.

[9] The Rev. Albert Victor Baillie (1864–1955). A chaplain to the Queen and to King George VI. Dean of Windsor 1917-44.

[10] Tree, *op. cit.*, pp. 16, 26-27 and 63. His retrospective description of his step father is that he was 'a very remarkable man in addition to being a very good looking one and very attractive to women. Without being in any way intellectual he possessed to a great degree gifts of leadership allied to an intuition that seldom deserted him, coupled with amazing courage and dash.'

[11] SLGF 12/1.

[12] George Meredith, *Modern Love,* Canto 50.

[13] SLGF 12/1.

[14] *ibid.*

[15] V. S. Pritchett, *The Gentle Barbarian* (Chatto and Windus, 1977) p. 154.

[16] SLGF 12/1.

[17] From unfinished biography of his father by George Godfrey-Faussett. SLGF 11/15.

[18] Elizabeth Longford, *Wellington. The Years of the Sword* (U.S. Ed. Harper and Row, 1969) p. 265.

[19] C. H. Dudley Ward, *A Romance of the Nineteenth Century* (Murray, 1923) has an account of the Godfrey-Faussett family.

[20] Godfrey-Faussett diary and letters, SLGF 11/15.

CHAPTER 3
Problems – Naval and Matrimonial, 1902-1913
Pages 40-58

[1] Beatty to Ethel 17th July 1909. Part quoted in *Chalmers*, p. 99.

[2] Dewar's book *The Navy from Within* (Gollancz, 1939) contains strong criticisms of the navy's pre-war training. Though sometimes overstated Dewar's strictures certainly had substance in them. Another 'intellectual' of

the period Commander Stephen King-Hall (Lord King-Hall, 1966) expressed similar views in *My Naval Life 1909-1929* (Faber, 1952).

³ Beatty to Godfrey-Faussett 1st May 1911. SLGF 2/3.

⁴ Geoffrey Bennett, *Charlie B. The Life of Admiral Lord Charles Beresford* (Peter Dawnay, 1968) pp. 136-7 and Ch. 11.

⁵ The Lord Chamberlain at the time was Viscount Althorp, who succeeded to the Spencer Earldom in 1910.

⁶ Ethel to Godfrey-Faussett 23rd May 1911. SLGF 2/3.

⁷ Arthur Ellis, of Lord Chamberlain's Office, to Godfrey-Faussett 5th March 1909. Underlining as printed. SLGF 2/1.

⁸ Beatty to Godfrey-Faussett 18th Oct. 1910. SLGF. 12/2.

⁹ Godfrey-Faussett to Beatty 19th Oct. 1910. SLGF 2/3.

¹⁰ Beatty to Godfrey-Faussett 1st May 1911 (19 pages, holograph) SLGF 2/2.

¹¹ ? George Crichton (signature not clear) of Lord Chamberlain's Office to Godfrey-Faussett 19th May 1911. SLGF 2/3.

¹² Extract from Ch. VII of Leslie's draft biography. SLGF 12/4.

¹³ Captain Agar to Leslie 10th May 1952. SLGF 8/1.

¹⁴ Quoted in Leslie's draft biography. SLGF 12/2.

¹⁵ Information on *Glencairn* and *Sheelah* from Lloyd's *Register of Yachts* 1912-15.

¹⁶ Captain Troubridge to Beatty 5th July 1911. Quoted by Leslie SLGF 12/2.

¹⁷ McKenna to Beatty 21st July 1911. Quoted *ibid.*

¹⁸ Beatty to McKenna 26th July 1911. Quoted *ibid.*

¹⁹ Troubridge to Beatty 26th July 1911. *ibid.*

²⁰ Beatty to Troubridge 26th July 1911. *ibid.*

²¹ Godfrey-Faussett to Beatty 19th Aug. 1911 from Bolton Abbey. *ibid.*

²² *Chalmers*, p. 107.

²³ Minutes of 114th CID meeting. Cab. 38/19/49.

²⁴ Churchill, *My Early Life* (Macmillan, 1934 Ed.), Ch. XV.

²⁵ Churchill, *The World Crisis* (Thornton Butterworth, 1923), I, pp. 37-8.

²⁶ *ibid.*

²⁷ Churchill to Asquith 5th Nov. 1911. *The World Crisis*, I, p. 82.

²⁸ Parl. Deb., Commons, Vol. XLV, Cols. 1875-1907. Mention of the Bridgeman letter to Battenberg of 25th Nov. 1911 is in Cols. 1898-9.

²⁹ Parl Deb., Commons, Vol. XLV, Col. 1897.

³⁰ Stephen Roskill, *Churchill and the Admirals* (Collins, 1978), pp. 295-9.

³¹ Beatty to Lord Stamfordham 21st Dec. 1912. RA. Geo. V. G. 414.

³² Geoffrey Bennett, *Charlie B.,* pp. 136-7

³³ Stephen Roskill, *Hankey. Man of Secrets*, I (Collins, 1970) pp. 99-100. Henceforth cited as Roskill, *Hankey.*

³⁴ Memo. of 1st Jan. 1912. Printed in the *Statement of the First Lord Explanatory of the Naval Estimates 1912-13.* Cd. 6106. See also Churchill, *The World Crisis,* I, pp. 82-4.

³⁵ Sir Ernest Cassel-Albert Ballin correspondence 1909-13. Broadlands Archives Trust. By courtesy of the late Earl Mountbatten a complete set of copies has been deposited in Churchill College. (Acc. 116).

³⁶ *Documents on British Foreign Policy*, VI, pp. 666-761. See also Churchill, *World Crisis,* I, pp. 97-104 and Arthur J. Marder, *From the Dreadnought to Scapa Flow,* I (Oxford U.P. 1961), pp. 272-87. The latter source is henceforth cited as Marder, *Dreadnought.*

37 Fisher to Admiral May 20th April 1904. Quoted Arthur J. Marder (Ed.) *Fear God and Dread Nought. The Correspondence of Admiral of the Fleet Lord Fisher of Kilverstone,* I (Cape, 1952), p. 308. Henceforth cited as Marder, *Fear God.*

38 Beatty to Ethel 27th May 1912.

39 Marder, *Dreadnought,* I, p. 320.

40 Lord Chatfield, *The Navy and Defence* (Heinemann, 1942), p. 100. Henceforth cited as *Chatfield,* I or II.

41 Churchill, *World Crisis,* I, p. 88.

42 Letter from Commander H. G. D. de Chair (the Admiral's son) to the author 12th Feb. 1968. See also the Admiral's memoirs *The Sea is Strong* (Harrap, 1961), pp. 150-2.

CHAPTER 4

The Battle Cruiser Squadron and Preparations for War, 1913-14
Pages 59-76

1 *Chatfield,* I, p. 115.

2 Beatty to Ethel 4th April 1913.

3 Copy in Drax papers (Churchill College) DRAX 4/1.

4 On German cryptographic successes in World War II see S. W. Roskill, *The War at Sea 1939-1945* I (HMSO, 1954), pp. 267 and 469-70. A detailed account of the subject and of the Anglo-German conference held in 1978 on the subject is in J. Rohwer and E. Jäckel *Die Funkaufklärung und ihre Rolle im Zweiten Weltkrieg* (Stuttgart, 1978).

5 First Fleet Temporary Memorandum 99 of 19th Mar. 1914. Copy in DRAX 1/9.

6 Peter Padfield, *Aim Straight. A Biography of Sir Percy Scott* (Hodder and Stoughton, 1966).

7 Fisher to Lord Tweedmouth 10th Sept. 1906. Marder, *Fear God,* II, p. 87. Italics in original.

8 Jellicoe to Oswald Frewen 8th July 1921. A. Temple Patterson (Ed.), *The Jellicoe Papers,* II (Navy Records Society, 1968), p. 142. Henceforth cited as Patterson, *Jellicoe Papers.*

9 Marder, *Fear God,* III, p. 56 *note* and *Dreadnought,* 1, p. 408.

10 Fisher to Julian Corbett 10th Mar. 1908. Marder, *Fear God,* III, p. 56 *note.* Also Dreyer papers (Churchill College) DRYR 1/2.

11 Correspondence about Dreyer's early inventions in DRYR 1/9.

12 The Dreyer papers contain 168 letters from Jellicoe to him, nearly all holograph, covering the period 1906-24.

13 Correspondence with Admiral Charles Briggs's sons Rear-Admiral T. V. Briggs and Captain E. W. Briggs, 1979.

14 Marder, *Dreadnought,* V. p. 324.

15 Pollen papers.

16 Jon T. Sumida, article *British Capital Ship Design in Dreadnought Era etc.,* Journal of Modern History, Vol. 51, pp. 205-30 (June, 1979).

[17] Pollen to Moore 11th April 1912. Pollen papers.

[18] Marder, *Fear God*, III, pp. 87 and 164, *notes*. There are identical references to Pollen in the same author's *Dreadnought*, II, p. 396 and III (2nd Ed.), p. 297, *note*. Mr. Sumida's doctoral thesis on the Pollen fire control system and Mr. Anthony Pollen's biography of his father, in which full use is for the first time made of the voluminous Pollen papers are both expected in 1980.

[19] Admiral Dreyer's papers on the appeal to the Royal Commission are in DRYR 2/1 and 2/2.

[20] Beatty's memorandum 015 of 15th April 1913. It was revised on 3rd Mar. 1914 after a year's experience, and in the revised form stressed the need for light cruisers to be attached to the battle cruiser force. On 17th June 1914 Beatty summoned all his Captains 'to discuss generally the duties of the Battle Cruisers in time of war' on the basis of that memorandum. DRAX 1/2.

[21] Mahan's three 'Influence' books were *The Influence of Sea Power on History* (1890), *The Influence of Sea Power upon the French Revolution and Empire* (2 Vols., 1892) and *Sea Power in its relations to the War of 1812* (2 Vols., 1905).

[22] Jonathan Steinberg, *Yesterday's Deterrent. Tirpitz and the Birth of the German Battle Fleet*. (Macdonald, 1965)

[23] Captain Sir John Colomb's most important works were *The Protection of Our Commerce and Distribution of our Naval Forces Considered* (1867) and *The Defence of Great and Greater Britain* (1880). Those of Admiral Philip Colomb were *Naval Warfare* (1891) and *Essays on Naval Defence* (1896), all published in London.

[24] Marder, *Fear God*, I, pp. 340–1.

[25] *Ibid.*, II and III, *passim*.

[26] For an excellent study of the works of the Colombs, Mahan, Corbett and other 'intellectuals' of the late 19th and early 20th century see D. M. Schurman *The Education of a Navy* (Cassell, 1965).

[27] To Ethel 4th April 1913.

[28] On the notorious row between Scott and Beresford over the signal sent by the former that 'paintwork appears to be more in demand than gunnery' see Padfield, *Aim Straight*, Ch. 9, Geoffrey Bennett, *Charlie B* p. 290 and Marder, *Dreadnought*, I, pp. 97–9.

[29] Letter by Scott published in *The Times* 5th June 1914.

[30] Marder, *Dreadnought*, I, p. 353. Beatty's letters of 24th and 25th June, quoted in *Chalmers*, pp. 125–6 make it appear that the exercises took place a month earlier than stated by Marder. But the fact that Beatty misdated those letters by a month is confirmed by Churchill's congratulatory message to Jellicoe, for his conduct of the Red (or German) forces, dated 27th July. See Patterson, *Jellicoe Papers*, I, p.29.

[31] The Invasion Sub-Committee of the C.I.D., which was revived in Jan. 1913, reported on 15th April 1914. C.I.D. 62A Cab. 38 26/12.

[32] Fisher's memorandum of 24th June 1912 to Churchill. Marder, *Fear God*, II, p. 469 and Fisher, *Records*, pp. 183–5.

[33] Memo. of May 1907. Quoted Marder, *Dreadnought*, I, p. 381. There is a clear contradiction between that historian's conclusion on p. 383 that 'British naval thinking in the pre-war decade did not anticipate the extraordinary degree to which blockade would throttle the German economy in 1914–18' and the statement in the same work, II, p. 372 that 'Pre-war British naval

thought and war plans placed a high value on the effects of economic pressure on Germany. I hold the latter to be the more correct.
[34] Beatty's memorandum 015 of 15th April 1913. The copy in the Drax papers is endorsed in Plunkett's (i.e. Drax's) hand 'DB wrote the draft of this with his own hand shortly after joining the *Lion*'. DRAX 4/1. The resultant 'Battle Orders for 1st Battle Cruiser Squadron' were dated 17th July 1913. They were reproduced in revised form with consolidated amendments on 18th Feb. 1915. Plunkett endorsed his copy of the original Memo 'the wording of 1 and 2 of Battle Cruiser Orders was Beatty's', though he (i.e. Plunkett) 'had drafted many sections of the orders'. DRAX 1/2 and 1/3. *Chalmers*, p. 120 dates this Memo to September 1913 which is surely incorrect.
[35] For a critique of British pre-war tactical training see K. G. B. Dewar, *The Navy from Within*. Though this work is too much of a *pièce justificative* of his own conduct later it does contain valuable and valid material on the tactics practised by the Royal Navy.
[36] Marder, *Dreadnought*, I. p. 401.
[37] Beatty to Ethel 12th and 16th Feb. 1914.
[38] Parl. Deb., Commons, Vol. LIX, Cols, 1896–1965. The debate was continued next day, 18th Mar. 1914.
[39] *Chalmers*, p. 128. Perhaps the best description of the battle cruisers' visits to Russian ports in June 1914 is to be found in the anonymously edited and neglected memoir *Harold Tennyson R.N.* (Macmillan, 1918) pp. 186–211. Tennyson, who was a grandson of the poet, was serving as a midshipman in the *Queen Mary*, and although his letters represent a 'gunroom eye' view they certainly provide a vivid and entertaining account of the principal events and the characters involved in them.

CHAPTER 5

The Test of War, 1914
Pages 77-105

[1] Parl. Deb., Commons, Vol. LIX, Col. 241.
[2] *ibid.*, Col. 1917.
[3] *The World Crisis*, I, p. 190.
[4] Quoted Marder, *Fear God*, I, p. 432 (*note*).
[5] Martin Gilbert, *Winston Spencer Churchill* (Heinemann, 1971), III, p. 15. Henceforth cited as Gilbert, *Churchill*.
[6] Beatty to Ethel 7th Aug. 1914 'You won't on any account come in the *Sheelah* will you?'
[7] Same to same 28th Oct. 1914.
[8] Same to same 19th Aug. 1914.
[9] Same to same 20th Aug. 1914.
[10] PRO. Adm. 137/288.
[11] Dewar, *The Navy from Within*, pp. 25–6 and 122–3.
[12] Marder, *Dreadnought*, III, 2nd Ed. (Oxford, 1978), p. 5.
[13] *ibid.*, pp. 29–32.

[14] Roskill, unpublished lecture given several times at Imperial Defence College *The Role of Maritime Forces. Lessons of World Wars I and II*. ROSK 10/6 (Churchill College).

[15] Personal experience in HMS *Warspite*, Mediterranean Fleet Flagship 1937-39, and conversations and correspondence with Admiral Sir Manley Power, who had served as Staff Officer Operations to Cunningham. See also Admiral Power's unpublished memoirs (Churchill College).

[16] Jellicoe to Admiralty 30th Oct. 1914. Marder, *Dreadnought*, II. pp. 75-6.

[17] For full account of the escape of the *Goeben* and *Breslau* and its aftermath see E. W. R. Lumby (Ed.), *The Mediterranean 1912-1914* (Navy Records Society, 1970) Parts II and III, and Marder, *Dreadnought*, II, Ch. II.

[18] Dated 'August 1914'.

[19] Beatty to Ethel 19th Aug. 1914 'I see Kitchener has stated that the war will be over in six months or two years i.e. if it is not over in six months it will last two years. This I cannot think possible for a moment. The money in the world will run short before then. . . .'

[20] *Chatfield*, I, pp. 124-5. The author tells how 'unburdened with responsibility, and eager for excitement, I said "Surely we must go in".'

[21] A. Temple Patterson, *Tyrwhitt of the Harwich Force* (Macdonald, 1973), p. 62.

[22] Beatty to Ethel 29th Aug. 1914.

[23] Same to same 2nd Sept. 1914.

[24] For example Nelson to his wife 2nd Aug. 1796 '. . . .had all my actions been gazetted not one fortnight would have passed. Let those enjoy their brag and one day or other I will have a large gazette to myself'. G.P.B. Naish (Ed.), *Nelson's Letters to his Wife* (Navy Records Society, 1958), p. 298.

[25] *Chalmers*, p. 155.

[26] Beatty to Ethel 23rd Sept. 1914 (continuation of letter begun on 19th).

[27] *ibid*.

[28] Churchill, *The World Crisis*, I. Ch. XV for his account of this episode.

[29] Beatty to Ethel 18th Oct. 1914. Next day Beatty wrote again that Churchill's 'flying about and putting his fingers into pies which do not concern him is bound to lead to disaster'.

[30] Admiral Sir Henry Oliver in conversation with the author many years later repeatedly stressed how he had pressed Churchill not to go to Antwerp. On the German view of the threat inherent in the British landings in Belgium see B. H. Liddell Hart, *The Real War* (Faber, 1930), pp. 79-81.

[31] Beatty to Ethel 11th Oct. 1914.

[32] Sir Alfred Ewing, *The Man of Room 40* (Hutchinson, 1939) and Admiral Sir William James (Hall's deputy), *The Eyes of the Navy* (Methuen, 1955), p. 29 ff. Sir Shane Leslie, who as a young man knew Count Benckendorff, the Russian ambassador in London at the time and his family well, recorded in his diary for 24th July 1914 that Benckendorff sent his son Constantine to St. Petersburgh whence he returned with the signal book. Leslie, *Long Shadows* (Murray, 1966) p. 168.

[33] See the anonymously edited *Harold Tennyson* (Macmillan, 1918), pp. 228-9. In Tennyson's letter of 18th Oct. 1914 he expressed the strongest admiration for Captain Hall and told his parents that 'Our new Captain is . . . Captain Bentinck'.

[34] Beatty to Ethel 29th Oct. 1914.

[35] *Chalmers*, pp. 203–4.

[36] Speyer was chairman of the merchant banking firm Speyer Bros. of London, Frankfurt and New York. Anti-German hysteria forced him and his family to emigrate to USA in 1915, whence he unwisely continued to correspond with his Frankfurt branch. His letters and cables were intercepted, and after the war he (and other ex-German naturalised British subjects) were called to appear before a Special Tribunal under Mr. Justice Salter to decide whether they should be allowed to retain their British nationality. In Speyer's case the decision of the Tribunal was against him.

[37] Beatty to Ethel 23rd Oct. 1914.

[38] Beatty to Churchill 17th Oct. 1914. No reply to this letter is printed in Vol. III of Gilbert, *Churchill*.

[39] For example on 4th June 1914 Percy Scott wrote in a letter to *The Times* 'that submarines and aircraft had entirely revolutionised naval warfare . . . That all naval strategy was upset. . . .' Similar arguments are constantly repeated in his memoirs *Fifty Years in the Royal Navy* (Murray, 1919).

[40] S. W. Roskill, *The War at Sea 1939–1945*, I, (HMSO, 1954) pp. 76–8.

[41] Marder, *Dreadnought*, I, pp. 417–8.

[42] Beatty to Ethel 16th Nov. 1914.

[43] Kenneth Young, *Arthur James Balfour* (Bell, 1963), p. 351.

[44] Beatty to Ethel 30th Oct. 1914. On 2nd Nov. Beatty wrote again and in almost identical terms, to Ethel about Fisher's return, but added that he expected the old admiral 'will rule the Admiralty and Winston with a heavy hand' – a prophecy which was not fulfilled. Gilbert, *Churchill*, III (Heinemann, 1971) p. 154.

[45] Same to same 29th Sept. 1914.

[46] S. W. Roskill, *The Strategy of Sea Power* (Collins, 1962) pp. 106–7 regarding the effects of the Declarations of Paris and of London. M. W. W. P. Consett, *The Triumph of Unarmed Forces* (Williams and Norgate, 1923) recounts how they were finally overcome.

[47] Beatty to Ethel 3rd Nov. 1914.

[48] *ibid*.

[49] Geoffrey Bennett, *Coronel and the Falklands* (Batsford, 1962), p. 95.

[50] Churchill, *The World Crisis*, I. p. 415.

[51] Beatty to Ethel 5th and 6th Nov. 1914.

[52] *ibid*.

[53] Admy. message No. 171 of 4th Nov. 1914.

[54] Beatty to Ethel 6th Nov. 1914.

[55] Same to same 7th Nov. 1914.

[56] Same to same 13th Nov. 1914.

[57] Roskill, *Churchill and the Admirals* (Collins, 1978), pp. 177–8 and *passim*.

[58] Filson Young, *With the Battle Cruisers* (Cassell, 1921), p. X.

[59] Beatty to Ethel 10th Dec. 1914.

[60] Beatty to Jellicoe 13th Nov. 1914. Patterson, *Jellicoe Papers*, I, pp. 97–8. The *Tiger* had only just joined Beatty's flag and was far from fully efficient.

[61] Beatty to Fisher 15th Nov. 1914. Marder, *Fear God*, III, pp. 70–2.

[62] Churchill's holograph order to the C-in-C, Devonport is reproduced in facsimile in Geoffrey Bennett, *Coronel and the Falklands* (Batsford, 1962), p. 119.

[63] Bennett, *op. cit.*, pp. 127–9.

[64] Beatty to Ethel 21st Nov. 1914.

[65] Churchill to Beatty 22nd Nov. 1914, holograph from Admiralty. Not mentioned in Gilbert, *Churchill,* III or reproduced in the relevant Companion Volume of documents.

[66] Beatty to Ethel 25th Nov. 1914.

[67] Churchill to Beatty 30th Nov. 1914, holograph from Admiralty. Not mentioned in Gilbert, *Churchill,* III or reproduced in the relevant Companion Volume of documents.

[68] Chatfield, I, pp. 105-6.

[69] Beatty to Ethel 2nd Dec. 1914.

[70] Same to same 4th Dec. 1914.

[71] Same to same 7th Dec. 1914. Most of the Beatty-Fisher correspondence is printed in Marder, *Fear God,* III.

[72] Same to same 10th Dec. 1914.

[73] Geoffrey Bennett, *Coronel and the Falklands* Ch. 5 for a full account of the battle. N. J. M. Campbell's *Warship Special No. 1. Battle Cruisers* (Conway Maritime Press, 1978) p. 9 has the latest and most detailed study of the gunnery and damage on both sides.

[74] Marder, *Dreadnought,* II, pp. 124-6. The *Dresden* was finally located at Juan Fernandez Island in the South Pacific on 8th March 1915 and scuttled herself.

[75] Neither Sir Julian Corbett nor Professor Marder made any serious study of the development and final rejection of the Pollen system, and its consequences.

[76] Padfield, *Aim Straight,* p. 219.

[77] Donald Macintyre, *The Thunder of the Guns* (Batsford, 1959), p. 187. Marder, *Dreadnought,* II, p. 126.

[78] Beatty to George V, holograph, 2nd Dec. 1914, RA. GV, Q.832/367.

[79] Sir Julian Corbett, *Naval Operations* (Longmans, 1921) II, p. 43.

[80] Beatty to Ethel 20th Dec. 1914. See also *Chalmers,* p. 175.

[81] Beatty to Jellicoe 20th Dec. 1914. Patterson, *Jellicoe Papers,* I, pp. 110-12.

[82] Leslie papers SLGF 12/1.

[83] On the *post-mortem* to the Scarborough raid see Marder, *Dreadnought,* II, pp. 142-9. Copies of Goodenough's and Beatty's reports are in the Beatty papers.

[84] Admiralty to Jellicoe M. 04953/14 of 6th Jan. 1915.

[85] Jellicoe to Admiralty 105/H.F. 0022 of 14th Jan. 1915.

[86] Admiralty to Jellicoe M. 0473/15 of 18th Jan. 1915.

[87] Beatty to Admiralty 134/01 of 26th Feb. 1915.

[88] John Pearson, *Façades* (Macmillan, 1978), p. 89.

CHAPTER 6

The Submarine Comes into its Own, 1915
Pages 106-135

[1] A. Temple Patterson, *Jellicoe* (Macmillan, 1969), p. 82.

[2] Beatty to Jellicoe 8th Feb. 1915.

³ Hugh L'Etang, *The Pathology of Leadership* (Heinemann, 1969) has case histories of this type.

⁴ Admiral Sir Reginald Bacon, *The Life of John Rushworth. Earl Jellicoe* (Cassell, 1936), p. 228.

⁵ Fisher to Beatty 6th Jan. 1915.

⁶ Beatty to Fisher. The draft is undated but was obviously written a few days after the letter from Fisher which initiated it.

⁷ Admiralty to Beatty M. 01032/15 of 8th Feb. 1915.

⁸ On Cowan's personality, his enjoyment of war and his service in the *Zealandia* (3rd Battle Squadron) and then in the *Princess Royal* see Lionel Dawson, *Sound of the Guns* (Pen-in-Hand, Oxford, 1949).

⁹ Hugo von Waldeyer-Hartz, *Admiral von Hipper* (Eng. Trans. Rich and Cowan, 1933), p. 148.

¹⁰ Churchill, *The World Crisis,* II, pp. 129-30.

¹¹ *ibid.*, p. 129. Churchill argues that a raid on the east coast 'was clearly to be expected'; but the intercepted German signals gave no indication whatever of such an intention. Churchill's account also shows how greatly he relished holding the destiny of fleets in the hands of himself and his naval colleagues in Whitehall. *op. cit.,* pp. 131-2.

¹² N. J. M. Campbell, *Warship Special No. 1. Battle Cruisers.*

¹³ Beatty to Keyes 10th Feb. 1915 from *Princess Royal.* I have been unable to trace the source of Beatty's quotation about the 'merry hunt' but it obviously comes from some poet of the chase.

¹⁴ Moore to Beatty 25th Jan. 1915, para 8. Moore does not make his case better by misquoting Beatty's signal here. It was 'Course North-East', as stated here. Moore runs the two flag signals which were flying simultaneously together and substitutes 'bearing' for 'course'.

¹⁵ Pelly to Beatty 31st Jan 1915, quoting Home Fleet Gunnery Order (HFGO) No. 15 regarding 'concentration on the leading enemy ships' in his defence.

¹⁵ᵃAddendum to diary for 24th Jan. 1915, DRAX 1/41.

¹⁶ Interviews with Leslie in 1950s.

¹⁷ Beatty to Jellicoe 8th Feb. 1915.

¹⁸ Beatty to Pollen 14th Dec. 1929. Pollen papers.

¹⁹ Beatty to Jellicoe 8th Feb. 1915.

²⁰ Fisher to Churchill 25th Jan. 1915. Gilbert, *Churchill,* Companion Volume III, p. 449.

²¹ Fisher to Beatty 27th Jan. 1915. Marder, *Fear God,* III, pp. 146-7.

²² Fisher to Beatty 31st Jan. 1915. Marder, *op. cit.,* pp. 150-1.

²³ On Pakenham's character and idiosyncracies see Geoffrey Lewis, *Fabulous Admirals* (Putnam, 1957) Ch. XVII.

²⁴ Churchill, *World Crisis,* II, p. 89.

²⁵ Fisher to Beatty 8th Feb. 1915.

²⁶ The reports which passed between Beatty, Jellicoe and the Admiralty on the Dogger Bank action, including the defence of their conduct by Admiral Moore and Captain Pelly, are printed *in extenso* in Patterson, *Jellicoe Papers,* I, pp. 131-150.

²⁷ Beatty to Admiralty 16th April 1915.

²⁸ Secretary of Admiralty to Beatty 30th June 1915.

²⁹ N. J. M. Campbell, *Warship Special No. 1,* p. 30.

30 Beatty to Ethel 12th Mar. 1915.

31 King George V's diary for 26th–28th Feb. 1915. Royal Archives.

32 Beatty's 017 of 18th Feb. 1915. Copy in DRAX 1/3.

33 Naval Staff Monograph No. 5 (1925).

34 Beatty to Jellicoe 21st Feb. 1915.

35 Jellicoe to Beatty 25th Feb. and 2nd Mar. 1915.

36 Same to same 7th Feb. 1915.

37 Same to same 25th Feb. 1915.

38 Beatty to Jellicoe 5th Mar. 1915.

39 Letters Admiral Carrington to the author of 7th Oct. 1957 and 9th Feb. 1958. ROSK 3/1.

40 DRAX 1/2. Plunkett's paper has the date 1913 written at the bottom, but that must have been added later. From its wording it was obviously written early in 1915.

41 Memo. 013 of 10th May 1915.

42 Beatty to Jellicoe 25th May 1915. On 23rd June U.40 was sunk by the submarine C.24 working with the trawler *Taranaki*. A second success was achieved on 20th July when the submarine C.27 and trawler *Princess Louise* destroyed U.23. Robert M. Grant *U-boat Intelligence* (Putnam, 1969), p. 183. This work revises the same author's *U-boats Destroyed* (1964), which gives a wrong date for the sinking of U.40.

43 G. M. Caroe, *William Henry Bragg* (Cambridge U.P., 1978) pp. 83–9.

44 Beatty to Hood 26th April 1915.

45 Beatty to Hood 26th April and 15th May 1915. Hood papers. See also Roskill, *Churchill and the Admirals* (Collins, 1978) pp. 37–8. Jellicoe also wrote to Hood in much the same vein as Beatty.

46 Interview with 6th Viscount Hood, who well remembers the association of his family with the Beatty children, Aug. 1978.

47 Beatty to Jellicoe 26th May 1915.

48 Beatty to Ethel 21st May 1915.

49 Marder, *Dreadnought*, II, pp. 279–93 and Roskill, *Hankey*, I, pp. 173–6 give full accounts of the Fisher-Churchill crisis and breach.

50 Marder, *Fear God*, p. 241, H. Nicolson, *King George V* (Constable, 1952), p. 263 and Roskill, *Hankey*, I, pp. 173–6.

51 Beatty to Jellicoe 31st May 1915.

52 Marder, *Dreadnought*, II, pp. 98–100 regarding the loss of the *Formidable* and the aftermath.

53 Pollen papers and correspondence with Mr. Jon Sumida 1978–9.

54 Beatty to Jellicoe 20th Aug. and to Balfour 21st Sept. 1915.

55 Balfour to Beatty 23rd Sept. 1915.

56 Grant, *U-boats Destroyed*, p. 27 regarding the *Baralong* incident and his *U-boat Intelligence*, p. 183. Curiously Professor Marder does not mention this incident in his *Dreadnought*, II.

57 Orders for gunnery practices. BCF 7 of 19th Nov. 1915. PRO. Adm. 137/2129.

58 Beatty to Jellicoe 21st Nov. 1915.

59 Jellicoe to Beatty 22nd Dec. 1915.

60 Beatty to Ethel 16th and 22nd Nov. 1915.

61 Beatty to Hamilton 14th Dec. 1915, 10th Jan. and 14th Feb. 1916. Hamilton papers, NMM 119. The *Sheelah* is not shown as attached to the

BCF in 1915 or 1916 Navy Lists, but Fripp and Shields appear under 'Temporary Consulting Physicians and Surgeons'.

[62] To Admiral May 20th April 1904. Marder, *Fear God*, I, p. 308. See also the same work, II, pp. 349 and 485 for Fisher's repetition of this prophecy in 1911 and 1913.

[63] The figures given here exclude fishing vessels sunk. They are taken from Archibald Hurd, *The Merchant Navy*, II (Murray, 1924), Appendix C.

64 Figures from Grant, *U-Boat Intelligence*, pp. 182-3.

CHAPTER 7

Stalemate, January – May 1916
Pages 136-148

[1] Beatty to Brand 1st Jan. 1916.

[2] Edyth Du Bois to Beatty 6th Jan. 1916. SLGF 11/2.

[3] Fisher to Bonar Law 7th Jan. 1916., Marder, *Fear God*, III, p. 290.

[4] *op. city.*, p. 274.

[5] Patterson, *Jellicoe Papers*, I, and Marder, *Fear God*, III for the Fisher-Jellicoe correspondence.

[6] Beatty to Asquith 3rd Feb. 1916. Asquith papers (Bodleian). Beatty said he excluded what he called 'the freak ships', *Furious, Glorious* and *Courageous* because their armament and protection would never enable them to engage the German battle cruisers. The *Furious* was originally designed to mount two 18-inch or four 15-inch guns, while the other two were to have four 15-inch. Campbell, *Battle Cruisers*, pp. 65-8.

[7] Jellicoe to Beatty 24th Feb. 1916.

[8] Beatty to Jackson 25th Feb. 1916.

[9] Beatty to Jellicoe 3rd Mar. 1916.

[10] Jellicoe to Beatty 10th Mar. 1916.

[11] Beatty to Jellicoe 10th Mar. 1916.

[12] Hamilton to Beatty 3rd Mar. 1916.

[13] Marder, *Fear God*, III, pp. 285-353.

[14] Beatty to Jellicoe BCF 016 of 13th Mar. 1916.

[15] Jellicoe to Beatty HF/119 of 15th Mar. 1916.

[16] Beatty to Jellicoe 7th April 1916.

[17] Jellicoe to Beatty 14th April 1916. The first part of this letter is printed in Marder, *Dreadnought*, II, pp. 423-4. The trials with the two submarines are described fully in Commander Ryan's report of 11th April to the C-in-C, Rosyth.

[18] Marder, *op. cit.*, p. 424.

[19] Beatty to Jellicoe 7th May 1916.

[20] Beatty to Jackson 6th May 1916.

[21] Douglas Robinson, *The Zeppelin in Combat* (Foulis, 1962), pp. 145-6.

[22] Beatty to Keyes 13th May 1916. Keyes papers (British Library).

[23] Beatty to Jellicoe 18th May 1916.

[24] Beatty to Jackson 14th May 1916.

[25] Same to same 21st May 1916.

[26] Unfinished typescript of book on Jutland. Chalmers papers.

CHAPTER 8
Jutland, 31st May – 1st June 1916
Pages 149-188

[1] Marder, *Dreadnought*, III. The student should use the 2nd Edition (Oxford, 1978). I have here followed the very thoroughly researched conclusions reached by N. J. M. Campbell regarding the hits scored and received by both sides in the battle – which sometimes disagree substantially with Professor Marder's figures. Attention may also be drawn to my account in *H.M.S. Warspite* (Collins, 1957 and Futura Paperbacks, 1974) and in *The Strategy of Sea Power* (Collins, 1962).

[2] Jellicoe to Archibald Hurd 27th Nov. 1922. Patterson, *Jellicoe Papers*, II, pp. 420-6.

[3] Letter of 30th Nov. 1951 addressed to 'My dear Admiral'. Copy in Leslie-Faussett papers SLGF 6/14.

[4] Enclosure to Jellicoe's letter of 27th Nov. 1922 to Archibald Hurd. The enclosure was the draft of a revised Appendix to Jellicoe's book *The Grand Fleet* (Cassell, 1919) if a new edition was published – which did not in fact take place.

[5] In a letter of 8th Jan. 1970 the late Donald McLachlan described to the author how Kapitän zur See Kupfer, who served in the German B-Dienst (the equivalent of Room 40) in both wars had described to him with pride the transfer of Scheer's wireless operator as well as his call sign ashore. ROSK 3/6.

[6] Lionel Dawson, *The Sound of the Guns* (Pen-in-Hand, Oxford 1949), pp. 133-4.

[7] Marder, *Dreadnought*, III, (2nd Ed.), p. 55.

[8] Jellicoe's 'Errors made in Jutland Battle', written in 1932, is printed in full in Patterson, *Jellicoe Papers,* II, pp. 447-52. It was produced, in his own words, 'so that others may benefit from our experience' and still stands as a moderately worded and fair critique which spares no one – including himself. Professor Marder prints part of Beatty's hostile reaction to Jellicoe's paper in *Dreadnought*, III, p. 79.

[9] This was one of the points on which Jellicoe later criticised Beatty in 'Errors made in Jutland Battle'. Patterson, *Jellicoe Papers*, II, p. 447.

[10] 'Remarks given to the USA Captain' of Dec. 1920. Dreyer papers DRYR 6/9.

[11] Georg von Hase, *Kiel and Jutland* (Eng. Trans., London, 1921) pp. 149-50.

[12] Hipper to Scheer 10th July 1916. Copy in Dreyer papers. *DRYR* 6/10.

[13] Churchill, *World Crisis*, III, p. 129.

[14] The original of *Southampton's* track chart (in Churchill College MRDN 1/1) shows a sharp turn away at 4.45 p.m. – presumably made just after the sighting of the High Seas Fleet.

[15] S. W. Roskill, *H.M.S. Warspite,* p. 117.

[16] Marder, *Dreadnought*, III, 2nd Ed., pp. 73-5.

[17] Beatty's despatch gave the range as 14,000 yards at this time, but all the evidence available to Captain J. E. T. Harper, who was charged with preparing the 'Official Record' of the battle, indicates that it was

considerably greater. After a strenuous argument Harper compromised by quoting the figure given in Beatty's despatch but gave the higher figure from 5.40 p.m. Harper, *Record*, pp. 23-4.

[18] In his remarks on the 'Admiralty Narrative of the Battle of Jutland' and in his 'Errors made in Jutland Battle' Patterson, *Jellicoe Papers*, II, Doc. 154.

[18a] PRO T 173/204 for Dreyer Table information. Cmd. 1068 (Jutland Despatches) for the Argo Tower data and GO 92/13 (n.d. but probably 1913) for 'Technical History and Technical comparison' of Pollen and Dreyer fire control systems.

[19] In Pollen papers, shown to the author by his son Anthony.

[20] Cmd. 1068. *The Battle of Jutland. Official Despatches with Appendices* (1920).

[21] Corbett, *Naval Operations*, III, Maps 29 and 30.

[22] Roskill, *H.M.S. Warspite*, pp. 122-7.

[23] Roskill, lecture I.D.C. Copy in ROSK 10/6

[24] Marder, *Dreadnought*, III, 2nd Ed., p. 134.

[25] Corbett, *Naval Operations*, III, pp. 370-2.

[26] Admiral Chalmers, who was plotting the flagship's movements at the time, explained exactly what happened in a memorandum for the author dated 25th Oct. 1957; but he made no mention of the turn in his biography of Beatty – because he considered 'there was no need to put it in'. He also showed me a print of the original track chart of the *Lion* in which the 360 degree turn was clear. The Chalmers memo. is now in Churchill College, ROSK 3/1.

[27] Marder, *Dreadnought*, III, pp. 148-50.

[28] Draft Ms. of biography. SLGF 12/1.

[29] Marder, *Dreadnought*, III, p. 130.

[30] *ibid.*, pp. 135-8.

[31] *ibid.*, p. 141.

[32] Corbett, *Naval Operations*, III, Map 40.

[33] Leslie, draft biography. SLGF 12/1.

[34] Marder, *Dreadnought*, III, p. 146. I am indebted to Mr. John Campbell for drawing my attention to the lack of any evidence in the records of the German 2nd Battle Squadron that it engaged British ships at this time.

[35] Marder, *op. cit.*, pp. 146-7.

[36] Jellicoe to Oswald Frewen. See also his 'Errors made in Jutland Battle' of 1932. Patterson, *Jellicoe Papers*, II, p. 451.

[37] Unsigned memo. criticising Admiral Harper's book *The Truth about Jutland* (Murray, 1927). Beatty certainly saw this memo. as he made some amendments to it.

[38] Marder, *Dreadnought*, III, p. 155, *note 8*.

[39] This was W. F. Clarke's view. See also Marder, *Dreadnought*, III, pp. 153-4 and *note 6*.

[40] Marder, *Dreadnought*, III, pp. 156-9.

[41] Langhorne and Gibson, *The Riddle of Jutland* (Cassell, 1934), pp. 219-20.

[42] Marder, *Dreadnought*, III, p. 168.

[43] *ibid.* pp. 171-2.

[44] Roskill, lecture to Imperial Defence College (ROSK 10/6) and Marder, *op. cit.*, pp. 175-6.

[45] Marder, *op. cit.* pp. 185-6.

46 *Chalmers*, p. 262.

47 Leslie, draft biography. SLGF 12/1.

48 Letter Mrs. Courage to Leslie dated Oct. 13th, probably 1948. SLGF 11/6.

49 Baillie to Leslie 22nd June 1948. SLGF 6/15.

50 Quoted in draft biography. SLGF 12/1.

51 Fisher to Beatty 9th June and reply by latter of 16th June. Marder, *Fear God*, III, pp. 355 and 357.

52 Letter Roskill to Chatfield 27th April and reply by latter of 29th April 1955. ROSK 3/1.

53 Cunninghame Graham papers and memoirs (Churchill College) and correspondence with the author.

54 Marder, *Dreadnought*, III, (2nd Ed.), p. 200.

55 *ibid*.

56 Article 'Something Wrong with our Bloody Ships' by A. P. P. (Commander Anthony Pellew) in *The Naval Review*, Vol. 64, No. 1 (Jan. 1976). See also the memoirs of Admiral Sir Francis Pridham, who was President of the Ordnance Board during World War II, which throw much light on the inefficiency of British shell and armour plating testing. (Churchill College).

57 Beatty to Evan-Thomas 4th June 1916. Evan-Thomas papers, British Library. Add. Mss. 52504–06. A complete set of copies is in ROSK 3/3.

58 An English translation of Scheer's despatch is in ROSK 3/5.

59 Article *The Naval Balance. Quality versus Quantity*. RUSI Journal, Vol. 123, No. 4 (Dec. 1978), p. 58.

CHAPTER 9

Investigation and Reappraisal, June – December 1916
Pages 189-201

1 Beatty to Jellicoe 9th June 1916. Patterson, *Jellicoe Papers*, I, p. 277. Copy in Dreyer papers DRYR 6/5.

2 Jellicoe to George V 11th June 1916. RA Geo. V. Q.832/423.

3 George V to Queen Mary 16th June 1916. RA Geo. V. CC4/148.

4 Marder, *Dreadnought*, III, pp. 237-8, *note*, quotes the 2nd Earl Beatty as recalling that his father had told how Jellicoe 'made the doleful confession "I missed one of the greatest opportunities a man ever had" '; and also Leo Amery's account of Jellicoe 'breaking down completely in his cabin at the thought of his failure' – which Amery got from Beatty. Later Leslie acquired similar evidence – from the same source, which can hardly be described as impartial.

5 The Committee's Report is dated 4th July 1916. Dreyer papers DRYR 6/10.

6 Madden to Dreyer 3rd Jan. 1924. Dreyer papers DRYR 4/3.

7 Beatty was much distressed by the death of his Fleet Engineer Officer Captain G. C. Taylor in the *Tiger* at the Dogger Bank action, and paid tribute to his Engineer Officers in many official and personal letters.

[8] Robert Rhodes James, *Memoirs of a Conservative* (Weidenfeld and Nicolson, 1969), p. 209 where he quotes Lord Davidson's recollections of the fight inside the Admiralty over improving the status of Engineer Officers.

[9] Marder, *Dreadnought*, III, p. 261.

[10] Pollen's paper and the minutes quoted are in DRAX 1/9.

[11] Pollen to Beatty 1st Aug. 1916. Pollen papers.

[12] Patterson, *Jellicoe Papers*, II, pp. 192 and 412. 'It fell to me to turn down his inventions on more than one occasion' (8th July 1921). *Note* 1 on page 192 gives a very unfair account of Pollen's invention; and his company was the Linotype Company, not Monotype as stated.

[13] See Jon T. Sumida, article 'British Capital Ship Design and Fire Control in the *Dreadnought* Era'. *Journal of Modern History*, June 1979.

[14] Cunninghame Graham memoirs and papers (Churchill College) and correspondence with the author.

[15] See W. F. Clarke, 'Retrospect' and 'An Admiralty Letter'. ROSK 3/6.

[16] Deleted.

[17] Douglas Robinson, *The Zeppelin in Combat* (Foulis, 1962), pp. 188–9.

[18] Marder, *Dreadnought*, III, p. 219.

[19] Patterson *Jellicoe Papers*, II, pp. 47–61 for the revised GFBOs issued on 11th Sept. 1916.

[20] Naval Staff Monograph, *Home Waters June-Nov. 1916* pp. 10–11. Copy in Naval Library.

[21] *ibid.*, pp. 10–12.

[22] Beatty to Jellicoe 27th July 1916. Beatty probably had in mind the Court Martial of Admiral Troubridge after the escape of the *Goeben* and *Breslau* in which the order not to engage 'superior forces' became an important issue.

[23] Beatty to Ethel 8th Aug. 1916, and Duff's diary for 6th Oct. 1916 (NMM); also Marder, *Dradnought*, III, pp. 246–7

[24] Jellicoe to Jackson 31st July 1916. Patterson, *Jellicoe Papers*, II, p. 41.

[25] Newbolt, *Naval Operations*, IV, pp. 36–7.

[26] Patterson, *Jellicoe Papers*, II, pp. 71–77 has Jellicoe's report on this conference.

[27] S. W. Roskill (ed.), *The Naval Air Service*, I, (Navy Records Society, 1969), Docs. 140 and 143 (pp. 389–404 and 412–22) give Curzon's attack and Balfour's reply in full. Doc. 145 (pp. 423–8) is Curzon's 'Last Words' on the controversy. Hankey aptly described the contest as 'the rapier versus bludgeon'. Roskill, *Hankey* I, pp. 271–2.

[28] Beatty to Admiralty 20th Nov. 1916.

[29] Marginal note to Fisher's letter to Jellicoe of 28th Nov. 1916. Marder, *Fear God*, III, p. 395.

[30] Masterton Smith (Balfour's Secretary) to Stamfordham 29th Nov. 1916. RA Geo. V. Q.1005/8.

[31] Stamfordham to the King 10th Nov. 1916. RA Geo. V. G. 1039.

[32] Balfour to the King 21st Nov. 1916. RA Geo. V. G. 1039/3.

[33] George V to Balfour 22nd Nov. 1916. RA Geo. V. G. 1039/4.

[34] George V to Beatty 3rd Dec. 1916. RA Geo. V. Q. 832.

[35] Beatty to George V 6th Dec. 1916. *ibid.*

[36] Pakenham to Beatty 27th Nov. 1916. SLFG 3/8.

[37] Beatty to Cowan 28th Nov. 1916.

[38] On the resignation of Asquith and the formation of the War Cabinet see Roskill, *Hankey,* pp. 320–32.

CHAPTER 10

Crisis for the Navy: Comfort for the C-in-C, January – June 1917
Pages 202-224

[1] Beatty to Ethel 1st April 1917.

[2] Diary 22nd Sept. 1917. Richmond papers. NMM. For study of Richmond's career and character see Arthur J. Marder, *Portrait of an Admiral* (Cape, 1952).

[3] Tyrwhitt to Keyes 18th Feb. 1917. Keyes papers. (British Library).

[4] Same to same 22nd June 1917. *ibid.*

[5] Shane Leslie, *Long Shadows* (Murray, 1966) p. 220.

[6] Marder to Drax 12th Feb. and reply by latter of 24th Feb. 1962. DRAX 6/18.

[7] Leslie, draft biography SLGF 12/2.

[8] Beatty to Eugénie 19th June and 19th Sept. 1916. Godfrey-Faussett papers. SLGF 15/1 for originals 14/1 for typed copies.

[9] Same to same probably 2nd Dec. 1916. *ibid.*

[10] Same to same 14th Dec. 1916. Beatty wrote in almost identical terms to Ethel on this matter on 5th Dec. 1916.

[11] Corbett, *Naval Operations,* III, pp. 267–70.

[12] Newbolt, *Naval Operations,* IV, Ch. VI, and Marder, *Dreadnought,* IV, pp. 99–101.

[13] Beatty to Balfour 15th Dec. 1916 and Cab. WC. 47 of 29th Jan. 1917.

[14] Roskill, *War at Sea 1939-45,* I, pp. 156–8.

[15] Beatty to Eugénie 4th Mar. 1917.

[16] Beatty to King George V 31st Dec. 1916. RA. Geo. V. Q.832/371

[17] Beatty to Ethel 15th Dec. 1916.

[18] Roskill, *Naval Air Service,* I, *passim.*

[19] *Op. Cit.,* Docs. 153 and 154.

[20] Beatty to Eugénie 19th Jan. 1917.

[21] *ibid.*

[22] Same to same 16th Mar. 1917.

[23] John Winton, *The Victoria Cross at Sea* (Michael Joseph, 1978) pp. 124–5.

[24] Beatty to George V 5th Feb. 1917. RA Geo V. Q.832/372

[25] Godfrey-Faussett diary 27th Mar. 1917.

[26] Beatty to Eugénie 13th April 1917.

[27] Same to same 13th April 1917.

[28] Roskill, *Hankey,* I, p. 216 for Hankey's diary entry for 11th Sept. 1915.

[29] Beatty to George V 22nd April 1917. RA Geo. V. Q.832/373.

[30] Beatty to Ethel in a number of letters of early May 1917.

[30a] Cabinet WC. 124.

[31] Miss Langton, Registrar, Royal Archives, to the author 13th Feb. 1979.

[32] Godfrey-Faussett diary 19th April 1917.

[33] Roskill, *Hankey*, I, pp. 377-8 for Hankey's diary entries for 18th-19th April 1917.

[34] Beatty to Eugénie 22nd April 1917.

[35] Beatty to Carson 13th Jan. and to Jellicoe 27th Jan. 1917. Jellicoe to Beatty 4th Feb. 1917. Patterson, *Jellicoe Papers*, II, pp. 142-4.

[36] M. W. W. P. Consett, *The Triumph of Unarmed Forces* (Williams and Norgate, 1923).

[37] Marder, *Dreadnought*, IV, pp. 40-41.

[38] *ibid.*, p. 45.

[39] *ibid.*, p. 31. See Chalmers, pp. 288-9, 316 and 317-8 for Beatty's letters of 1917 to Ethel expressing his ardent desire for offensive action.

[40] This brief summary is based on the GFBOs of 12th Mar. 1917. Marder, *op. cit.*, Ch. 2 deals more fully with Beatty's changes to the GFBOs.

[41] Marder, *Dreadnought*, IV, p.34.

[42] Roskill, *Naval Air Service*, I, Docs. 156 and 158 for Beatty's letters of 11th and 21st Jan. 1917 to Admiralty.

[43] *ibid.*, Doc. 161 for Beatty's letter of 7th Feb. 1917 to Admiralty. On the conversion of the *Furious* see N. J. M. Campbell, *Warship Special No. 1. Battle Cruisers*, p. 68.

[44] Roskill, *op. cit.*, Doc. 186.

[45] Beatty to Carson 30th April 1917. Quoted *Chalmers*, pp. 447-9.

[46] Beatty to Ethel 3rd and 8th May 1917.

[47] Same to same 10th May 1917.

[48] Beatty to Tyrwhitt May 1917. Marder, *Dreadnought*, IV, p. 179.

[49] *ibid.*, pp. 180-1.

[50] Beatty to Eugénie 2nd May 1917.

[51] For a complete statement of shipping losses see the Admiralty's *Statistical Review* (Copy in Naval Library). Slightly different figures will be found in C. Ernest Fayle, *Seaborne Trade* (Murray, 1923), II, Appendix 1A and Sir A. Hurd *The Merchant Navy* (Murray, 1919), Appendix C; but the broad trend is the same in all sources.

[52] Grant, *U-boat Intelligence*, pp. 182-90

[53] Marder, *Dreadnought*, IV, Ch. V.

[54] Jellicoe to Beatty 4th Feb. 1917.

[55] Beatty to Admiralty 6th Feb. 1917. He gave similar views to Carson at their conference in January.

[56] Cabinet Paper GT. 611 of 27th April 1917.

[57] Marder, *Dreadnought* IV, pp. 107-8 and R. Pound, *Evans of the Broke* (OUP, 1963) pp. 148-54.

[58] Marder, *op. cit.*, Ch. VI.

[59] *ibid.*, pp. 115-6.

[60] *ibid.*

[61] Fayle, *Seaborne Trade*, II, Ch. 2.

[62] See for example Jellicoe to Beatty 23rd Dec. 1916. 'The shipping situation is by far the most serious question of the day, I almost fear it is nearly too late to retrieve it.' Patterson, *Jellicoe Papers*, II, Doc. 19. Also the account by Admiral W. S. Sims, USN of his first meeting with Jellicoe on 10th April 1917 described in his *Victory at Sea* (Murray Ed., 1920), pp. 6-7 – though Jellicoe later denied that he had expressed any such views.

[63] Cabinet Paper GT. 519 of 22nd April 1917 and WC 215.

64 Fayle, *Seaborne Trade*, III, pp. 90-100. Marder, *Dreadnought*, IV, pp. 146-150.
65 Churchill to Hankey 16th Oct. 1937. Roskill, *Hankey*, I, p. 357. Lloyd George's opinion of Hankey's part was expressed to Lord Riddell in July 1919. See his *Intimate Diary*, p. 104 and Roskill, *Hankey*, I, p. 384.
66 Beatty to Eugénie 10th May 1917.
67 Same to same 23rd May 1917. Also letter to Ethel of 18th May 1917 quoted *Chalmers*, p. 315.
68 Godfrey-Faussett diary for 16th and 17th July 1917.
69 Wilfred Owen, *Mental Cases*.
70 John Pearson, *Façades* (Macmillan, 1978) p. 105.
71 Beatty to Eugénie 31st May 1917. Also letters to Ethel of 24th and 31st May quoted *Chalmers*, pp. 316 and 317-8 in which he expressed similar, though less strongly expressed thoughts about Jutland.
72 Same to same 6th June 1917. The date can be read as 1915 but the context obviously makes it two years later.
73 J. W. Wheeler-Bennett, *King George VI* (Macmillan, 1958), pp. 100-2.
74 Beatty to Eugénie 9th July 1917.
75 King George V's diary 21st-26th June 1917. Royal Archives.
76 Beatty to Eugénie 24th June 1917. Misdated 1916.
77 Same to same 28th June 1917.
78 Bryan Godfrey-Faussett's diary 2nd July 1917.
79 Beatty to George V 4th July 1917. RA Geo. V. Q.832/374.

CHAPTER 11

A Fleet in Frustration, July – December 1917
Pages 225-248

1 Beatty to Ethel 11th July 1917.
2 Beatty to Eugénie 22nd July 1917.
3 Same to same 1st Sept. 1917.
4 Godfrey-Faussett diary July-Aug. 1917.
5 For full statistics of losses July-December 1917 see the Admiralty's 'Statistical Review' (Naval Library).
6 Grant, *U-boat Intelligence*, pp. 184-6.
7 *The Times*, 7th May 1917.
8 Marder, *Fear God*, II, p. 35 and *passim*.
9 *Sunday Pictorial* 24th June 1917.
10 Roskill, *Churchill and the Admirals*, Ch. 8.
11 Beatty to Ethel 10th May and 3rd July 1917.
12 Roskill, *Hankey*, I, Chs. 14 and 15.
13 Marder, *Portrait of an Admiral* (Cape, 1952), pp. 219-20.
14 The head of the new section was Captain A. D. P. R. Pound who was to become 1st Sea Lord 1939-43. Marder describes him as 'the supreme centralizer' and 'not an ideal choice', with which I fully agree. See *Dreadnought*, IV, p. 197.
15 'Notes for Conference' of July 1917. Bellairs Papers, formerly in the Naval Library but now location unknown.

16 Beatty to Ethel 29th June 1917.

17 Such an operation, called 'Rosegarden' was tried again in 1943 – and with exactly the same result. D. A. Rayner, *Escort. The Battle of the Atlantic* (Kimber, 1955), Ch. VI.

18 Beatty to Jellicoe 27th June 1916.

19 Godfrey-Faussett diary 26th Aug. 1917.

20 Roskill, *Hankey*, I, pp. 354-5 and 404-5.

21 Lord Geddes, *The Forging of a Family* (Faber, 1952), p. 242.

22 Geddes was 'read in' as First Lord on 20th July 1917. Admiralty records.

23 Cabinet Paper GT. 2003. Lloyd George, *Memoirs*, III, pp. 1177-8 gives a full account of the changes made in the Admiralty in the autumn of 1917.

24 Admiral H. T. Mayo USN to Beatty 11th Sept. 1917. SLGF 3/12.

25 Beatty to Eugénie 10th Sept. 1917.

26 Same to same 27th Sept. 1917.

27 Beatty to George V 16th Oct. 1917. RA. Geo. V. Q.832/375.

28 Beatty to Ethel 10th Oct. 1917.

29 Roskill, *Hankey*, I, p. 406.

30 Grant, *U-Boat Intelligence*, pp. 183-7.

31 Beatty to Carson 18th July 1917.

32 Beatty to Geddes 25th Sept. 1917. For Richmond's obsession with these operations see his diary for 12th Dec. 1917. NMM.

33 Roskill, *Churchill and the Admirals*, pp. 93-4.

34 Beatty to Geddes 25th Sept. 1917.

35 'Record of Conference' held on 10th Oct. 1917. Bellairs papers. See Marder, *Dreadnought*, IV, p. 239, *note*.

36 WC. 227 of 3rd Sept. 1917.

37 'Additional Notes on the Naval Offensive', with diary entry for 23rd Aug. 1917. Richmond papers. NMM.

38 Richmond diary 25th Aug. 1917. NMM.

39 Beatty to Admiralty 11th Sept. 1917. Adm. 1/8486. Roskill, *Naval Air Service*, Doc. 189.

40 *ibid.*, Doc. 194.

41 Beatty to Admiralty 7th Oct. 1917. *ibid.*, Doc. 197.

42 Admiralty to Beatty 20th Oct. 1917. *ibid.*

43 Newbolt, *Naval Operations*, V, pp. 149-58 has a detailed account of this disaster. Marder, *Dreadnought*, IV, has some interesting amplifications – especially on the Intelligence side.

44 Beatty to Eugénie, dated 'Tuesday' – almost certainly 23rd Oct. 1917.

45 Godfrey-Faussett diary 24th Oct. 1917.

46 Beatty to Eugénie 30th Oct. 1917. Parts of this letter are reproduced in *Chalmers*, pp. 321-2 but it is badly misquoted there – which suggests that Beatty's first biographer never saw the originals of any of the letters.

47 *Marmion*, c. XVII.

48 Beatty to Eugénie 5th Nov. 1917.

49 Same to same. Undated but obviously early Nov. 1917.

50 Same to same 23rd Nov. 1917.

51 Newbolt, *Naval Operations*, V, pp. 164-7. Marder, *Dreadnought*, IV, pp. 299-310.

52 *ibid.*

53 Beatty to Eugénie 29th Nov. 1917.

[54] Same to same 10th Dec. 1917.

[55] Newbolt, *Naval Operations*, V, pp. 184–94. Marder, *Dreadnought*, IV, pp. 311–15.

[56] Beatty to Jellicoe 14th Dec. 1917. Jellicoe papers.

[57] Roskill, *Naval Air Service*, 1, Doc. 172.

[58] *ibid.*, Docs. 69, 146 and 165.

[59] *Ibid.*, Doc. 175.

[60] Geddes to Beatty 11th Aug. and reply by latter of 12th Aug. 1917. *ibid.*, Doc. 175(2) and (3).

[61] Beatty to Geddes 15th Aug. 1917. *ibid.*, Doc. 177.

[62] *ibid.*, Docs. 178 and 182.

[63] *ibid.*, Doc. 184.

[64] *ibid.*, Doc. 207.

[65] Geddes papers. PRO. Adm. 116/1807.

[66] Beatty to Eugénie 24th Dec. 1917.

[67] Marder, *Dreadnought*, IV, Ch. XII, Patterson, *Jellicoe Papers*, II, Docs. 102-5 and Roskill, *The Dismissal of Admiral Jellicoe*, Journal of Contemporary History, Vol. I, No. 4 (Oct. 1961).

[68] George V to Beatty 10th Feb. 1918.

[69] Marder, *Dreadnought*, IV, pp. 328–31.

[70] Beatty to Eugénie 30th Dec. 1917.

[71] Beatty to George V 28th Jan. 1918. RA Geo. V. Q.832/376.

[72] The papers of both Secretary Daniels and Admiral Benson are in the Library of Congress, Washington. For a summary of their characters see Roskill, *Naval Policy between the Wars*, I, pp. 50-1.

[73] Beatty to Eugénie 19th Jan. 1918.

[74] Beatty to Admiralty 29th Sept. 1917. Adm. 1/8536.

[75] Letter of 29th Sept. 1917. Adm. 1/8536 and 1/8539.

[76] PRO. Adm. 1/8536.

[77] *Chalmers*, pp. 306-8.

[78] Roskill, *H.M.S. Warspite* pp. 143-4.

[79] These are the figures given in David Woodward, *The Collapse of Power* (Arthur Barker, 1973) p. 77. See also Daniel Horn, *Mutiny on the High Seas* (Rutgers University 1969 and Leslie Frewin 1973) Chs. IV and V. The latter work is, however, too much of a polemical indictment of the German Navy's disciplinary and judicial system to command confidence.

[80] Roskill, *Naval Policy between the Wars*, II, Ch. IV.

CHAPTER 12

Victory – of a Kind, January – November 1918
Pages 249-280

[1] 'Discussion at the Admiralty on Occasion of the Visit of the Commander-in-Chief, Grand Fleet'. Marder, *Dreadnought*, V, p. 142.

[2] Admiral Sir Sydney Fremantle, *My Naval Career 1880-1928* (Hutchinson, 1949) p. 244.

[3] Beatty to Wemyss 31st Jan. 1918. Wemyss papers.

[4] Wemyss to Beatty dated 'Saturday', almost certainly 4th May 1918.

[5] Same to same 30th Mar. 1918. Wemyss papers.

[6] Beatty to Geddes 9th April 1918. Geddes papers. Adm. 116/1804-10.

[7] Wemyss to Beatty 26th Mar. 1918. Wemyss papers.

[8] Beatty to Ethel 1st Feb. 1918.

[9] Beatty's memo. 'Situation in the North Sea' of 9th Jan. 1918.

[10] Geddes's memo. 'Naval Situation in North Sea' of 17th Jan. 1918. Marder, *Dreadnought*, V, pp. 131-8.

[11] Roskill, *Hankey*, I, pp. 477-82.

[12] *Der Krieg in der Nordsee*, VII, p. 225.

[13] Beatty to Eugénie 11th Jan. 1918.

[14] Peter Avery of King's College, Cambridge to the author 15th Mar. 1978 (now attached to Beatty to Eugénie letter of 24th April 1918 SLGF 15/1).

[15] Beatty to Eugénie 24th April, 3rd and 20th May 1918.

[16] Same to same dated only '1st March' but obviously written in 1918.

[17] Same to same undated but obviously March 1918.

[18] Same to same 19th March 1918.

[19] Geddes papers, Adm. 116/1804-10.

[20] Beatty to Eugénie 19th Mar. 1918.

[21] Beatty to Ethel 7th April 1918. Quoted *Chalmers*, p. 324. Also to Wemyss. 20th April 1918. Wemyss papers.

[22] Roskill, *Hankey*, I, pp. 486 and 530-1.

[23] Beatty to Eugénie 29th March 1918.

[24] Same to same 9th April 1918.

[25] Grant, *U-Boat Intelligence 1914-18* pp. 182-90.

[26] Beatty to Wemyss 13th Feb. 1918. Wemyss papers.

[27] Beatty to Wemyss 26th April 1918,˙ Wemyss papers, and to Eugénie 20th May 1918.

[28] Same to same 10th Aug. 1918, *ibid.*, and to Balfour 21st Aug. 1918. Balfour papers. (British Library)

[29] Letter of 23rd Aug. 1918 by Lord Robert Cecil (Under Secretary, Foreign Office) to Lloyd George tells how, after discussion with Beatty he had given instructions that the Foreign Office was 'not to threaten the Norwegian Govt. with forcible action until further orders'. Lloyd George papers F/6/5/39.

[30] Grant, *U-Boat Intelligence* gives this figure.

[31] Beatty to Eugénie 15th April 1918.

[32] Wemyss papers.

[33] Roskill, *Hankey*, I, Ch. 18 has his diary entries for May-July 1918 which give perhaps the most vivid account of those critical weeks. Hankey was of course present at all the Inter-Allied conferences and discussions. The quotation is from Basil Liddell Hart, *History of the First World War* (Cassell Ed. 1970) p. 540.

[34] Beatty to Eugénie 15th April 1918.

[35] Same to same 24th April 1918.

[36] Same to same 20th May 1918.

[37] Beatty to Wemyss 5th May 1918. Wemyss papers.

[38] Same to same 26th April 1918.

[39] Same to same telling how 'despite a pea Soup fog' the fleet had got to sea within 1½ hours of receiving the signal. *ibid.* He also gave Eugénie a graphic

description of this feat. Letter of 20th May 1918.

[40] The escort comprised an Armed Boarding Steamer and two destroyers, and the covering force was the 2nd Battle Cruiser Squadron and 7th Light Cruiser Squadron.

[41] This short account is based on *Newbolt*, V, pp. 230-40 and Marder, *Dreadnought*, V, pp. 148-55.

[42] Fisher to Lloyd George 14th Mar. 1917. Marder, *Fear God*, III, pp. 438-9.

[43] Cabinet Paper GT 217 of 16th Mar. 1917. Cab. 24/8

[44] Roskill, *War at Sea*, I, Ch. IX. But Churchill later declared that he had never believed that an invasion was likely. Roskill, *Churchill and the Admirals* p. 121.

[45] Beatty to Wemyss 3rd June 1918. Wemyss papers.

[46] Same to same 24th Mar. 1918, quoting his letter to Geddes. *ibid*.

[47] Beatty to Ethel 2nd July 1918.

[48] Wemyss to Beatty 6th Aug. and reply by latter of 10th Aug. 1915. Further letter by Wemyss of 15th Aug. 1915. Wemyss papers.

[49] Same to same 6th Aug. 1918.

[50] Deleted.

[51] Beatty to George V 16th June 1918. RA Geo. V. Q.832/377.

[52] *ibid*.

[53] Beatty to Eugénie 30th May 1918.

[54] Same to same 12th June 1918.

[55] Same to same 15th June 1918 with addendum dated 20th June.

[56] Same to same 29th June 1918 with addendum dated 1st July.

[57] Same to same 10th July 1918.

[58] Same to same dated 'Saturday Night' – probably 14th or 21st July 1918.

[59] Pershing to Beatty 16th June and reply by latter of 28th June 1918. SLGF 6/4.

[60] Beatty to Eugénie 6th Sept. 1918.

[61] Same to same dated 'Sunday' – probably 8th Sept. 1918.

[62] Same to same dated 'Wednesday' – probably 18th or 25th Sept. 1918.

[63] Beatty to Eugénie 6th Sept. 1918.

[64] Same to same dated 'Sunday' – probably 8th Sept. 1918.

[65] Same to same dated 'Wednesday' – probably 18th or 25th Sept. 1918.

[63] Admiralty 'Statistical Review of the War Against Merchant Shipping'. Naval Library.

[64] See Roskill, *War at Sea*, III, Part II, Ch. XXIX and Appendices Z and ZZ.

[65] Admiralty to Beatty 4th June 1918.

[66] Grant, *U-boat Intelligence* pp. 184-90.

[67] Geddes to Beatty 27th Sept. 1918, and his notes for guidance in conference with U.S. Navy Department of Sept. 1918. Geddes papers. Adm. 116/1804-10.

[68] Sims to Josephus Daniels 5th April 1918. USN Operational Archives

[69] Article 'From Petitions to Reviews' by H. P. (Commander Harry Pursey) in *Brassey's Annual*, 1937, pp. 105-7.

[70] Wemyss to Beatty 2nd Sept. 1918.

[74] Same to same 3rd Sept. and reply by latter of 4th Sept. 1918. Wemyss papers.

[72] Wemyss to Beatty 12th Oct. 1918. *ibid*.

73 Beatty to Eugénie dated 'Friday' – probably 4th or 11th Oct. 1918.

74 Same to same 5th Oct. 1918.

75 Same to same 9th Oct. 1918.

76 Beatty to Wemyss 2nd Oct. and reply by latter of 4th Oct. 1918. Wemyss papers.

77 It is printed in full in *Chalmers*, pp. 332–4.

78 Beatty to Wemyss 17th Oct. and reply by latter of 18th Oct. 1918. Wemyss papers.

79 Same to same 19th Oct. and reply later, date uncertain but the pencilled entry '? 10th Nov.' on his copy must be wrong. *ibid*.

77a Beatty to Hankey 23rd October 1918 with enclosure. Hankey papers.

80 Wemyss to Beatty 26th Oct. 1918. *ibid*.

81 Beatty to Eugénie 31st Oct. 1918. Parts of this letter are printed in *Chalmers*, p. 336.

82 Fremantle to Beatty 27th and 29th Oct. 1918.

83 Beatty to Eugénie 9th Nov. 1918. Parts printed in *Chalmers*, pp. 341-2 but there misdated 12th Nov.

84 Beatty to Wemyss 5th Nov. 1918 and reply by the latter of same day. Wemyss papers.

85 Same to same 7th Nov. 1918. *ibid*.

85a Beatty to Eugénie 9th Nov. 1918.

86 Beatty's case is stated in Cabinet Paper GT 6107 of 23rd Oct. The War Cabinet's decision is in WC 491B of 26th Oct. 1918.

87 IC 87 covers the Supreme War Council's meetings of 31st Oct.-4th Nov. 1918.

88 On Benson's attitude and purposes see Roskill, *Naval Policy between the Wars*, I, pp. 73-5.

89 Beatty to Wemyss 5th Nov. 1918. *Chalmers*, pp. 338-9.

90 The final terms of the armistice are in Cd. 9212.

91 Beatty to Geddes 8th Nov. and reply by latter of 9th Nov. 1918.

92 Wemyss to Beatty 14th Nov. 1918. Wemyss papers. See also Lady Wemyss, *The Life and Letters of Lord Wester Wemyss* (Eyre and Spottiswoode, 1935), p. 399. Henceforth cited as *Wester Wemyss*.

93 *ibid*.

94 From Captain Basil Jones's memoirs *And so to Battle* (Privately printed, 1979), p. 16. Copy in Churchill College.

95 Beatty to Admiralty 12th Nov. 1918. Adm. 116/1825. Roskill, *Naval Policy*, I, p. 75.

96 Lady Seymour, *Commander Ralph Seymour* (Glasgow U.P., 1926) reproduces her son's letter of 19th Nov. 1918.

97 Beatty to Eugénie 19th Nov. 1918. Part printed in *Chalmers*, p. 343.

98 Same to same 26th Nov. 1918. Part printed in Chalmers, pp. 344-6.

CHAPTER 13
Interlude – and an Admirals' Quarrel, 1919
Pages 281-296

1 Leslie holograph notes dated 29th Jan. 1948. SLGF 6/17.

2 Beatty to Eugénie. Dated 'Monday' – probably 6th Jan. 1919.

[3] Same to same 14th, 16th, 22nd and (probably) 29th Jan. 1919.
[4] Same to same 22nd Jan. 1919.
[5] *ibid*.
[6] Unpublished holograph memoirs. Wemyss papers.
[7] Beatty to Admiralty 29th July and 1st Aug. 1918. Adm. 116/1803.
[8] Wemyss memoirs.
[9] *ibid*. Also *Wester Wemyss*, pp. 420-1.
[10] *ibid*.
[11] Long to Beatty 21st Mar. and reply by latter of 25th Mar. and further letter by former of 27th Mar. 1919.
[12] Memo. by Long of 5th May 1919. Lloyd George papers F/33/2/42(B).
[13] Wemyss memoirs.
[14] *ibid*.
[15] *ibid*.
[16] Beatty to Eugénie dated 'Monday' – probably 6th Jan. 1919, the date of the article in *The Times*.
[17] Long to Stamfordham 9th Mar. 1919. RA GV. G. 1474/1.
[18] Long to Beatty 25th Feb. 1919.
[19] Same to same 4th Mar. 1919.
[20] Wemyss to Beatty 28th Feb. and reply by latter of 1st Mar. 1919. Copies in SLGF 3/14 and in Wemyss papers.
[21] Wemyss memo. of 2nd Feb. and Sir Oswyn Murray's of 6th Feb. 1919. Wemyss papers.
[22] Beatty to Eugénie 10th April 1919.
[23] Marder, *Fear God*, III, pp. 241-3.
[24] Long to Lloyd George 9th Mar. 1919. Lloyd George papers F/33/2/21, Long to Stamfordham 9th Mar. 1919 RA GV G. 1474, Long to Beatty 13th March and reply by latter of 15th March 1919.
[25] *Evening Standard* 15th March: *The Times* 7th and 24th April 1919.
[26] Wemyss to Long 10th March 1919. Copy in Wemyss papers.
[27] Parl. Deb., Commons, Vol. 115, Col. 90. Long was answering a question addressed to the Prime Minister by Commander Carlyon Bellairs.
[28] *Chalmers*, pp. 453-4.
[29] *op. cit.*, pp. 353-4.
[30] Beatty to Eugénie 10th April 1919.
[31] Same to same 19th April 1919.
[32] Same to same 25th April 1919.
[33] Same to same 30th April 1919.
[34] Same to same 8th May 1919.
[35] Interview with 6th Viscount Hood who knew the Wemyss family well, Aug. 1979.
[36] Beatty to Eugénie 22nd May 1919.
[37] Churchill to Lloyd George 1st May 1919. Lloyd George papers F/8/3/46.
[38] Beatty to Eugénie 22nd May 1919 from Monte Carlo.
[39] Long to Stamfordham 14th June 1919. RA GV. G. 1474/3.
[40] King George V diary 12th and 22nd June 1919. Royal Archives.
[41] Stamfordham to Lloyd George 15th Nov. 1918. Lloyd George papers F/29/2/60. On behalf of the King Stamfordham proposed that Viscountcies should be conferred on both Haig and Beatty.
[42] Churchill to Lloyd George 11th April 1919. Lloyd George papers F/8/3/39.

[43] Parl. Deb., Commons, Vol. 119, Cols. 183-5 and 415-48.
[44] *Wester Wemyss*, p. 439.
[45] Beatty to Eugénie 26th July 1919.
[46] Same to same 4th Aug. 1919.
[47] Same to same 25th Oct. 1919.
[48] Fisher to Beatty 1st Nov. 1919. Copy in SLGF 12/1.
[49] Marder, *Dreadnought*, V, p. 210.

CHAPTER 14
First Sea Lord. The First Phase, 1919 – 1923
Pages 297-321

[1] Beatty to Eugénie dated 'Sunday' – probably 9th Nov. 1919.
[2] Same to same dated 'Sunday' – probably 21st Dec. 1919.
[3] Same to same 25th Dec. 1919.
[4] Same to same 24th Feb. 1920 with endorsement by George Godfrey-Faussett on typed copy.
[5] Roskill, *Naval Policy*, I, p. 127, *note*.
[6] *ibid*. pp. 127-9.
[7] Minute of 17th Nov. 1922. Quoted *ibid.*, p. 128.
[8] Roskill, *Naval Policy*, I, Ch. 3.
[9] Geoffrey Bennett, *Cowan's War* (Collins, 1964) pp. 67-8 and 198-203.
[10] Beatty to Eugénie 30th July 1920.
[11] Memo. of 6th Jan. 1920. Adm. 116/1774.
[12] Beatty's memo. of 28th May 1920. Lloyd George papers F/202/1/30.
[13] Roskill, *Naval Policy*, I, pp. 103-4.
[14] Harold Nicolson, *Curzon: the Last Phase* (Constable, 1934) p. 186.
[15] Roskill, *Hankey,* II, pp. 166-8.
[16] Beatty to Eugénie 9th April and 22nd May 1920.
[17] Same to same 11th Aug. 1920.
[18] Roskill, *Naval Policy,* I, pp. 117-18 deals fully with the 1919 pay codes, which were published in Cmd. 270 (officers) and Cmd 149 (men).
[19] *op. cit.*, pp. 119-20.
[20] *opt. cit.*, pp. 126-7.
[21] Memo of 12th Aug. 1919. Adm. 116/1774.
[22] Roskill, *Naval Policy*, I, pp. 214-5.
[23] See Arthur J. Marder, *The Anatomy of British Sea Power* (Frank Cass, 1964 Ed.) p. 17 and *passim*.
[24] Memo. of 8th July 1920. Adm. 1/8602.
[25] Roskill, *Naval Policy*, I, pp. 220-4.
[26] Godfrey-Faussett diary 7th May 1920.
[27] Memo. of 14th Dec. 1920. Adm. 116/1775. Also CID papers N4 and N5 of same date.
[28] Beatty to Long 1st Mar. 1921. CID NSC 11 of 2nd Mar. 1921.
[29] Beatty to Eugénie 28th Aug. 1920.
[30] Same to same 1st and 9th Sept. and 5th Oct. 1920.
[31] Same to same 31st Dec. 1920.
[32] *Chalmers*, pp. 351-2. The speech to Edinburgh University is printed in full in Appendix VII.

[33] Roskill, *Naval Policy,* I, pp. 252-3.
[34] Minute of 24th Oct. 1919. Adm. 1/8574.
[35] Roskill, *op. cit.*, p. 255.
[36] *ibid.*, p. 260.
[37] Beatty to Eugénie dated 26th Jan. 1921 but from internal evidence probably written on 28th.
[38] Same to same 2nd Feb. 1921.
[39] Note by George Godfrey-Faussett on typed copy of Beatty's letter of 26th (or 28th) Jan. 1921.
[40] Roskill, *Naval Policy*, I, Ch. IV.
[41] Beatty to Eugénie, undated but c. March 1921.
[42] Same to same dated 'Monday', probably 30th May 1921.
[43] Same to same dated 'Saturday', probably in Aug. 1921.
[44] Roskill, *Naval Policy*, I, pp. 289-95.
[45] *ibid.* Copy (undated) in Beatty papers.
[46] Stamfordham to Lloyd George. Lloyd George papers F/29/4/83.
[47] Beatty to Ethel 28th Oct. 1921. *Chalmers*, p. 367.
[48] Beatty to George V 12th Nov. 1921. RA GV O.1735/74
[49] *ibid.*
[50] Eugénie to Ethel 14th Nov. 1919 and reply by latter (undated). SLGF 6/5.
[51] Beatty to Eugénie 23rd Nov. 1921.
[52] H. and M. Sprout *Towards a New Order of Sea Power* (2nd Ed. Princeton UP, 1943) and Roskill, *Naval Policy*, I, Chs. VIII and IX. The former treats the conference mainly from the American and the latter from the British point of view.
[53] Quoted in Leslie's draft biography.
[54] Beatty to Eugénie 23rd Nov. 1921.
[55] Roskill, *Naval Policy*, I, pp. 319-20.
[56] Cmd. 1581 of 14th Dec. 1921. Roskill, *Naval Policy*, I, pp. 230-3.
[57] General Wilson to Lloyd George 15th and 16th July 1919. Lloyd George papers F/47/8/26.
[58] Beatty to Ethel 19th Jan. and 24th Feb. 1922.
[59] Beatty to Eugénie probably 29th Dec. 1921 and 9th Jan. 1922.
[60] *Chalmers*, p. 424.
[61] Roskill, *Naval Policy*, I, pp. 338-41.
[62] King Albert to Beatty 12th Aug. 1922. SLGF 12/1.
[63] Deleted.
[64] The original of this letter is in SLGF 6/5A and it is reproduced as here in the typescript (SLGF 12/2) of Leslie's biography. As it is dated 'Sunday' and Beatty ended 'All good luck to you and yours in 1923' it can be dated confidently to 22nd or 29th Dec. 1922.
[65] Leslie's Ms. note, undated but almost certainly mid-Oct. 1921. SLGF 12/1.
[65a] Beatty to Leslie dated 'Friday' but endorsed by Leslie 'Oct. 15th 1921', SLGF 6/5A
[65b] *The Times* 5th, 6th and 7th Oct. 1922.
[66] Letters Horatia Seymour to Leslie 1942-62 in SLGF 10/1, also Leslie's draft on the subject for his biography of Beatty – which, at the Seymour family's request, he suppressed. Also the author's correspondence with Horatia Seymour 1962-65 in ROSK 3/1.

[67] *Commander Ralph Seymour RN*, (Glasgow U.P., 1926)
[68] SLGF 10/1.
[69] Cmd. 2029.
[70] Beatty to Bonar Law dated 'Wednesday', almost certainly 14th Feb., and reply by latter of 21st Feb. 1923. Bonar Law papers 111/5/23 and 24.
[71] CID. ND 12. (April 1923)
[72] Cmd. 2029, pp. 277 ff.
[72a] Beatty to Amery 31st July 1923. Roskill, *Naval Policy*, I, pp. 378-82.
[73] Lord Templewood, *Empire of the Air* (Collins, 1957) pp. 63-5 and Andrew Boyle, *Trenchard: Man of Vision* (Collins, 1962) pp. 489-91.
[74] Chatfield to Keyes 5th Jan. 1937. Keyes papers 8/9. Paul Halpern (Ed.) *The Keyes Papers*, II (Navy Records Society, 1980) pp. 361-2.
[75] Cmd. 2029, Part VII. Roskill, *Naval Policy*, I, pp. 372-85.
[76] Parl. Deb., Commons, Vol. 161, Col. 1089. c.f. *Chalmers*, p. 465.
[77] The Anderson Committee of Mar. 1923 was set up 'to enquire into the present standard of remuneration and other conditions of employment of all government servants'. Roskill, *Naval Policy*, I, pp. 401-2.
[78] CID 221C.
[79] Cmd. 1987, Section XII.
[80] Roskill, *Naval Policy*, I, pp. 411-12.
[81] Beatty to Eugénie 2nd Jan. 1924.
[82] George Godfrey-Faussett to the author 19th Aug. 1978.
[83] I am indebted to Sir John Colville for this quatrain which he remembered very well; but its attribution to Belloc is uncertain.
[84] Commander Colin Buist, an intimate friend of Lord and Lady Brownlow, to the author 11th Mar. 1963. SLGF 16/15.
[85] For example to Eugénie 31st Dec. 1920.

CHAPTER 15

The Jutland Controversy, 1919 – 1927
Pages 322-339

[1] Earl Jellicoe, *The Grand Fleet. Its Creation, Development and Work* (Cassell, 1919) and Commander Carlyon Bellairs, *The Battle of Jutland. The Sowing and the Reaping* (Hodder and Stoughton, 1920).
[2] Cmd. 1068.
[3] Beatty to Ethel 31st May 1917. *Chalmers*, p. 317.
[4] Richmond diary for 4th May 1917. NMM.
[5] In *The Naval Review*, Vol. 12 (1924), p. 183.
[6] Harper's 'Observations' on Beatty's remarks on the *Record*. Adm. 116/2067
[7] Parl. Deb., Commons, Vol. 311, Col. 1538. The motion was agreed *nem. con.*
[8] Wemyss's memo. of 23rd Jan. 1919 to Long. Harper's appointment became effective on 6th Feb. 1919.
[9] Memo. by Harper, British Library, Add. Ms. 54477-80.
[10] Parl. Deb., Commons, Vol. 120, Col. 648.

[11] *ibid.*, Vol. 122, Col. 374 and Vol. 125 Cols. 370–1.

[12] *ibid.*, Vol. 125, Cols. 870–1.

[13] *ibid.*, Vols. 120–205. Also Harper, *The Truth about Jutland* (Murray, 1927), pp. 7–8.

[14] This comparison is now in ROSK 3/10, as is my correspondence with the RUSI Council when I tried to get all the Harper papers released in 1959–63.

[15] Navy Records Society, 1968.

[16] Patterson, *Jellicoe Papers*, II, p. 462.

[17] Board Minute 1607 of 8th Mar. 1923. Adm. 167/68.

[18] These are Harper's words. Patterson, *Jellicoe Papers*, II, p. 483.

[19] *Jellicoe Papers*, II, pp. 478–9.

[20] Harper to Chatfield 23rd Dec. 1919 and minute by Beatty of 11th Feb. 1920.

[21] *Jellicoe Papers*, II, p. 467.

[22] Harper to Chatfield 20th Feb. 1920, minuted 'Approved' by Chatfield.

[23] *Jellicoe Papers*, II, p. 467.

[24] Harper to Long 24th Feb. 1920. Minute by Beatty 'The written orders issued to Captn. Harper by me are cancelled'.

[25] Harper to Chatfield and Long 12th Mar. 1920.

[26] Harper to Naval Secretary for First Lord 14th May 1920.

[26a] See for example Jellicoe to Frewen 12th Feb. 1920. Patterson, *Jellicoe Papers*, II, Doc. 128.

[26b] Dreyer Papers, DRYR 3/4 contains 168 letters, nearly all holograph, from Jellicoe to him.

[27] Jellicoe to Long 5th July 1920. Patterson, Jellicoe Papers, II, Doc. 130.

[28] Patterson, *Jellicoe Papers*, II, p. 469.

[29] *ibid.*, p. 470.

[30] *ibid.*, p. 471.

[31] Board Minute 1251 of 6th Aug. 1920. Adm. 167/60.

[32] *Jellicoe Papers*, II, p. 472–4.

[33] Frewen to Evan-Thomas 22nd Feb. 1927. Evan-Thomas papers, originals in British Library Add. Mss. 52505 and 52506. Complete copies are in Churchill College ROSK 3/3.

[34] Long to Beatty 10th Sept. 1920.

[35] Beatty to Long 18th Sept. 1920.

[36] O. Murray's minute of 23rd Sept. 1920.

[37] Parl. Deb., Commons, Vol. 133, Cols. 1716–17 (27th Oct.), Vol. 134, Cols 42–4 (1st Nov.) and Cols. 566–7 (4th Nov.).

[38] Parl. Deb., Commons, Vol. 136, Col. 452.

[39] Sims to Moreton Frewen 3rd Dec. answering his letter of 16th Nov. 1920. SLGF 6/2.

[40] Long to Moreton Frewen 9th and 12th Nov. 1920. Copies in SLGF 6/3.

[41] Brock to A. C. and K. G. B. Dewar 15th Nov. 1920.

[42] Jellicoe's remarks on 'Admiralty Narrative of the Battle of Jutland'. Copy in Evan-Thomas papers. See also his letters to Frewen and to the Admiralty of 25th Aug., 6th Nov.–27th Nov. 1922 in *Jellicoe Papers*, II, Docs. 140, 142 and 143.

[43] Roskill, *Naval Policy*, I, pp. 559–60 regarding the notorious '*Royal Oak* Incident' of 1928. K. G. B. Dewar was the Captain of the ship.

[44] Brock to Dewars 15th Nov. 1920.

[45] *Evening News* 29th Nov. 1920.

[46] K. G. B. Dewar, *The Navy from Within*, p. 267.

[47] Minute by Chatfield of 14th Sept. 1921.

[48] Interview with Sir Shane Leslie 1961.

[49] *Jellicoe Papers*, II, p. 482, *note*.

[50] Memo. by Keyes of 20th Dec. 1921.

[51] *Jellicoe Papers*, II, Doc. 140.

[52] *ibid.*, Doc. 143.

[53] Now numbered ROSK 3/13.

[54] Keyes and Chatfield to Beatty 14th Aug. 1922.

[55] *Jellicoe Papers*, II, Doc. 143.

[56] Evan-Thomas to Rear-Admiral W. H. Haggard (DTSD) 14th Aug. and to Captain M. Hodges (Naval Secretary to 1st Lord) 18th Sept. 1923. Evan-Thomas papers.

[57] Based on notes by Admiral Sir Geoffrey Barnard, Evan-Thomas's nephew, now in the British Library. Copies in ROSK 3/31.

[58] Jellicoe to Frewen 12th Feb. 1920, 8th July 1921 and 6th Nov. 1922. *Jellicoe Papers*, II, Docs. 128, 133 and 142. Copies of many more letters from Jellicoe to Frewen 1920-27 are in ROSK 3/11.

[59] Rear-Admiral W. H. Haggard (DTSD) to Keyes 7th Feb. 1923.

[60] Chatfield to Keyes from H.M.S. *Cardiff* Jan. 1923. Keyes papers (British Library).

[61] Hutchinson, 1924.

[62] Thornton Butterworth, 1927.

[63] Churchill to Beatty 11th Nov. 1924. Quoted *Chalmers*, p. 401.

[64] *The Times*, 13th Feb. 1927.

[65] Chatfield to Beatty 9th Mar. 1927.

[66] Parl. Deb., Commons, Vol. 205, Cols. 1606-7 (4th May 1927).

[67] Minutes by Beatty of 10th May and Bridgeman of 12th May 1927. Adm. 1/8722-290/27. Harper, *The Truth about Jutland* (Murray, 1927) and with J. Langhorne Gibson, *The Riddle of Jutland* (Cassell, 1934).

[68] Proof and published copies (Benn, 1930) interleaved with letters from Beatty, Jellicoe, Madden and other participants in the battle, together with many reviews of the Epic, are in SLGF 13/1-8. Leslie-Beatty letters are in SLGF 6/1-17.

[69] Heinemann, 1933. Copy, interleaved with letters, in SLGF 13/2.

[70] SLGF 6/1-17.

[71] Chatfield papers CHT 8/2 dated 8th Mar. 1938. NMM. (Signature illegible).

[72] I owe a debt to Mr. John Barnes of the London School of Economics for drawing my attention to this aspect of Beatty's involvement in the Jutland controversy.

CHAPTER 16

First Sea Lord. The Second Phase, 1924 – 1927
Pages 340-360

[1] RA. GV. K.1918/184B

[2] Sir Alan Lascelles (Private Secretary to Queen Elizabeth II) to Sir Owen Morshead, 3rd June 1952. RA. GV. K. 1918/184A.

[3] Beatty to Ethel 23rd Jan. and 15th Feb. 1924. *Chalmers*, pp. 394 and 396.

[4] Same to same 25th Jan. and 15th Feb. 1924. *ibid.*

[5] Endorsement by George Godfrey-Faussett on Beatty to Eugénie 17th Jan. 1924.

[6] Beatty to Eugénie 'Sunday' – probably 27th Jan. 1924.

[7] Same to same 30th Jan. 1924.

[8] Same to same dated 'Sunday' probably 20th and 27th Feb. 1924.

[9] Air Ministry letter of 11th Jan. and Chelmsford's reply of 14th Feb. 1924. Adm. 116/2236 and 2230.

[10] CID 503B.

[11] Roskill, *Naval Policy*, I, pp. 389-98.

[12] *ibid.*, pp 412-13 and 416-17.

[13] The full programme is in Adm. 1/8672-230/24 which was sent to the Cabinet on 4th April 1924.

[14] Cabinet Paper CP. 15(24) of 20th Feb. 1924.

[15] RS(24) 1st and 2nd Meetings. The quotations above are taken from the minutes of the second meeting. Cab. 18(24) and 20(24) record the Admiralty's fight against cancellation. David Marquand, *Ramsay MacDonald* (Cape, 1977) pp. 315-16 has a good summary of the discussions as viewed from the government's standpoint.

[15a] CP. 15(24) of 20th Feb. 1924.

[16] Beatty to Eugénie 4th March 1924.

[17] Parl. Deb., Commons, Vol. 171, Col. 320. The correspondence with the Dominions was published in Cmd. 2083.

[18] Undated draft memo. in Beatty papers.

[19] Adm. 1/8672-230/24.

[20] Parl. Deb., Commons, Vol. 169, Col. 1971 ff.

[21] *ibid.*, Vol. 171, Cols. 275-406 and 743-804.

[22] Oliver memoirs NMM.

[23] Beatty to Eugénie misdated 23rd Feb. 1924. Should surely read March.

[24] Same to same 26th March 1924.

[25] *ibid.*

[26] Minute of 23rd April 1924. Adm. 1/8683-131/25.

[27] Parl. Deb., Commons, Vol. 173, Col. 709.

[28] Interview with 6th Viscount Hood, Aug. 1979.

[29] SLFG 12/1.

[30] *ibid.*

[31] Beatty to Eugénie 29th Sept. 1924.

[32] CID meeting of 28th July 1924.

[33] CP.450(24) of 27th Sept. 1924.

[34] Roskill, *Hankey*, II, pp. 381 and 393-9, and *Naval Policy*, I, pp. 429-31. David Marquand's *Ramsay MacDonald*, pp. 354-6 has a fair account, rather

more favourable to the Labour Government's standpoint.
35 *The Times*, 20th Nov. 1924.
36 Beatty to Eugénie dated 'Monday', probably 16th Dec. 1924.
37 Same to same dated 'Tuesday night', probably 31st Dec. 1924.
38 Same to same dated 'Sunday', probably 18th or 25th Jan. 1925.
39 Same to same dated 'Saturday'. The reference to 'Bacon's bl—dy book' about Jutland dates it to about April 1925.
40 Its sale was advertised in *The Times* of 21st Feb. 1925.
41 Beatty to Ethel 11th and 16th Feb. 1925. *Chalmers*, pp. 406-7.
42 Beatty to Eugénie dated 'Monday', probably 23rd or 30th Mar. 1925.
43 Beatty to Dewar 23rd April 1925. Dewar papers DEW/3. NMM.
44 Robert Rhodes James, *Memoirs of a Conservative*, (Weidenfeld and Nicolson, 1969) pp. 205 and 208.
45 General Lord Bridgeman's unpublished memoir of his father, p. 574 (typescript). Copy in Churchill College.
46 Beatty to Ethel, undated but postmarked 8th Jan. 1925. Part quoted in *Chalmers*, p. 402.
47 Board Minute 1989 of 11th Dec. 1924. Adm. 167/69.
48 Roskill, *Naval Policy*, I, pp. 445-6.
49 Admy. memo. of 4th Feb. 1925. Cabinet Paper. CP. 67(25).
50 Beatty to Ethel 2nd Feb. 1925.
51 Bridgeman, memoirs p. 107 (typescript).
52 The other members were Lord Peel (First Commissioner for Works), Mr. E. Wood (Earl of Halifax 1944), Churchill and Bridgeman.
53 Roskill, *Naval Policy*, I, p. 449.
54 Beatty to Ethel 1st and 7th July 1925. *Chalmers*, pp. 408-9.
55 Beatty to Eugénie 17th June 1925. *Chalmers*, p. 408.
56 Roskill, *Hankey*, II, pp. 403-4 and 463.
57 Parl. Deb., Commons, Vol. 186, Cols. 2421-3. Also Roskill, *Naval Policy*, I, pp. 451-2. The building programme was published in detail in Cmd. 2476.
58 Parl. Deb., Commons, Vol. 187, Cols. 457-75.
59 Roskill, *Naval Policy*, I, pp. 473-84.
59a *ibid.*
60 Bridgeman to N. Chamberlain 16th Jan. 1926. Quoted Bridgeman memoir p. 559a (typescript).
61 Beatty to Ethel 11th Mar. 1926. *Chalmers*, p. 411.
62 *The Times* 29th June-12th July 1926.
63 Board Minute 2164 of 11th Feb. 1926. Adm. 167/73.
64 Amery to Baldwin 8th Feb. 1926. Baldwin papers, Vol. 96. Cambridge University Library.
65 *The Times*, 5th Nov. 1926.
66 Copies in Churchill College.
67 SLGF 12/2.
68 Robert Rhodes James, *Memoirs of a Conservative*, pp. 252-3.
69 *ibid.*, p. 252.
70 *ibid.*, p. 208.
71 Beatty to Ethel 13th Oct. 1926.
72 Editorial Note by Admiral W. H. Henderson, *The Naval Review*, Vol. I, No. 1 (Nov. 1913).

[73] A full account of the history of the Naval Society and its journal, including the details of the Hon. Editor's battles with authority, was published in its Jubilee Number, (Vol. II, No. 1 Jan. 1963).

[74] The story of the suspensions and the ultimate granting of freedom to the *Naval Review* is told at length in Ch. 5 of Barry D. Hunt's unpublished Doctoral Thesis entitled *Richmond: The Intellectual Admiral* (Royal Military College, Canada, 1979). The relevant Board Minutes quoted are in Adm. 1/8708 and 167/73.

[75] *The Times* 6th Mar. 1968.

[76] Beatty to Eugénie, dated Monday – probably written late in 1926 or early 1927. The contents of Eugénie's letter of protest are clarified by the recollections of her son George and her maid and confidante Doris Taylor that Beatty was pursuing a woman who was also being sought by the Prince of Wales. Eugénie, knowing the Prince's jealousy, warned Beatty 'to stay clear', but he immediately told the lady who in turn told the Prince. Though he took no offence, Eugénie 'was furious' and it was probably this anger which she communicated to Beatty. George Godfrey-Faussett letter to the author of 7th Aug. 1978.

[77] Beatty to Eugénie 17th Jan. 1927.

[78] Bridgeman diary p. 163.

[79] L. C. M. S. Amery, *My Political Life*, II, p. 475.

[80] Article *Memories of Beatty*, Quarterly Review, Vol. 290, No. 593 (July 1952).

[81] Beatty to Ethel 14th June 1927. *Chalmers*, p. 413.

[82] Beatty to Eugénie, undated. *ibid.*

[83] Beatty to Ethel, 17th Jan. 1927. *ibid.*, p. 142.

[84] Bridgeman, memoir, p. 656 (typescript).

[85] Beatty to Ethel 21st June 1927. *Chalmers*, p. 414.

[86] *The Times* 30th April and 2nd May 1927.

[87] Beatty to Eugénie 12th July 1927.

CHAPTER 17

Last Years, 1928 – 1936

pages 361 – 369

[1] Letter of 22nd April 1928 to Bryan Godfrey-Faussett, signature almost certainly 'Fritz' the name by which Sir Frederick Ponsonby was known. Godfrey-Faussett papers.

[1a] Beatty to Eugénie 11th Mar. 1928. Part quoted in *Chalmers*, p. 417.

[2] Beatty to his son David 8th June 1930. Copy in SLGF 12/2.

[3] Beatty to same, Good Friday 1930. *ibid.*

[4] Leslie's Ms. biography SLGF 12/2.

[5] *The Times*, 9th July 1925 and 21st June 1928.

[6] *ibid.*, 19th Dec. 1929.

[7] *ibid.*, 23rd Dec. 1930.

[8] *ibid.*, 20th Dec. 1932.

[9] *ibid.*, 3rd May 1934.

[10] *ibid.*, 6th Feb. 1935.

11 *ibid.*, 3rd Dec. 1935 and 7th Feb. 1936.
12 Leslie, draft biography. SLGF 12/1 and 12/2.
13 Beatty to Eugénie 15th July 1932.
14 Beatty to Cowan 20th July 1932.
15 Hankey to Beatty 30th April 1927.
16 Leslie's draft biography. SLGF 12/1 and 12/4.
17 *ibid.*
18 Original in SLGF 11/11.
19 Article by Leslie *Memories of Beatty*, Typescript and proof in SLGF 12/4.
20 Eugénie to Leslie 14th Sept. 1947. SLGF 7/2.
21 Leslie manuscript notes. SLGF 12/1.
22 Beatty to Leslie 27th Sept. 1935. SLGF 7/1A.
23 Chatfield to Beatty dated only 'Tuesday'. SLGF 7/1.
24 SLGF 12/1.
25 Parl. Deb., Commons, Vol. 311 Col. 1538 ff.
26 Copy of Souvenir Programme in SLGF 11/12.

EPILOGUE
The Last Naval Hero
Pages 370 – 375

1 Stephen King-Hall, *My Naval Life* (Faber, 1952) pp. 97 and 222.
2 SLGF 11/2.
3 *ibid.*
4 Thomas Carlyle, *On Heroes and Hero-Worship* (Ward, Lock and Bowden, 1896 ed.)
5 *King Henry V*, Act. III, Scene I and Act IV, Scenes I-VIII.
6 *op. cit.*, p. 145.
7 Five Volumes (London, 1858 (two), 1862, 1864 and 1865).
8 H. R. Trevor-Roper, *The Last Days of Hitler* (Macmillan, 1947), pp. 106–8 and 252–4.
9 Iris Origo, *A Measure of Love* (Cape, 1957), pp. 152 and 197.
10 See for example Newbolt's volume of poems *Drake's Drum* (Hodder and Stoughton, n.d. but c. 1915).
11 Three volumes, first published by Longmans 1907-1911 and constantly reprinted up to 1939, when they appear to have been dropped from the RNC Dartmouth's curriculum.
12 Marder, *Dreadnought*, V, p. 338.
13 By Charles Owen (Allen and Unwin, 1975).
14 Admiral Sir Ian McGeoch, who was captain of the 17th *Lion*, to the author 14th Aug. 1979.
15 Millicent, Duchess of Sutherland, to Leslie 8th Jan. 1949. SLGF 11/4.

Index

NOTE: *The Ranks and Titles given are the highest to which any person rose.*

411